Tribal Livelihood

Editors

S.N. Chaudhary
Sarit K. Chaudhuri

GYAN

ISBN : 978-81-212-1425-4

First Published, 2018

Published by

Gyan Publishing House
5, Ansari Road
Daryaganj, New Delhi-110002
Phone: 9811692060
E-mail: books@gyanbooks.com

Printed at: G. Print Process, Delhi.

Contents

Preface

The concept of tribal livelihood occupies prominent space in tribal studies. The history of tribal studies denotes that culture initially dominated the analysis of tribes, especially among the sociologists and social anthropologists. Development issues occupied prominent position after independence. Tribes were analyzed in relation to issues directed to development. But since 1991, the tribals are analyzed with reference to mega development projects, environment, development, displacement and rehabilitation related issues and so on. Also, the tribal development is discussed in the light of PESA Act 1994, Forest Rights Act 2006, MNREGA, New Panchayati Raj system, Self-Help Group, seasonal outmigration, new social movements going on in tribal areas and so on. The issue of tribal livelihood has attracted attention of cross-section of scholars and researchers, during this phase. Most of them have examined the impact of globalization and other interventions on the status and condition of tribal livelihood. They have examined how such initiatives are influencing the tribal livelihood functionally or dys-functionally. Scholars and others are discussing the livelihood related issues keeping in view of the basic need approach and human rights approach.

Keeping these issues, a two-day national seminar was organized by Rajiv Gandhi Chair in Contemporary Studies with partial financial support from Indira Gandhi Rashtriya Manav Sangrahalaya, Bhopal during Dec. 06-07, 2016. We received pragmatic and academic cooperation from different institutions and individuals in holding the seminar. It is our moral and ethical obligation to acknowledge them.

At the very outset, we are extremely thankful to Dr. M.D. Tiwari, Ex-Vice-Chancellor, Barkatullah University, Bhopal for his needful support and cooperation. We are thankful to the contributors and participants, who have attended the seminar and contributed in a meaningful manner. Prof. D.K. Verma needs special appreciation for delivery of Rajiv Gandhi Memorial Lecture on the occasion. We also acknowledge fruitful issues and arguments raised by Professor M.N. Karna and Professor S.B. Chakrabarti in their keynote and valedictory address, respectively. Several research papers were presented in the technical sessions of the seminar, but after needful editing work, we could receive 18 articles for inclusion in the volume. We are extremely thankful to them who took pains to complete editing work on time. However, the views expressed in the articles are of the respective contributors and not necessarily of the editors.

Last but not the least, we are thankful to the research staff and administrative staff of Indira Gandhi Rashtriya Manav Sangrahalaya, Bhopal, Rajiv Gandhi Chair in Contemporary Studies and Barkatullah University, Bhopal for their needful support and cooperation.

S.N. Chaudhary
Sarit K. Chaudhuri

Contributors

Abhik Ghosh, Professor, Department of Anthropology, Panjab University, Chandigarh

Chaturbhuj Sahu, Former Head, University Deptt. of Anthropology, Vinoba Bhave University, Hazaribag, Jharkhand

D C Sah, Professor Emeritus, MP Institute of Social Science Research, Ujjain, Madhya Pradesh

D.K. Verma, Professor, Dr. B.R. Ambedkar University of Social Sciences, Mhow, Madhya Pradesh

Debashish Debnath, Faculty, Indian Institute of Forest Management, Bhopal, Madhya Pradesh

Gaya Panday, Faculty, Department of Anthropology, Ranchi University, Ranchi, Jharkhand

Jayent Behera, Faculty, Department of Sociology, I.G.N. Tribal University, Amarkantak, Madhya Pradesh

K.G. Iyer, (late) Former Professor, Punjab University, Chandigarh

M C Arunkumar, Professor, Social and Cultural Anthropology, Department of Anthropology, Manipur University, Imphal, Manipur

Neelu Rawat, Assistant Professor, Dr. Hari Singh Gour University, Sagar, Madhya Pradesh

Nisheeth Rai, Assistant Professor, Department of Anthropology, M.G. Antarrashtriya Hindi Vishwavidyalaya, Wardha, Maharastra

S.K. Chaudhuri, Director, Indira Gandhi Rashtriya Manav Sangrahalaya, Bhopal, Madhya PRadesh

S.N. Chaudhary, Professor of Sociology and also Professor Rajiv Gandhi Chair in Contemporary Studies, Barkatullah Univeristy, Bhopal, Madhya Pradesh

S.N. Tripathi, Professor of Economics, Gokhale Institute of Politics and Economics, (Deemed University), Pune, Maharashtra

Satya Ranjan Mahakul, Research Associate, Madhya Pradesh Institute of Social Science Research, Ujjain, Madhya Pradesh

Shailendra Prasad Sinha, Asst Professor (Rtd), University Dept. of Anthropology, Ranchi University, Ranchi, Jharkhand

Sunil K. Yadav, Senior Research Fellow, Rajiv Gandhi Chair in Contemporary Studies, Barkatullah University, Bhopal, Madhya Pradesh

Sushila D. Mahant, Research Scholar, School of Anthropology & Tribal Studies, Bastar University, Jagdalpur, Chhatisgarh

Swapan K. Kolay, Associate Professor & Head, School of Anthropology & Tribal Studies, Bastar University, Jagdalpur, Chhatisgarh

Tapas K. Dalpati, Assistant Professor, Sociology, Madhya Pradesh Institute of Social Science Research, Ujjain, Madhya Pradesh

Chapter - 1

Introduction

Livelihood refers to capabilities of the people and means of their living. It includes sufficient hygienic food; continuous flow of income to ensure food supply and other basic requirements. It also refers to the availability and freedom to own and use both tangible and intangible assets. Tangible asset includes resources such as land, irrigation, trees, cattle, farm equipments, tools, utensils, stores and so on. And intangible asset refers to various **claims** and **demands**. Both these set of assets contribute to each other. In other words, tangible asset i.e., stores refers to food stocks to ensure food security, gold jewellery to mortgage or sale in the stress situation, readymade textile and cash saving in formal institutions. And intangible asset includes claims and access. Claims cover demands and appeal for material, moral and other support. The demand may be for food, fertilizer, implements, loans, gift, work employment and so on. These claims may be made on the individuals, agencies, relatives, employers, NGO, government etc.

The individual or families must have access to various resources such as material, technological, employment oriented activities, transport facility, education, health services, information technology, security system and so on, to ensure sustainable livelihood. The people decide their livelihood and also its security upon these tangible and intangible resources. It further empowers them achieve higher level resources, which in turn positively affect their quality of life and standard of living, if those resources were available. These are traditional and modern. The tradition and modernity help each other, in numbers of cases. Hence, if a person is born in a resourceful family, he is likely to avail the available resources for furthering higher order resources, which in turn improves the quality of life and social status.

The scholars are divided about the socio-economic status of tribes - pre-British period, but believe majority of them to hang on in villages and engaged in primary occupation for livelihood. Their socio-economic status is low and the process of class formation is very slow among them in spite of various institutional and non-institutional initiatives, although there were many political elites among them.

The survey of literature revealed they don't have any serious threat for livelihood. Majority of them instead were in the safer zone. A sound status of local ecology and environment, plenty of life sustaining natural resources like forest and forest produce, low population pressure, life around the basic requirements, and insignificant and limited contact with outside world – have collectively ensured their livelihood. Tribes developed culture, institutions, mechanisms, religious activities etc; with the help of local ecology and such cultural heritage ecology was encouraged and protected on to establish symbiotic relationship between the tribals and local resources, animate and inanimate, respectfully continued. The existence of totem is one of the best examples of organic relation between the culture and environment. According to A. Sen and E. Lalhrietpuri (2006: 205-10), 'In pre-colonial days, there was greater diversity of landscapes, and sacred groves and shifting cultivation contributed to this diversity'. Similarly, according to A. Kothari (1996), the totemic social organizations have contributed to the protection of flora and fauna. Also, as late as in 1953, an eminent botanist N.L.Bor (1963), reported 'the largest deodars (Himalayan Cedar) are those which were planted near temples, venerated and protected them from injury'. According to Guha (1994), "For forest dependent communities like charcoal iron makers and shifting cultivators, control over the forest was vital to their economic and cultural life. As Elwin demonstrated for

Baiga and Agaria their rituals, myths, and sense of self were all deeply interwoven with their forest world. Consequently, the takeover of forest by the state and their subsequent working on commercial lines, when coupled with the alienation of tribal agricultural land to outsiders, destroyed their livelihood and culture. This process has resulted in a deep sense of helplessness, or what Elwin termed a 'loss of nerve' (p.14)". It was because of past glory of tribes that a group of scholars talk about not storation rather restoration of human rights and dignity of tribes.

Gradually their interaction with outside world has increased. Since, the interaction between the tribals and others was that between two unequal partners, two unequal wants and two distinct cultures; therefore, gradually the non-tribal culture has dominated over the tribal culture, material and non-material. An interaction was one way and largely in favour of non-tribals. What were the factors and mechanism to encounter uncalled for dictation of non-tribal culture, which in one way or another negatively affected the local ecology, affecting the livelihood as an issue which needs to be examined. According to Kosambi (1956) "when Gupta Emperors made attack on them, with the help of indigenous technique, they challenged it and retained their autonomy and independence." According to Srivastava (2008) "Tribes have themselves done a lot for their own improvement, they have led movements for environment protection, saving their cultural and human rights, throwing the exploiters out of their territories, regaining rights over their lost land and other resources, closing liquor shops in their area, curbing practices of conspicuous consumption and putting a full stop to all those practices that reduce their respect in the eyes of others" (p. 35). More specifically, one of the scopes of a national seminar was to underline the socio-cultural initiatives taken by tribals in the past and today to encounter negative forces to ensure their livelihood.

There was serious commodification of natural resources available in tribal areas, since the inception of **British Rule** till 1947. These resources were directly or indirectly snatched away without respecting the needs and requirements of local population. The **voices of protest** such as Kol revolt (1821),

Bhumij revolt (1832), Santal revolt (1763), Birsa Munda Movement (1890), Tana Bhagat Movement (1915) and Jharkhand Movement (1950) in present Jharkhand state, the Revolt in Bastar (1911), protests in Gudem-Rampain (1920s), Worli revolt (1945-46), Juang Movement (1837-56) and Kaujhar Movement (1891-93) in Orissa state and Gond revolt (1911) and the movement for separate Gond State (1940) in Madhya Pradesh may be cited as few among several other revolts/ movements; but these movements were either unsuccessful or had ad-hoc arrangement and therefore, localized impact on the storation [restoration] of livelihood resources of tribal masses. These revolts were forcefully suppressed by the alien and local power structure (Chaudhary, 2016). Hence, it may be said that by the time, India became free tribals' interaction with outside forces increased and with this condition, their livelihood got pruned. Acculturation had its intended and unintended negative consequences in the local society, particularly from the point of view of livelihood. How tribals have accommodated with adverse environment to meet their basic requirements? How exchange mechanisms and barter system have responded to this challenge? These issues were seriously debated in the seminar.

Various institutional[1] and non-institutional efforts have been made to protect and promote the livelihood of tribal masses without wondering on three major sociological dilemmas of development i.e. **Cultural part of Development, Environmental part of Development** and **Equity part of Development,** between 1947 and mid-1991. How the issues were managed by respective policies, provisions, schemes and agents of change and development from the point of view of livelihood of tribal masses needs to be seriously examined. There is a strong belief that these dilemmas and dimensions of development were by and large left unattended in the wider interest of non-tribals and capitalistic model of development. In other words, there is a strong belief that ongoing capitalist model of development has ruined the tribal culture, damaged local ecology, environment and contributed to assimilation and whatever benefits it has delivered, it has been cornered by only few from among them. The majority of tribes have been left at their own fate. Question is seriously and strongly raised that how Top-Down model of development can move side by side with environmental sustainability, respect for local culture and how benefits of development may be inclusive and equitable?

The globalisation is formally going on in the country since 90's. It is neither friendly to tangible and intangible tribal heritage nor geographical space historically inhabited by tribals. There is massive expansion of mega-development projects in the tribal dominated areas. The resources available in those areas were perceived as the haven for industrial and corporate houses. It is claimed that these houses have snatched the available resources in many tribal areas. Thousands of tribals were displaced from their century-old place of residence without any suitable and meaningful rehabilitation packages (Chaudhary 2013). Today, in many pockets, it appears that they were uncalled for and unwanted. In some pockets, the corporate houses are working for their welfare under **Corporate Social Responsibility** (CSR) scheme. How these two initiatives and interventions have affected the livelihood of tribal masses needs to be examined from close quarter. This needs to be seriously analyzed, because the doubt is being raised about the functioning of CSR. Questions are being raised that how unrepairable environmental damage directly or indirectly caused by corporate houses may be repaired through CSR? Also, inspite of increasing state initiatives through various schemes like New Panchayati Raj Institution, PESA, Forest Rights Act, MNREGA, Rehabilitation and Resettlement Policy, Land Acquisition Act, Food Security Act and host of others steps conclusions are drawn that quality of life of tribes is even lower in comparison to SCs. How and to what extent these interventions have succeeded from livelihood point of view?

Transportation and communication technology were popularized in some tribal villages. All weather roads were built. The cropping pattern has been patented. Under the given situation, how and to what extent the tribals at large feel safe and secured? How technology is tribal friendly from their livelihood and quality of life point of view? How and to what extent tribes in general and primitive tribes (PVTGs) in particular have come out of the trauma of what **Cernea** (2000) called *impoverishment, landlessness, Joblessness, Homelessness, Marginalization, Food Insecurity, High Morbidity* and *loss of access to community property resources*? Why it is so that inspite of various livelihood schemes at the village level the cases of seasonal outmigration, merely for the fulfillment of basic requirements, is increasing day by day? Question is also raised about the role of outmigration in meeting basic requirements of tribals. All these issues were discussed in the seminar.

Objectives

The specific objectives were as under:

(1) To understand concept and philosophyof tribal livelihood in the changing scenario;

(2) To examine different sources of livelihood found in tribal areas either through the external initiatives or from their own cultural heritage (both tangible and intangible);

(3) To explain the status of different conventional and non-conventional sources of livelihood in the current context;

(4) To underline process and consequences of erosion of livelihood on their basic requirements, human rights, development, empowerment and social institutions and cultural practices;

(5) To explore coping mechanisms adopted by tribals to overcome stress situation created by livelihood crisis in a successful/unsuccessful manner;

(6) To find out role and status of new technology of all types in meeting concerns and issues related to livelihood; and

(7) To understand and suggest ways and means to strengthen their livelihood keeping in view their present and future requirements, existing and upcoming challenges and also their carrying capacity.

II

The volume contains 18 articles. The opening article by S.N.Chaudhary is primarily based on the review of literature and field opinion portraying tribes of central India are historically the victim of uncontrolled variety of acculturation which in turn have forced them to move towards insecurities. Their support base had been eroded largely by the external forces which in turn have massively ruined their identity, coping mechanisms and survival strategies. They have tested state initiated coping mechanisms only in a notional manner. The new coping mechanisms including Panchayat (Extension to the Scheduled Areas) Act – 1996 (PESA) and the Scheduled Tribes and Other Traditional Forest Dwellers (Reorganization of Forest Rights) Act – 2006 (FRA) and host of other schemes are largely failed to restore their human rights. Social movements, rehabilitation promises and seasonal outmigration are also significantly incapable to address their problems. Their mobility towards insecurity and deprivation is aheading unwaited and under the globalization driven socio-economic scenario they are further likely to be marginalised. Hence, the paper presents an unilinear explanation of marginalization of scheduled tribes of central India.

The contribution of D.K.Verma is primarily based on the secondary source. It covers multiple dimensions. The author raises question on the notion of primitive and particularly vulnerable. He shares the broad conclusion that non-tribal economy is primarily responsible for economic underdevelopment of tribes. He infers the dependency theory of development call for further development of strong group so that under-development of so-called under-developed group gets through in a pre-condition. He describes the history of pauperization among three primitive tribes of Madhya Pradesh like Baiga, Bharia and Saharia in a historical perspective. The thesis also laments on poor functioning of welfare schemes.

K.G.Iyer in his attempt examined the role of Forest and NTFP as an important source of livelihood for the Jharkhand tribals. It is an empirical study in the districts of West Singhbum and Khunti. The role of Kendu leaves, Sal leaves, Mahua, Tamarind and other important minor forest produce have been examined to see whether it will serve as some source of livelihood. In this context, the role of lac cultivation in the livelihood of the tribals in Khunti district in particular has been analysed.

The study also intends to examine the role of Forest Rights Act, 2006 in the state of Jharkhand in the districts mentioned above. The study also concentrates on a comparative understanding of the impact of the Forest Right Acst in the left extremist districts of Jharkhand and Orissa.

The main objective of the attempts from S.K. Kolay and S.D. Mahant was to explore the issues, demand and benefit of entrepreneurship establishment in urban fringe for tribal peoples. It was focused on evolving recommendations for economic development by entrepreneurship for tribal people. Data collection was done by primary and secondary tools. The primary data relates to the general information about the family, enterprise, acceptance and denying reasons for women entrepreneurship, information about the self-income and that of the family through interview, FGDs, schedule/questionnaire, observation by semi participatory method etc. The findings depict opportunities for economic development through entrepreneurship in urban fringe. It was mooted the deterioration of traditional occupation, art, craft and culture parallelly comes through entrepreneurship development, which creatdes a lot of socio-cultural problems, migration, health hazard, anti-social activities, livelihood migration and illiteracy.

According to the article of D. Debnath, tribes mainly live in the forests or in the vicinity of the forests. Hence, their economy is the outcome of the reciprocating relationships with the forests. Once in the common property resource (CPR) management regime they developed their self-sufficiency in their traditional livelihoods. But in course of time, while the forests were brought under state management regime, they were alienated and day-by-day became poor in the modern market economy. This was despite several developmental schemes of the state to protect them from exploitation and preservation of traditions. Later a watershed change occurred in state policy when the forest department attempted to involve them in the forest management. The adoption of 'sustainable livelihood' approach in the fringe forest village through natural resource management led to people's participation, community empowerment, income generating activities and equitable benefits sharing. By doing so, the paternalistic form of development was transformed into participatory development with the accumulation of natural, human, social, physical and financial capital. This proposition underlines traditional economic organization with recent sustainable livelihood approaches with dynamic social change and human development in the process of Globalization.

D.C.Sah argues that, under a shock, access failure to natural, human, social, financial and physical capital victim tribal households enter in the trap of poverty from some 688 household. The study tries to highlight the intensity of poverty in tribal villages is significantly higher than dryland as well as dry-industrial villages. Annual income from various occupations in the villages such as forest, agriculture, casual labour, NREGA, and traditional occupation etc; is unable to meet the annual consumption of households as one move from industrial to dryland to tribal villages. In order to bridge this expenditure gap, members from seriously affected households in dryland villages and more so in tribal villages have to migrate. Among migrant households, this expenditure gap in all the three locations is significantly higher to pressurise the households to migrate more as a coping mechanism.

The tribal livelihood is ever changing. The state initiatives were on in the post-colonial era. Tribal societies have spruced up. These have focused on the occupation pattern and livelihood, life-styles of the tribal societies. Moreover, the communities in urban centres in the neo-liberal era have their own problems. M.C. Arunkumar, through his thesis, examines the tribal livelihood particularly among, the Kabui (Rongmei), a scheduled tribe living in three different contexts: hill, plain rural and urban areas. The changing pattern of the tribe is being studied in these socio-economic settings.

Neelu Rawat wonders how it was difficult to separately demarcate the communities. It was so due to to partial loss of traditional economic system they are being involved in various activities for survival and perform several economic activities together, so broadly they can be classified as - settled agriculturist, agricultural labourer, wage labourer, forest dweller, artisans, self-employed, nomad and pastoral etc. Over the time, various schemes were formulated and implemented to ensure their livelihood security. Traditional economy was tried to be replaced by the modern economy. It came true at some sort that finds replicated in change and continuity in their pattern of earning livelihood. However, the question of livelihood security still remains unresolved, due to one or other reason.

T.K. Dalpati in his submission argued that tribal households were facing crucial challenge to maintain their livelihood. They were unable to resort to the traditional bases of livelihood due to widespread deforestation, narrowing down of habitat and fragmentation of land holding over the generations. Most of them were unable to cope with the financeial turmoil and their land resources were being dragged into the process. The transfer of land to the non-tribal finds restricted under law, but several informal tactics were adpted in the process of land transfer from the tribal to non- tribal hands. His thesis highlights the trajectory and nature of transfer of Kondh land to the non- tribals in the highland of Kalahandi district of Odisha. The thesis posits the vicious circle of lease-mortgage and sale incurred from financial constraint is the root cause of land alienation among Kondh tribe due to which their livelihood situation was bleak.

S.P.Sinha, has found the role of culture vital in overcoming the problems related to gathering, producing, growing, storing, processing, consumption, distribution, exchange, trade and marketing etc; of food items among the studied tribes. He believed the change in scenario after *tsunami* in December 2004. He argued indigenous coping mechanisms include the worship of deities and ancestors by the tsunami affected victims particularly of the Katchal Nicobarese of Tihunyu islands. Ancestors of the Katchal were considered as very important in sundry ways. Nearly 10 km area got submerged. The data was retrieved from the west bay and Kapand village of Katchal besides Jula, Junshin, Upper katchal and Pounda villages. *Tsunami* erupted on the early hours of December 26, 2004, in the Indian Ocean. It owed to the most powerful earthquake of its kind in 21^{c}. Katchal are mongoloids, traditionally dependent on the forest and seas. They had developed a belief system in the harmony with distinct ecological setting. The victims lost strength in terrestrial and aquatic resources – an irreparable damage. But, Katchals tried their level best with the existing situation even among the survived, with the help of adhoc welfare measures.

Chaturbhuj Sahu, recollected the tribal communities to have adapted to ecological setting since centuries. On the economic aspect, they hung out as foodgatherers to settled agriculturist and to become skilled and employed. The livelihood of Jharkhand tribals aggregating to about 26.3 per cent of the state population relied on land and land-based activities. They were found primarily subsistence-oriented and earning livelihood from forest, agriculture, pastoralism etc. Now modern means, especially daily wage-work has metamorphosed their lives. The primary source of livelihood of the Birhor and Korwar tribe was forest. Asur, Birjia, Lohara, Karmali, Munda, Chickbaraik proved to be efficient artisans, whereas the shifting cultivation was the means of livelihood of Sauria Pharia and Mal Paharia tribes. Agriculture was the source of income for the developed tribes viz Santhal, Oraon, Munda, Ho, Kharia, Chero, Kherwar, etc. It was characterized by low productivity and monocropping pattern. Aadvanced technology and hybrid seed mode of farming mobilized them cultivate **Aghani** as well as **Bhadai** and **Rabi** crops. Sahu has elaborated the cropping pattern on the basis of assorted agricultural regions and suggested for need-based improvement.

The contribution of Nisheeth Rai focused on the strategies adopted by Kolam, a P.V.T.G. of the state of Maharashtra. He has examined their survival strategy through the DFID model with an ethnographic touch. He recounted over the historical factors and relevant conditions for the current state of affairs among Kolam tribe in particular today, particularly from the point of view of their livelihood.

The tribal livelihood is no longer the kind predefined and noted by anthropologists some two decades before. Many of the tribes seldom follow the routes of traditional livelihood that once defined them as a community. They follow other routes, which were more in tune with random market forces active. For tribes, the contribution of Abhik Ghosh depicts, for researchers as well as the development experts, a new set of paradigms. On the one hand, the tribal heritage and knowledge system was found gradually eroded by addition from generations ahead, which made them ignore what they have inherited earlier. On the other hand, the development experts were keen to add a whole new repertory of issues to the tribal livelihood that may often forget about the human and environmental factors. It may be good for the current market trends or the national economy. Ghosh attribute his analogy through Jharkhand tribes and believes that a standardized development practice would not fit into a pan-Indian situation. He anticipates the tribes seldom develop unless we stop aping the development practices of others from elsewhere.

The contributor S.R. Mahakul examines cultural perceptions of Juang tribes of Odisha for utilizing the Common Property Resources (CPRs) in general and the agricultural land in particular in a tribal village of Keonjhar district. He wants to ascertain the position of socioeconomic impact of CPR utilization in terms of livelihood support and the problems encountered by various sections of the village communities. He believes the privatization and outsiders' intervention have throttled the existing CPRs. The changing patterns of CPRs owe to the resources at the time of utilization. The livelihood needs, as such, finds regulated by socio-cultural practices and institutions. His thesis proposed a comprehensive strategy for CPR-based development planning and management. He believed that it will certainly provide the outcome with the involvement of community on the grounds of cultural and social perceptions and values.

The contributor S.N. Tripathy denotes the concept of tribal livelihood as most textured and varied, the most basic working definition comprising the capabilities, assets, and activities required for a means of living. Especially, the livelihood issues relates to the tribes of India, presuming the significance of traditional means of obtaining livelihood. The access to land and control over the natural resources has gone a radical change, post-independence. On the one hand, the state has monopolized its ownership over nature; and on the other hand, non-tribals have begun to use these resources without considering the ecological balance, as a result of which; the ecological degradation has proliferated. The pattern of development has virtually affected the tribals' access to customary land and forest-based livelihood source. There is concern over as to how to protect the current sources of livelihood and to promote their economic development, viz., may be through Forest Rights Act (FRA). However, a decade later, it was found ineffective with parameters of field variance. Tripathy explained how the Wadi-project had served as an alternative avenue for sustainable livelihood of Koraput district [Odisha] tribe.

The paper of J.K. Behera deals with how the forest department determines the livelihood pattern of the tribals. The extensive poverty, illiteracy, malnutrition, deficiency of safe drinking water and sanitary conditions, poor maternal and child health services etc. determines their livelihood pattern. In present time tribal development is a major issue. He claims the researchers to have followed policy makers in removing dilapidated conditions of tribals. Inspite of efforts, the tribals have suffered from problems galore. He wondered whether certain interacting factors could determine the livelihood and problems related to the development of those communities. He focused on what they think about their livelihood and what they actually do with regard to seeking their right or resorted to action-oriented development.

Gaya Pandey believed various government policies, acts, and programmes certainly have had effect on keeping the tribals on to their culture. Tribes are now not in isolation. They have been integrated in the mainstream of our nation. Change in livelihood is also true for tribals. Some are still continuing with their hereditary livelihood, while others have adapted to the change in traditional livelihood. Members of the new generation prefer modern mode of survival. Older generations still subsist on the hereditary strategies. Some families have given up the traditional means of livelihood on this ground of *perestroika*. Karmali, Lohara, Mahili and Chickbraik were known Jharkhand artisans. The ratified forest policies, acts and introduction of development inputs, have made the majority of families abandon traditional means of livelihood. Some of them have become service doers and small businessman, while others have become labourers. Their craftsmanship has received a heavy doll due to forest and mining policies, acts, and urbanization and industrialization. Some artisan tribes have witnessed positive change in the livelihood, in contrast with gloomier aspect of some others.

Author Sunil Kumar Yadav describes the livelihood status of Bharia tribe in the framework of continuity and change. He underlies the economic and non-economic reasons responsible for the apathy eclipsing their future. He laments neither uniform development strategy nor any formulation of welfare mechanism in isolation from cultural heritage could empower their status in the society.

III

It is apparent from an overview of abstract of articles that researchers were divided on the status and source of livelihood of tribal mass across the country. Majority of the tribes live in village or cluster of villages in islands. However, in many villages, one observes an alien culture. They were found on primary sources of livelihood. The latter refers to the resources directly or indirectly related to the local available natural resources. Their status has largely deteriorated subjected to the modern law restrictions imposed on the tribal lot in accesing those resources. Various state authorities have adopted the need-based, solution-oriented measures, with the country subjected to Open Door Policy [1991]. However, there is a dilemma that traditional resources seldom cope with the requirements, when the tribes have notional access to modern life chances and opportunities available within or outside their villages. Only small segments of them have availed the benefits of opportunities anew at the cost of social, psychological and cultural development. Some new initiatives such as PESA, Forests Rights Act, Popularization of SHG in tribal areas, popularization of the PDS and the health services, increasing number of primary schools in tribal villages, seasonal outmigration by tribes etc; were insignificantly successful in meeting the basic need and requirements of tribes. Even CSR, modern NGOs, expansion of transportation and communication network etc; have very limited impact on tribes from the point of view of meeting basic requirements. The process of social capital formation is very slow. Most of them do not have linkage with local level changers. In short, the contributions included in this volume, broadly agree upon the issue that in the broader sense, the term status and quality of life of tribal masses was not up to the mark from the point of sustenance. Contributors have suggested certain mechanisms to ensure their perpetual livelihood. How and to what extent such suggestions were practical and enforceable is a matter which needs rethinking in the current context in the aftermath of globalization, such as individualism, apathy, reluctance, limited commitments etc., were found especially among the catalysts working at the village or panchayat level.

Reference

Bor, N.L. (1963): *Manual of Indian Forest Botany.* New Delhi: Oxford, p-18.

Canera, Michael M. (2000): 'Poverty Risks from Population, Displacement in Water Resources Development', *HIID Development Discussion paper No. 355, Cambridge,* Mass: Harward.

Chaudhary, S.N. (2016). (ed): *Social Movements in Tribal India.* Jaipur: Rawat.

Chaudhary,S.N. (2013): (ed.) *Globalisation, National Development and Tribal Identity.* Jaipur: Rawat.

Guha, R. (1994): *Sociology and the Dilemmas of Development.* New Delhi: ICSSR.

Koshambi, D.D. (1956). *An Introduction to the Study of Indian History.* Mumbai: Popular.

Kothari, A. (1996): 'Is Joint Management of Protected Areas Desirable and Possible', in Ashish Kothari, N. Singh and S. Suri (ed.), *People and Protected Areas: Towards Participatory Conservation in India.* New Delhi: Sage.

Sen, A. and E. Lalhrietpui. (2006): 'Scheduled Tribes (Recognition of Forest Rights) Bill: A View from Anthropology and Call for Dialogue', *EPW,* Vol. XII (39): pp 4205-10.

Srivastava, V.K. (2008): "Concept of Tribe in Draft National Policy" in *EPW,* Vol. XLII, No. 50, Dec. 13.

Chapter - 2

Tribal Livelihood: A Historical Overview on Central India

— *S.N. Chaudhary*

Introduction

Livelihood refers to the capabilities of the people and means of their living. It includes the availability of sufficient hygienic food; continuous flow of income to ensure food supply and other basic requirements. It covers on the availability and freedom to own and use tangible and intangible assets. Tangible asset includes the resources viz., land, irrigation, trees, cattle, farm equipments, tools, utensils, stores etc. And intangible asset refers to various **claims** and **demands**. These set of assets contribute to each other. In other words, the tangible asset i.e., stores refers to food stocks to ensure food security, gold jewellery to mortgage or the sale in stressed situation, readymade textile and cash saving in the formal institutions. And intangible asset includes the claims and access. Claims cover demands and appeal for material, moral and other support (Chamber and Conway, 1991). The demand may be for food, fertilizers, [agricultural] implements, loans, gift, work, employment etc. These claims may be made on individuals, agencies, relatives, employers, NGOs, corporate houses, government etc. In order to ensure livelihood, the individual/families must have access to the resources such as material, technological, employment, transport, education, health services, protection, information technology etc. People decide their livelihood and ensure its security on the basis of such resources. If these resources are available, it further enables them achieve more valued resources, which in turn positively affect or tend to affect their lives. These resources are traditional and modern, per se. Here in many cases, tradition and modernity help with each other. If a person is born in a resourceful family, he is likely to avail the available resources for furthering higher order resources, which subsequently improves the quality of life in comparison to those who are born in a relatively families without resource.

The condition is more frustrating today, if we examine the livelihood of tribes (Scheduled Tribes) of the Central Indian States[1]. It will be so, particularly from the point of view of their quality of life and that too in an era of planned development and globalization in comparison with the situation before British Raj. Often, the frequency of interaction between the tribal and non-tribal societies was insignificant. Today, it appears that there is massive deterioration in the traditional livelihood resources. The cultural practices were incapable to address with the livelihood crisis. The extraneous coping mechanisms have largely failed to address the demands and claims. The tangible and intangible assets have equally failed to stop the shift towards insecurity. Does it mean the degree of livelihood insecurities will increase as the unequal and unregulated variety of interaction between tribal and non-tribal societies jack up? If it is so, how will it be and why should it be? What are the status and consequences of institutional measures, NGOs initiatives, social movements and efforts made by tribes on their livelihood? The thesis is an attempt to search answer of these questions.

The British Raj

During pre-British days, tribes (Adivasis and Vanbasis) generally lived their lives autonomously. They lived in no-man's areas. These areas were geographically isolated, largely disconnected from the so-called mainstream society, in terms of social and economic sense. Tribes (a colonial construct) constructed the autonomous coping mechanisms. They have developed instruments, institutions, cultural practices etc., to regulate their vital demographic events like birth, marriage and death etc; suiting to local ecology. They had their own perceptions of natural resources[2]. They have developed youth organization, to socialize with younger generation. They became animists, because they were living in and around nature. When tribals perceived the local ecology as object, they have made every effort, through culture, to establish and retain the symbiotic relationship that sustained for generations. They had their own cultural interpretation of environment like trees, animals, birds, mountain, water, land and so on. Sowing of seeds, harvesting of crops etc; all were regulated through cultural practices. Culture sustained local ecology. The latter contributed to their culture. In fact, the latter emerged in the light of local ecological and environmental context. Low population pressure, limited needs and isolation from vested interests, self-generating status of resources etc; have retained symbiotic relations. Generally, there was no question of livelihood crisis. The health status of local resources was sound enough to fulfill limited needs. In certain pockets, if there was stress situation on temporary basis, there were cultural capsules such as barter system, shifting cultivation etc, to overcome stress.

The interaction over time increased between the tribals and the non-tribals. And with this, the issue of livelihood gradually became problematic in different parts of Central India. Take the case of Bhils of M.P., Maharashtra, Gujrat and Rajasthan as an example. As and when excesses were on them, they made unsuccessful attempts to survive amongst the mixed race. According to **Koshambi** (1956) "When Gupta Emperors made attack on them, with the help of indigenous techniques they challenged it and retained their autonomy and independence."

The situation changed adversely during the Muslim period. The Muslim rulers of the neighboring states, particularly from Gujarat, made attempt to crush the independence of Bhil with the help of modern weapons. The Muslim rule gradually expanded into non-tribal areas. This development forced the latter, particularly Rajputs of Rajasthan to runaways in the Bhil areas for protection. Dense forest of Jhabua of Madhya Pradesh, for example, became an important destination. Bhils came in direct contact with the inmigrant Rajputs. It had negative consequences, particularly from their culture and identity point of view. Gradually, these Rajputs gained and retained power in the area and subsequently forced the tribals to pay tax and do ***Begar* [Unpaid labour]**. Expansion of Maratha rule in the area further contributed to their marginalization, (Manohar (2001) said: "The rise of the Marathas in the mid-seventeenth century onwards for the first time led to serious inroads into the Bhils' homeland. They carried sustained campaigns against the Bhils, to develop trade and settled agriculture, in augmenting of the revenue, when refused to endorsing the incursion into their lifestyles. The peasants and traders from Gujarat and Maharashtra were encouraged to settle in the Bhil regions and the forests were cleared to bring land under the plough. Thousands of Bhils were massacred when they rose in revolt against this policy" (p.3).

The major parts of Madhya Pradesh were ruled by **Marathas**. They levied taxes on tribes and tribal rulers as per their own choice. In western Madhya Pradesh, the tribes were directed to clear forest and produce foodgrains for Maratha rulers. Since tribes were not habituated to produce cereals, many of them refused, and they were taught lesson. Non-tribals belonging to agricultural background from Gujarat were encouraged to inmigrate, settle over there, log the tree and produce cereals for tax payment and for market. And in this way, non-tribals rule was strengthened in the area. From the tribal livelihood point of view, this development was dysfunctional. It gradually ruined the environment-based sources of livelihood. In many pockets, through the number of restrictions, tribals' access to forest and forest produces were also restricted. It also led to the laying of the foundation stone of tribal indebtedness (Rahul; 2011).

Natural resources were perceived before industrial revolution, as objects in different societies; but the values generated have re-defined them as resources within England, and also in its colonies. Once the nature of relation between man and objects changed, the objects were perceived as the resources, for human population. Argument was made in favour of technological modernization. It was argued by the sociologists and the social anthropologists of the 19th Century representing the evolutionary school; that as the level of technological modernisation will increase, the amount of exploitation of natural resources will also increase, which in turn will bring material progress in the society. The third world countries will come out of the trap of backwardness. Faith in the technological modernization led process of development had also supported the core premises (see Banuri, 1989) of classical/orthodox theory of development. According to the classical theory, the western countries were developed and non-western countries were underdeveloped, people all over the world have equal capacities, hence inequality is not natural and it can be mitigated through concerted and planned human efforts with the help of science and technology, national government may play vital role in this context and development can only be measured in objective terms like the Gross National Product (GNP), the Gross Domestic Product (GDP), the Per Capita Income (PCI) and so on, and for this country has to move from the primary sector to secondary and tertiary sector. It was argued that only this model of development can bring prosperity.

The forest resources played the crucial role in the life of tribes during this period. According to Guha (1983), an adequate forest cover was ecologically necessary to sustain cultivation on the hilly terrains, whether it was **jhum** (Shifting Cultivation) or cultivation of the terraced variety. In addition, the forests themselves provided the year-long consumable food that could be utilized throughout the year. The Indian Famine Commission of 1881, has detailed 31 spices of trees, whose produce was consumed as food by the tribes of Satpura Hills, in different seasons- including fruits, flowers, buds, young shoots, seeds etc., both in raw and cooked form (in fact, peasants and tribals in forest areas normally know of over a hundred natural products, besides the staples, that can be gathered without cultivation). And where animal husbandry was a valuable appendage to cultivation (as in the Himalayan foothills), the forests were a prime source of fodder, in the form of grass and leaves. He further said that the organic linkages between tribals and forests were institutionalized through a number of socio-cultural mechanisms. According to a Government of India Report (1967), 'It is striking to see how many of the myths and legends, the deep sense of identity with the forest is [being] emphasized'. According to Brandis (1897), the first Inspector General of Forests, a large number of sacred groves were found in the Indian forests. These groves have been analyzed as an ancient strategy for the sustainable use of forest. Groves are part of the belief systems among many tribal groups, which have been used as the conservation mechanism. According to A. Sen and E. Lalhrietpuri (2006: 205-10), 'In pre-colonial days, there was greater diversity of landscapes, and sacred groves and shifting cultivation contributed to this diversity'. Similarly, according to A. Kothari (1996), totemic social organizations have contributed to the protection of plants and animals. Also, as late as in 1953, an eminent botanist N.L.Bor (1963) reported that 'the largest deodars (Himalayan Cedar) are those planted near temples and which are venerated and protected from injury'. According to Guha (1994), "For forest dependent communities, like charcoal iron makers and shifting cultivators, control over the forest was vital to their economic and cultural life. As Elwin demonstrated for Baiga and Agaria tribes, their rituals, myths, and sense of self were deeply interwoven with their forest world. Consequently, the take over of forest by the state and their subsequent working on commercial lines, when coupled with the alienation of tribal agricultural land to outsiders, destroyed their livelihood and culture. This process has resulted in a deep sense of helplessness, or what Elwin termed a 'loss of nerve' (p.14)".

The increasing inclination of a section of tribals, particularly tribal kings, in favour of the Hindu culture directly or indirectly contributed to the loss of livelihood and cultural degeneration, which in turn became problematic from the point of view of livelihood. The following case may be taken as an example. In order to increase their social status, some of the tribal kings in present Jharkhand state invited p**riests [also called Purohit]** from plains to perform the rituals. The p**riests** (Brahmins) subsequently settled and managed with the situation in their own favour, which had its impact on tribal economy. According to J. McDougall (2008: 5), 'Among the Santhals, there were headmen, who possessed authority over the whole groups of villages. Many centuries before the British assumed control over Ranchi district, one of these superior headmen emerged as the chief of such headman. This headman, who came to be known as the **Maharaja** (or chief) of Chotanagpur, was paid nominal rent by Adivasi villagers, and seems to have occasionally provided them with military protection. However, his position changed markedly in 17th century, after one Maharaja came into closer contact with the Mughal Empire. He began aspiring to high caste Hindu status, and brought non-Adivasis from the Gangetic plains to serve as priests, artisans and soldiers. Adivasis supported the new commerce through higher rents, forced labour and the expropriation of Adivasi lands by the newcomers'. This is one of the examples of Hinduisation of tribes. Many more examples may be cited. This process promoted a march towards marginalization in the social and economic life of tribal masses, directly or indirectly.

The British regime gradually crushed Marathas and other Hindu rulers to establish its own rule. However, it retained Maratha's policy measures to deal with tribes. They established the **Zamindari** system in the area. They encouraged logging for various purposes. The Land Acquisition Act-1894, The Indian Forest Act-1865 (revised in 1878), The Forest Policy of 1894, and The Forest Act-1927 etc., were ratified to establish the state monopoly on forests. They encouraged the non-tribals in the area, who could clear the forests; do farm work; produced grain, deposited revenue and foodgrains to the Britishers on time. According to Rahul (op. cit.): the British followed the policy of Marathas and brought in Kunbi, Patidar and Jat farmers from Gujarat and Rajasthan, respectively and got them settled on the Bhil lands in the plains, so as to multiply the earnings from land revenue and commercial agriculture simultaneously tame the militant Bhils. Non-adivasi farmers got converted into serfs and bonded labourers" (pp. 4-5).

Around 1850, there was the expansion of railway network in the area and logging in the forest of western M.P. particularly Jhabua district played crucial role. The expansion of railways contributed to deforestation. Nath (1960) claims, "For the smooth logging, good quality roads were also built in the forest area. And for all these purposes, heavy tax was imposed on tribals. The tribals were forced to become commercial agriculturist so that they can remain busy and also can pay taxes to the British Raj easily".

The shifting cultivation was an important source of livelihood of various tribes. But for taxing purposes, the Britishers discouraged shifting cultivation and forced tribals to become settled agriculturists and do farm work on lands, which were made clear after massive deforestation. If we examine the literature on shifting cultivation, two types of literature were available. Most of the British writers have perceived the shifting cultivation negatively. Writings of Dr. M.L. Bor, who was the Botanist of the Forest Research Institute, Dehradun and Nicholson, was the conservator of forests in Orissa, perceived the shifting cultivation negatively and M.D Chaturvedi, M.S. Sivaraman and S.H.Howard, et al have perceived the practice in a relatively positive manner (as quoted in Dhebar Commission Report, 1961: PP.145-148). Since negative interpretation of shifting cultivation was more powerful due to administrative support, efforts were made therefore, to discourage with the procedure. Some hundreds of shifting cultivators were displaced from their only source of livelihood, because of this effort alone.

The Britishers also brought radical changes in the revenue collection. For instance, during earlier days revenue was collected at the village level and village head was responsible for it. But, in the British regime, the process of revenue collection was made formal. It was centralised with the creation of the post of ***Malgujars***. The role of village headman was abolished. The *Malgujars* were empowered to collect and increase the revenue as per their choice, as a result, land revenue in the central and western Indian regions has increased to the level of about 65 per cent of the production of the farmer from around 25 per cent prevailing during earlier days (Mishra, 1956). All these steps have created a serious disruption in the traditional livelihood of tribes of the western Indian region (Hardiman, 1987).

The tribals' interaction with non-tribals increased in the later part of the British rule. This encouraged infiltration of large number of non-tribal vested interests in the tribal areas. Many of them became unbearable for tribals to such an extent that these outsiders were termed by them as **DIKU** (outsider having bad connotation) in the area today known as Jharkhand State. An overview of related literature depicts the impact of British rule on tribes of central regions in particular was dysfunctional. Views of three scholars, for example, may be cited to support the argument:

> **Hutton** (as quoted by Dhebar: op.cit.) said, "Far from being of immediate benefit to the primitive tribes, the establishment of British Rule in India did most of them much more harm than good. It may be said that the early days of British Administration did very great detrimental thing to the economic position of tribes through ignorance and neglect of their rights and customs... many changes have been caused incidentally by the penetration of the tribal country, the opening up of communications, the protection of forests and the establishment of schools, to say nothing of the openings given in this way to Christian Missions. Many of the results of these changes have caused acute discomfort to the tribes" (p. 21). More or less, similar observation was made by Elwin (1939, 1943a and 1943b).

Ghurye (1959) supported the views expressed by Hutton. He said, "The acuteness of discomfort was very often so great that it led to apathy, indifference, moral deterioration and even a decline in population" (p.21).

Baviskar (2004) observed that classification of forests under different categories during the British period and the formulation of distinct laws to regulate the relationship between tribes and forest was functional for Britishers and dysfunctional for tribes. The state control over forests during the colonial period meant the traditional sources of livelihoods for STs became the property of the state. It has forced the tribes to become tenants, trespassers and poachers.

From the livelihood point of view, development which took place in the tribal areas during British period was problematic.

Land, water, visitation community (such as community pastures, common dumping and threshing grounds, watershed, drainage, village tank, rivers and rivulets and wastelands) are the important resources on which tribals were historically dependent. But over the time, due to the state appropriation of these resources for revenue, expansion of railways, the construction of ship, industrialization, privatization and the establishment of development projects with the help of different Acts and Policies, the British administration prepared a foundation for the weakening status of tribes as well as natural resources.

The interaction between the tribals and the non-tribals refers to the encounter between the two unequal partners. Because of the poor bargaining power of tribes, the direction of their interaction with non-tribals was in favour of the latter. This encounter gradually led to the weakening of livelihood sources. Some of the new packages declared by the British Raj could not reach the poor tribals. No concerted effort was made in favour of human rights of tribals. The freedom struggle also could not address the problems of tribal masses in honest, deep and sustained manner, because the movement was largely confined to the plain areas. There were revolts and movements against the British administration and other vested interests such as Kol revolt (1821), Bhumij revolt (1832), Santal revolt (1763), Birsa Munda Movement (1890), Tana Bhagat Movement (1915) and Jharkhand Movement (1950) in present Jharkhand state, Revolt in Bastar in 1911, protests in Gudem-Rampain the 1920s, Worli revolt of 1945-46, Juang Movement (1837-56) and Kaujhar Movement (1891-93) in Odisha state and Gond revolt (1911) and movement for separate Gond state (1940) in Madhya Pradesh but these movements were either unsuccessful or had ad-hoc and localized impact. These revolts were forcefully suppressed by the power structure (Chaudhary, 2016). Hence, it may be said that by the time India became free, the tribal interaction with outside forces increased and with this condition, their livelihood has siganificantly decreased.

Post- Independence

India adopted democracy after independence. National

leaders also realized about the pitiable condition of tribes. Therefore, they made number of constitutional provisions[3] to extend social justice to them. Area specific and target group specific schemes were also launched over the time. The number of NGO's was also working in favour of tribes. But, from the basic need and livelihood point of view, the picture was unsatisfactory, rather frustrating. The model of development was capitalistic. It is not accountable to the tribes. Change agents working in villages were accountable to their boss and not to the very tribes. Even tribal change agents followed the same pattern of indifference.

Critically speaking, from the livelihood point of view, there were two broad consequences of trickle down approach of development on tribes: Some tribes (except primitive tribes) among whom class formation was slowly on. These tribes were numerically dominant. In Madhya Pradesh, these tribes are Gond, Bhil and Bhilala. Elites have emerged among them. Today, one can see hundreds of village, block and district level panchayat representatives. Also, as per reserved seat, their presence is found in the state assembly, parliament and other elective bodies. They take part in the decision making. And panchayat representatives are directly involved in the implementation of schemes at the local level. But their presence in middle and upper level bureaucracy, media, judiciary, entertainment world, trade and commerce etc., is largely missing. The inclusion of common tribes, even from among the dominant tribes, is not visible. Majority are being excluded. The tribal elites are also partially blamed for this state of affair. There is a feeling of in-group and out-group. It is argued that the tribal emerging elites such as panchayat representatives have imitated the style and functioning of non-tribal established Panchayat representatives (Chaudhary, 2004).

It is claimed that **DIKUs** are now also found among tribes. Majority of tribes are unable to integrate themselves with the so-called mainstreaming process. They are both left out and further marginalized. The majority of tribes in Central India live in villages. Most of them are poor. Their level of education, health status, social standing etc; is low. They are dependent on primary occupation. There is poor social capital formation among them. Their life resolves around the fulfillment of basic needs. Water, forest and land occupy key position in their life. The dilemma with them is that on the one hand for want of essential requirements they have miserably failed to avail such benefits of new opportunity and on the other hand due to continuous environmental degradation, they are unable to meet even their fundamental requirements. They are the serious and immediate victims of environmental degradation[4]. Because of unregulated acculturation coupled with the expansion of market forces and the expansion of communication and transportation network, they have become the victims of '**relative deprivation**'. Planning Commission Report (2002) rightly observed that non-tribal outsiders who converge into these areas corner both land and the new economic opportunities in commerce and industry. The incomplete rehabilitation of the displaced tribals has further compounded their woes as they are pushed into a vortex of increasing assetlessness, unemployment, debt bondage and destitution (p.67)[5].

The tribal youth, who are in large number, are now aspiring to live and behave like their non-tribal counterparts. The forces of modernization are enhancing their aspiration. But, the available resources are not permitting them fulfill the same. This is enhancing the amount of frustration, outmigration in search of better life; some of them are associating with the extremist forces in certain pockets in central India. The crisis also contributes towards the trafficking of tribal girls. The shrinking of local natural resources have contributed to intra-group conflict at the local level. Many new crimes are reported even in the villages of Vth Schedule areas. These crimes are handled by the police and the court and not by customary laws/ informal panchayats of elders due to logistic reasons (Chaudhary, 2012: 177-84).

The tribes have tested all the traditional coping mechanisms to ensure livelihood viz., they have curtailed the expenditure on essential items, have sold assets, taken loan, mortgaged household and agricultural assets, formed self-help groups (SHGs), adopted alternative sources of livelihood, availed the benefits of PDS, MNREGS, availed help from friends, relatives, NGOs etc; and many of them have also adopted seasonal outmigration, but these efforts are by and large have failed to deal with livelihood crisis created due to decline in labour work, decline in wage rate, decline in forest and farm yield, decline in common property resources, decline in water table, decline in rainfall, growth in population size, decline in farm size, loss of assets, lower bio-economic production, illness, increasing violence, drought, crop failure and so on.

No seriousness was observed among the change agents at the implementation level in villages - no matter these were tribal or non-tribal, local or outsider, specific. The scene is full of corruption and manipulation and the result is further pauperization. Equity and social justice dimension is missing. This conclusion may be supported from the findings made by the following three reports.

(1) A decade after independence, the Home Ministry, GoI, constituted a committee headed by Varrior Elwin (1960) to enquire into the functioning of government schemes in tribal areas. It was found that the officials in-charge of these schemes "were lacking in any intimate knowledge of the people (and) had very little idea of general policies for tribal development." Worse, there was "a tendency for officials to regard themselves as superior, as heaven-born missionaries of a higher culture. They boss the people about; their **chaprasis** abuse them; in order to get things done; they do not hesitate to threaten and bully. Any failure is invariably placed at the tribal lore,...the block officials blaming everything on the laziness, the improvidence, the suspiciousness, the superstitions of the people (pp. 20 and 192).

(2) U.N. Dhebar Committee report (1961) identified land alienation, the denial of forest rights and the displacement by development projects as among the major problems facing the adivasis. Sometimes, the state policy had failed to come to the rescue of the tribals; at other times, it had only worked to impoverish them further. The state machinery had been unable to

prevent the loss of land to outsiders, or to check the exploitative activities of moneylenders.

(3) 28th and 29th reports of the Commissioner for SCs and STs (1988 and 1990) headed by B.D. Sharma said that the major problems faced by tribals were land alienation, restrictions on their use of forests and displacement by dams and other large projects. He pointed out that "the tribal people are at a critical point of their history...". They were "losing command over resources at a very fast rate but are also facing social disorganization which is unprecedented in their history". And yet the "tales of woes from tribal areas are hardly heard outside. And when they come they are not taken seriously...". What was worse, "the state itself sometimes tends to adopt a particular role and become a privy even for actions not quite legal simply because the matter concerns voiceless small communities" (quoted by Guha: 2007: pp. 3306-8).

The review of other related literature supported the argument that tribes were yet to avail the benefits of development rather many of them were the victims of development. Remedial measures have largely failed to arrest pauperization. Instead of protecting their human rights and integrating them with mainstream process they have been left at their own to encounter challenges of globalisation.

During-Globalisation

The globalisation was formally introduced in the country in July 1991. The tribal areas with having ample amount of state owned land and natural resources, particularly coal, iron, bauxite, water etc's; are heaven for globalization. As expected, hundreds of industrial plants/power projects have been established in the tribal areas and outside which are dependent on raw materials available in tribal belt. 121 MOUs have been signed since 1991 in states of Chhattisgarh and Odisha[6]. During the new development regime thousands of acres of land have been taken over by these industrial concerns without serious efforts for the rehabilitation of the displaced tribal masses. Forest Conservation Act-1980 makes it clear that forest land shall not be used for non-forest work without the approval of GOI but in spite of that large part of forest land is used for different activities. Authentically it is very difficult to estimate number of tribes who are the victim of displacement, however, some unofficial studies, particularly by Fernandes (2008) estimates this figure at around 60 million for the period from 1947 to 2004 involving 25 million ha. of forest and six million ha. of other Common Property Resources. It is estimated that of the total displaced people 40 p c were tribals. Hardly a third of the displaced persons, including tribals, have been resettled. Sahu (2009) said that at least 90 per cent of tribal population displaced by development projects, experience a drastic drop in their standards of living. His findings regarding the impact of construction of upper Indravati reservoir in southwest Odisha showed that about 40,000 tribals were displaced due to this project. They were promised many things, but no promise was fulfilled. Today, they live with lack of water, money, electricity, education, medical facilities, and food. If anyone gets seriously, ill in resettlement villages they are simply left to die. It appears that they were the victim of 'internal colonialism' (Sengupta, 1982). According to Ekka (2000) in Jharkhand nearly 90 per cent of those displaced by various projects between 1951 and 1995 were tribals. The displacement has led to what Shah (2007) calls a "Log-jam of adverse conditions", for these affected. Their productive assets and income sources are lost, they have experienced a new pattern of economy which they are least acquainted, their community systems and social networks have weakened and cultural identity, traditional authority and trait of mutual help have diminished (Beck, 2009).

Of course, some efforts were made through social movements[7] against the development projects and in favour of rehabilitation of displaced tribals or the victims of what Padel (2013) called 'Investment Induced Displacement', but these movements were few and far between to address the plight of these displaced people rather the number of MOUs with the industrial houses to establish projects in these areas are increasing day by day. Maximum number of social movements is shining on paper. Some of these movements were as dysfunctional as industrial and corporate houses. Large number of tribals in Chhattisgarh, Jharkhand and Orissa were the victims of naxalite movement and the state-sponsored terrorism. Significant number of innocent tribals have been killed and humiliated by police and naxalites in these states during last couple of decades[8]. There are cases of rape of tribal women by the security forces. Roy (2010) mentioned that large number of tribal teenage girls and boys were joining Maoist movement in desperation on finding their beloved raped and murdered, with justice impossibile. She observed how Himanshu Kumar was driven out of Chhattisgarh. And what has happened to the adivasis, whom he had encouraged to stand up and be witnesses to the atrocities, they have experienced? Sodi Sambo, who had survived a group shooting to be the witness, was arrested and disappeared under police care. Is she still alive? Soni Sori, whose nephew trained to be a journalist and recorded atrocities, taken into custody apparently just because she was a witness, was tortured with stones forced into her private parts. Padel (2013) also reported similar incidence of violence from the state of Odisha.

Social, economic and cultural aftermath of globalisation was imagined by the state. It was felt that India will make progress in different spheres and its economy will significantly improve, a neo- middle class will emerge and gradually its size will increase, market forces, consumer culture, information technology related devices etc., will reach to the village, urbanization and industrialization will get momentum and new jobs will be created, particularly in the private sector but the gap between the rich and the poor, the developed regions and the underdeveloped regions and the dominants and the dependents will also increase. And if increasing inequality is not addressed; the problem of rural violence in the form of suicide, crime against women, group conflict, robbery etc; are likely to increase. Therefore, in order to address the emerging resentments in tribal areas, improve the status of tribal livelihood and their quality of life, besides the functioning of plethora of welfare schemes after 1991, two major steps have been exclusively taken by the state. These are PESA-1996 and FRA-2006.

The PESA came into existence on December 24, 1996 in Schedule V Areas in the states of Andhra Pradesh, Gujarat, Himachal Pradesh, Madhya Pradesh, Chhattisgarh, Maharashtra, Orissa, Rajasthan and Jharkhand. In the principle, PESA is aimed to empower village panchayats and **Gram Sabhas** in the scheduled areas, in such a manner that they can own resources, manage affairs and decide course of action for development. But the Act could not become main stream policy (Sinha, 2011), some states had misinterpreted the concept of **Gram Sabha** and equated it with the meeting of the **Gram Panchayat** (**The Telegraph**, Guwahati edition, April 09, 2012). In the case of Pachwara coal mines project in Jharkhand, for example, at no point of time, any consultation in any form with the affected Santal and Paharia households, the villagers and the **Gram Sabha** was made (Iyer, 2013), the purpose of PESA has not been understood, either by the politicians or by the bureaucracy. The people at large were not aware of the provisions of PESA (Tripathy, 2013). In many cases relating to land acquisition, dubious method was used through coercion and brutal force to obtain consent of villagers (Das, 2005). The level of participation of people in **Gram Sabha** has been very low, its meeting is rarely held and if it is organized, only few people attend the meeting. **Gram Sabha** is almost like a non-functional organization (Sisodia, 2009). Even if **Gram Sabha** meeting is organized qorum is not fulfilled and in many cases decisions were taken on those issues, which were not as per PESA spirit (Chaudhary, 2013). It is widely believed that PESA has not been implemented in spirit. Also, the tension has been noted between the functions of the **Gram Sabha** and functions of the **Gram Panchayat** (Saxena, 2004: Upadhyay, 2007).

Similarly, the Forest Rights Act was passed on 18 December, 2006 and notified on 31 December, 2007. There is a provision to provide Land Title Rights to locals, (both individuals and communities), they have right to use non-timber forest produce (NTFPs), use grazing land, enjoy forest management rights and right for proper rehabilitation etc. The number of studies is available to see the functioning of this project. Chaudhary (2014) observed that in Madhya Pradesh till March 2010 altogether 404, 591 claims were received from both individuals and community, but only 109, 000 (about 25 per cent) claims were cleared. Altogether, 359, 520.09 acres of land were allotted under 89, 035 titles. It is also claimed that the **pattas** distributed were not accepted as negotiable instruments for receiving subsidies or accessing bank loans. Iyer (2013) has cited the summary report on implementation of the Forest Rights Act prepared by Council for Development, New Delhi in September 2010. It says "all of the key features of this legislation have been underlined by a combination of apathy and sabotage during the process of implementation. In the current situation, the rights of majority of the tribal and other traditional forest dwellers were being denied and the purpose of the legislation was being defeated. Unless immediate remedial measures were taken, instead of undoing the historical injustice to tribal and other traditional forest dwellers, the Act will have the opposite outcome of making them even more vulnerable to eviction and denial of fare customary access to forests....Both the Central and State government had actively pursued policies that are in direct violation of the spirit of the Act" (pp 48-49).

These findings prove that inspite of innovative character and good intensions these interventions were ineffective. Following the findings support the argument that all interventions-internal and extraneous – are by and large failed to improve status of tribes. For instance, during 2005-06 Infant Mortality Rate (IMR) was 43.8 per cent among the tribes, but it was 36.1 per cent among others. 64 per cent pregnant women of non-ST categories could access a doctor for ante-natal care, but its percentage was only 28 among tribal women. The incidence of stunting and wasting, number of underweight children and number of 12-13 months children, who could not receive vaccination was higher among STs in comparison to others. According to the World Bank report (2011) 63.3 per cent, STs were below poverty line [1983]. It decreased to 43.8 per cent in 2004-05. But, 45.6 per cent, non-STs were below the poverty line [1983] and their number decreased to 27.5 per cent in [2004-05]. M.P. had 20.3 per cent of tribal population with having 50.2 neo-natal, 25.2 post-natal, 75.4 infant, 41.6 child and 117.0 under five mortality rate per 1,000 live births [2005] (p .50). A World Bank Study (2007) in Orissa finds that the child and infant mortality rates were higher among the tribals. This is largely due to the poverty (lower levels of income and assets), the low level of education and the poor access and utilization of health services. Sharma et al. (2009) observed that the lowest and the second lowest wealth quintiles (based on an asset index) have experienced the highest under five mortality (119 and 97 deaths per 1,000 respectively) compared with respectively 66 and 28 deaths per 1,000 among the children of families belonging to the **'Top to Quintiles'.** In other words, the children in the poorest households were four times as likely to die before their 5th birthday compared with those in the richest quintile (p.53).

Micro studies on food insecurity among the tribes provide a contextual picture of the causes of chronic mal-nutrition. A 2005 survey of Adivasi areas in two Indian states has found that 99 per cent of the sample Adivasi households faced chronic hunger, 1-0.25 faced semi-starvation during the previous week and not a single household had more than four out of ten assets from a list that includes such the basic items as a blanket, a pair of shoes and a radio (CEFS, 2005: 58). Mal-nutrition, sickness on the regular basis and infrequent treatment or the delayed treatment increases the mortality rate among tribes.

The medical practiceners generally link poor health outcome among the tribes to lack of demand or ignorance. The reluctance of tribal women to accept modern treatment contributes to the higher level child and infant mortality. In Rajasthan, about 86 per cent births occur at home and over three-fourths were conducted by the untrained **dais** or other untrained personnel largely, because ante-natal care was not accepted and was not considered necessary in the tribal societies (Nagda, 2004:61). A longitudinal study in the tribal dominated Bolangir district of Orissa found that villagers took young children to the hospital only, if the condition of the children was critical, this is because the condition of road was poor and it was very costly to hire a vehicle. They have also identified giving birth as a risk, because mothers could not reach health centers, because of inadequate road access. (p.63). Absence of doctor, nurses and medicine etc; contributes to disinterest in favour of hospitals.

The average land holdings have declined among all groups in the country from 1983 to 2004-05, but it has declined sharply among tribals[9]. This reflects the alienation of tribals from traditional lands. Besides, the loss of housing and land, the loss of control over water and forests has forced the tribal to become chronically poor. It has compelled them to remain away from the public schemes, affected their traditional food practices and forced them outmigrate to cities to work under harsh conditions.

Why this state of affair?

If we see number of welfare projects introduced for the development of tribal masses alone, we cannot even imagine such a poor state of affair coupled with low quality of life. On the one hand, they lose their cultural heritage, which helps them to lead life, since long and on the other hand, they are largely failed to avail the benefits of new development projects. Even seasonal outmigration, NGO intervention, under the banner of corporate social responsibility and social movements going on in the tribal belt etc; are largely incapable to arrest ongoing pauperization among them. Only small number of tribes of central India have availed the fruits of development. But, they have been made dependent prone and are habituated to pay social, psychological and cultural cost of development. Why this state of affair? A number of scholars commented on this issue. As an example, the opinion of three scholars is being presented below to know the roots of underdevelopment and backwardness among the tribal lot of the central India in particular.

According to (Guha, 2011), there are eight broad reasons responsible for this. These are (a) tribes live in the affluent resource areas, which are haven for investors and corporate houses. These areas are forced to supply raw materials without taking care of socio-economic and environmental consequences, (b) tribals have failed to produce a fighter like. Dr. BR Ambedkar therefore, their plight is neither properly represented at the macro level nor it is honestly addressed, (c) Tribals at large are geographically scattered population. Therefore, they are not perceived as assertive critical vote bank by political parties which in turn make the parties insensitive to tribal problems, (d) Tribals of central India are found in less number in the country level bureaucracy like their counterparts of north-east India. As a result, the top level bureaucracy either does not understand their plight or they are indifferent on the very issues, (e) Tribals were known for indigenous knowledge system. It has helped them lead life in a peaceful manner, since centuries. But, such knowledge does not command respect in the non-tribal society. The latter depends on modern knowledge system, which is a product of research institutes and laboratories; (f) Recognition of tribal language is a pre-condition for educational and subsequently socio-economic development of tribes. Unfortunately, only Santali language was recognized. The tribal children speak in their mother tongue in the family, but in the school, they are taught either in Hindi or in the local language spoken by non-tribals. As a result, their performance level is poor, (g) Today, many tribal areas are conflict-prone. It is reported that there are 83 extremist-affected districts in the country of which 42 districts are found in the scheduled areas. As a result, the development projects are compelled to suffer, and (h) It is said that media is the 4th pillar of democracy. Over the time, the importance of electronic media has increased, but the electronic media does not provide proper space to the tribal issues in its programmes. Therefore, the people at large do not know problems and the challenges faced by tribes.

Oommen (2014) has identified four broad reasons, which are responsible for underdevelopment of tribes. These are - (a) tribal voice is weak at different forums. For, their population size is small and therefore, their representation in elective bodies is also small, (b) Since they are scattered here and there, therefore the history and status of collective mobilization against the violation of human rights and in favour of protective discrimination mechanism in ineffective, (c) Historically, they do not have reference group with whom they can compare, as the SCs compare themselves with upper caste Hindus. A poor tribal compare himself with another poor, because, others were unfound and only poor tribals were found in many villages; and (d) As a result, they have no feeling of common shared disability to unite themselves against marginalization, as it is done by dalits, primarily, because of the practice of untouchability against them.

Xaxa (2014) identified seven interconnected reasons, responsible for the deprivation and marginality among tribes. These are: (a) The government of India adopted integration approach in post-independence, for tribal evelopment. It was forcefully said that neither isolation nor assimilation, but integration will solve the problem. But, unfortunately instead of adopting **bouquet** technique, it followed **melting pot** technique, which has forced them loose their identity in favour of others, (b) Elwin promoted isolation approach, which was endorsed by Pt. Jawaharlal Nehru. It encouraged the political integration, but socio-cultural isolation, (c) There were plenty of development schemes, but these schemes were poorly implemented and local elites were indifferent, (d) Tribals at large, who live in villages have traditional lifestyle. They depend on **Jhar-Phunk** [mumbo-jumbo] technique instead of modern treatment techniques on many occasions. Therefore, they are not serious on the functioning of **PHC** and **Aanganwadi Kendra**, (e) Since long, there was misappropriation of tribal/ forest land, either by the state or by the vested interests, without any meaningful rehabilitation package therefore, landholding tribe is forced to become landless labourer without exposure to the modern technology, (f) India is known for adopting capitalistic model of development, since the British days, which believes in top-down approach. Can we achieve the socialistic goal with capitalistic path?, and lastly (g) there was popularization of left wing extremism in the central India due to which most of the welfare projects were either half-heartedly introduced or were non-functional.

The net result is that there is lack of opportunity, lack of capabilities, denial of entitlement etc, which inhibit their social inclusion.

Conclusion

It may be inferred that the marginalization of tribes of Central India, which began during the pre-British period, gradually became forceful and speedy with the passage of time. Pro-active efforts could not arrest the marginalization, although it led to the emergence of small number of tribal elites. The role of these elites in the development of tribes is debatable. It is reported that the elected representatives take interest in the passing of Acts and provision for tribal development, but they were indifferent at the level of implementation. More or less, similar is the situation at the local level. Some of these local level tribal elites were almost like a '**Diku**'. The change agents working at the panchayat and block level were not accountable to the targeted population, primarily due to the absence of effective checks and balance. After 1991, the speed of erosion of livelihood sources remained very fast. The available resources are being misappropriated by the vested interests. For want of required resources and capabilities such as knowledge of English, Computer, social capital, economic resource etc; majority of tribes of central India have failed to avail the benefits of new opportunities, rather they are compelled to suffer. They are also forced by consumer culture to spend their insignificant and minimum savings. And in spite of various efforts, they are forcefully compelled by the negative forces, particularly globalization today, to further move towards insecurities. Looking to the state of affairs, it appears that under the given context, it is very difficult to restore their human rights and discontinue their march towards livelihood insecurities and deprivation.

End Notes

The states in the Central India refers to Odisha, Chhattisgarh, Jharkhand, M.P. and Rajasthan which are being inhabited by 22.8, 30.6, 26.2, 21.1 and 13.5 per cent tribal population, respectively, from their concentration point.

According to Padel (2013) Niyam Raja, the Dongria Konds, the manifestation of the supreme deity of Niyamgiri is an example of tribal societies' ecological values. Dongria have maintained a 'Nigam' (rule), over many generations, of no cutting of forest on top of mountains. The hill slopes they often cultivate, but never the top- unlike other tribes. This is why Niyamgiri is the dense forest on its summit of all the bauxite- capped mountains in South Odisha and Nort-East Andhra.

(1) Important among these are Article 15, 16, 19, 23, 29, 46, 164, 330, 332, 335, 338, 339, 342 and 371, all protection-oriented, Article 15, 16, 19, 46, 275 and 339 for development, Article 334,338 and 339 is administration related and applicable in the Sixth Schedule

areas and finally Articles 330, 332, 334, 335 and 340 are for expanding the reservation facility in job and admission issues (see Chaudhary; 2009).

(2) Besides the economic loss, environmental degradation contributes to serious health loss. Uranium mining and its processing near the Subarna Rekha River has even led to radioactive pollution. According to the Planning Commission (2008), mining dust causes pneumoconiosis (a group of lung deseases), eye infection, conjunctivitis, corneal ulcers, glaucoma and squint trachoma, silicosis is caused by dust from coal, mica, silver, lead, zinc and manganese mines, pottery and ceramic units, sand blasting, metal grinding, building and construction work, rock mining, iron and steel plants, slate pencil factories, etc.

(3) Canera (2000) underlined the indicators of impoverishment among the victims of displacement due to globalisation. These are: landlessness, joblessness, homelessness, marginalization, food insecurity, high morbidity, loss of access to CPRs and community disarticulation. These indicators are also available among tribes of Central India- no matter whether they are direct victim of displacement or not.

(4) The total proposed budget of these MoUs was Rs. 1, 92,126 crore. About half of them have already started functioning. In M.P. 324 MOUs were signed of which 12 MOUs have been implemented and 18 are in process. The areas where MOUs have been signed are agriculture and food processing, forest and herbal industries, infrastructure, minerals, power, textiles and tourism. In Odisha, 235 MOUs were signed during the above period. These were in the following sectors: Air Products (04), Alumina and Aluminium (12), Aviation (01), Cement (P.26) Ferro Products (09), Food Processing (08), Mining (03), others (13), Paper (05), Palletisation (14) Petroleum (05), Power (63) and Steel (72) (Source: Different websites of the concerned state governments dated June 24, 2014).

(5) There are twelve reasons responsible for unrest in tribal areas. These are: absence of self governance, defective forest policy, defective excise policy, land related issues, various types of exploitation, humiliation, political marginalization, land alienation, displacement, faulty implementation of welfare schemes in scheduled areas, indebtedness and violence by the state (Planning Commission Report: op. cit.).

(6) Dungdung (2013) reported that in Jharkhand 557 people were killed in so-called crossfire and people have been put behind bars (P.29). He quoting data from National Crime Records Bureau (NCRB) revealed that from 2001 to 2010, 6075 adivasi women were

raped, 12730 cases of atrocities and 383 cases of untouchability practices against adivasis were registered in different police stations across the country. 5000 adivasi women were sexually exploited in Chhattisgarh during the anti-naxal operations, which grow every day in the Red Corridor across nine states of the country (p. 80).

(7) **The Times of India,** Bhopal Edition (Nov. 12, 2013) reported that in seven states like Gujrat, Rajasthan, Madhya Pradesh, Maharashtra, Chhattisgarh, Jharkhand and Odisha number of agricultural labourers have increased by 35 percent between 2001 to 2011 at the national level but among the tribals of these states, the spike was a mind boggling 52 per cent. As a result, 48 per cent of all tribal workers are now agricultural labourers, compared to 38 percent a decade ago. At the national level, 30 per cent of the workers are agricultural labourers, slightly up from 27 per cent a decade ago.

References

Banuri, Tariq (1989): *Modernisation and its Discontents: A Perspectives from the Sociology of Knowledge*, Helsinki: World Institute of Development Economic Research.

Baviskar, Amita (2004): *In the Belly of the River: Adivasi Battles over 'Development in the Narmada Valley*, New Delhi: Oxford.

Beck, H (2009): 'Development Induced Displacement: A Cause of Concern', paper presented at the International Seminar on *Adivasi/ST Communities in India: Development and Change,* New Delhi: August 27-29.

Bor, N L (1963): *Manual of Indian Forest Botany,* New Delhi: Oxford, p-18.

Brandis, D (1897): *Indian Forestry*, Working, p-12.

CEFS (Centre for Environment and Food Security) (2005): *Political Economy of Hunger in Adivasi Areas: A Survey Research on Hunger in Adivasi Areas of Rajasthan and Jharkhand*, New Delhi: CEFS.

Canera, Michael M (2000): 'Poverty Risks from Population, Displacement in Water Resources Development', *HIID Development Discussion paper No. 355, Cambridge,* Mass: Harward.

Chamb ers, R and G R Conway (1991): *Sustainable Rural Livelihoods: Practical Concepts for the 21st Century*, IDS Discussion paper 296.

Chaudhary S N (2004): *Dalit and Tribal Leadership in Panchayat,* New Delhi: Concept.

Chaudhary S N (2009): *Tribal Development Since Independence,*(ed.), New Delhi: Copncept.

Chaudhary S N (2012): *In Search of Sustainable Development: Scenario in a Tribal Village of Madhya Pradesh,* Delhi: Serials.

Chaudhary S N (2013): *Globalisation, National Development and Tribal Identity* (ed.), Jaipur: Rawat.

Chaudhary S N (2016): *Social Movements in Tribal India, (ed.),* Jaipur: Rawat.

Dhebar, U N (1961): *Report of the Scheduled Areas and Scheduled Tribes Commission,* New Delhi: Government of India Press.

Duggal, R (1990): 'Health and Population in Three Tribal Villages' in *Demography of Tribal Development (ed.),* A. Bose, R.P. Tyagi and U.P.Sinha, New Delhi: BR Publishing Corporation.

Dungdung, G (2013): *Whose Country is it Anyway?*, Kolkata: Adivani.

Ekka, A (2000): 'Jharkhand Tribals: Are They Really a Minority?', *EPW,* Vol. 35 (52-53): pp 4610-12.

Elwin, V (1939): *The Baiga,* London: John Murray.

Elwin, V (1943): *The Aboriginals*, Bombay: Oxford.

Elwin, V (1955): *A Philosophy for NEFA*, London: Oxford.

Fernandes, W (2008): 'Sixty Years of Development Induced Displacement in India' in Mathur H. M. (ed.), *India Social Development Report 2008: Development and Displacement,* New Delhi: Oxford.

Ghurye, G S (1959): *The Scheduled Tribes* (third edition), Bombay: Popular.

Government of India (1960): *Report of the Committee on Special Multipurpose Tribal Blocks,* New Delhi: Manager of Publications.

Government of India (2002): *Tenth Five Year Plan-2002-2007,* New Delhi: Planning Commission.

Government of India (2008): *Development Challenges in Extremist Affected Areas: Report of an expert Group to Planning Commission,* New Delhi: Planning Commission.

Guha, R (1983): 'Forestry in British and Post-British India: A Historical Analysis', *EPW,* Vol. XVIII (44): pp 1882-96.

Guha, R (1994): *Sociology and the Dilemmas of Development,* New Delhi: ICSSR.

Guha, R (2007): 'Adivasis, Naxalites and Indian Democracy', *EPW,* Vol. 42(32): pp 3305-12.

Hardiman, David (1987): *The Coming of the Devi: Adivasi Assertion in Western India,* Delhi: OUP.

Hutton, J J (1931): *Census of India,* Delhi: Gian.

Iyer, K G (2013): 'Globalisation, Jharkhandi Identity and Rural Transformation', in (ed.) S.N. Chaudhary, *Globalisation, National Development and Tribal Identity,* op.cit, pp. 48-49 and 57-81.

Koshambi, D D (1956): *An Introduction to the Study of Indian History,* Mumbai: Popular.

Kothari, A (1996): 'Is Joint Management of Protected Areas Desirable and Possible', in Ashish Kothari, N. Singh and S. Suri (ed.), *People and Protected Areas: Towards Participatory Conservation in India,* New Delhi: Sage.

MacDougall, J (2008): *Tribal Resistance,* New Delhi: Critical Quest.

Manohar, D (2001): *Bagh Ke Bachche Hain Hum (We are the children of tiger),* Hoshangabad: Disha Samvad.

Mishra, D P (1956): *The History of the Freedom Movement in Madhya Pradesh (ed.),* Nagpur: Government Press.

Nagda, B L (2004): 'Tribal Population and Health in Rajasthan', *Studies of Tribes and Tribals,* 21(1): 1-8.

Nath, S (1960): *Bhils of Rataamal: An Analysis of the Social Structure of a Western Indian Community (Dissertation),* Baroda: University of Baroda.

Padel, F (2013): 'Tribal Identity and Real Development in a Rapidly Globalising World' in *Globalisation, National Development and Tribal Identity* (ed.) S. N. Chaudhary, Jaipur: Rawat.

Rahul (2011): *Sahukars Rule the Root-Status of Informal Rural Financial Market in Adivasi Dominated Regions of Western Madhya Pradesh,* opted from www.scribd.com/doc/47224758/Sahukars-Rule-the-Roots

Roy, Arundhati (2010): 'Walking with the comrades', *Outlook,* March 29.

Sahu, Subrat Kumar (2009): *DAM-aged,* Documentary Film.

Saxena, N C (2004): *Policies for Tribal Development: Analysis and Suggestions,* New Delhi: National Advisory Council.

Sen, A and E Lalhrietpui (2006): 'Scheduled Tribes (Recognition of Forest Rights) Bill: A View from Anthropology and Call for Dialogue', *EPW,* Vol. XII (39): pp 4205-10.

Sengupta, Nirmal (1982): *Jharkhand: Fourth World Dynamics,* Delhi: Authors Guild.

Shah, A (2007): *Pattern Processes of Reproduction and Policy Imperatives for Poverty in Remote Rural Areas: A Case Study of Southern Orissa in India,* Working Paper 179, Ahmedabad: Institute of Development Research.

Sharma M, B.L. Sarangi, J Kanungo, S Sahoo, L Tripathy, A Pathak, J Tewari and A D Rath (2009): 'Accelerating Malnutrition Reduction in Orissa', *IDS Bulletin* 40(4): pp 78-85.

Sinha, Ratnawali (2011): 'Governance in the Scheduled Areas: Expectations and Realities', *Man in India,* Vol. 91(3-4): 429-40.

Sisodia, Y S (2002): 'Decentralised Governance in Madhya Pradesh: Experience of the Gram Sabha in Scheduled Areas', *EPW*, Vol. 37(40): pp 4100-04.

The World Bank (2007): *Achieving the MDGs in India's Poor States: Reducing Child Mortality in Orissa*, Report, New Delhi.

The World Bank (2011): 'Perspectives on Poverty in India: Stylized Facts from Survey Data', *India Poverty Assessment*, New Delhi: Poverty Reduction and Economic Management Network.

The World Bank (2011): *Poverty and Social Exclusion in India*, Washington, D.C.

Times of India (2013): *Tribal Loose Land, Forced to Become Farm Workers*, November 12.

Tripathy, S N (2013): 'Paradox of Development and the Plight of Tribes in India', in (ed.) S.N. Chaudhary, *Globalisation, National Development and Tribal Identity,* op. ct., pp. 95-113.

Upadhyaya, S (2007): 'Assessment of Orissa PESA: Legal Perspective', Paper prepared for the Study of Poverty and Social Exclusion in India, New Delhi: Indian Institute of Dalit Studies.

Chapter - 3

Baiga, Bharia and Saharia Tribes in Madhya Pradesh

— ***D.K. Verma***

Robert John Haylock Chambers[1] essentially conceptualized the livelihood in the context of poverty and tribals were never poor people. Poverty is a non-tribal concept and juxtaposing poverty-centred concept of livelihood in tribal areas is ontologically erroneous, I would empirically explain in my following discussion. Chambers and Conway elaborated the concept comprising the capabilities, assets (stores, resources, claims and access) and activities required for a means of living and a livelihood is sustainable which can cope with and recover from stress and shocks, maintain or enhance its capabilities and assets, and also provide sustainable livelihood opportunities for the next generation; and which contributes net benefits to their livelihoods at the local and global levels and in the short and long term. It was economics while for tribal it is ecology.

'Livelihood' and further 'Sustainable Livelihood' are further *mis*-conceptualization in the context of PVTGs with the increase in 'outside intervention' heterogeneity; the habitat erosion and the dependency on non-tribals have increased. How PVTGs could be empowered in a sustainable manner appears as the "*trauma of primitiveness*".

The contents, as such focused on [i] the review of various policies and perspectives implemented and advocated by the intellectuals, the ideologues and the interventionists on the Primitive Tribal Groups (PTGs) or particularly Vulnerable Tribal Groups (PVTGs or Most-VTGs). [ii] the methodological and empirical base was developed from the research studies on Baiga, Bharia and Saharia in Madhya Pradesh. [iii] The convergence on empirical understanding about the identities by Baiga, Bharia and Saharia tribes. The status characteristics generalization (SCG) theory by Cecilia Ridgeway (2014) in support of a new type of social status was conceptualized as 'Affirmed Status' besides ascribed status explained by Ralph Linton (*The study of Man*, 1936). The latter explains the emergence of the affirmed status with the extension of 'Social Devolution Theory' by the author[2] to answer why Baiga, Bharia and Saharia are at the critical stage?

The tribes were found to have identified their position about their land and love on being simple and natural. Albeit, perspectives of intellectuals, ideologues and interventionists differ, but they (Baiga, Bharia and Saharia) ask how come 'we are disparaged with primitive or particularly vulnerable identities'? Besides, their imposed identities as primitive or particularly vulnerable, they (discontent youth among Baiga, Bharia and Saharia) also question 'why such policies and programmes are designed that deliberately keep them poor in their own ecologically-rich areas that are isolated in such a manner that they cannot use their own land and forests for economic-opportunities but who are the people in which ecologically-poor areas who become rich due to our isolation'? and 'how come the globalized market evades that isolation which is also one of our imposed characteristics?

Albeit, empirical evidences gathered from the field in the form of 'what they say' are juxtaposed certain perspectives (rather beliefs) were found to have selectively advanced as the contribution to knowledge by well-known ideologues, but to invoke or suppress the facts to promote certain ideologies or serve some vested interests. The author laments that field-based academician get very low priority being encased in university libraries, but book-review writings by intellectuals were available at shops in the airport lounges, make them popular among bureaucrats and legislatures, who quote and cite references of such ideologues, draw policies having packages of (un)welfare programmes. Different perspectives appear just reel-fiction for execution, entertainment or exploitation; because their socio-economic status in the post-modern-context remains unchanged, as the outside world still identify them as primitive or particularly vulnerable.

Varrier Elwin and Ram Chandra Guha were indeed great ideologues and renowned intellectuals. Elwin at the time of Independence and living for almost two decades with tribals advanced non-interference ideology and Guha after his very famous work *Savaging and Civilized* writes in the recent blog ("Where are the conservative intellectuals in India?", March 15, 2015, Caravan) finds Arun Shourie as the only intellectual, socially conservative in India. He also identifies G S Ghurey as old-fashioned scholar, who considers the task for the nation-in-the-making was to bring tribals ever closer to the (Hindu) mainstream. But what *so-called old-fashioned* academician aspired six decades back, tribals want to achieve even now, after living as 'identified *inassimilable'* (notified or de-notified, stigma of notification as de-N continues) like untouchables for more than six decades of freedom from the British Raj, in geographically isolated areas in independent India (one tribal youth called it *economic-imprisonment* like embargo), be it in the name of environment/forest/tiger/bio-sphere reserve or natural resources and its mining as state-owned for national produce (largely for non-tribals) or under the Nehurivian *Panchsheel policy* advocated as 'non-interference in tribal areas' by Varrier Elwin, but now deconstructed by the tribal themselves as more in favour of making the Modern Temples of India.

Baiga, Bharia and Saharia *premunire* state-sponsored social stigma of being identified as 'primitive' or 'particularly vulnerable', which was considered by them more derogatory than 'Criminal Tribals' as notified by British during pre-independence period. They were not primitive, but non-tribal economy has made them poor, despite their ecologically-rich habitat. They were not vulnerable, but their economic-political exploitation to siphon out economic benefits from the affluent natural resource areas without giving their due share made them particularly vulnerable.

The tribes were neither primitive nor vulnerable, but proud who *premunire, a social writ against the continued British Raj policy challenging* socio-environmental injustice and wrongs done to them by the state, the intellectuals, the ideologues and the interventionists. Limitations were of course there with regard to the interpretation of what they say and what we 'deconstruct' as their meaning, but respecting their 'identities' as they wish to reveal to the world, we need to review interventions.

Tribal people, variously called as Adivasis, Janjati, Vanvasi are better known as a category of those people/communities designated as the Scheduled Tribes under the Constitution of India, so as to empower them with special provisions for education, economic and social welfare in general and for their representation in political, education and services in particular. According to Oxford Dictionary "A tribe is a group of people in a primitive or barbarious stage of development acknowledging the authority of a chief and usually regarding them as having a common ancestor." But other than constitutionally designated category as scheduled tribe ST, there is little agreement among the social scientists including the anthropologists and the sociologists about the definition of tribe.

Albeit, scholars have viewed tribal societies in the light of evolutionary theory and sought to demonstrate tribes being represented as type of social organization, as well as stage in social evolution by the comparison of contemporary tribes as primitive societies. The British Anthropologists distinguish analytically between the band, the segmentary system and the chiefdom. But, they have continued, by and large, to apply the same term tribe to the three hundred units that comprise the Scheduled Tribes of India. It covered the modes of tribal organization from the band to the chiefdom, as classified systematically by the colonial administration.

The tribes in Indian continent orginate from the language families like Andamanese, Austro-Asiatic, Dravidian and Tibeto-Burman. These tribals belong to different language families, live in distinct geographic settings. The major tribal belts in India include Andaman, Nicobar and Lakshadweep islands; the

Himalayan belt: (Assam, Meghalaya, Arunachal Pradesh, Nagaland, Manipur, Mizoram, Tripura, hills of Uttar Pradesh and Himachal Pradesh); the central India belt, where more than half of the tribal population of the country live, in the states like Bihar, West Begal, Orissa, Chattisgarh and Madhya Pradesh.

The western Indian tribal belt include these communities in Rajasthan, Maharashtra, Gujrat, Goa, Dadra and Nagar Haveli and the Dravidian region including Karnataka, Andhra Pradesh, Kerala and Tamil Nadu. Some bands of hunters and gatherers still exist among the Andaman Islanders or on the mainland among the Birhors were more common. The segmentary mode of tribal organization was also more common in Orissa, Madhya Pradesh, Bihar and other areas. But there were chiefdoms as well in addition to these.

Among the chief characteristics of Indian tribes include the kinship as an instrument of social bonds, lack of hierarchy among men and groups, absence of strong, complex, formal organization, communitarian basis of land holding, little value on surplus accumulation on the use of capital and on market trading, lack of distinction between form and substance of religion and a distinct psychological bent for enjoying life. The tribals preserved and retained their identity as that of mutual exclusion as they lived in forests and hills without any contact with the civilization and as there was no non-tribal population pressure on their resources, which remained unchanged till Muslim period, but thereafter military campaigns extending for a short spell into and/or through tribal areas deprived many aboriginal tribes of their socio-political autonomy.

The tribals conflict have been recorded since late 17th Century, but more specifically their movements became evident, when the Administrative officers during the British Raj introduced uniform methods of revenue collection over the tribal system of land tenure, compelling their alienation and the availability of tribal land to non-tribal populations.

As academically worked out, there were 11 distinctive characteristics of tribes in India including their definite common topography, sense of unity, endogamy, common dialect, ties of blood-relationship, protection awareness, distinct political organization, common culture, kinship, egalitarian values and rudimentary type of religion.

Robert Goodland has given the following characteristics –

The geographical isolation or semi-isolation; Unacculturated or partially acculturated into national society; largely or entirely independent of the national economic system; Ethnic distinctiveness from the national society; Economic base tightly dependent on their, specific environment; Possessing leadership but no more national representation, and few, if any political rights.

Tribals either withdrew further into hills and tracts of marginal land, or accepted the economic status of tenants or agricultural labourers on the land their forefathers had owned, on being unable to resist their alienation from ancestral land. There were some tribes, however, who rebelled against an administration beginning in Bihar in 1772, followed by revolts in Andhra Pradesh, Andaman and Nicobar Islands, Arunachal Pradesh, Assam, Mizoram and Nagaland. The important tribes involved in revolt in the 19th century were Mizos (1810), Kols (1795 and 1831), Mundas (1889), Daflas (1875), Khasi and Garo (1829), Kacharis (1839), Santhals (1853), Muria Gonds (1886), Nagas (1844 and 1879) and Konds (1817). In Chhota Nagpur and the Santhal parganas in 19th 17th Century, where it was recorded that about 10,000 Santhals to have lost lives in 1855. The British system of landownership and revenue trebled beyond the tribal cultivators' paying capacity. Many non-tribals began to settle in the tribal areas offering credit facilities, which initially provided reliefs to tribals, but gradually became exploitative.

The tribal societies have least problems within traditional organization, but faced more problems, because of their discrimination and demarcation between the tribal and the non-tribal society in the context of Indian society.

The tribes have existed at the margins during pre-independence civilization in India from time immemorial. However, these margins have been vague, uncertain and fluctuating acknowledging the distinction between tribe and caste, one confined to the isolation of hills and forests and the other settled in villages and towns with a more elaborate division of labour. The establishment of heavy industries, construction of dams and launching of development plans in those tribal zones has necessitated displacement of local population. Thousands of tribal families were being displaced from traditional habitats contact situations with outsiders have been equally detrimental.

The tribal lands were occupied by moneylenders, zamindars and traders by advancing credits. Opening of mines in the heart of tribal habitat and even a few factories provided wage labour as well as opportunities for employment, but also brought increasing destitution and displacement. The forest land and its resources provide the best means of livelihood for the people, but when outsiders exploited their land and resources, the natural life cycle of tribal ecology and tribal life got greatly disturbed. Majority of the people live under chronic poverty, for they followed simple occupations based on simple technology that fell into the primary occupations such as hunting, gathering and agriculture. There was no profit and surplus making in such economy. Hence, the per capita income was very meagre, making them heavily indebted in the hands of local moneylenders and Zamindars. They often mortgaged or sold land to the moneylenders, to repay debt.

In many parts of India, the population suffers from chronic infections and diseases out of which water borne diseases are life-threatening. They also suffer from deficiency diseases. Leprosy and tuberculosis were common. Infant mortality was very high. Malnutrition is quite common. It has affected the general health of children, as it lowered the ability to resist infection, leading to chronic illness and sometimes leads to brain impairment.

The ecological imbalance like tree felling have increased the distances between villages and the forest areas, forcing women to walk longer distances, in search of forest produce and firewood. Another important cause for their backwardness was their withered economic base-shifting agriculture, hunting, fishing and forest produce formed the mainstay of their economic base.

Use of forests products and shifting agriculture were very important parts of the tribal economy.

However, the imposition of land revenue settlement mobilized non-tribals expand agriculture in tribal areas or surplus forest cover led to the erosion of tribal traditions of joint ownership and increased their socio-economic differentiation in the egalitarian structure of the tribal society.

The increasing demand for wood from early nineteenth century for the Royal-Navy and then Railways, lead to the increasing control of government over forests lands. Why would this be a problem? The establishment of a Forest Department in 1864, Government Forests Act (1865) and Indian Forests Act (1878) established complete government monopoly together over the Indian forest land. Shifting agriculture, a widespread practice amongst various tribal communities was banned from 1864 onwards in the 'reserved' forests. The restrictions were imposed on the previously sanctioned timber and grazing facilities. The extention of settled agriculture led to the influx of non-tribals in the tribal areas.

The outsiders exploited them and extension of settled agriculture led to their loss of land, which reduced them becoming agriculture labourers. The work of Christian missionaries brought about changes in their socio-economic and cultural equation with the mainstream society. Plus, in turbulent times, the tendency of missionaries to abandon arms or in discouraging the people from revolt against the government mobilized the missionaries to be viewed as the extensions of colonialism and was often attacked by the rebels.

Some of the tribal uprisings took place in reaction to the efforts of landlords to levy taxes on the customary use of timber and grazing facilities, police extractions, new excise regulations, exploitation by lower country traders and moneylenders, and ther estrictions on shifting cultivation in forests. The rebellions by the non-frontier tribals were usually reactions against outsiders (dikus), local landlords and rulers, the support provided to the latter by the British administration and their intervention in the tribal life. The indigenous names for these tribal movements were *meli, hool* and *ulgulan.*

The introduction of the notion of private property made their land bought, sold or mortgaged, which led to an overall loss. In other words, the reasons for tribal backwardness in the contemporary India could be seen as consequential to the indifference from administrators and bureaucracy in dealing with their grievances, harsh and unfriendly forest laws and regulations, lack of legislation to prevent the passing of tribal land into the hands of non-tribals, lack of credit facilities, ineffective government measures to rehabilitate tribal population, delay in implementation of recommendations of different committee and discrimination in implementation of reform measures.

A number of merchants, moneylenders, landlords, petty officials etc. from the non-tribal community disrupted their lives, during the colonial era. In central India, their land was acquired, and exploited them in their own business at a lower cost. Thus, over the past two centuries, in central India, the tribal people have been increasingly subjugated by the state agencies, landlords and money lenders. The loss of their agricultural lands through privatization, and degradation of forests have made them poorer, left them alienated, disempowered and vulnerable to exploitation. They suffer from exclusion, neglect and under-development, which can be attributed to their geographical isolation and separation from the mainstream.

The politics of tribe started long before independence. It owed to an anthropological notion of them being people in an "imperfect state of being civilized". It was seen as the solemn duty of the British to protect them from the mainland forces and to "cause them to be civilized". The approach was highly protectionist, as the latter were thought to be simplistic and easily exploited people, if left to govern themselves. The debates of the British Parliament provide us with rich insight into how the tribal lot was thought of, when the first laws to regulate their lives were passed for the colonies.

The tribals are neither Marxists nor Maoists, because their communities were not only alien to such ideologies, but such explanations were rather methodologically extra-tribal in the empirical reality. Albeit, scholars and administrators do take their respective stands, either to justify their perspectives or disguise their academic sponsorship/methodological shortcomings under the umbrella of certain ideologies, which were often wrongly accounted for and/or explain nothing about the real issues from the tribal perspective, but certainly impose non-tribal perspective on the contemporary social movements in tribal areas, to justify the pro-capitalist political-economic issues, where the socially alive indigenous tribal identities were stigmatized against a virtual mainstream of non-tribal (including state and its people where a majority of them were also deprived and poor) constructed by the Marxian, British-minded-Indian academics to justify rights of left wing.

Following the British policy of divide and rule, methodologically untrained British Anthropologists however, were successful in implanting non-empirical-alien (NEA) concepts of Aryan (non-tribal) and Dravidian (Tribal) races. It was the cause for infusing clash between the non-existing-civilizations, exploitation of resources in the tribal areas or superimposed ideology (Marxism) confirming class-struggle (in fact that did not exist) against socio-economic exploitation of isolated tribal communities. There was violent rebellion (projected Maoism) in the tribal areas at a much social distance away from the mainland. However, these policies and approaches were based on the assumption that considered tribal life as a kind of wild-life to be enclosed within socio-ecologically fenced areas. Even a majority of tribal communities were notified as criminals under Criminal Tribals Act (CAT) of 1871 and at the time of independence that Act was imposing upon thirteen million tribal people belonging to 127 tribal communities under the surveillance, search and arrest without any warrant, if found outside their (notified tribal) precincts. Albeit CAT was repealed in 1949 and the [tribal] communities were denotified, (but still DNT stigma haunts them) the Habitual Offender Act of 1952 continues to provide sanctity to the state-sponsored isolation and sustain the stigmatized tribal identities.

The Nehruvian Panchsheel policy of exclusion of tribal and their areas under the influence of Verrier Elwin during the early years after Independence, the state made deliberate attempts to restrict non-tribal interference in the tribal socio-cultural milieu, which resulted in the continued isolation and their exclusion with the areas. Thereafter, in the name of modernization and mechanisms adopted therefore by the state after independence (mega projects called as Modern Temples of India) displaced tribals from their areas and still they were found struggling for the rehabilitation and resettlement. The state encroachment over tribal areas for resource-exploitation to develop and modernize the non-tribal India and the denial of tribal socio-culture-livelihood rights in the tribal areas like Bio-sphere, National Park, Sanctuaries, Tiger Reserves, Forests, to restore ecological balance was found disturbed by non-tribal population need to be discussed in the context of contemporary social movements in tribal areas.

We need to reorganize our policy, planning and programmes as well as future empirical research from tribal point of view. Ethnographic methodology employing tribal concepts could be more meaningful rather than content analysis or review of pro-capitalistic-Marxian-British-minded-academics and sponsored project-based research. The relative position of tribal communities is in fact the major concern. Falsely, the tribals were considered backward in relation to the non-tribal culture, be it western or eastern. Sociologist G.S. Ghurye has even argued that tribals were "backward Hindu" and suggested for their development to mobilize them merge into the mainstream. Several studies on tribal communities and social movements in their areas not only confirm such stand, but recommended such transformation for development till they become non-tribal. After partition of Chhattisgarh, so far peaceful tribal areas of Madhya Pradesh need urgent empirical attention in this regard.

The author attempted over to analyse isolation, displacement and exclusion of tribal communities and emerging social movements in those areas for their inclusion into and against from the mallstream four or six-lane highways meandering through their areas, the mainstream that was developed through Special Economic Zones (SEZs) located in their areas or the mainstream that is powered with multipurpose mega projects situated in tribal areas.

End notes

1. British academic and development practitioner, who was infamously turned down for a professorship at IDS on the grounds of insufficient publications in academic journals and regaining only in 1995 at the age of 63, early worked in Kenya and the UK on resettlement and irrigation schemes, and public administration. In 1980s his works on rapid and participatory forms of appraisal were developed. He is a leading team of advocates for putting the poor, destitute and marginalized at the centre of the processes of development policy. In particular he argues the poor should be taken into account when the development problem is identified, policy formulated and projects implemented. He popularized within development circles such phrases as "Putting the last first".
2. Verma D.K. has coined two new terms, namely 'social devolution' and 'affirmed status' to understand the status of reserved categories in the post-modern society.

   Verma D.K. (2004): *Social Devolution: A Sociological Perspective on Affirmed Status of dalits in India, The Asianists' ASIA, Vol III (Paris) Summer 2004, ISSN: 1298-0358, published by Centre de Recherches sur les Etudes Asiatiques Paris, France on August 5, 2004, Association n 0941011951.*

   <http://www.stateless.freehosting.net/AA3ContentsPage. htm contd>

   <http://www.stateless.freehosting.net/Affirmed Status of Dalits in India.htm>

   The new concept 'Affirmed Status' and the proposed theory 'Social Devolution' were also discussed in the session organized by Prof. Cecelia Ridgeway, the then President of American Sociological Association at the ISA XVI World Congress, Durban, South Africa 23-29 July 2006:

   Verma D.K. (2006): Social Devolution: A Sociological Perspective on Affirmed Status of Dalits in India, In: Newsletter International Sociological Association, Research Committee on Social Psycology, p4, may 2006. <http://www.isa-sociology.org/pdfs/rc42newsletter.pdf>

Reference

The concept was also discussed during two sessions on "Globalisation, Social Inequality and status Characteristics I & II" organized by the author at the XVII ISA World Congress of Sociology, 2010 in Sweden and as submitted paper in the XVIII ISA World Congress of Sociology, 2014 in Japan:

Verma DK (2010): Globalization, Social Inequality and Affirmative Status Generalisation in India.

< http://www.isa-sociology.org/pdfs/rc42newsletter_may_2010.pdf.>

Verma DK (2014): Relative Deprivation, Affirmative Status Generalisation and Social Identities, In: Facing an Unequal World: Challeges for Global Sociology, RC42-708.3, p1029, Pacifico, Yokohama, Japan.

<http://isaconf.confex.com/isaconf/wc2014/webprogram/paper50057.html.>

Chapter - 4

Non-Timber Forest Products among Tribes of Jharkhand

— K. Gopal Iyer

Introduction

An attempt is being made to discuss forest product as an important source of livelihood for the poor particularly Scheduled Tribes of the state of Jharkhand. It examines the prominent role of lac cultivation and marketing in the livelihood of adivasis in the state. Accordingly, the specific objectives of the study are the following:

- To know potentiality of major NTFP in the state of Jharkhand.
- The review earlier studies on NTFP by relevant scholars.
- To find out important Forost Produce available in the West Singhbhum district.
- To analyse policies on NTFP in the state of Jharkhand, and
- To describe significance of Lac cultivation, production and processing in the state of Jharkhand.

The methodology of the research on NTFP is based, on the secondary and primary data. The secondary data is mainly based on the sources of Jharkhand government particulary, Forest department, statistical published sources, and review of studies. The primary data has been collected from the districts of West Singhbhum, Khunti, Saraikela-Kharsawan and East Singhbhum. The main techniques of primary data have been non-directive interview, case studies, focus group discussion and interview schedule. More intensive study on NTFP is confined to the districts of West Singhbhum and Khunti districts.

Jharkhand literally means 'Forest Region', where the forests play a central role in the economic, cultural and socio-political systems. The entire lives and livelihood of a majority of the people revolve around forests and forestry. Forest-based livelihoods mainly revolve around the collection, processing and utilization/ selling of various NTFPs throughout the year along with some seasonal subsistence agriculture in the forest fringe areas. About 29 p c land is covered by the forest area in the state containing vast resources of coal and minerals. The forest cover in the State (based on interpretation of satellite data), is 22,977 kms which is 28.82 p c of the state's geographical area.

The tribal communities and forest dwellers of Jharkhand have lived in harmony with the nature since ages: for them every aspect of life and livelihood is dependent on NTFP (Kataisag, Putkal, Banskari, Fruits, Mahua fruit, Kendu fruit etc): fibres and tubers are being derived from the seeds or fodder for their animals: the house they live in, the medicines they use to cure themselves and other necessities of life are being derived from forest produce. These produce have been supporting tribals for more than 6-8 months a year, both in terms of subsistence and cash income. However, the pertinent aspects of NTFP production and productivity, their role in livelihood, analysis of market trends and potentials, gap analysis and associated challenges have not been comprehensively studied in Jharkhand. Jharkhand is blessed with many non-timber forest produce of economic value. Tradionally, these resources only cater to the rural economy. Some of NTFPs traded most are - Harra, Bahera Chiraunji, Karanj, Jamun Chiraita, Bamboo shoots, Tamarind, Mahua, Dori, Sal seeds, Neem seeds, Honey, Satabri etc. *The dependence is maximum on produce like kendu leaf, mahua lac, char, tamarind, sal seed, amla etc.*

Table 1 - Major Non-Timber Forest produce

Botanical Name	*Name of NTFP*	*Annual Production (App in MT.)*	*Value Added Products*
Buchanania	Chiraunji	2,000	Dry fruit, used confectionary
Pongamia pinnata	Karanj	5,000	Antibiotic oil, ointment, spray etc
Terminalia chebula	Harra	2,000	Harra powder & Triphala churna
Emblica ooficinalis	Amla	2,000	Amla Powder, Triphala churna & morabbam
Terminalia belerica	Bahera	2,000	In Triphala churna
Syzigium cumini	Jamun Pulp and Kernel	5,000	Jamun syrup and Jamun powder
Swertia chiraita	Chiraita	2,000	Antibiotic chiraita powder
Babusa spp	Bamboo Shoots	2,000	Pickles and vegetables
Tamarindus indica	Tamarind	200,000	Packed without seed, paste
Madhuca indica	Mahua	200,000	Wine
-do-	Dori	20,000	Oil/Soap
Shorea robusta	Sal seeds	100,000	Oil/Feed
Schleichera oleosa	Kusum	10,000	Oil/Feed
Arundinella csetisa	Hill Broom	200	Broom
Anstida setacea	Thorn Broom	200	Broom
Asparagus racemosus	Satabari	200	Medicine
Bauhinia vahili	Adda leaves/ Mahulan Patta/ Siali leaf	500	Plate
Apis spp	Mahua/Honey	100	Food
Embelia ribes	Baividang	N.A.	Medicine
Andrographis paninculata	Kalmegh	N.A.	Medicine
Woodfordia fruticosa	Dhawai Phool	N.A.	Medicine
Azadirachta indica	Neem Seed	500	Oil/Soap
Rauwolfia serpentine	Sarpagandha	500	Medicine
Withania somnifera	Aswagandha	500	Medicine
Butea monosperma	Palas/Tesu Phool	1,000	Colour
Diospyros melanoxylon	Kendu Leaf	N.A.	Biri
Other important minor forest produce like honey, medicinal plants, herbs gums and resins.			

Source: Jharkhand State Minor Forest Produce Co-operative Development and Marketing Federation Limited

The medicinal plants were found in abundance in Jharkhand. Amla, Harra, Bahera, Karanj and various other herbs and shrubs over hundred species not only can be grown but also processing units both at rural and urban centres can be setup. The livelihood of the poor rural and tribal families depend on a range of forest produce such as, tassar, lac, honey, mahua, chironji, medicinal plants and a number of NTFPs. *Key issues and challenges related to NTFPs in the state are* NTFP Collection, Trade and Value Addition, lack of marketing focus, *Market constraint and ineffective value chain sequence.*

Value Chain Development

Every stage of the produce attracts opportunities for value addition.

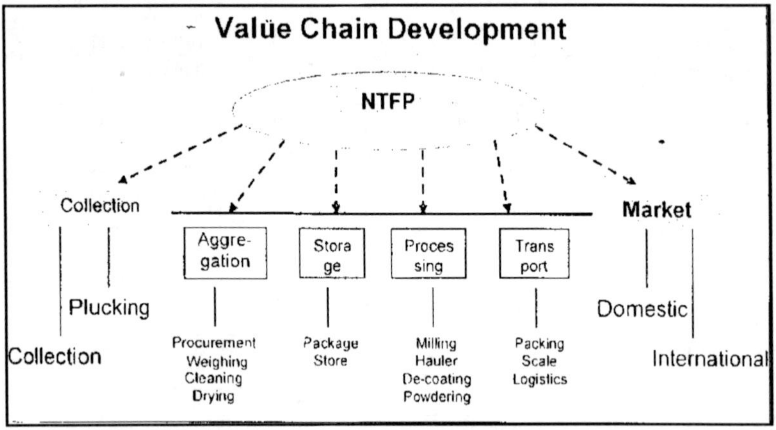

Table 2: Seasonality of NTFP Collection and Trading

Name of the NTFP	*Jan*	*Feb*	*Mar*	*Apr*	*May*	*Jun*	*Jul*	*Aug*	*Sep*	*Oct*	*Nov*	*Dec*
Tamarind		C	C									
		PT	PT	T								
Mahua			C	C								
Flower			PT	PT	T	T						
Mahua Seed						C	C					
						PT	PT	T	T			
Sal Leaf	C	C			C	C	C	C	C	C	C	C
	T	T			T	T	T	T	T	T	T	T
Siali Leaf						C	C	C	C	C	C	C
						T	T	T	T	T	T	T
Char Seed				C	C							
				PT	PT	T	T					
Kusum Lac						C	C			C	C	C
						PT	PT			T	T	T

C - Collection Season **PT** - Peak Trading Season **T** - Trading Season

Source: NTFP Survey Report, Strengthening NTFP based livelihood systems through a market led approach, Mart-Noida.

The different NTFP collection and trading takes place in different months of the year. For example, Tamarind is procured during the months of Feb-March: Mahua flowers in the months of March-June: Mahua seed is procured during the months of June and July. The Sal leaves are ever green NTFP which is procured and marketed by the tribals during all the months in the year except March and April. Similarly, Siali leaves is procured by the the tribals of Jharkhand during the months of June-December, Char seed is procured during Apri-May and Kusum lac is procured and marketed during the months of June,July,October,November and December.

Use of NTFPs

- Household use for food fodder, fibre, fuel and beverage and other uses.
- Used to market the NTFP for money for livelihood security.
- Market NTFP for earning money through Bicholia (Middle men),
- Medicinal Plants: Used by local practitioners or collected for selling in local market to Bicholias, finally goes to big markets of Jharkhand and other states.
- NTFP Semi processed for value addition by villagers such as Bamboo, Mahua, Chiraunji, Sal, (Patta Datun), Tamarind, Sabai grass, Leaves (Khajaur), fruits, such as, Jamun, Amla, Jangli Bel, Jangli Ber, Beeju aam (Mango grown by seeds in forests).

Table 3 - NTFPs primarily used for household consumption

Sl. No.	*Local Name*	*Botanical Name*	*Household consumption and Commercial use*	*Regeneration status*
1.	Sal	Shorea robusta	Very important supplement of livelihood through the year for Pattal and Dauna making (leaf plates). Seeds are also important cash crop of sustenance.	Regeneration status is very good depending upon the type of the forest and locality where they are grown.
2.	Karanj	Ponamia Pinnata	Important as oil yielding tree species. Fruits and seeds are in high demand and gives money for 2-3 months during the season.	Population is decreasing day by day and quantity coming in markets is declining.
3.	Mahua	Madhuca Indica	Fruits are good supplement of food and beverage of local people. Seeds are important source of commercially important oil.	All old trees are preserved and new generation are coming up in good number: this tree is not harvested for fuel and timber.
4.	Chiraunzi	B. Nuchanania Lanzan	Fruits used as valuable dry fruits and supplementing the economy of tribals.	Population is decreasing as evidenced by less quantity coming in market.
5.	Tamarind	Tamarindes indica	Collected for house hold use, but sold in major markets such as Jamshedpur and Chakardharpur.	Its population is diminshing in Ranchi and Hazaribagh districts; Chaibasa region has good concentration
6.	Gum Karaya	Sterculia urens	Unorganized collection from forest areas; not being optimally utilized	Primarily present in dry deciduous forests of rocky hills; population is declining throughout the state.

Collection of Kendu Leaf

Kendu Leaf is an important forest produce, but is still being handled by the state and particularly by the state forest department. The collection and price being paid to pluckers is listed below:

Table 4 - Position Between 2002 ~14 and the price being paid to pluckers

Year	*Rate paid to labour per bag of Kendu leaf*	*Collection in lakh bags*	*Price paid to KL Pluckers in crores*	*Gross premium to corporation*	*Total Sale (in lacs amount)*
2002	401	5.09	20.413	7.680	28.093
2003	426	3.87	16.491	6.484	22.975
2004	431	4.74	20.423	6.416	26.839
2005	451	3.48	15.692	5.619	21.311
2006	456	3.06	13.978	7.538	21.516
2007	471	7.50	35.311	15.298	50.609
2008	501	5.65	28.326	14.862	43.188
2009	551	5.68	31.299	16.463	47.762
2010	601	5.68	34.164	20.757	54.921
2011	651	4.19	27.307	28.256	55.563
2012	701	7.69	53.906	41.244	95.150
2013	901	4.13	37.211	23.105	60.316
2014	901	4.13	37.211	23.105	60.316
2015	**1066**	**3.01**	**32.035 (62.11 p c)**	**19.130 (37.38 p c)**	**51.165 (100 p c)**

Source: Forest Corporation, Forest Department Government of Jharkhand, 1995.

Some 3.01 lac kendu leave were collected [2015], by the **adivasis** in the state out of which the sale aggregated to Rs. 51.165 lac and the price being paid to pluckers was 62.11 per cent of the sale and further 37.38 per cent of the sale was the gross premium to the corporation. During the past two to three years, particularly between 2014-15 and 2015-16, collection in the state has considerably declined due to the strong Left Wing Extremism, particularly in the districts of West-Singhbhum, Khunti, Latehar and Palamau. The contractors couldn't partake as the Left Wing Extremist activists demanded ransom. The decline was a huge loss of income to the **adivasis** wherein the women were the major beneficiaries. Similarly, in the procurement of other NTFP, the **adivasis** couldn't do so, in the extremist affected districts of West Singhbhum, Khunti, Ranchi, Lohardaga, Latehar, Garwah, Palamau, etc.

Position - West Singhbhum District

An empirical study was conducted in the distrit [2013-15]. The products collected by Adivasis include Jhadu grass, Kendu leaves, Karanj, Kusum, Mahua flowers, Mahua seeds, Mango, Mushroom, Sal leaves, Tamarind, etc. Major products being sold at the *haats* by local tribals could be ascertained. (*Source: Report of Jharkhand State Agriculture and Marketing Board. The Total and Average products collected (at a time) by the tribals of West Singhbhum.)*

The important NTFP found in the forests are Kendu leaves, abundant in the Kolhan division. Of late sal seed, like kendu leaf, has gained importance from the revenue point of view. Since 1977, this is being done departmentally through the state forest development corporation. Ahua and Kusum were the most important among the oil seeds produced. The corolla of Mahua flowers is being collected on a very large scale from trees growing from within and outside the forest. It plays a significant role in the economy of rural population. *The fruits of Harra (Terminaliachebula), Bahera (T. belerica), and Amla (Emblica officialis) jointly known as myrabolan have since long been collected for medicinal use.* The villagers collect and sell the fruits to local vendors in the hats. The kernel of Buchanania lanzan nut is known as *Chiraunji*. It is collected by villagers and sold in the local hats during season. The steam of the climber is used for rope making by villagers and the leaves were used for making Pattal (leaf plates). The Pattal made of *mahulan* leaves has good market in the south. The sal ('sarjom' as locally named by the Ho tribes of the region) tree holds a special position in the socio-economic life of tribals as each part of the tree (wood, seed, leaves, young shoots) finds used every day by forest dwellers. Sleeping mats made from khajur leaves are being used in most rural areas of West Singhbhum and were exported to Bihar and West Bengal. Tribals collect a number of different wild vegetables, tubers and flowers; sometimes they were unable to differentiate with. In West Singhbhum district alone, at least seven types of wild and leafy vegetables were regularly collected from local forest areas; many being gathered by tribal women when they return from the fields during the agricultural season.

Vegetables like tomato, lady's finger, brinjal and cucumber were also sold in the haats by the tribals, which they grow in farms. Once, these vegetables get ready for the *haat*, they were taken to local haats by women as headload and sold at a minimum price.

One of the most important fruit products in [West Singhbhum] is Mango. Mango trees were abundant in forest throughout the West Singhbhum district, as a natural associate of sal, and many were planted aside the road and village wastelands. Ripe mango fruits were both consumed domestically and sold in local markets. There was also a lot of market demand for both the fruits and seeds of the tamarind tree. The sale of tamarind fruit and seeds is major source of income in West Singhbhum district. *The main tree generating oil seeds in Kolhan are sal, kusum, neem, karanj and mahua.* Oilseeds of tree origin are quite important for the income needs of tribal households in remote locations of West Singhbhum. In West Singhbhum, *Mahua Seeds are one of the main sources of income and subsistence during the lean summer months (April –July) for many poor tribal families.*

In the West Singhbhum district, neem trees can be found in large number in villages and in the forests. The tribals of the villages basically use its seeds for extracting oil and twigs for *datun* (tooth brushes). They also use their leaves and barks for curing certain diseases. Sal leaves were used for domestic consumption and increasingly (among the poorest families) for the manufacture of sal leaf plates for the sale in urban markets. Sal leaves are being collected throughout the year at weekly or sometimes at monthly intervals and generally speaking, it is women and children, who undertake the share of their collection. The leaves are being collected mostly by the women belonging to different age, right from children to old aged. They spend whole day in the forest for collecting them. They roam through the farmlands and collect the khajur leaves cutting with datrom (hasua). The process of making mats is quite time –consuming. It takes some five to six weeks to prepare a mat of a standard size [7 × 3 ft]. The prepared mats were generally used for household's activities, but were also sold in the market between

Rs. 200 and 400. Karanj oil is being used widely in the district as a source of oil for lamps, body massage and occasionally for cooking and medicinal purpose.

On the one hand, there were products, which the tribes bring to the market with lot of efforts and on the other side; there were non-tribal controlled haats, where you will find non-local highly-competitive persons who're impersonal. This results in exploitation of those products, as well as the tribal people, who produce such products. According to Buriuly (2013) in this process of capitalist encroachment to the tribal economy, the local tribes of Kolhan get entangled in the vicious circle of capitalist structure of this market system. In this sense, they were at the 'tail-end' of the capitalist value chain. They were already dependent on the markets for livelihood and become more vulnerable to such exploitation.

Review of NTFP

We won't have any input about the NTFP as a source of livelihood. An attempt is being made to review available studies. *Ashish K. Gharai* et al (2009), *Md. Ajaz-ul-Islam* et al (2013), *Sanjay Kumar Verma, et al (2016), R K Yogi et al (2016), Sudeep Kumar and Ankita Choudhary (2016)* have attempted to analyze with the output.

Gharai and Chakrabarti (2009) have made a study of perception of the commercialization potential of selected NTFP in the three districts of Jharkhand, mainly Gumla, Hazaribagh and Simdega. The NTFPs available in each area were studied, but the main analysis is being based on four major NTFPs i.e., Mahua, Lac, Karanj and Chironjee. The data collection was mainly done through household surveys, focus group discussions and collation of secondary data. Sample size was approximately 30% of total number of households in each village.

- The people were more dependent on income from agriculture and agricultural labor than from NTFP.
- Average percentage of annual income from NTFP in the villages surveyed was in the range of 10p c – 31 p c in Hazaribagh: only two items (Karanj and Mahua) were collected.

- Simdega has many NTFP resources but lack of proper market and infrastructure for processing various items, makes NTFP related livelihoods less profitable.
- In Gumla, nearly half of the households surveyed were found to be involved in agriculture and the rest were marginal farmers, who engaged themselves in NTFP collection.
- Simdega district is rich in NTFP resources and almost all the household surveyed were involved in NTFP collection along with agriculture and allied activities.
- The four major NTFPs which were taken into consideration are Karanj, Chironjee, Lac and Mahua. Out of these four items, only Lac is collected during winter and rest all are collected in summer. Out of the four main NTFPs studied, there is no problem with storage & processing of Chironjee and Lac. Storage of Karanj has its problems with pest infestation and degradation due to weather. But the maximum storage problems are associated with Mahua.- pests, weather, lack of storage facilities & money required, leakage, lack of knowledge on storage mechanisms etc.
- *On an average, 16 p c of total household income in the villages studied comes from collection, value addition and sale of NTFPs.* Mahua generates maximum income followed by Karanj and Chironjee where as Lac on the other hand generates less income than them. *Mahua is widely collected across all of these studied villages for which they spend on an average of 23 days in the summer season. During this period they collect an average of 2,264 kgs of Mahua per village.* More than 85 p c of Mahua collected is used in making alcohol and thus storage of raw and processed material becomes a huge problem. *Mahua is available in abundance in Simdega district but major problem in collection is that the area is affected by Naxalite activities.* The price per kg in Simdega is Rs.4-5 and in Gumla it is from Rs. 7-8. Mostly wine is prepared from dried mahua flower. Wine is for self consumption and it is also considered as a

tradional drink. The cost of a bottle in the local market is Rs.12. It is used as food, fodder and medicine.

- Value addition is done only for Mahua and Karanj (with Karanj they prepare pickle). As Mahua is used for preparing wine, they generally use a specially designed indigenous machine for this purpose. Women play a very important role in collection of NTFP. It was found that around 83 p c of women are involved in NTFP collection.
- *Chironjee* is collected for 26 days on an average, during summer season. *Karanj is mostly found in Gumla. The villagers sell seeds directly to small traders @ cost of Rs. 7 to Rs. 8: on an average 415 kgs are collected per day and the maximum amount is Rs. 3,320 per day. Lac is available mostly in Simdega district. Lac is sold @ around Rs. 100 to Rs. 120: on an average 1,840 kgs. of lac are collected each day.*
- Transport is one of the most crucial factors which decide the fortune of NTFP trade. In Jharkhand, lack of proper roads and transport facility in the rural areas affects the trade. In the villages surveyed, the major mode of transport is cycle (84 p c) which has a direct impact on the NTFP trading as it is difficult to use cycles for this purpose, especially when the distance to the market is long. About 12 p c of NTFP is transported through head-loading and only 3p c is carried by aut omobile (van). NTFP collectors come to the traders to sell and sometimes traders go to the collectors directly for procuring material. During peak season, NTFP products are procured by them 3-5 times a month. Each trader covers around 35-40 villages for procurement of NTFPs.

The average market price per kg of Mahua is Rs. 10-12, Karanj - Rs.6-7, Lac - Rs 120 and Chironjee - Rs.100-120. The traders will purchase some processed/value added products (only Karanj and Mahua in the study area). *A price comparison shows that an unprocessed kg of Mahua is procured at Rs 5- but the processed one at Rs 11-14kg. Unprocessed Karanj is being procured at a price of Rs 8- per kg and the processed Karanj is procured at Rs 28- to Rs 32- per kg.* Women play a vital role in the context of NTFPs, right from the stage of collection, processing, value addition, transport till its marketing. In each of the stages of NTFP trade women's involvement is quite significant. *Thus, it can be said that in the villages where study was conducted, women are actively involved in the collection, processing and marketing of NTFPs.*

Mohammad Ajaz-ul-Islam et al (2013) in their study on "Livelihood Contributions of Forest Resources to the Tribal Communities of Jharkhand" have analyzed the livelihood contribution of forest Resources to the Tribal Community of Bundu block in Ranchi district of Jharkhand. The capability of agriculture and livestock production to form sustainable livelihoods of tribal poor is in continuous decline. Consequently, the tribal people are constrained to earn their livelihoods from forest resources. The main tribal communities in the *Bundu* block are *Munda, Oraon, Lohara etc.* They are socially, educationally, economically and politically backward with accompanying impediments of illiteracy, poverty, malnutrition, superstitions, addictions, ignorance and exploitation. The land area under cultivation is 53.06 p c of the total geographical area in the sample villages. Majority (75.74 p c – 100 p c) of the population in the villages are dominated by schedule tribes. The literacy rate is very low varying between 24.52 to 44.87 p c. Average sized land holding per household was found to be 1.89 ha. *The average size of forest based direct paid employment among surveyed population was 19.82 mandays/ household/ annum and the mean income earned from these activities was Rs. 2,199.70 household annum in the area. Sal leaf fetched highest earning (Rs 20, 8000 annum) among surveyed households in the area followed by lac* (Rs 1,00,500 annum), fuel wood (Rs 89,600 annum), tooth brush (Rs 67,200 annum), fodder (Rs 64,000 annum), *mahua* flower (Rs 56,760 annum), mango (Rs 31,000 annum), *chironji* (Rs 25,200 annum), *ber* (Rs 24,000 annum), *mahua* seed (Rs 17,424 annum), *jamun* (`Rs 16,800 annum), tamarind (Rs 13,000 annum), *koinar* tender leaf (Rs 9,600 annum), *bhelwa* (`Rs 9,600 annum), bamboo corn (Rs 7,200 annum), *kachnar* flower (Rs 7,200 annum), *kusum* seed (Rs 5,850 annum), *chiraita* (Rs 4,200 annum), *phutkal* lessaf buds (Rs 4,000 annum), *tendu* fruit (`Rs 3,500 annum), toot ( Rs 3,200 annum), *bel* (Rs 2,991 annum), jackfruit (Rs 2,625 annum), dassal seed (Rs 2,250 annum), *rugra* and *khukhri* (Rs 2,250 annum), *karanj* seed (`Rs 2,200 annum), *jirhul* flower (Rs 1,800 annum), *harra* (Rs 1,500 annum), *bahera* (Rs 1,200 annum) and *barhar* (Rs 1,100 annum).

The NTFPs markets are by and large imperfect and tribes do not get a fair return for their labour. The poor marketing infrastructure and lack of storage facilities force them to sell off their produces to the first market contact that is generally the haat or the petty trader who is known to them. The selling of almost all the forest resources is predominantly done in the local weekly markets where transaction takes place on a mutually agreed price quote between vendors and petty traders. *The middlemen invariably exploit collectors of NTFPs on account of prevailing malpractices, forced and distress sales. The present situation reflects that all the major NTFPs are available for around 2-3 months except for fuel wood, fodder, sal leaf, lac and tooth brush and bulk (peak) trading seldom goes beyond 3-4 months.*

Sanjay Kumar Verma and Sujit Kumar Paul (2016) in their study "Sustaining the Non-timber Forest Products (NTFPs) Based Rural Livelihoods of Tribals in Jharkhand: Issues and Challenges" tried to explore the spectrum of rural livelihood contributions of Non-Timber Forest Product (NTFP) through a sample of 50 respondent randomly selected from two villages in Bishunpur Block, Gumla district. All the households collect NTFPs irrespectively of their income contribution; *but income contribution from crop cultivation is higher than that from NTFPs. To make NTFPs collection by tribals sustainable various issues and challenges needs to be addressed.*

R K Yogi et al (2016) undertook a study entitled "Current Scenario and New Policy Interventions in the Lac Sector". They argue that the dynamic complex of lac host plants like ber (Ziziphus mauritiana), kusum (Schleichera oleosa), Palas (butea monosperma) and semialata (Flemingia semialata) and lac insect (Kerria spp.) are an important means of life support system for tribal communities across the major lac producing states of India. Natural resins secreted by the insect Kerria lacca (Kerr) is known as lac and categorized as a Non-Wood forest product (NWFP). *Jharkhand state alone contributes around 40 p c of the total national lac production. A paradigm shift of lac growers from rangeeni to kusmi strain (both Kerria species) was observed during recent years due to failure of rangeeni crop. Kusmi lac fetched a greater price comparatively.* Lac and its value added products make a significant contribution to the country's foreign exchange earnings. *Policy interventions like Minimum Support Price (MSP) for Non-Wood Forest Products including lac may be helpful to support lac cultivation activities and the strengthening of its marketing system. Thus, the dissemination of lac cultivation technologies and strengthening of value chain and farmer-industry linkages may play a key role to harness the opportunities available for the forest and sub-forest dwellers, lac processors, manufactures, exporters and other stakeholders.*

Sudeep Kumar and Ankita Choudhary (2016) in their study entitled " Enhancement of Livelihood Activities Through Non-Timber Forest Products: A Study in Jharkhand's Ranchi and Simdega Districts" have argued that Jharkhandis having a rich agriculture for its rural people still search for alternatives livelihood opportunities is required for smallholders. Agriculture is passing through a difficult phase due to the increasing frequency of unseasonal and extreme weather events creating difficulties in managing risk, thereby leading to livelihood insecurity. NTFPs act as a subsidiary source of income for rural dwellers. This paper examines the collection, processing and marketing of NTFPs, and attempts to analyze the differences in rates obtained and the number of people involved in the NTFP business. *The findings reveal that rural women actively participate in carrying out various NTFP practices,and that there is a need for more awareness generating interventions among the rural people.*

Policies on NTFP Management and Trade

The Present Scenario

Generally the rights admitted inside the forest are:

- Right to take firewood. An average family is allowed 168 cft. stacked firewood, which is subjected to change depending on the capacity of the annual coupes and can be limited or reduced.

- Right to graze cattle in the forests except in coupes up to five years of age.

Besides the above rights a number of concessions have been admitted from time to time and they are:

- Concession to take head load of dry firewood by the poor and landless people without any payment, for their own use, sale or barter, vide Revenue Department govt. of Bihar letter No. C/F-5076/54-67-RT dated May 09, 1954.
- Concession to remove all edible flowers and fruits free of any royalty.
- Concession to remove "Jhanti Jhuri" of thorny species for "Gherawan" purposes.
- Turis (a community engaged in making of bamboo based products) are to be given bamboo at concessional rate vide Govt. letter No. 226/69-1669 dated June 06, 1969.

Government Regulation in NTFP Trade

The first major policy level shift for the state government had taken place a year before in the form of The Bihar Kendu Leaf (Control of Trade) Act 1972. This act was the first to initiate the nationalisation of an NTFP in the state of Bihar. The Kendu Leaf became a big revenue earner for the state. *Secondly its aim to check the exploitation of the tribal and give them their due share of the price, also was achieved to some extent.* Bihar State Forest Development Corporation trading in Sal seeds (Nationalised in 1977 itself) was initiated in the year 1977. The Bihar State Forest Development Corporation was extended to include Harra fruit and seed, Palas fruit and seed, Aonla fruit and seed and Bahra fruit and seed. An act was framed in the year 1984 known as the Bihar Forest Produce (Regulation of Trade) Act, 1984. The Act talks of appointing one or more than one agent for all or any specified Forest produce. It visualises greater role of Gram Panchayats, LAMPS, PACS, Vyapar Mandal or the Bihar State Tribal Co-operative Development Co-operation Ltd. The Act also expanded the range of products coming under the State's purview. The new addition to the list were: fruit and seeds of Maula, Kamla, Chironji, Kacheria, Flowers of Mahua, Gums and Resins of Karaya, Katila, Dhaura, Sal resin, Salai resin, Sabai grass, lac, Tasar, Mahulan and Sal leaves, Khair, bamboo and medicinal and fibre yielding plants. The Bihar State Forest Development Corporation was given the responsibility of carrying out the trade (collection & marketing), by the State government (Department of Environment and Forest), of Kendu Leaf in the state in the year 1987. This meant that now the Bihar State Forest Development Corporation would undertake collection and marketing on commercial basis and all the expenses vis-a-vis collection and marketing of the produce will be borne by the agency itself.

The Panchayat (Extension to scheduled areas) Act of 1996 gives powers to the **Gram Sabhas** and panchayats to safeguard and preserve the traditions of the local population, This Act provides useful directives and guidelines to the State government for formation of appropriate forest laws and Acts to the benefit of villagers living in and around the forest. This Act was further streamlined and amended.The Bihar Panchayat Raj Act, 1993 was amended in the year 2000 and known as The Bihar Panchayat Raj (Amendment) Act, 2000. As per the guidelines given in the Panchayat Act of 1996 *The Bihar Minor Forest Produce (Endowment of Ownership to Gram Sabha) Act 2000 was introduced in the State endowing the Panchayats appropriate ownership of Minor Forest Produce.*

The major markets trading in various NTFP/NTFP based products in the State are: Daltonganj, Garhwa, Latehar, Chatra, Hazaribagh, Gumla, Giridih, Ranchi, Jamshedpur, Chaibasa & Chakradharpur. The main traders of these markets get collected NTFP from sub-trader/regional wholesaler/agents and depending upon the utility and demand of a particular NTFP it is traded in the domestic or export market. *There is a general disenchantment among the next generation of primary collectors, towards taking up NTFP collection as their source of income. This generation is not interested in going to the forest because in their opinion this work is not up to their standards. The naxalite movement in the interiors is also a great problem for the primary collectors because they are the ones who get directly affected.*

Lac Cultivation, Production and Processing

Lac is a natural resin secreted by an insect Kerrialacca (Kerr), which thrives on the tender twigs. The raw lac is the source of three valuable, natural and renewable products i.e. resin, dye and wax. Rangeeni and Kusmi are the two strains of lac insect which are classified based on the preference of the insect for specific host plants. *Lac cultivation is an important source of income for livelihood of the forest dwellers in Jharkhand. Besides, it had high potential for generating employment for both men and women in forest and fringe areas of Jharkhand.*

Lac production Scenario

Jharkhand state ranks first in production of lac followed by Chhattisgarh, Madhya Pradesh, Maharashtra and West Bengal. These five states contribute around 97 per cent of the national lac production. Regarding share of different crops *jethwi* ranks first (32.60 per cent) followed by the *baisakhi* (27.25 per cent), *aghani* (24.32 per cent) and *katki* (15.82 per cent) in national lac production. In the year 2012-13, the production of all the crops in comparison to previous year production has increased. At the national level, the production of lac was around 8.24 per cent more than the previous year arrival.

Major Lac producing districts

Table 5 - Lac production [2012-13] (in tons)

Districts	*Name of the Crops*				*Total*
	Baisakhi	*Jethwi*	*Katki*	*Aghani*	*Production*
Ranchi	650	2,150	430	1,020	4,250
Simdega	40	1,480	100	1,100	2,720
Gumla	40	1,200	30	1,000	2,270
West Singhbhum	160	400	50	300	310
Palamau	50	0	150	10	210
Latehar	15	20	20	15	70
Garhwa	20	0	40	0	60
Others	180	120	150	80	530
TOTAL	**1,155**	**5,370**	**940**	**3,555**	**11,020**

The districts producing over 1,000 tons of lac during 2012-13 were Ranchi (Khunti, 4250 tons), Simdega (2,720 tons) and

Gumla (2,270 tons) and their all India rank is respectively 1, 2 and 3 respectively.

Lac processing Scenario

The total quantity of sticklac processed during 2010-11 was 13,600 tons which also included the imported lac in India. There are twenty eight lac processing units in Chhattisgarh, 15 units in Jharkhand. Six units in Maharashtra, two units in Madhya Pradesh and 143 units in West Bengal. West Bengal ranked 1st (42.7 per cent) followed by Chhattisgarh (26.5 per cent), Jharkhand (25.7 per cent), Maharashtra (5.1 per cent) and Madhya Pradesh (0.7 per cent).

The Lac processing Centers in Eastern-India during 2001-11 were Jharkhand and West Bengal. The districts having lac process centers were the highest in Ranchi district (10 processing units), followed by Simdega (two units) and Daltonganj (two units) and the districts of Saraikela-Kharsawanand and West Singhbum had one unit each. In West Bengal Purulia (Balrampur) had the largest number of processing unit numbering 110, followed by Purulia Tulin (30) and Purulia (Jhalda) had 3 processing unit. These processing units were producing seed lac, Button lac, Shellac and bleach lac.

Table 6 - Amount of Stick lac processed in India [2010-11]

States	*Quantity processed (tons)*	*Percentage share in lac processing*
West Bengal	5,800	42.33
Chhattisgarh	3,600	26.28
Jharkhand	3,500	25.55
Maharashtra	700	5.11
Madhya Pradesh	100	0.73
Total	**13,700**	**100.00**

Export Scenario

Almost 75 per cent of lac produced in India is exported to different countries of which the main customers are USA, UK, Germany, Italy, France, Japan, China, Sweden, Brazil,

Argentina and Russia. The total export of lac and its value added products [2010-11] was 6,339.05 tons valued Rs. 211.13 crore.

Table 7 : Export of lac and its value added products [2010-11]

Sl. No.	*Name of the product*	*Export in 2010-11*	
		Quantity (tons)	*Value (Rs. lakh)*
1	Shellac	4,616.18	13,565.14
2	Seedlac	1,089.55	3,659.44
3	Dewaxed shellac	200.125	1,051.68
4	Bleached lac	336.13	1,598.86
5	Aleuritic acid	64.00	1,118.13
6	Gasket lac	4.32	6.62
7	Shellac wax	28.75	113.05
	Total	**6,339.05**	**21,112.92**

Critical gaps and interventions in Lac Processing

Though Jharkhand produce 56.88 p c of sticklac in the country, it process only 25.74 p c of the lac. The rest of the lac produced in Jharkhand is despatched to the neighbouring states, mostly West Bengal, for its processing and state lose revenue by supplying lac as a raw material to these states.

The Cultivation of Lac

Indian Institue of Natural Resins and Gums, Namkum Jharkhand has played yeoman service in promoting the lac cultivation in Jharkhand, Bihar, Uttar Pradesh, Orissa Chhatisgarh, West Bengal, Rajasthan and other states in India. It is located in Ranchi from where it imparts In-Campus Orientation Programme, Demonstration of lac cultivation technologies in different states, field visit programmes to different districts and states, Impetus to production, marketing including export, conducting workshops and seminar, having direct face to face interaction with the lac farmers, promoting shellac industry and monitoring scientific lac cultivation, processing and utilization. *It has been of seminal benefit to the tribals of the Jharkhand and other states. It would be apt to depict some of the success stories of the tribal cultivator in Jharkhand due to the intense effort of the Indian Institue of Natural Resins and Gums, Namkum Jharkhand.*

Lac as an important source of livelihood– Case studies

Case 1: Income Generation through kusmi lac cultivation

Description of the lac cultivation activity: Jagdish Hansda came into the contact with the Joydeb Mahto (Master trainer under capacity building programme at IINRG, Ranchi) in 2011. He was inspired to join the occupation of lac cultivation. But, he was not able to do this in the absence of host trees with him. Hence, he took the 75 host plants of ber on lease from the locality during 2011. He is doing the scientific lac cultivation by adopting the technologies for pruning of lac host, selection of good quality broodlac, bundling of broodlac and inoculation on plan, phunki removal, spraying of recommended pesticides and use of synthetic net.

Impact: Jagdish Hansda has purchased good quality kusmi broodlac (31kg) and inoculated on 75 ber plants in June-July 2011. He got 3.12 quintal kusmi lac production. This produce (broodlac) was again inoculated for jethwi crop on 34 kusum tress. In June-July, 2012, he purchased 6.17 qt (Rs.4.31 lac) broodlac for inoculation on 217 ber and 21 kusum trees. On 4th February 2013 he harvested the bumper crop of kusmi lac (about 20 qt). *At the current price of Rs.700/kg he earned the gross income Rs.14 lakhs and thus, net profit of about Rs.9 lakhs.* Out of this, he also shared the 25% with his partners (14 farmers who have given the host plants on lease). In addition, he also developed two acres land with 14,000 F.semialata host plants. This improved the living standard of Hansda along with the farmers in his locality.

Case 2: Enhancing income through lac cultivation- Story of a small tea vendor

Yogendra Ahir, aged 57 years living in Banta village of Silli block in Ranchi district. He ran a small tea stall from which he earned around Rs.3, 000 per month which was insu fficient to support the family requirements. He is the father of four daughters (three married) and one son, aged 12 years. He owned around 60 decimal lands for paddy cultivation under rain fed condition. He does not have any lac host tree but is aware of potential of lac cultivation. He met Shri Ramesh Chandra, an ex-trainee of Indian Institute of Natural Resins and Gums (IINRG), Ranchi who motivated Shri Ahir to initiate lac cultivation. He acquired three trees of Z.mauritiana from his fellow farmer and inoculated 3 kg of kusmi broodlac (worth Rs.1, 500) in July 2011 with the pre-condition that production will be shared. The tree was pruned during February 2011 on advice of Shri Ramesh Chandra. After six months of inoculation, he harvested 30 kg broodlac worth Rs.15,000 during January 2012. Out of this, he retained 13 kg for his own purpose and rest 17 kg given to owner of tree. In order to fulfill the broodlac requirement every year in July for inoculation on ber trees, he searched for lease tree in other areas and involved one of his relative (Village: Bundiaru, Block, Rahe, Dist. Ranchi) to take summer crop by giving him broodlac. Thus 13 kg broodlac was inoculated on one lease a tree during January 2012. After six months, his relative harvested 100 kg broodlac from single kusum tree. Shri Ahir has taken back 20 kg broodlac from his relative during July 2012 and re-inoculated ber trees with 15 kg broodlac in his own village (on share basis). Rest 5 kg broodlac, was given to another relative (Village-Chirgaldih, Block: Sonahatu, Ranchi), who inoculated on 10 ber trees.

When lac crop matured after six months in January 2013, he harvested 65 kg kusmi broodlac worth Rs.32, 500 during January 2013 from 15 kg inoculated by him. Out of 65 kg produced, he sold 30 kg @ 500 per kg and earned cash income of Rs.15, 000. *The* rest 35 kg was given to another relative with the condition that he will return twice the quantity given to him after six months when crop will mature as he required broodlac every year in July to inoculate ber trees. He gets back 70 kg broodlac in July 2013 which was marketed with cash income of Rs.28, 000. Shri Ahir inoculated 20 ber trees during July 2013 with 40 kg broodlac which was given to him in lieu of broodlac he had given to his first relative during July 2012. He added an income of Rs. 8,000 from Phunki scraped of Rs.40 kg. The standing crop on ber trees is developing well. He adopted all the scientific methods of lac cultivation including pruning of trees for availability of tender shoots and crop protection measures recommended by IINRG, Ranchi.

Shri Ahir is basically doing commercial broodlac production on ber trees. A part of his production, he is giving to other farmers every season but takes back broodlac from fellow farmers every year in order to fulfill his own requirement to inoculate ber trees and also to market and earn cash money every six months. Year by year his income enhanced as he has adopted more farmers. Basically this is how a resource poor farmer arranged lac host trees (ber) from other farmers, became self reliant for broodlac and enhanced his income to Rs.36, 000 per season in two years by a meager investment of Rs.1, 500 only. *The technology of lac cultivation is also being transferred from farmers to farmers.* Encouraged from this, he raised 150 numbers of Flemingia semialata, a quick growing busy lac host plant with tomato as intercropping. The lac crop on F.Semialata is growing well. Now Shri Ahir is supporting his family very well. Thanks to Shri Ramesh Chandra for motivating and supporting Shri Ahir at initial stage.

Case 3: Income generation through kusmi lac cultivation

Smt. Albina Marki was the member of Self Help Group (DEEPAK). She came into the contact with the Centre for Women Development (CWD), Torpa Khunti (under DPO sponsored project on lac cultivation and processing unit) in 2011-12. Her husband Shri Phillip Marki was inspired to join the occupation of lac cultivation with scientific interventions during various exposure visits by the officials from IINRG, Namkum, Ranchi and CWD, Torpa. He was identified from SHG group as direct beneficiary under this project. He came to the institute for training and visited that Institute Research Farm where scientific cultivation of lac was demonstrated by experts. He was trying lac cultivation on kusum and ber but could not succeed due to poor quality broodlac. His efforts were directed towards scientific lac cultivation and experts from IINRG demonstrated the technology at the Baghiya village and inputs were supplied by CWD, Torpa.

Now, he has adopted scientific lac cultivation and is well aware about time of pruning, selection of good quality broodlac, bundling of broodlac and inoculation, Phunki removal, spraying of recommended pesticides etc. Family of Smt. Albina has got good quality Kusmi broodlac from the project (7 kg) and also purchased good quality kusmi broodlac (10 kg) and inoculated on 15 kusum trees in Feb. 2013. They also arranged about 20 kg broodlac for inoculation. Thus, a total of 37 k broodlac was inoculated. Marki family got a total of 270 kg kusmi lac production. *In September 2013, they earned Rs.1.15 lakh by the sale of first harvest of the kusmi crop.* This produce (brood lac) was again inoculated for next crop by their family and other farmers in the locality.

Broodlac was purchased by CWD, Torpa and distributed to the other interested member of SHGs in identified lac growing areas. This improved the standard of living of the farmers in his locality also. Moreover, with the initiative of all the partners including District Planning Office, Khunti, IINRG, Ranchi and CWD, Torpa beneficiaries from three different SHG from Rania block were honoured on 12 September 2013 on the occasion of Foundation Day Celebration of the Khunti District. Hon'ble Chief Minister, Jharkhand. Shri Hemant Soren handed over a cheque of Rs.4 lakh. Broodlac was purchased from these beneficiaries for distributing further. *Besides this, lac worth of Rs.5.00 lakh was sold by the beneficiaries in the open market with good price during the year by the members of SHGs.* This achievement has brought in a lot of interest towards lac cultivation in this area.

Case 4: Field visit/Demonstration/Training to farmers

Twenty five field visits were undertaken for interaction with farmers and monitoring of lac crop time to time in adopted villages of Jamtara and Dumka districts by the experts of IINRG, Namkum (Ranchi). A total of seven demonstrations were carried out for rangeeni lac cultivation on B. monosperma tree, one in each village namely Karmatand and Nawadih villages of Jamatra district; Jiyathar, Sagbehari, Guhijori (block: Dumka), Sarepahari and Maghi Santhali village of Dumka districts; A total 39 farmers from Jamtara and Dumka districts successfully completed two days training on "Scientific lac cultivation on palas tree" at IINRG, Ranchi during 15th and 16th July 2013.

The case study of the farmers field demonstration in the block of Dumka shows that the highest income by the individual farmer named Sh. Ram Hansda was Rs.9, 300 from Sagbehri and Rs. 8, 600 for Isahak Hembram from village Jiyathar. In Jamtara block another tribal farmer Sh. Baldev Marandi could secure an income of Rs. 7, 800 from Karmatand village, another tribal farmer Sh. Ram Murmu from Jhilimtand could earn Rs. 5, 100 and Sh. Shivlal Tudu from Nawadih village could earn Rs.5,400 per annum. The total number of farm family involved were 38 in the employment and income generation during 2013.This shows the important contribution IINRG, Namkum, Ranchi in providing motivation and stimulous to the adivasis families in Jharkhand and elsewhere. These efforts are still in the initial stage and would enhance the further capability of the adivasis in Jharkhand region to augment their income and support from their livelihood through the active intervention of IINRG, Namkum, Ranchi. *Source (Indian Institute of Natural Resins and Gums Namkum)*

MARKETING CHANNELS OF LAC

Private Channels Lac Growers => Agent => Paikars=> Rakhiwals => Arhatdars => Wholesaler => Manufacturer

Cooperative Channels

Farmers => Agent => Purchase Committees => LAMPS; PACS; VMSSS Marketing of Lac - A Cooperative Approach

Lac Cooperative in Jharkhand

There are a good number of important haats in the lac growing areas, where lac is grown in abundance. As it is a non-nationalised item, it is being handled by many intermediaries. Big manufacturers distribute money to the *paikars* on the basis of individual purchasing capacity in the morning of each *haat* day. These *paikars* purchase stick lac in the *haat* at price dictated by the principal buyers. In the evening, they bring purchased stock to the buyer and take their commission. The commission is generally five to seven rupee per maund (40 kg): where the commission includes the transport cost from *haats* to buyer's godowns.

Some *paikars* bring the stock to manufactures in the areas and negotiate on rates with them. If the rates are acceptable to *paikars* they deliver the stock and receive commission at the rate of Rs. 10 to Rs. 20 per maund. There were also some *arhats* in some towns. *These arhats are in Ranchi, Chandwa, Daltonganj and Ranka (Garwah).* The function of these *arhats* generally is to arrange stic klac for the potential buyers. The buyers' approach these arhats, and indicate requirements. Arhatdars contact paikars or lac traders in locality for the required stock. Their commission is three per cent of the value of the stock transacted. They extract commission from the buyers and sellers. In most of the *haats*, lac growers bring stick lac for sale, but there were *haats,* where *paikars* collect stick lac from interior areas and bring the stock on horseback for sale. *These haats are at Ranka (Palamau district) and Tamar (Ranchi district).Presently, there being no processing unit in Uttar Pradesh, the entire stock of sticklac produced is smuggled to Jharkhand.* The rates are very cheap in those areas. *The field study has revealed that Ranka Haat situated on the borders of Uttar Pradesh, is being dominated by middleman, who collect stick lac from the surrounding villages bring stock in the haat and sells it.*

The Role of JASCOLAMPF

JASCOLAMPF operates in lac growing areas. It extends support price to farmers through Vyapar Mandals and multipurpose agricultural societies. There are about 178 affiliated societies with the JASCOLAMPF in the whole of Jharkhand, basically in Palamua, Ranchi and Chaibasa, but about 50 to 60 societies were involved in the lac marketing. The presence of JASCOLAMPF the price of stick lac in the market was only Rs. 30.00 (thirty) per kg [2002], but traders hiked its rate, when JASCOLAMPF declared Rs. 50 per kilo. The lac growers have had good price through the LAMPS, PACS and V.M.S.S.

The primary multipurpose agricultural cooperative societies are called LAMPS, (Large Area Multi-Purpose Cooperative Society). There are about 1000 members in each of the LAMPS which covers 15 to 20 square kilometers area. There are 834 LAMPS in Jharkhand but only 152 LAMPS are affiliated to JASCOLAMPF. Most members of the LAMPS depend upon the farming of minor forest produces like lac, tamarind and mahua etc. But among these, lac is an important produce of the tribal farmers. Primary Agricultural Cooperative Societies are called PACS. There are 476 PACS in Jharkhand and 152 are affitiated with the JASCOLAMPF. 16 PACS are doing lac marketing with it in the area of Palamua and Garwah. JASCOLAMPF is trying to eradicate the exploitation of farmers by the middleman. (J. Kumar, 2011).

The role of women

Lac cultivation can be suitably taken up as rural enterprises on existing natural hosts like palas, ber and kusum. Besides, it can be taken up on plantation basis, by introducing the host – plants like Flemingia macrophylla, F. semialata and Albiza lucida. In general, lac cultivation operations carried out involve climbing on trees. Thus pruning, typing of broodlac bundles on host-tree at a different places, harvesting and spraying of pesticides etc. are done by male laborers' while bundling and selection of broodlac and scrapping of lac encrustation from host twigs etc. can be carried out by women.

Lac cultivation on 100 tree - palas resulted into generation of 35 mandays for women out of a total of 80. For producing one quintal of brood lac: women can contribute around 43 p c of the total manpower involved. Similarly, on 100 trees of ber, out of a total of 157 mandays, 110 mandays were generated for women. For producing one quintal of sticklac 14 mandays for women are generated which constitute 70 p c of the total manpower. Similarly, for trees of kusum, out of a total 192 mandays, 85 mandays were generated for women. The production of one quintal brood lac from kusum tree will result into generation of six mandays for women.

The employment generation from lac cultivation on major host – trees like Palas contributed 55 male mandays and 35 female mandays. Similarly, in another host tree of Ber unit (100 trees), the number of male mandays generated was 67 and female man-days generated was 110. In the Kusum host tree, the number of male mandays generated was 147 and female mandays generated was 85. The above description clearly demonstrates that in Palas, Ber and Kusum cultivation; the female labor days were quite substantial and in ber lac cultivation in particular, the female labor days were much higher than male labor days. (K.K Kumar, 2011). In the lac processing, sieving, drying of seedlac and winnowing is carried out exclusively by women, while for crushing, washing and conservation of seedlac into shellac, women assist men counterparts. Overall, in the indigenous methods, women contribute 50-55 p c of the physical input in terms of labour up to preparation of seedlac stage.

Lac resin is such a versatile product that it makes its presence felt in most of the sectors like varnish, paints, inks, adhesive, food, cosmetics, leather, electrical, pharaceuticala industry, besides some uses of miscellany. The wax obtained from lac insect finds uses in shoe. The automobile and floor polish, bottle sealer, tailor's chalk, crayon, lipstick and fruit coatings were some of the outlets. From a very small-scale cottage unit consisting of three to five persons to a very big lac based unit of more than 100 persons, can be established.

Manufacture of lac-bangles and ornaments unit can be started with only Rs. 10,000 as a capital investment. Many units at present are being run exclusively by women in many parts of the country. A unit with three working women can earn around Rs. 100-200 per day. The advantage is that such units can be developed in the very village and provide ample opportunities to rural women for livelihood. The manufacture of sealing wax like lac bangles, women can run by women. A unit of three women can give earning of about Rs. 100 per women per day. The simple method of preparation of varnish for wooden furnitures and its application can involve them in this particular field. Besides, there are many big lac-based units manufacturing bleached lac, de-waxed decolorized lac, lac-dye etc. which involves women at various steps.

Lac Crop Calendar and production Areas

LAC CROP CALENDAR

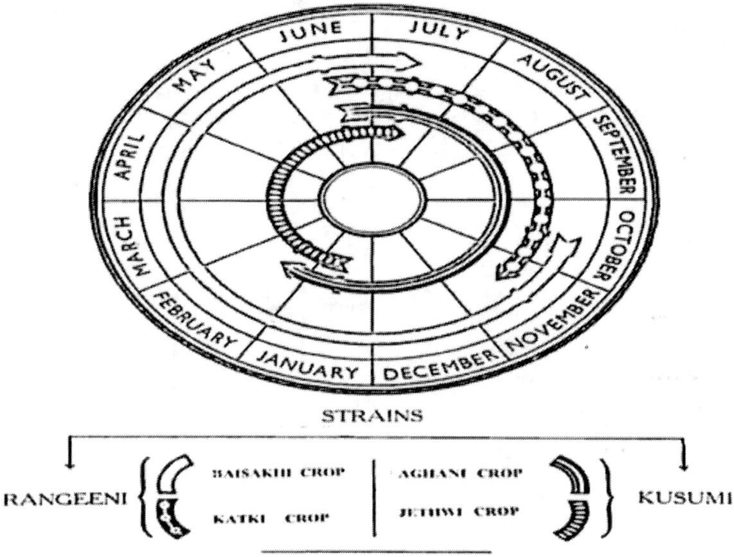

The position of lac production in different districts was:

Bihar/Jharkhand:	Ranchi, Palamau, Singhbhum, Hazaribagh, Dhanbad, Gaya and Santhal Parganas.
Madhya Pradesh/ Chhattisgarh:	Bilaspur Balaghat, Sahdol, Surguja, Raipur, Seoni, Jabalpur Mandla, Durg, Raigarh and Hoshangabad.
West Bengal:	Purulia, Murshidabad and Bankura.
Gujarat:	Bhandara, Chnada, Panch Mahals and Baroda
Meghalay:	Mikir hills, Garo hills and khasi, and jainthia hills.
Odisha:	Mayurbhanj, Keonjhar Dhenkanal and Kalahandi.
Uttar Pradesh:	Mirzapur and Varanasi.

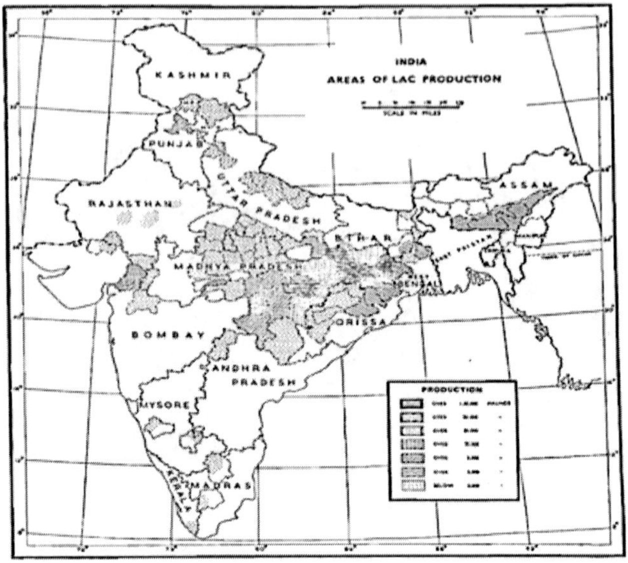

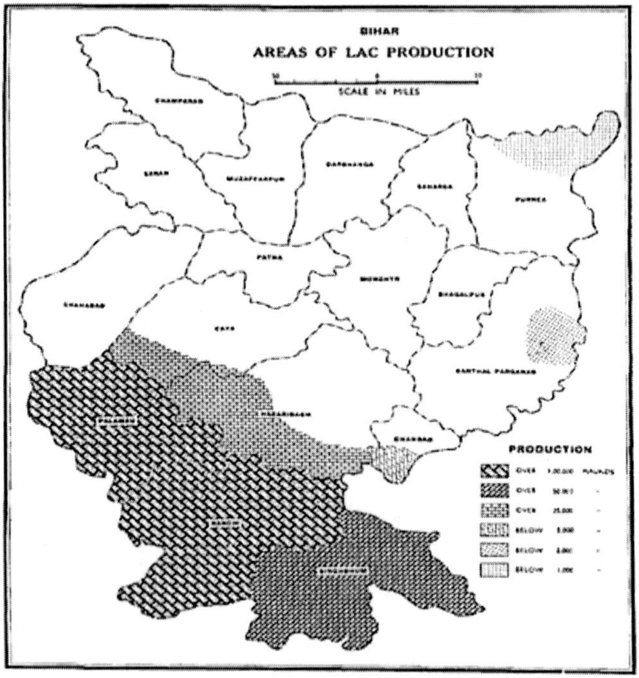

Areas of Lac production in Jharkhand

Lac Cultivation and Processing Unit - District Khunti (The field of empirical study)

This project has been initiated by District Planning Office, Collectorate Khunti, Jharkhand [2014-15] to address the major issues of the poor resource constraint faced by the people inhabiting in forest and sub-forest areas through scientific interventions and utilization of locally available natural resources. Lac cultivation is one of the viable interventions to provide livelihood support for sub forest and forest dwellers with additional opportunity of employment at industry level and better utilization of degraded land with biodiversity conservation. The District Planning Officee, Collectorate, Khunti has taken initiatives and provided funds through the District innovative funds to Indian Institute of Natural Resins and Gums, Ranchi for developmental activities in Khunti district. Three institutions namely, District Planning Office (DPO), Torpa Rural Development Society for Women (TRDS), Torpa and Bioved Lac Resource Training Centre, Khunti, has come forward to work together in collaboration with IINRG, Ranchi under the project to demonstrate improved technologies of lac cultivation on existing lac host trees (kusum, ber and palas) and establish Flemingia semialata farms as well as small scale lac processing unit and imparting skill development for preparation of lac based handicraft items.

The work will be carried out in Torpa and Rania Blocks of Khunti district through formation of SHGs (31) and total 415 families will be covered under the project. Six farmers across three villages of Khunti district were identified and 1,200 seedlings of quick growing bushy lac host, Flemingia semialata were distributed for planting in farmer's fields. Some Butea monosperma (palas) trees were identified in nearby villages for raising rangeeni summer season (baisakhi) lac crop. Two quintals of rangeeni broodlac have been distributed to 93 members of eight SHGs across six villages in two blocks of Khunti district. The demonstration of bundling and inoculation of broodlac as well as monitoring and technical guidance in five villages of Torpa block was conducted.

Conclusion

Some of the NTFPs traded most in the state are - Harra, Bahera Chiraunji, Karanj, Jamun Chiraita, Bamboo shoots, Tamarind, Mahua, Dori, Sal seeds, Neem seeds, Honey, Satabri etc. The dependence of adivasis is also considerable on produce like kendu leaf, mahua, lac, char, tamarind, sal seed, amla etc. Medicinal plants are also found in abundance in Jharkhand e.g. Amla, Harra, Bahera, Karanj and various other herbs & shrubs. Apart from this, the livelihoods of the poor rural and tribal families depend on a range of forest produce such as, tassar, lac, honey mahua, chironji, medicinal plants and a number of NTFPs.

Key issues and challenges related to NTFPs in the state are NTFP Collection, Trade and Value Addition, lack of marketing focus, Market constraint and ineffective value chain sequence. The Different NTFP collection and trading takes place in different months of the year. For example, Tamarind is procured during the months of Feb-March: Mahua flowers in the months of March-June: Mahua seed during the months of June and July. The Sal leaves are ever green NTFP which is procured and marketed by the tribals during all the months in the year except March and April. Similarly, Siali leaves is procured by tribals of Jharkhand during the months of June-December, Char seed during Apri-May, and Kusum lac during the months of June,July,October,November and December.

The major use of NTFP by Adivasis and marginalized sections are for household use, marketing for livelihood security. NTFP are also semi-processed for value addition by villagers such as Bamboo, Mahua, Chiraunji, Sal, (Patta Datun), Tamarind, Sabai grass, Leaves (Khajur), fruits, such as, Jamun, Amla, Jangli Bel, Jangli Ber, Beeju aam (Mango grown by seeds in forests). The role of middleman is important in the market transaction of NTFP and medicinal plants are also used by intermediaries for profit. The tribals are fleeced in this process.

Some 3.01 lac kendu leaf were collected by the adivasis [2015-16], out of which the total the sale amount was Rs. 51.165 lac and the price paid to leaf pluckers was 62.11 per cent of the total sale; further 37.38 per cent of the total sale was the gross premium to the corporation. The Kendu Patta collection in the state declined considerably [2014-15 and 2015-16] due to the strong left wing extremism particularly in the districts of West-Singhbhum, Khunti, Latehar and Palmau. The contractors stopped partaking in the tender since the extremists demanded heavy ransom as their earning.

The decline in kendu leaf collection is a huge loss of income and livelihood to the adivasis of the state of Jharkhand, wherein the incidence of women participation was very high. Similarly, in the procurement of the other NTFP, the adivasis were not able to collect and lost their income and livelihood; particularly in the left extremist affected districts of the West Singhbhum, Khunti, Ranchi, Lohardaga, Latehar, Garhwa, Palamau, etc. This is a tremendous blow to their economic source of earning for future as well. The products collected by the adivasis in West Singhbhum District include Jhadu grass, Kendu leaves, Karanj, Kusum, Mahua flowers, Mahua seeds, Mango, Mushroom, Sal leaves, Tamarind, etc. During the last three years of empirical study [2013-14, 2014-15 and 2015-16]. It has been found to have some considerable decline in its procurement in West Singhbhum district by the adivasis, due to left extremism, dwindling women mandays.

The studies conducted by the few authors on NTFP in Jharkhand in the districts of Hazaribagh, Simdega and Gumla give us a glimpse of the dependence of the adivasis in Jharkhand on NTFP. An average percentage of annual income from NTFP in the villages surveyed was in the range of 10 to 31 per cent in Hazaribagh. Simdega has many NTFP resources, but lack of proper market and infrastructure for processing various items, makes NTFP related livelihoods less profitable. In Gumla, nearly half of the households surveyed were found to have been involved in agriculture and the rest were marginal farmers, who were in NTFP collection. Simdega district is rich in NTFP resources with almost all the households surveyed were involved in their collection along with agriculture and allied activities. The four major NTFPs taken into consideration are Karanj, Chironjee, Lac and Mahua. Out of these four items, only Lac is collected during winter and remaining three were collected in summer.

There was no storage and processing problem for Chironjee and Lac. The storage of Karanj has its problems with pest infestation and degradation due to weather. The maximum storage problems were associated with Mahua.- pests, weather, lack of storage facilities and money required, leakage, lack of knowledge on storage mechanisms etc. around 83 p c of women were involved in their collection. NTFPs acted as the subsidiary source of income for rural people. The findings reveal that rural women actively participate in various NTFP practices, and that there was a need for mobilizing awareness among the rural folks.

Before its formation as a state in 2000, Jharkhand was a part of the state of Bihar. Certain policies on NTFP were still based on the formulation by Bihar government. The first major policy level shift for the state government had taken place a year before in the form of The Bihar Kendu Leaf (Control of Trade) Act 1972. This Act was the first to initiate the nationalisation of NTFP in the state of Bihar. The Kendu Leaf became a big revenue earner for the state. Secondly, its aim was to check the exploitation of tribals and give them their due share of price, which was achieved to some extent. Bihar State Forest Development Corporation trading in Sal seeds (Nationalised in 1977 itself) was initiated in the year 1977.

The Bihar State Forest Development Corporation was entrusted with the task of procuring Harra fruit and seed, Palas fruit and seed, Aonla fruit and seed and Bahra fruit and seed. In this regard, an Act was framed in the year 1984 known as the Bihar Forest Produce (Regulation of Trade) Act, 1984. The Act envisages the appointment of one or more than one agent for all or any specified Forest produce. It visualises greater role of Gram Panchayats, LAMPS, PACS, Vyapar Mandal or the Bihar State Tribal Co-operative Development Co-operation Ltd. The Panchayat (Extension to Scheduled Areas) Act of 1996 emowers the Gram Sabhas and panchayats to safeguard and preserve the traditions of local population, This Act endorses useful directives and guidelines to the state government for formation of appropriate forest laws and Acts to the benefit of villagers, living in and around the forest.

The major markets trading in various NTFP/NTFP based products in the State are: Daltonganj, Garhwa, Latehar, Chatra, Hazaribagh, Gumla, Giridih, Ranchi, Jamshedpur, Chaibasa and Chakradharpur. The empirical study was conducted in the district of West Singhbhum. The important NTFP as the source of livelihood in this district were kendu leaves, mahua flowers, kusum, haara, behra, amla, chironji, khajur leaves, tomatoes, lady finger, brinjal, cucumber, mango, tamarind, neem, sal leaves, karanj, mahua seed and lac. However, the interest of the young generation in the NTFP procurement is considerably dwindling. The major markets in various NTFP/NTFP based products in the state are: Daltonganj, Garhwa, Latehar, Chatra, Hazaribagh, Gumla, Giridih, Ranchi, Jamshedpur, Chaibasa and Chakradharpur. There is a chain of traders vertically. The main traders of these markets get collected NTFP from sub-trader/regional wholesaler/agents and depending upon the utility and demand of a particular NTFP it is traded in the domestic or export market.

Lac cultivation is an important source of income for the forest dwellers. Besides, it has high potential for generating employment for men and women in forest and fringe areas of Jharkhand. The districts in Jharkhand produce over 1,000 tons of lac [2012-13] were Ranchi (Khunti, 4250 tons), Simdega (2,720 tons) and Gumla (2,270 tons) and their All India Rank was respectively 1,2 and 3. The main varieties of lac were Baisakhi, Jethwi, Katki and Aghani. The Lac processing Centers in Eastern-India during 2001-11 were Jharkhand and West Bengal. The districts having lac processing centers were highest in Ranchi (10 processing units), followed by Simdega (two units), Daltonganj (two units), Saraikela-Kharsawan and West Singhbum [one unit each]. In West Bengal Purulia (Balrampur) had the largest number of processing unit numbering 110, followed by Purulia Tulin (30) and Purulia (Jhalda). These processing units were producing seed lac, button lac, shellac and bleach lac.

Almost 75 per cent of lac produced in India is exported to different countries of which the main customers were USA, UK, Germany, Italy, France, Japan, China, Sweden, Brazil,

Argentina and Russia. Its total export with value-added products [2010-11] was 6,339.05 tons, valued at Rs. 211.13 crore. Indian Institue of Nadtural Resins and Gums, Namkum Jharkhand has played yeoman service in promoting its cultivation in the states of Jharkhand, Bihar, Uttar Pradesh, Orissa Chhatisgarh, West Bengal, Rajasthan and other states in India. It is located in Ranchi. It imparts in-campus orientation programme, demonstration of cultivation technologies in different states, conducts field visit programmes to different distrcts and states, provides impetus to production, marketing including export, conducting workshops and seminar, having direct face-face interaction with the lac farmers, promoting shellac industry and monitoring scientific lac cultivation, processing and utilization. It has been of seminal benefit to tribals of Jharkhand and other states. This has been amplified through some of the success stories. These case studies refer to Sh. Jagdish Hansda, Sh.. Yogendra Ahir and Smt. Albina Manki of the district of Khunti, and adjacent districts of Jharkhand. The case studies demonstrate that the tribals of Jharkhand are able to earn good deal of income through lac cultivation and marketing as also to use it as sustainable source of livelihood. They procure mostly raw lac brood and sell them directly to the arahat.

Twenty five field visits were undertaken for interaction with farmers and monitoring of lac crop time to time in adopted villages of Jamtara and Dumka districts by the experts of IINRG, Namkum (Ranchi) and considerably contributed to the enhancement odf income generation of several families in these two districts. It has a good impact on the neighbouring villages of the two districts to adopt lac as an important source of livelihood. A lac project has been initiated by District Planning Office, Collectorate Khunti, Jharkhand [2014-15] to address major issues of poor resource constraint faced by forest and sub-forest inhabitants through scientific intervention and utilization of locally available natural resources.

Lac cultivation is one of the viable interventions in this direction to provide livelihood support for sub forest and forest dwellers with additional opportunity of employment at industry level and better utilization of degraded land with biodiversity conservation. The district of Khunti is one of the empirical areas for the present research. These arhats are in Ranchi, Chandwa, Daltonganj and Ranka (Garwah). The role of arhats generally was to arrange stick lac for potential buyers. The buyers approach them with requirements. The tribals were squeezed by arhats and traders in the absence of market facilities provided by the state government. Even the traders from West Bengal come in large number to Jharkhand to procure the lac from the tribal farmers for a song.

Lac cultivation can be suitably taken up as rural enterprises on existing natural hosts like palas, ber and kusum. The women contribute considerably in the labour participation for lac cultivation. Lac cultivation on 100 tree of palas resulted into generation of 35 mandays for women. out of total 80 mandays. For producing one quintal of broodlac, women can contribute around 43 p c of the total manpower involved. Similarly, on 100 trees of ber, out of a total of 157 man-days, 110 mandays are generated for women. For producing one quintal of sticklac 14 mandays for women are being generated, which constituted 70 p c of total manpower. Similarly, for the kusum trees, out of a total 192 mandays, 85 mandays were generated for women. The production of one quintal broodlac from kusum tree will result into generation of six man-days for women. In Palas, Ber and Kusum cultivation, the female labor days were quite substantial and in ber lac cultivation in particular, the female labor days were much higher than male labor days.

Lac resin is a versatile product. It make its presence felt in most of the sectors like varnish, paints, inks, adhesive, food, cosmetics, leather, electrical, pharaceuticala industry, besides some miscellaneous uses. Manufacture of lac-bangles and ornaments unit can be started with only Rs. 10,000 as a capital investment. At present, many units are being run exclusively by women in many parts of the country.

A comparison of the status of NTFP as a source of livelihood in Jharkhand and Orissa shows that the dependence of the vulnerable sections is considerably higher in the state of Jharkhand than Odisha. One of the important reasons was the active intervention in the state policy by the govermnet of the

Odisha to promote NTFP through recogniztion of Gram Sabha and Panchayats as holding the owenership right of MFP for 69 produces. The intervention by various agencies like Forest Department, ORMAS, TDCC and MART has considerably activated the SHGs in the procurement, marketing and income earning through various NTFP in the state of Orissa.

The role of government of Jharkhand appears to be very tenuous. As a result, the young generation seems to be getting alienated from the NTFP as an important siource of livelihood unlike their adivasis counterparts in Orissa. Women play significant role in the procurement and marketing of the NTFP in Orissa. The future of the adivasis in Orissa on the dependence of NTFP as an importance source of livelihood is very promising. The state government almost appears to be lukewarm to attend to the MFP needs of vulnerable sections. Another constraint therein was the role of left extremist forces. It was counter-productive to the procurement of NTFP as a source of subsistence. Certain forest produce, like mahua flower, mahua seed (char seed), tamarind, sal leaves, siali leave, karanj, chironji, and lac are still procured by the adivasis in Jharkhand. In the otherwise gloomy situation in Jharkhand, the role of IINRG, Namkum, Ranchi appears very encouraging, where they have made positive impact in few districts of the state like Khunti, Jamtara, Ranchi, etc. which is a welcome augury.

Appendix I

Total NRG Production, export and import [2012-13]

Particulars	*Production (Tons)*	*Export*		*Import*	
		Quantity (Tons)	*Value (Rs. lakh)*	*Quantity (Tons)*	*Value (Rs. lakh*
Guar gum	8,07,541.68	3,31,497.58	21,14,672.40	460.35	2573.72
Lac	19,575.00	4,361.30	48,027.58	NA	NA
Karaya um (Indian Tragcanth)	212.50	5,764.40	2,220.80	71.92	197.86
Other NRGs	10,251.78	3,949.48	11,197.83	89,214.06	75,763.32
Total	**8,37,580,78.00**	**3,40,384.76**	**21,76,118.61**	**89,746.33**	**78,534.90**

Source: Indian Institute of Natural Resinsand Gums Namkum, Ranchi, (Jharkhand), [2013-14]

References

Buriuly, Bace (2013): "Tribal Weekly Market (HAATS): A Study in West Singhbhum District of Jharkhand (Unpublished report)", Centre for Social Entrepreneurship, School of Management and Labour Studies, Mumbai: Tata Institute of Social Sciences.

Gharai .A.K, & Chakrabarti, S. (2009): A study on NTFP related Livelihood dependency and people's perception of the commercialization potential of Selected NTFPs in selected Locations of Gumla, Hazaribagh & Simdega Districts of Jharkhand, Secunderabad: Central for People's Forestry.

J. Kumar, (2011): "Marketing of lac– A Cooperative Approach", K.K. Sharma and R. Ramani (ed), 2011," Recent Advances in LAC CULTURE", Indian Institute of Natural Resins and Gums, Namkum, Ranchi.

Kumar S and Ankita Chaudhary (2016): "Enhancement of Livelihood Activities through non-Timber Forest Products: A Study in Jharkhand's Ranchi and Simdega Districts", Jharkhand Journal of Development and Management Studies XISS; Ranchi, Vol.14, No.1, March 2016, pp 6919-30.

Kumar J (2011): "Marketing of Lac: A Cooperative Approach", in (eds.) "Recent Advances in Lac Culture", K.K.Sharma and R.Ramani, Ranchi: Indian Institute of Natural Resins and Guns, pp 269-73.

Kumar, K.K, (2011): "Lac as a Rural Enterprise for Women", in Sharma K.K. and Ramani R (eds) 2011, "Recent Advances in Lac Culture", Indian Institute of Natural Resins and Gums, Namkum, Ranchi *(ICAR)*, pp, 274-81.

M.A. Islam, S.M.S.Quli, R.Rai and Angrej Ali " (2014): "Exploration of Variables Predicting Livelihood Assets Status of Tribal Communities subsisting in Forests of Jharkhand", India, J Hum Ecol, 47(3): 241- 49.

Yogi, R.K. R.KSingh, A Bhattacharya, A.K.Jaiswal and Alok Kumar (2016) "Current Scenario and new Policy Interventions in the Lac sector", Indian Institute of National Resins and Guns, Namkum, Ranchi, Jharkhand Journal of Development and Management Studies, XISS, Ranchi, Vol.14, No.1, March 2016.

Verma, Sanjay Kumar and Sujit Kumar Paul (2016): "Sustaining non-timber forest products (NTFPs) based rural Livelihoods of Tribals in Jharkhand: Issues and Challenges", Ranchi:, Jharkhand Journal of Development and Management Studies XISS, Ranchi, Vol.14, No.1, March 2016, pp. 6865-83.

Chapter - 5

Contemporary Forest Management Systems

Debashis Debnath

Introduction

The tribal livelihoods have been borne out of survival mechanism by reciprocating interactions with the surrounding environment in an ecosystem and obviously revolved around the forest resources. The evolution and development of tribal livelihoods, comprising their assets, capabilities assets required for living, carried its own institutional arrangements of common property resources with their social institutions and cultural practices to lead their life on their own. Thus, in the socio-evolutionary processes, their resource management is common property resource management, whose ownership hangs on with the community-based institutions with use-rights on community. They live in a natural environment, where there is no distinction of economic, religious and magical activities, though they are being categorised broadly into four varieties with socio-evolutionary process and economic pursuits as:

1. Hunter-gatherer bands that are generally egalitarian
2. Tribal societies with limited instances of social rank and prestige.
3. Stratified tribal societies led by chieftains.
4. Civilizations, with complex social hierarchies and organized, institutional governments.

As per 2011 census, their population constitute 8.6 per cent (104.28 million) of the Indian population. As the 60-70 p c of our tribals are living either inside or in the vicinity of forest, they were either known as forest-dwelling or forest dependent communities, which in Indian connotation, known as *Vanabasi* or *Vanyajati* as well as 'the Scheduled Tribe' (a constitutional category), as their affinity with forest from time immemorial. In the forest economy, they are found in collection of forest products, including small-timber and non-timber forest products including medicinal herbs, timber, fuel wood, fodder and bamboo for their self-consumption and selling surplus in the local market at nominal prices. In the changing sphere, they have been exposed to modern education and technology, which perforce them into various occupational patterns, to adopt services and business. Being a constitutional category, they were found in large numbers in government services and in private services. They can be seen in small business, like petty shops, outlets for agricultural and forest products, and crafts, etc.

Today, the socio-economic life of Indian tribal is based on their organizations, environment and spate of challenges, due to lack of livelihood opportunities for tribal people as one of the chief causes of their backward status as compared with the other social groups. This issue is aggravated by the high rate of degradation or depletion of natural resources and displacements faced by tribal people due to various infrastructural developments, which also causes loss of livelihood for them among other things.

Brief History of Tribal Economy

In order to examine the dynamics of tribal livelihoods and economy, this is well-observed since industrial revolution and its aftermath the change occurred in tribal economy with the alterations of the concept of natural objects into natural resources and introduction of capitalistic ideology with the maximization of profit on forest resources. Later, with the imposition of Forest policies and laws by the British Rulers with massive logging of woods for administrative and commercial purposes coupled with the classification of forests. They introduced the policies and legislations to exploit the natural and human resources. Diversion of forest lands were taken place for various purposes, specially into to the agricultural lands, as it has got priority in the Forest policies 1894. Similar practices and arrangements in the light of colonial government's interests helped the custodial, centralized and controlled state management regime to influence and destroy the autonomy of the tribal economy by simply alienation from the rest of the people and exploitation of them with the help of zamindars, landlords and contractors. Other historical incidents like the rise of Marathas from the mid-seventeenth century onwards for the first time led to serious inroads into the Bhil homelands (Monohar, 2001, quoted from Chaudhary 2010). In order to develop trade and settled agriculture to boost up their revenues carried out sustained campaigns against the Bhils who refused to agree to this incursion into their lifestyle. Peasants and traders from Gujarat and Maharashtra were encouraged to settle in the Bhil regions and forests were cleared to bring land under the plough. Thousands of Bhils were massacred when they rose in revolt against this policy. In this manner, according to Luard (1908, quoted from Chaudhary 2010), the British Raj followed the policy of the Marathas and brought KunbiPatidar and Jat farmers from Gujarat and Rajasthan respectively and settled them on the Bhil lands in the plains to increase the revenue and commercial agriculture and to tame the militant Bhils. "While some of the Bhils withdrew into the hills, most others were converted into serfs or bonded labours of these non-adivasi farmers. Thus, net results of the acculturation process of different varieties between tribal and non-tribal there was near breakdown of the tribal autonomy of their both material and non-material culture. A new and alien way of life was gradually imposed on them and the process of pauperization and ruinization among them started during pre-British days by rulers and kings became common among them. British Raj maintained distance with socio-cultural practices in principle but in practice its natural resources management mechanism was designed and introduced in such a fashion that it contributed to erosion of social and cultural heritage along with economic deterioration" (Chaudhary, 2010: 3). The state management regime was imposed on the declaration of Charters of Indian Forests by Lord Dalhousie in 1885 on the 3rd August. The tribals were driven away from their homelands and became labours in the silvi cultural operation of the so-called Scientific Forest Management. They made the 5000 forest villages for the regular supply of labour and made some concessions to meet up the fulfilment of fuel woods, fodder or the pastoral activities. Towards the dawn of independence, the dominant change agents, especially the state and civil societies, recognized historical marginality of tribals. This realization led to the formulation and implementation of different policies, acts, plans, programmes and schemes for the protection and promotion of human rights of tribal masses especially in the light of problems and provisions of Indian Constitution. Many civil society organizations commenced various activities viz. protest movements as well as capacity building oriented efforts, emerged for their development. So one side the roles of individual philanthropists and social reformers were significant and on the other side the suppression of the indigenous knowledge system relating to different aspects of life, custom, tradition, and seasonal migration caused pauperization and marginality of the tribals from their rights and ownership. This was reflected from the Tribal Commissioners' reports viz. the reports of Dhebar and ShiloAo Commissions. This continued till declaration of the National Forest Policy in 1988, which is recognized as pro-poor and pro-tribal policy and the paradigm changes occurred.

Objectives

The author attempts to rationalize the concept:

1. Traditional economic Organizations and Ownership of Indian Tribals; and
2. Sustainable livelihood approach in natural resource management.

Tribal Economic Organization

The tribal economic organization is mainly concerned with producing to meet their daily needs. These activities are very much determined by the geographical environment. As they are living in the remote and inaccessible world, they generally carry out production without adequate technological aids resulting into their backwardness and poverty. Thus the chief aim of economic activities in a tribal society is to fulfil the community duties. Thus, the organization of most of the economic activities is cooperative and communal. In their holistic economy there is no distinction of economic, religious and magical activities, rather there is a tendency to mix up all these. In the economic activities also religious and magical activities are utilized to attain economic ends. Many superstitions in this respect are prevalent among the tribals, for example, among Nagas there was a custom of human sacrifice and sprinkling human blood over land in order to increase its fertility.

In the absence of sufficient technological aids and scientific knowledge regarding agricultural and other production, the tribal people generally produce as much as they require only to consume. Hardly anything is left for exchange or hoarding. They do not use currency in deciding the price of commodities and in exchange. There are no banks of economic exchanges in their societies. They hardly carry out any exchange of economic goods with outside groups. There are no regular markets found in tribal societies and, therefore, there is no competition, monopoly, business or trade in their economic organization. There is absence of profiteering in tribal economic organization due to two important causes. Firstly, the absence of currency to fix the price of commodities and secondly the connection of unity sentiments with economic activities. There are no specialists in different branches of economic organization in tribal societies, with the result that there is no division of labour and specialization.

The above mentioned characteristics of tribal economic organization account for their economic backwardness. They do not know the new changes and inventions in different fields of production.

Ownership of lands

This section presents the distribution of ownership holdings among the households of Scheduled Tribes and all householders at the National level. The following Table gives the details of distribution of landownership. Holdings at all-India level among rural, urban, and combined areas for Scheduled Tribes and all other groups [2002-03]. In rural areas, a substantial proportion of Scheduled Tribes own very little land. Among them, 12.81 per cent of the householders own only up to 0.002 hectare of land, while the aggregate of all groups under this category is 10.0 per cent. In the marginal category, among Scheduled Tribes 63.16 per cent of households own 26.96 per cent of land in rural areas. It shows that the marginal category among Scheduled Tribes is less equitable than the all-social groups. Significantly, the zero and marginal categories together account for 75.97 per cent among Scheduled Tribes, while it is 79.60 per cent for all householders. In small and above categories, the relative share of area is greater than their respective shares of household of Scheduled Tribes in rural areas.

Table 1: Distribution of ownership holdings

Categories/ Ownership	*General population*	*Scheduled Tribes*
Large	0.6	0.3
Medium	3	2.2
Semi-medium	6	7.31
Small	10.8	14.21
Marginal	69.6	63.16
Landless	10.0	12.81

Source: Report of the High-level Committee on Socio-economic, Health and Educational Status of Tribal Communities of India (2014)

Occupational Distribution

Table 2: Percentage of Main ST workers in rural sectors

	Year	*Cultivators*	*Agricultural Labours*	*Non-farming*
Percentage of total main workers of Scheduled Tribes	1971	55.6	33	9.4
	1981	54.43	32.67	12.9
	1991	54.32	32.69	12.81
	2001	54.32	29.88	15.8
Percentage of total main workers of General population	1971	43.9	26.9	30.2
	1981	41.5	24.94	33.48
	1991	38.75	26.15	35.1
	2001	31.7	26.5	41.5

Source: The high-level Committee report on Socio-economic, Health- Educational Status of Tribal Communities of India (2014)

The present occupational distribution [All India level from 1971-2001] with respect to Scheduled Tribes and General Population projects the percentage of Scheduled Tribe cultivators to the total Scheduled Tribe main workers as the highest, when compared to the general population in all the NSSO surveys. The percentage of agricultural labourers and non-farming workers to the total main workers among Scheduled Tribes were consistently higher than the general population. While among Scheduled Tribes, the percentage of cultivators has decreased from 55.6 per cent to 54.32 per cent between 1971 and 2001, the percentage of non-farming workers has increased from 9.4 to 15.8 percent in the corresponding period.

Table 3: Household Income, Expenditure and poverty Scheduled Tribes and in All [?]

Social Groups	*Average Income (Rs)*	*Average Consumption (Rs)*	*Percentage of poor*
Scheduled Tribes	3,2345	29,523	49.6
General Population	72,717	65,722	12.0

Source: Report of the High-level Committee on Socio-economic, Health and Educational Status of Tribal Communities of India.

Sustainable Livelihood Approach

One of the widely used terms [often quoted definition] 'sustainable livelihoods' (SL) was put forth by Robert Chambers and Gordon Conway. The verbatim definition is as follows: "A livelihood comprises the capabilities, assets (stores, resources, claims and access), and activities required for means of living. A livelihood is 'sustainable' when it can cope with, and recover from stresses and shocks, maintain or enhance its capabilities and assets, and provide sustainable livelihood opportunities to the next generation: and which contributes net benefits to other livelihoods at the local and global levels and in the short and long term" (Chamber, R; Conway, G 1992). The simplified conceptual framework developed for the study comprises three key basic concepts. They are (a) livelihood resources and capabilities, (b) livelihood activities, and (c) outputs obtained from performing activities for fulfilling the livelihoods needs. These three concepts collectively form a comprehensive whole that captures the various aspects of livelihood reality of rural people. They are also observed to be intrinsically interlinked and interdependent on each other.

Today, the economic development in the tribal lands has taken place, bringing the trend in favour of monetised economy by the process of industrialization,information, technology or globalization in terms of possession of household and agricultural assets, savings and indebtedness, health management, education, entertainment and lifestyle. It was also assumed that the benefits of macroeconomic growth would reach the bottom-most sections of the society through the 'trickledown' process. The two main routes envisaged for the trickle down processes are (a) 'chain reaction' of the economic enterprises/activities and, (b) the state-supported income redistribution program through specific poverty alleviation and welfare schemes for the poor. The destruction of bio-mass to meet the urban and industrial needs leading to deforestation is having a major impact on the lives of tribal peoples who live within the non-monetized, biomass based subsistence economic (Mishra, 2005).

In tribal areas, in the last two decades and a half these have been prime attempts for fulfilling the various livelihoods needs, these households rely on varied and multiple livelihood sources (such as land, forest, water and so on). Various livelihood needs (such as water, food, fodder, shelter and so on) are fulfilled through multiple livelihood activities (such as forest collection, fishing, wage labor, cultivation). Thus, different livelihood needs of the majority of the tribal households are being fulfilled through various activities and using differentresources. Therefore, viewing the livelihoods reality of rural poor in terms of the conventional, urban-industrial, middle class framework of 'employment-cash income purchase of goods and services-fulfillment of needs' is completely incorrect. In this context, there is an urgent need to evolve an alternative development approach with different conceptual core. This conceptual core will have to transcend the limitations imposed by the conventional view of livelihoods (in terms of 'employment-income-nexus'). It will also have to become comprehensive and be able to capture the livelihoods reality of the rural poor.

There are several reasons behind the failure of the mainstream's approach to anti-poverty programs. One of the fundamental and important reasons behind the failure of poverty eradication programs relates to the problems in the conceptual core of the mainstream approach. The major lacuna in this conceptual core, which is dominated by the 'economist' thinking, is the restricted meaning of the term 'poverty'. Accordingly, poverty is equated with "low income or lack of adequate income" and, it is assumed that, as a consequence of low income, people are not able to buy adequate quantity of goods and services. In other words, it means that the households having low income are not able to afford (to buy) the goods and services that are necessary for fulfillment of basic livelihood needs. This results into "low standard of living", which is considered as "poverty".

For eradicating the poverty of the rural marginalized households, the first step would be fulfillment of all minimum basic needs on a regular basis. However, only this much is not enough, as these households in the rural areas continuously face various economic, political, social, natural, and familial difficulties and threats. These difficulties and threat shave adverse effects on their livelihoods, which directly affect fulfillment of their needs and further result into making their livelihoods vulnerable. Threats to the livelihoods include sudden shocks (e.g., floods, draughts, earthquake, storm or sudden change etc.) as well as long-term stresses (for e.g. chronic illness, addiction, debt, seasonal shortages, food deprivation etc.). Shocks are sudden, unpredictable and have dramatic impacts, while stresses are pressures, which are typically continuous and cumulative, predictable, and distressing.

Therefore, the main objective should be to ensure security of livelihoods against these threats. This would mean creating a situation in which the deprived households will be able to successfully deal with these threats and fulfill livelihood needs on a continuous basis.Here, the term 'security' means "freedom from the negative impact of the shocks, stresses, and threats to the livelihood".

Participatory Forest Management and Development

Joint Forest Management Programme is a collaborative forest Manage mentor Co-management forestry initiated on the declaration of the resolution on the 1st June 1990, following up the National Forest Policy in 1988, which paved the way for active participation of the people in the protection, management and development of forests. This strategic approach has led the Government of India to issue guidelines for the participation of communities residing nearby the forest areas as partners in management.

In the JFM programme the attempts were made to achieve the sustainable forest management with the livelihood improvement in the decentralized process. Thus, the benefits were derived in the two major ways; forest endowments (i.e., rights to forest) and forest entitlement (i.e., economic benefits from forest). Thus forests in the state can play an important role as a source of income and a basis for the livelihoods of forest dependent people. The principle services and products from forest include Non-Timber Forest Products by collection, processing, value-addition, marketing, watershed projects for the enhancement of agricultural livelihood, environmental services i.e. ecotourism, and other nature based entertainment programmes.

In the umbrella scheme of National Afforestation Programme, the developmental Authority i.e., Forest Developmental Agency (FDA) has been a registered body formed by selected Joint Forest Management committees in order to fulfil the goals of livelihood generation and developmental interventions. For the community participation sustainable livelihood Approach (SLA)is an attempt in tune with the basic intention of the scheme in which role of formal and informal institutions is significant. In this case, on the basis of the above background, the attempt was made to fulfil the following objectives:

1. Social equality in participatory process in the institution affecting NAP.
2. Personal empowerment to SL under NAP.
3. Community mobilization in participatory process.

In this context two case studies were developed in Madhya Pradesh showing the sustainable livelihoods attempts in the National Afforestation and Forest Development Agencies.

Sustainable Livelihood Approach: Two Case Studies

Case 1: Convergence of indigenous knowledge and government schemes in Sericulture activities in Betul district of Madhya Pradesh

Guvasen forest village is situated at a distance of about 40 km from Betul in Chicoli range under West Betul forest division of Madhya Pradesh. The village is situated near the main road. The village is dominated by the Korkus. There are about 300-400HH of Korkus and 25 HH of Yadavs and about 10-12 HH of Gonds. Table 1 gives a profile of the village

Table 4: Profile of Guvasen Village

Total population	*Male*		*Female*		*Sex ration*					
	399	*49.6 pc*	*405*	*50.3 pc*	*0.98*					
Occupation	Agriculture		Agri-Labour		Non-agri-Labour		Forest collection			
	78	60 pc	32	24.62 pc	22	16.9 pc	40	30.8 pc		
Land holding	Landless		Marginal		Small		Medium		Big	
	13	10 pc	78	60 pc	39	30 pc	Nil	Nil	Nil	Nil
Education	Lit		Primary		Secondary		Grad		PG	
	326	40.5 pc	260.82	32.4 pc	228.2	28.3 pc	Nil	Nil		

In the year 2012, the forest department under the UNDP-GEF project initiated an income generating activity for the women JFMC members of the village. A Self-help groups (SHG) of 20 women were formed for the activity of extracting threads from the silk cocoons. Ten machines were purchased by the JFMC fund of Guvasen FPC that was formed in 1996. These women were provided with training by the sericulture department. The sericulture department gives cocoons to the women members and purchases the silk thread from them. The payment is based on the grades of thread extracted. The women members involved in this activity earn monthly income of Rs 4,

000-Rs 6, 000. This activity was done in collaboration with the sericulture department of Madhya Pradesh Government. The department of sericulture provides cocoons to the women.In one day, women weave about 100-200gm of cocoons. This activity is undertaken in the room provided by the forest department at the free of cost. The Department has provided them the infrastructure and the Department of sericulture provides them trainings to undertake this activity.

The women who are involved in this activity are very happy and satisfied with the work and the income earned. This has greatly reduced their dependency on forest resources and the migration has declined considerably. Women members have become more confident and feel more secured and independent. About 70% of the women were confident that they had the ability to demonstrate their skill to other women. Women were very proud of their skills and ready to demonstrate it to others. Women members come as far as Bhopal to sell their products in Van melas.

Case 2: An innovative income generating activity of Paper mesh craft making in Bamnai

Bamnia forest village is about 30-35 km from Obdullaganj Forest Division under Dahod range in Raisen district. This village is situated near the Bhopal –Indore main Road. The village is a multi-ethnic village of Gond, Korkus and Basods. The Eco-development committee of Bamnai was formed in 2006. This EDC come under Ratapani Wild life sanctuary. The village is surrounded by rich miscellaneous forest of Teak, Saja and other species. Table 2 gives a profile of the village.

In Bamnai, women have grouped themselves into a SHG and are engaged in making toys and handicrafts from paper mesh/waste paper. The forest department has imparted training for this activity through NGOs/institutes. These toys are sold at herbal melas (van melas) organized by the Forest department, which are held regularly at different places of the state. These are also exhibited in Delabadi Ecotourism center. This is a very cost innovative marketing mechanism initiated by the department. It provides them raw material like waste paper,

Table 5: Profile of Bamni Village

Total population	***Male***		***Female***		***Sex ration***					
	398	51 pc	383	49.0 pc	1.03					
Occupation	Agriculture		Agri-Labour		Non agri-Labour		Forest collection			
	108	60 pc	108	60 pc	90	50 pc	36	20 pc		
Land holding	Landless		Marginal		Small		Medium		Big	
	69	38 pc	111	62 pc	Nil	Nil	Nil	Nil	Nil	Nil
Education	Lit		Primary		Secondary		UG		P G	
	572	73.2 pc	343.20	43.94 pc	286.00	36.62 pc	Nil	Nil	Nil	

gum etc. required for making toys. Their products were sold by the department and women members engaged in this activity get about Rs. 80 per day. During the initial years, this activity was a success and members engaged in this activity were appreciated and recognized for their work. Now it is on full swing under the initiation of the beat guard Ms Ganga Thakur since 2008. Besides, their daily chores and other activities, they do it in their own convenience at home. As per demand, they make the materials and supply it either to the forest department or to individuals.

The percentage of women members acquiring training has increased considerably,due to the active involvement of the beat guard. It has helped in increasing their income and reduced their dependency on forest resources. Women were more confident about the skills acquired. They go along with the beat guard to Bhopal melas to sale their goods and demonstrate their skills.Earlier, they were involved in felling and selling wood, which was discontinued by the state government intervention, making them involve in JFM activities.

Conclusion

In India, the decentralization and participation in forest management was initiated in the early 1990's as an outcome to National Forest Policy (NFP) – 1988. Since then the partnership between state and people for protection, management and development of the patches of the forests with the villagers of the fringe forests have initiated to build a common property resource situation to eradicate the poverty of the people involving them in the decision-making processes in the participatory way. The decentralization of forest management responsibilities to local communities came into practices since 1990s as an efficient forest management practice leading to good governance. Currently, the involvement of local communities in it, is widely spread and practiced throughout the country. As on date, more than one lakh village-level forest committees, popularly known as Joint Forest Management Committees (JFMCs) have been formed. This decentralization has led into twin inter-related objectives- (i) development of livelihood opportunities for forest dependent communities leading to alleviation of rural poverty; and, (ii) the restoration of forest wealth of the country to ameliorate the environment. Later since Tenth five year plan an approach of Eco-development in the fringe forest villages on the formation of Forest Development Agencies (FDAs) as an institutional mechanism to develop forest range villages, where the communities were substantially dependent on the local forest resources. The FDAs in collaboration with the village-level forest committees (JFMCs) are working as a two-tier mechanism, wherein the communities at village level are supported and guided by forest division level FDAs.

Attempts were being made at the grassroots level to make the sustainable livelihood approach through the natural resource management. This was a first step to achieve the Sustainable Development in short time. This people-centric, people-responsive and pro-democratic approach was made for conservation and the sustainable use of forest and other natural resources in the micro-level or at the grass-roots with various interventions in livelihood development. Thus, the new avenues of species conservation, biomass enhancement, village institutions, institutional development through social rules, norms and beliefs and organizational development with the formation of self-help groups and small and micro-enterprises have been opened up for increasing jobs and speeding up income flows. The vulnerability and poverty reduction, with gender mainstreaming and women empowerment, have been pronounced. Thus the various livelihood options and development took place which has given the morale boost to mainstream the tribal development by promotion of traditional vocations or adopting the new alternative livelihoods as illustrated in the aforementioned cases developed in this context.

Reference

Berger, Peter, HeidemannFrank. (2013): *The Modern Anthropology of India: Ethnography, Themes and Theory*. Oxon: Routledge.

Chambers, R. and Gordon *Conway. (*1991): *Sustainable Livelihoods: Practical Concept for the 21st Century*, IDS Discussion paper 296.

Chaudhary, S.N. (2010): *Tribal Economy at Crossroads*. Jaipur: Rawat Publications, pp2-3.

Debnath, D. (2010): "Forest Management vis-à-vis Tribal Economy: Livelihood Generations for the Reductions of Poverty of the Tribals of Madhya Pradesh", in S.N. Chaudhary (ed), *Tribal Economy at Crossroads* (266-287). Jaipur: Rawat Publication.

Luard, C.E. (1908): *Central Indian Gazetter series: Western States (Malwa),* Vol. V, Bombay : British India press.

Manohar, D. (2001): *BaghkeBacche Hai Hum (We are the Children of the Tiger).*Hoshangabad :DishaSamvad.

Ministry of Tribal Affairs, Government of India. (2014): *Report of the High level Committee on Socio-economic, Health and Educational of Tribal Communities of India,* New Delhi.

Mishra, N. (2007): *Participatory Water Management and Sustainable Tribal Livelihood: Study of a Pani Panchayat in Southern Orissa,* Unpublished Thesis Submitted to University of Hyderabad, Hyderabad.

Chapter - 6

Tribals Livelihood in Urban Fringe

— *Swapan Kumar Kolay and*
Sushila D. Mahant

Introduction

Entrepreneurial resources have been considered as the significant input in the process of economic development (Tomar, 2014). It has been observed that large number of tribals were illiterate, but their traditional handicraft was significant which can generate income after the establishment of entrepreneurship with proper skill development training and marketing of products. Timmons (1986) stated the entrepreneurship to be an ability to create and build something practically. We cannot deny that entrepreneurship is an important source of economic growth along with social development. Deolankar (2003) observes that entrepreneurship among the weaker section that constitutes a large section of the Indian masses needs to be brought into the main stream of development.

Artists and traditional artists suffer from economic hardship despite their seasonal experience and background. A few tribals' communities are known as agriculturists, but depend on monsoon for farming and search alternate way to acquire income. At present, the tribals seldom keep away from the non-tribal population, but their least knowledge make them nomads to search better livelihood away from their habitat and wander here and there, for food and shelter. Apart from the government having launched economic development programmes for tribals, but an important factor which tribals' welfare schemes, in the state has ignored could be some regional variation in the pattern of living on their basic attitude. It is observed that many problems were common to tribals all over the state or even the county, but the precise nature of problems and the approach to solution ought to vary from region to region, upon the environmental, cultural, social and historical factors, So far, there have been schemes applicable to the whole state. Many of these have proved to be futile in other regions of the state. For real and substantial welfare work, it is essential that a regional approach should be developed and the individual region should be left largely free to evolve own schemes. As Grigson (1947) rightly argues that we need to introduce among the tribal such kind of education and motivation that could restore confidence and equip them face boldly and experience the exogenous forces of modernization. Therefore, the authors elaborate here on the outcome issues after the establishment of entrepreneurship by tribals in urban fringe as well as the demand for economic development.

Objectives

- to explore the issues of entrepreneurship establishment in urban fringe for tribal people.
- to introduce the benefit and demand of entrepreneurship for tribals, and
- to recommend for economic development by entrepreneurship for tribal people.

Methodology

This concept of entrepreneurship development in urban fringe with its impact issues and demands among tribals in rural India ought to be more precise with positive impact. The primary data depend ed on general information about family, enterprise, acceptance and denying reasons for women entrepreneurship, information about income of self and family etc. were gathered by interview, FGDs, schedule/questionnaire, observation by semi participatory method.

Some 25 households were selected as sample in Nerli village, Dantewada from among Dhurwa, Halba, Bhatra and Muriya tribes. The respondents above 15 years of age for male and female were selected. The secondary data relied on extensive literature review by published articles, books and news bulletin.

The characteristic feature of the Nerli Village reflects that it was subjected to the impact of modernization, as it was some three km away from NMDC Iron Ore Mine Deposit 5, 10 and 11. Thus, it necessitated the tribals to search for secondary option for economic growth despite holding jobs.

Results

Table 1 show that the female population above 18years of age (53.85 per cent) was larger than that of male counterparts (46.15 per cent) with latter's literacy higher than female. The educational status was not good because the majority of respondents have had primary level of education (62.50 per cent) and very few respondents studied up to college level (2.50 per cent). The status of primary occupation was not growing despite majority of them dependent on agriculture (24.00 per cent) and private job (24.00 per cent). The second group of respondents was daytalers (20.00 per cent). The rest of the lot held government jobs, or small business etc. The males (63.49 per cent) and females (36.51 per cent) played beneficial role to establish entrepreneurship, but the participatory rate of male was greater than female participation. Varieties of entrepreneurship were prevalent, but majority of them perform traditional art and craft it has attracted outsiders and businessmen. The tribals sold animal and forest products with bye-products. Their annual income lie between Rs 50,001 to Rs. 1,00,000 with second group's income hung between Rs. 1,00,001 to Rs.2,00,000, but this money was not enough, because tribals live in the joint family and the expenditure increases with increase in their number. After the establishment of any business 33.33 per cent respondents earned less than Rs 3,000 per month, while 28.58 per cent entrepreneurs earned between Rs 3, 000 to Rs 5,000. Some respondents (26.98 percent) earned beyond Rs.5, 000 upto Rs.10, 000 while the rest got over 10,000 per annum.

Table 1: Socio-demographic Distribution

Sl. No.	*Variables*	*Categories*	*Total*	
			Number	*Percentage*
1.	Population (More than 18 years age group in 25 HHs)	Male	42	46.15
		Female	49	53.85
		Total	**91**	**100**
2.	Education	Illiterate	51	56.04
		Literate	40	43.96
		Total	**91**	**100**
		Primary school	25	62.50
		Middle school	6	15.00
		High school	4	10.00
		Higher Secondary	3	7.50
		College	1	2.50
		Other	1	2.50
		Total	**40**	**100**
3.	Primary Occupation (HHs=25)	Agriculture	6	24.00
		Daily Wage Labour	5	20.00
		Business	1	4.00
		Private Job	6	24.00
		Govt. Services	3	12.00
		Others	2	8.00
4.	Frequency of Entrepreneurs amongst Selected Households (HHs=25)	Male	40	63.49
		Female	23	36.51
		Total	**63**	**100**
5.	Annual Income (HHs=25)	>Rs.50,000	6	24.00
		Rs. 50,001- 100000	9	36.00
		Rs. 1,00,001- 200000	7	28.00
		Rs.2,00,000<	3	12.00
6.	Kind of Entrepreneurship (n=63)	Traditional Handicraft	21	33.33
		Sale of Animals' Products	12	19.05
		Sale of Animals' Biproducts	7	11.11
		Sale of Forest Products	7	11.11
		Sale of Forest Biproducts	9	14.29
		Grocery Soap	1	1.59
		Fruits and Vegetables Vendors	3	4.76
		Others	3	4.76
7.	Status of Entrepreneurs' Monthly Income (n=63)	>Rs.3000	21	33.33
		Rs.3000- 5000	18	28.58
		Rs.5000- 10000	17	26.98
		Rs.10,000 <	7	11.11

The entrepreneurship promotion and development was not only identified as one of the key components of the nation's economic development strategy, but was important to increase individual's income also. **Table 2** revealed that income from primary occupation was not up to the mark among tribals, but it increased after participation of family members in other

Table 2: Status of Financial Growth by Entrepreneurship in Urban Fringe

Annual Income From Primary Occupation (Po)		*Monthly Income From Entre-preneurship (E)*		*Average Annual Income of Respondents*				*Annual Income (Po+E)*	*Increasing Rate (Monthly)*
Range	*(n=25)*	*Range*	*(n=25)*	*Po*	*(n= 25)*	*E*	*(n= 63)*		
>Rs.50,000	6	>Rs.3000	4	47,689.58	6	27,286.79	21	74976.37	+2,799.87
50,001-1,00,000	9	Rs.3000-5000	9	72,587.36	9	49,119.66	18	121707.02	+4,269.69
1,00,000-2,00,000	7	Rs.5000-10,000	9	1,60,587.59	7	77,992.59	17	238580.18	+6.843.72
2,00,000<	3	Rs.10,000 <	3	2,15,136.96	3	99,899.48	7	315036.44	+12,854.36

activities. **Table 2** reflected a minimum level increase of Rs. 2,799.87 while the maximum one Rs. 12,854.36 is increased maximum in individual entrepreneur. The household's income was dependent on the income of head of the family, but the entrepreneurship made a channel of family members with their involvement in small business to make them self dependent.

Table 3 depicts the opinion of respondents about the acceptance and problems regarding entrepreneurship, who already stood as entrepreneurs. Towards the objectgive, decision making was crucial for them, some 40.66 per cent respondents felt fear to take decision while 45.05 per cent take decision boldly with fear for the purpose of their economic growth. The access of entrepreneurship is very low (57.14 per cent) because of the money risk and lack of proper management of the business. Along with the knowledge and awareness about the government programmes for entrepreneurship is also very low (45.05 per cent), because the majority of respondents were illiterate and education level was poor amongst educated people. It was significantly observed that the ability of risk taking behaviour to establishment of entrepreneurship is medium (59.34 per cent) in scale, because their need and poverty has inspired them to wake up for high income. It was observed that the majority of respondents had medium entrepreneurial characteristic, which is a clear indication of the progressiveness of the tribal entrepreneurs. Further, it demands for the amplification of educational efforts and policy support to the entrepreneurs by the field extension workers of development departments, the NGOs and private organizations to make them more enterprising. The tribals have a confusing mind status about the success of business, so there was no accurate result (low: 34.06 per cent; medium 32.97 per cent; high: 32.97 per cent) about the opinion regarding this. Confusing mindset created lacking ability of the leadership (low: 56.05 per cent) to manage any kind of business. Apart, other prevalent problems, i.e., lack of training (53.85), marketing problems of products (56.04), lack of infrastructure and amenities (69.23), money risk in establishing entrepreneurship (51.65) and lot of paper work for loan from government institution (67.03 per cent) were very high in scale amongst the tribals.

Table 3: Problems of Entrepreneurs

Sl. No.	*Qualities of Entrepreneurs*	*Level*	*Total (n=91)*	
			Number	*Percentage*
1.	Decision making for the Acceptance of Entrepreneurship	*Low*	13	14.29
		Medium	41	45.05
		High	37	40.66
2.	Access of Entrepreneurship	*Low*	52	57.14
		Medium	29	31.88
		High	10	10.98
3.	Knowledge and Awareness about Entrepreneurship	*Low*	41	45.05
		Medium	30	32.97
		High	20	21.98
4.	Ability to become Entrepreneur	*Low*	17	18.68
		Medium	54	59.34
		High	20	21.98
5.	Confidence about the success of Entrepreneurship	*Low*	31	34.06
		Medium	30	32.97
		High	30	32.97
6.	Ability of leadershipto deal Business	*Low*	51	56.04
		Medium	25	27.48
		High	15	16.48
7.	Lack of Training	*Low*	10	10.98
		Medium	32	35.17
		High	49	53.85
8.	Marketing Problems of Products	*Low*	6	6.59
		Medium	34	37.36
		High	51	56.04
9.	Lack of Infrastructure and Amenities	*Low*	8	8.79
		Medium	20	21.98
		High	63	69.23
10.	Money Risk in Establishing of Entrepreneurship	*Low*	9	9.89
		Medium	35	38.46
		High	47	51.65
11.	Lot of Paper Work for Loan from Government Institution	*Low*	5	5.49
		Medium	25	27.48
		High	61	67.03

Inhibiting Factors

Following eight factors works as inhibiting factors in the promotion of entrepreneurship.

(1) Uprooting from Habitation

The tribal habitation is in the forest areas. They are forest dwellers. It was found that Naxals and the paramilitary CRPFs have encroached the areas. Local tribals, as such have migrated to safer zone, with urban pocket nearby, affecting their rate of survival and livelihood. Any kind of displacement has usurped their livelihood, because their communal territory was sufficient to fullfill the need within the area, but after becoming the part of urban population, they could not have proper nourishment, whether on sociological, economical or cultural grounds. For example, there has been displacement of tribal people, yet there was enhancement of tribal population in the Naxalite affected camps, as well as in urban slum, which have resulted in the loss of birth rates, high morbidity, mortality, malnutrition and improper living style etc.

(2) Migration for Livelihood

The tribal population is simply agriculturists, though it supplements the cultivation with hunting, gathering, fishing and other work. Tribal agriculture however, is being characterized by the unproductive and uneconomic holdings due to lack of facilities, lack of irrigational skills and primitive implements. In general, the tribals raise only one crop during rain and have to fall back upon other types of subsidiary works. Their style of life is marked with seasonal and agricultural festivals, ancestor worship, drinking, dancing and singing. Thus, the insufficient agricultural outcome insists them for migration for livelihood and they are moving from the birth place to urban areas. This kind of migration increases number of manual workers in the urban fringe and their traditional culture is moving towards extinction. The tribals are unaware of any kind of modern entrepreneurship as well as their traditional art and craft are sometimes not accepted by urban counterpart. In this way, the tribals are losing livelihood opportunities in urban areas and the crime often generates from here, when they feel deprived. Migration from one place to another not only degrades their family life, but also affects their physical and mental health.

(3) Increasing Child Labour

The increasing demand of money in urban areas makes hurdles for tribal people. They fascinate towards any kind of livelihood opportunities, whether it is legal or illegal and child labour is one of that kind of popular livelihood opportunities in the city areas. Tribal area as well as rural-urban areas have lately been emerging as hub of child labour from where the children are being enslaved not only for domestic work in metro cities, but also forced into child labour in chilly picking, thread weaving, brick kilns and poultry farming, in places including Tamil Nadu, Andhra Pradesh, Karnataka, Uttar Pradesh and Goa and other urban cities. It has been also noted that tribals believe that earning money is better than school going and they like to send their children for work rather than school for study.

(4) Fear from Alien Group

The Nerli village is situated in the forest area where territorial communities are living in the relative isolation of hills and forests. Their comparative isolation, in some ways has kept them apart from the main stream of society which creates fear among tribals from other communities. The distinctive ethos raises for them a series of tangled problems of social, economic and cultural adjustment, arising fear for entrepreneurship among tribal women. It has been observed that voluntary social service agencies have done considerable humanitarian work in the tribal areas, but often their idealism and spirit of service have not been matched by their understanding of tribal organisation, values and problems. They sometimes went into the tribal areas with an omnibus solution to the tribal problem as they understood it, while in reality the problems for different tribal groups and even for sections of one tribe, were often different. They failed to realize that their well intentioned reform may be injurious to the tribes with special reference to women in term of their socio-cultural integration.

(5) Occupational stress

The tribal's occupational transition from traditional to modern modes thwarted their health with mental stress. So, cultural or ethnic identity describes a process and outcome for a person's sense of 'who they are' and 'how they might be perceived' by others in their living and working environment. The rural tribals were more peaceful and satisfied as compared with urban, because amongst the urban tribals, the crises of cultural or ethnic identity has some bearing on a person's coping with the harmful effects of life and work stress and mental health, while the empirical evidence for this is limited, it is argued that a strong cultural or ethnic identity buffers the harmful effects of stress.

(6) Avoidance of Women Entrepreneurship

In tribal communities, women are very hard workers as compared with men and they do all kinds of household work, raring children, fetching water and wood from river and forest, respectively but were not allowed to work in unknown or strange surrounding or outside the communities. According to Mehta and Mehta [2011], women in India live protected lives. A woman is taught to depend on the male members of her family from birth. She is not allowed to take any type of risk, even if she is willing to take and has the ability to bear with. The women are neither mentally nor economically self-reliant. A strong mental outlook and an optimistic attitude amongst them create a fear of committing mistakes, while doing work (Goyal and Parkash, 2011). The family members and the society are unwilling to stand by them with entrepreneurial development potential. Rao (2007) observed that poverty and illiteracy are being the basic reasons of the low rate of women entrepreneurship in our country. The educational level and professional skills also influence their participation in the field of enterprise. According to Ghani et al. (2011) mobility is one of the important problems in their entrepreneurial development. They are not ready to leave their place for business activities and prefer staying at their residential areas. These traits were important as entrepreneurs tend to start businesses in the current local area and are thus disproportionately found in their region of birth (Dahl and Sorenson 2007). The belief that women should not, or cannot do work out of home and therefore elder head member of the family eliminate women from the participation on work. This opinion and believe do not support to establish women entrepreneurship in tribal community in urban fringe.

(7) Poverty, Urban Slum and Literacy Rate

For isolated tribal people, filling one's stomach and keeping it filled is a never ending problem. Too many people try to obtain food from forest and their little land. They not only become landless, but go fully without work, hopeless and fearful, on leaving their habitat. The necessary facilities are mostly lacking. They were pressurized to live in slum areas, and it is not wrong, if we are saying that this kind of population is creating urban slum. People are objectively uncomfortable during adverse climate and conditions and proliferating diseases reflected on them. The mortality rate among female and children sustains for many years. Apart, the literacy level among male and female find stymied in this area. We would say that tribal life is vulnerable in urban area without any livelihood opportunities.

(8) Traditional Art, Craft and Culture

Tribals in general are experts to make artifacts and handicrafts. On the other hand, urbanization offers them livelihood choices and enables them better access to services and infrastructure. The processes in many cases have posed threat to their traditional livelihood. The situation and the monetized economy therein have significantly affected the natural resource based primary economic activity which in turn have led to poverty and vulnerability to the livelihood of poor people. The new kind of enterprises is not easy to develop denying traditional frame.

The Demand for entrepreneurship

The educational level of tribals is very low. Removal of illiteracy is an important component. (Patel, 1989). Their socio-economic development depends on the educational advancement. Education is more than a mere asset for some tribal communities; investment in education is, in a way, crucial for their existence (Mehta, 1976). Without education, a person can ever be illiterate, but entrepreneurship can bring an abundance of education. The entrepreneurship, especially in tribal areas is very beneficial, because they can pay a lot for education and will get educated at higher level by paying the cost approximately equal to nothing and a gentle flow of education will bring good literacy status amongst those tribals.

Not only in improvement of literacy and education, but entrepreneurship ever helps to access financial growth. Mostly, tribals cultivate on small pieces of land. It does not result in sufficient income. To overcome this, entrepreneurship is a great solution. Small business like selling bi-products of forest and animals etc., could help to maintain the economy. Consequently, if a tribal person does farming that means full of its income depends on it, but in the case of famine health and nutritional problems arise from poverty, whilst a good financial condition helps to live in healthy way by availing nutritional food and hygienic surroundings. For healthy and disease-free life, good health institutions are essential. Available evidence regarding the immediate version of longer-term effects of economic downturn and recovery on population health is somewhat ambiguous, however. For example, there is some evidence that economic pressure may lead more women to seek reproductive services, and, in par-ticular, long-term contraception, and abortions (Economic Recession Prompting California Women to Seek Health Care in Clinics, 2009). At the same time, there is some evidence suggesting that, at least in previous recessions, decreased access to or use of prenatal services has been associated with a higher incident of adverse pregnancy outcomes such as anemia and low-birth weight infants in some low-income populations (Fisher, E. et al., 1985).

The tribals usually are unknown about various diseases and their treatment. They won't go for hospital, because of the intrinsic financial problems, but the financial growth can be through only by entrepreneurship with the development of socio-economic strata. They will get high identical status when compared to the earlier status of life. It has been observed during study that entrepreneurship establish them strongly in the field of business with their own identity. The entrepreneurship creates a scene of self respect, sense of responsibility and definitely provides a special survival tools in modern competitive world.

Recommendations

- Tribals should be motivated to come out of traditional occupation for accepting more challenging and rewarding economic activities. Concurrently, an environment should be arranged to enable their participation.

Primarily, this could necessitate them in motivating the funding agencies to be sympathetic towards their entrepreneurship. So, there is a need for the government policy makers ought to reevaluate strategies on the development of tribal entrepreneurship.

- Skill development training is important for unskilled tribals labour force in maintaining the skilled work force in the study area. It would help to upgrade the existing business like dairy, poultry and other crafts in modern business venture. The government should arrange various training programmes, especially for the entrepreneur swerver from ignorance about the state-of-art technology and knowhow about the present market. Instead of this institution, like business incubator, different NGO's can play major role in their development in tribal as well as Maoist areas.
- The nationalized banks and state Financial Corporations, NABARD, SIDBI and District Industries Centre's should extend loans to entrepreneurs on preferential basis. The government should provide link with other educational institutions outside the rural area to bring the available technical expertise and provide adequate knowledge about the banking procedures and various schemes of government, meant to develop their entrepreneurship. The other promotional and regulatory agencies should be motivated to be considerate, understanding and helpful towards entrepreneurs.

Conclusion

India is the habitat of tribals. The tribal communities constitute a large part of our national population. The percentage of tribal population is 8.6 in the country (Census 2011). There are 705 tribes, whereas the government of India has recognized some group as being primitive, granting special plans for their overall development. In spite of many central and state development programmes, entrepreneurship is the purposeful activity of an individual or a group of associated individuals, undertaken to initiate, and maintain profit by production or distribution of economic goods and services. Absence of an appropriate entrepreneurial climate and lack of access to relevant technology appear to be the crucial constraints for the developing communities to achieve a meaningful economic development. The tribals' economy is highly dependent on their habitat. They live with socio-cultural entrepreneurship. So, there is a need of proper intervention of entrepreneurship within traditional framework for tribal communities in the urban fringe.

References

Census of India (2011): *Scheduled Tribe of India,* As revealed in Census, India Ministry of home Affairs.

Dahl, M. S. & Sorenson, O. (2007): "Home sweet home: Social capital and location choice." MIMEO.

Deolankar, V. (2003): "A Profile of Entrepreneurship Development", Yojana May.

Economic Recession Prompting California Women to Seek Health Care in Clinics (2009): *Medical News Today*, The Advisory Board Company, Also see www.medicalnewstoday.com/articles/150896.php.

Fisher, E. et al. (1985): "Prenatal Care and Pregnancy Outcomes during the Recession: The Washington State Experience," *American Journal of Public Health*, Vol. 75, No. 8, pp. 866-9.

Ghani et al. (2011): Promoting Entrepreneurship, Growth, and Job Creational in Ejaz Ghani (ed.) Reshaping tomorrow, Oxford, UK: Oxford University Press.

Grigson, W.V. (1947): *Challenge of Backwardness*, Hyderabad: Government Press.

Mehta, Om (1976): *Tribal* Development*: The New Strategy*, Government of India, New Delhi, p.2.

Patel, M.L. (1989): "Some Aspects of Educational Development of Tribes", *Bulletin of Cultural Research Institute*, Calcutta, Vol. X, No. 3 and 4.

Rao, P. S. (2007): "Entrepreneurship Development among Women: A case study of self help Groups in Srikakulam District, Andhra Pradesh" *The Icfai Journal of Entrepreneurship Development* Vol.1V No. 1.

Timmons, J.A. (1986): "Characteristics and Role Demands of Entrepreneurship" *Journal of Small Business* Vol. III, No. 1.

Tomar, T.S. (2014): *Women Entrepreneurship :An empirical Study Financing and Earning Perspectives,* New Delhi: The Women Press.

Chapter - 7

Livelihood Struggle and Coping with Poverty in Madhya Pradesh

— D C Sah

This paper depicts the interrelationship among poverty, livelihood struggles and seasonal migration in dryland of Madhya Pradesh, especially its tribal belt. A voluminous literature was available explaining the migration that mirrors the discipline and ideological underpinning of the researcher. Although, social scientists like Lee (1966) has conceptualised migration as the play of negative and positive forces that push a migrant from the place of origin and pulls him to the place of destination, neoclassical economists construct has dominated the explanation. Locating migration decisions at the household level and arguing about such decisions are being based on opportunities and constraints that the households face, the neoclassical theorists propagated human capital theory (Sjaastad, 1962; Todaro, 1969, 1980). This construct has argued that the inclination to migrate is being determined by the difference in income between the source and the destination of migration, resulting in equating the expected income. Given their skills, decisions about where to live are based on where the individuals can optimise the present value of their discounted stream of expected future earnings.

Stark (1980) identifies the transaction cost, imperfect information and credit, land and labour markets as the main determinants of migration. Lucas (2004), in the same vein, argued that labour transfer to skill-incentive urban economy is being driven by gains of agglomeration. Migration according to Saxena (1977) may be motivated by a desire to seek skill and leads to development, urbanisation and socio-economic transformation. On the other hand, researches driven by the Marxist ideology (Breman: 1985; Olsen and Murthy: 2000) identified structural constraints of the capitalist system, as the main source of exploitation of migrant labours. In absence of alternatives, in extreme cases, monopoly creditor also becomes a monopsony buyer of the migrant's labour (Olsen and Murthy, 2000).

Breman (1996) shows that while for resource poor, migration is a coping mechanism that provides means for debt servicing, for the well endowed it increases the households' earnings, creditworthiness and ability to manage crisis. Breaking away from the neoclassical interpretations of determinants of migration, Mosse *et. al.* (2002) argue that migration is not an external factor impinging upon or undermining agrarian society. Existing social relations and inequalities, which define differential opportunities, constraining experiences and social outcomes, profoundly shape it. It is also been argued that access failure to capitals (Sah and Tomar, 2014) as well as constraints on markets influence occupational diversification, including seasonal migration.

Using data from 688 households from seven dryland districts of Madhya Pradesh, the author argues that, under a shock, access failure to natural, human, social, financial and physical capital traps households in poverty. The study tries to highlight that intensity of poverty in tribal villages is significantly higher than dryland as well as dry-industrial villages. Annual income from various occupations in the villages — forest, agriculture, casual labour, NREGA, and traditional occupation — is unable to meet the annual consumption of households, as one move from the industrial to dryland and tribal villages. In order to bridge this expenditure-gap, members from seriously affected households — in dryland villages and more so in tribal villages — have to migrate. Among the migrant households, this expenditure-gap in the three locations is significantly higher to pressurise the households to migrate more.

Theoretical Framework

In a resource poor economy, the existing economic hierarchy collapses during a shock like crop failure, drought, sickness, death, marriage, *Notra* (gifts in social ceremonies), *Bhanjhagda* (dispute settlement), population pressure, *etc;* In this economy, capital — physical, natural, financial, human and social — is unequally distributed, owing to historical exigencies as well as contemporary shocks. Livelihood in this economy is agriculture-based with a section of population depending on labouring. More often, it is not the improved efficiency due to commercialisation that allows some of the workforce to seek employment outside; rather it is sheer survival that forces some of the vulnerable sections to seek such an option. Under shock, heads of even larger landholding households also have to borrow to meet with the eventualities. Using constructs of Todaro (1980), Ellis (2000), Lucas (2004) and Sah and Bhatt (2008), in what follows, we have tried to establish that during a shock depletion of assets, shrinking livelihood opportunities and related borrowings have strong positive influences on intensity of poverty. In order to maintain their level of living and also for hedging the risk of declining consumption, the only strategy the affected households have is seasonal migration. This is so, because in dryland areas under crop failure, annual income — from agriculture, forest, casual labouring, MNREGA and other village sources — is unable to support the households' consumption. Postulate a village consisting 'n' households with per capita expenditure of the ith household c_i such that during normal years, the available income with the households G_i is able to support the expenditure at the minimum per capita expenditure at an acceptable level c^* for all M_i of its members for rest of the d_i days till the new harvest arrives. During a shock there are, however, households whose per capita expenditure falls short of c^* by an amount s_i for remaining days. Under such circumstances, in order to maintain the minimum level of expenditure, m_i out of M_i members of household migrate for D_i days in such a way that:

$$c^*. (M_i - m_i) D_i + c^*.M_i. (d_i - D_i) < G_i$$

The following implications relating to the seasonal migration may be noted. First, higher the unmet expenditure, the higher will be the pressure on the family to migrate. Second, during a shock existing expenditure finds augmented to s_i by taking a loan from the local *bania* or the middleman. Those who have faith on middleman borrow more from them and seasonally migrate. On the other hand, those who have more faith on local *bania*, borrow from him and work as causal wage earners. Under the situation, the labour market finds locked with the credit market. Third, the duration of seasonal migration finds controlled by households' perception about the shortfall in consumption expenditure s_i. As soon as the shortfall is overcome and borrowed loan repaid, the migrating members are free to rejoin the family; i.e., no sooner $m_i.c^*. D_i = s_i$ in such a manner that savings from migration are enough to repay the loan, the time to return is opportune. Fourth, after the decision to seasonally migrate has been taken, there may not be many households whose expenditure falls below c^*. In fact, among the 'n' households in the village, those opting for seasonal migration may be the ones with relatively higher expenditure levels. It can be seen from the above construct that if the migrating members from a household choose to stay for more than the required days at their destination, the expenditure of the remaining members of household may be maintained at higher levels than c^*. In a scarcity situation, it is highly probable that the consumption expenditure of the remaining members of migrating households is higher than of the members of non-migrating households in the village. These households may also create some savings and assets over the time. Fifth, the decision to migrate could confer larger societal benefit provided: (a) the migrants are employed in profitable industries where their wages and productivity is higher than source villages; (b) the consumption levels of migrant is maintained at least at c^* level at the destination without adversely affecting the wage rate; or (c) the state intervenes to support the minimum consumption of the migrant through (i) Public Distribution System, or (ii) creating investment climate for additional employment creating a wage bouncy. None of these options is closed in an economy, where the policy makers are sensitive to the emerging crisis of displaced migrants. But such public actions are not only ineffective, but also are seldom taken. Lastly, the decision to migrate is not taken by any individual in isolation; seasonal migration is a group decision taken by the household as a whole, perhaps even by several households together. The cost of information relating to destination, movement of the group, type of work and wage contract, dwelling at the destination and payment to middlemen *etc.* may be shared by households that perceive seasonal migration inevitable for the larger interest of their families. Although, it is difficult to establish the above construct fully, evidence provided by this research indicates the operation of the process.

The data for the study was generated by first listing drought prone districts of Madhya Pradesh. According to Central Water Commission, Dhar, Jhabua, Khargone, Ratlam, Khandwa, Jabalpur, Rewa, Sidhi, Damoh, Panna, Rajgarh, Dewas, Raisen, Betul, and Seoni are districts which are recognised as drought prone. These districts (a) face severe drought once every 10 years, (b) have less than 20 per cent of gross cropped area under irrigation. The discussions with agricultural experts revealed that among these we can select Jabalpur, Rewa, Damoh, Panna, Jabalpur, Dewas and Indore because in these locations (i) rainfall pattern is erratic (ii) agricultural based livelihood has become highly uncertain (iii) are mainly dryland and tribal (iv) human development index is relatively poor (v) except Indore and Dewas, industrial development is poor, and (vi) rural labour market is undeveloped, wage rates are low hence migration from rural areas is high. From these seven districts, we purposively selected two blocks which were agriculturally undeveloped. From these blocks, we have selected two villages, where migration was relatively high. From these villages, we have randomly selected twenty migrant and eight non-migrant households. This way, we have randomly selected 502 migrant and 186 non-migrant households for the study (see, for details, Sah and Tomar, 2014). The reference year remained 2010-11.

Access to Capitals, Employment and Food Insecurity

It is pertinent to understand the dimensions of poverty in different parts of drylands of Madhya Pradesh, where labourers and marginalised groups dominate, as multidimensional poverty finds significantly higher among the labours and dalits compared to others (Bhide and Mehta, 2007). Shah (2005) argues that dryland agriculture is highly diversified, upon variations in rainfall pattern, soil type, cropping pattern and management of rain water. Owing to such variations across locations, there is intense competition between agriculture and seasonal migration in those areas (Sah and Tomar, 2014). The dryland agriculture in Madhya Pradesh is being characterised by (a) dominance of soybean and pulses in cropping pattern; (b) market-friendly cultivators; (c) relatively large landholdings; and (d) risk taking farmers (*Ibid*). Drylands of Madhya Pradesh have experienced scarcity during 1990s and early 2000s, and faced deceleration in agricultural production. This resulted in decline in per capita availability of foodgrains and oilseeds. This food crisis of early 2000s has taken a new twist in the form of environmental crisis; the main source of irrigation in Madhya Pradesh is ground water (Sah, 2007) but by mid-2000s, the over-exploitation of ground water turned into an environmental crisis. Because of this, the drylands of Madhya Pradesh are trapped in an unsustainable agriculture. But poverty in non-tribal drylands is transitory in nature; during normal years, level of poverty is low and only a part of landless labourers and marginal farmers face severe poverty. But during abnormal agricultural years, incidence of poverty increases significantly. In these hard times, along with labourers, small and middle size cultivators fall into poverty. This is termed as transitory poverty of dryland.

As against this, in tribal areas (a) agriculture is kharif based and rainfed; (b) landholdings are relatively small; (c) farmers are risk aversions and cereals dominates the cropping pattern; (d) yields are significantly lower than non-tribal drylands; (e) soil erosion is high and poverty- borrowing-migration cycle forces the farmers to cultivate marginal lands that are not fit for cultivation; (f) this results in still more severe soil erosion; and (g) are also experiencing institutional crisis; the unwritten rules governing use and distribution of produce from commons are being disregarded, resulting in deterioration in environment sustainability. These forces are creating challenges for sustainable agriculture in the tribal Madhya Pradesh. Owing to all this, a large section of small farmers and landless labourers are trapped in poverty year after year. The poverty in tribal areas is chronic in nature (Sah and Bhatt, 2008).

Appendix I shows that access to various capitals — natural (forest and land), physical, social (trust within and on outsiders), human (education and health) and financial (access to financial markets and income) — is extremely constrained in the drylands. But, this access failure is severe in tribal areas followed by non-tribal drylands, and industrial dry areas. **Appendix I** reveals that despite diversifying their occupational pattern, the income from activities in village — forest, agriculture, casual labouring, MNREGA and traditional occupations — is lowest for tribals and highest among households located in industrial dry villages. The food security is also highly fragile among tribal households whose agriculture produce lasts for only two months as against four months for households located in industrial dry villages.

Table 1: Poverty, Income-Consumption Gap and Migration

	Industrial dry villages[p c]	*Dryland Villages [pc]*	*Tribal Villages [p c]*	*All [p c]*
Poverty across Locations				
Very Poor	29.2	29.5	58.6	37.8 (260)
Poor	38.1	44.4	27.3	37.6 (259)
Non-poor	32.7	26.0	14.1	24.6 (169)
All*	100.0	100.0	100.0	100.0 (688)
Village Income – Expenditure (Rs per year)				
Migrant	+2,497 (119)	-1,847 (230)	-9,149 (153)	-3047 (502)
Non-migrant	+10,544 (85)	+7,638 (58)	+15,889 (45)	+ 10,931 (186)
All **	5,791 (202)	+63 (288)	-3,459 (198)	732 (688)
Migration Intensity				
Person days***	75 (119)	140 (230)	160 (153)	131 (502)

Figures in brackets are total respondents
* Chi Square = 55.4 (.000), R = -0.24 (.000)
** F= 9.9 (.000)
*** F= 9.9 (.000)
Source: All the Tables in the paper are derived from primary data, for details, see Sah and Tomar (2014)

The incidence of poverty is relatively low among households located in the industrial dry areas compared to households located in dryland or tribal villages. Interestingly, income occurring from various sources in village is unable to meet the annual expenditure of households, as one move from industrial dry to drylands to tribal villages (**Table 1**). This expenditure-gap puts a pressure on tribal households. In order to meet this additional expenditure, the households in tribal areas are forced to migrate seasonally. It needs to be noted that in each of the three locations, the un-met expenditure among migrant households is significantly higher compared to non-migrants. The higher the un-met expenditure, the higher is the pressure on household to migrate seasonally. Despite the fact that pressure on households to migrate in industrial dry villages is nil, if some households are migrating, it indicates that such migration is for accumulation and not as a livelihood alternative. On the other hand, in dryland villages and tribal villages, seasonal migration is a necessity to survive. This is also reflected on number of migrants and the duration of migration in the three locations (**Table 1**); the migration intensity (number of migrants as well as period of migration) in industrial dry villages is only 75 person-days, while the migration intensity increases to 140 person-days in dryland villages and in tribal villages, migration intensity further increases to 160 person-day.

Table 2: Some Important Differences between Migrants and Non-migrants

	Migrant	*Non-migrant*	*All*	*F*
Adults	4.6	4.73	4.63	NS
Worker	3.68	3.78	3.71	NS
Land Acre	1.22	4.40	2.08	80.9 (.000)
Assets [Rs]	40,559	1,03,685	57,625	92.9 (.000)
Agricultural Production[Rs]	3,678	15,101.	6,766	71.7 (.000)
Loan [Rs]	4,319	5,299	4,584	NS
Loan Repaid [Rs]	860	1,031	906	NS
Outstanding Loan [Rs]	2,938	8,174	4,353	NS
Food Security Months	2.1	4.2	2.7	29.0 (.000)
Bonding Social Capital	2.2	2.0	2.1	16.2 (.000)
Bridging Social Capital	1.2	1.5	1.3	7.9 (.005)
Rs Income without Migration	21,443	39,229	26,252	99.9 (.000)
Annual Expenditure [Rs]	24,491	28,298	25,520	14.1 (.000)
Village income – expenditure	-3,048	10,931		(.000)

Table 2 gives the differences between migrants and non-migrants: Access to land and agricultural income is significantly high (about four times) among non-migrants. The income of non-migrants from various village activities is about two times higher compared to non-migrants and so is the case of food security. What is also evident is the growing expenditure gap among

migrant households compared to non-migrants. As agriculture, the main livelihood activity in source villages is unable to provide sustenance for whole year for households in tribal Madhya Pradesh, those severely affected by crop failure, are forced to migrate. It is argued that a shock, in the form of crop failure, induces a complex socio-economic process like access failure to food, debt and repayment, and migration. In fact, shock not only has repercussions that disrupt the economy but also has socio-cultural implications. It is also argued that social capital manifests differently among migrants and non-migrants, and that trust on local moneylender versus middleman significantly govern the choice to stay in village or seasonally migrate.

Odd-ratios have been used to examine the impact of drought on (i) migrants and non-migrants, (ii) poor and non-poor, and (iii) landless and landowning households (**Table 3**). If the odd-ratio is significantly higher than 1, than it can be argued that impact of the shock on, for example, migrant is highly adverse compared to non-migrants. It is found that owing to drought migrants compared to non-migrants are (i) 31 times more likely to deplete their animal heard rather than not; (ii) 16 times more likely to sell trees, rather than not; (iii) 14 times more likely to withdraw their children from school, than not; (iv) five times more likely to mortgage their land than not; and (v) thrice more likely to increase migration than not. These evidences (**Table 2**) clearly reveal that effect of drought is significantly adverse on poor, landless and migrants. An important question is if the social network of these affected groups differs compared to others?

Table 3: Effect of Draught between Migrant and Non-migrant, Poor and Non-poor, Cultivators and Landless Households

Effect of Draught	*Odd Ratio* [a]		
	Migrant	*Poor*	*Landless*
Started doing laboring	1.2	1.2	0.47*
Mortgage Land	5.0*	1.2	
Sold Land	1.5	78.0*	
Sold Trees	16.0*	78.0*	0.54*
Faced Foodgrains shortage	1.0	1.10	0.44*

(Contd...)

Increased Migration Intensity	3.1*	2.7*	0.48*
Animal Heard Depleted	31.0*	71.0*	1.12
Borrowing Increased	1.0	1.9*	1.00
Children were withdrawn from school	14.0*	32.0*	1.12
Old persons were sent to relatives	4.0*	0.57*	1.00
Could not pay doctor's fee	0.6	36.8*	5.30*

[a] Taken an action rather than not between:(i) Migrant-and non-migrants, (ii) Poor and non-poor, (iii) Landless and landowners.

*Significant at 5 % or low

The importance of social network, customs and social capital in influencing livelihood patterns cannot be overemphasised (Deshingkar, 2007). The social-cultural constructs have yet to find space in explaining development except for use of culture as a construct obstructing development. It has however, been argued that migration is significantly associated with social network the migrant choose (Sah, 2005; Sah and Bhatt, 2008; Sah et al, 2008). Using Widmalam (2004), Sah (2005) has argued that labour market and social capital are strongly interlinked. Sah and Bhatt (2008) have argued that trust within (bonding capital) manifests during a shock for the survival in the form of commodity exchange and sharing of information on migration. But trust on the outsiders (bridging capital) manifested only by non-poor in order to manipulate decision making at the grassroots democratic institutions (*Ibid*). Our analysis of trust reveals that migrants are three times more likely to trust middlemen, compared to non-migrants. On the other hand, the non-migrants are two times more likely to trust local moneylender- cum-large farmer compared to migrants. This is so because, non-migrants in order to get loans and labouring opportunity from large farmer-cum-moneylender trust them while the migrants depend on middlemen for labouring opportunities, small loans, healthcare expenses and information.

Migration Income [Remittances]

Of late, mobile phone has changed the migration process in more ways than one: (i) earlier the middlemen (the contractors and their *Munims*) were major source of information about destination, type of work and wages. But now over half the migrant find out the destination their own, only five per cent households depend on middlemen, (ii) earlier over 90 per cent of seasonal migration was rural-to-rural. But, now over half of the seasonal migration is rural-to-urban. While Delhi and NCR, Jammu, Himachal, Punjab, Mumbai, Western Uttar Pradesh, Rajasthan, Haryana and Gujarat are preferred destination outside Madhya Pradesh, Bhopal, Indore, Gwalior, Morena, Beena, Damoh, Katni are the locations for migration within state. And (iii) the happenings of the source village reach the migrants without time-lag. In city, migrants work as semi-skilled labourers in construction, hotels, security, while skilled labourers are employed in transport, factories and construction industry. Migrants when move to rural areas are employed in agriculture and mining. It should be noted that tribals are predominantly employed in construction industry.

Table 4: Migration Income and Savings

	Industrial dry villages	*Dryland villages*	*Tribal villages*	*All*	*F*
Migrant Persons	1.3	1.4	1.8	1.5	4.5 (.01)
Working Persons	1.2	1.3	1.8	1.4	8.8 (.00)
Migration Days	75	140	161	131	14.2 (.00)
Working Days	61	109	143	108	14.2 (.00)
Unemployed days	10	17	18	15	16.6 (.00)
Migration Income[Rs]	10,765	16,811	23,998	17,568	NS
Migration Expenditure[Rs]	1,529	1,657	1,582	1,604	5.0 (.01)
Migration Savings[Rs]	9,236	15,154	22,416	15,964	21.5 (.00)

On an average, two persons per household migrate for about 131 days and get employment for about 108 days, at the destination. This results in an average per household Rs 17,600 earning from migration. After the upkeep, average saving that is brought back to village is about Rs 16,000 per household. Migration from tribal dry belt is significantly higher compared to dryland as well as industrial dry areas (**Table 4**). Consequently, migration income and remittances are significantly higher in tribal areas and are lowest in industrial dry land villages. Migration income accounts for about 51 per cent of total income of migrant tribal households. Remittances are being used for a number of purposes, like meeting day-to-day expenses, purchasing property, investment in agriculture, repaying old debts, as well as in sickness. On an average, about three-forth of the remittances are used for day-to-day food expenses. An important dimension of remittances is the financial bridges it makes between urban and rural area, apart from its role in healthcare, education, gender equality (Ray Chaudhari, 1993; De Haan, 2007). In the tribal areas, the main use of remittances is sustenance while in industrial and dryland villages its use is varied (Table 5).

Table 5: Remittances and its Use

	Industrial Dry Villages	*Dryland villages*	*Tribal villages*	*All Migrants*	*F*
Migration Savings					
Migration Income[Rs]	10,765	16,811	23,998	17,568 (502)*	NS**
Migration Saving[Rs]	9,236	15,154	22,416	15,964 (502)	6.0 (.00)
Use of Remittances			Percentage		
Property	4.8	1.3	3.7	2.8 (46)	NS
Agriculture	1.8	1.7	-	1.1 (42)	NS
Repaying Debt	6.9	9.3	0.2	5.6 (129)	NS
Day-to-day Food Expenses	60.3	65.5	93.1	74.7 (458)	.00
Sickness	10.2	10.1	0.7	6.7(273)	NS
Others	9.3	11.1	1.2	7.1 (297)	.02

*Total Respondents

** Significance of F

NS Mean not significant across the three locations

It should be noted that over 97 per cent remittances are carried back home by migrants, whenever they return in tribal areas. Over 93 per cent of remittances were used for food purchase (**Table 5**). Studies by Oberai and Singh (1983), Ray Chaudhari (1993) and De Haan (2007) reveal that remittances are governed by mgration intensity, income, duration of stay and expenditure made by migrants at the destination. Ray Chaudhari argued that households, who stay for longer time, remit relatively higher proportion of their earnings. Although, there is no significant difference in intensity of saving between males and females, as female work participation is relatively less, their contribution, as will be seen, is relatively low compared to male. It is hypothesised that variation in working days, dependency among migrants, unemployment at source and also during migration, explain variations in remittances. It is also argued that those who (a) are employed for more days; (b) have higher food expenditure back home; (c) have faced higher unemployment at the source; (d) are working in construction industry than other places will have significantly higher income and hence their remittances are higher. It is also hypothesised that as one moves for industrial to dry and to tribal area, remittance will be higher. The results Linear Regression Analyses — with remittance as dependent variable and factors as explained above – do indicate towards this process **(Table 6)**.

As only 25 per cent of variations in remittances across households as explained by the construct developed **(Table 7)**, it clearly indicates that some important variables explaining variations in remittances are missing. Apart from these independent variables agricultural land, contribution of females, dependency and education were also used in explaining remittances; but their effect was found insignificant. The model with significant F value, nevertheless, indicates the process of explaining remittances have explanatory variables that are significant. The following interpretation is worth nothing.

Table 6: Determinants of Remittances across Migrating Households, Results of Linear Regression

	Coefficient	*Std. Error*	*Beta*	*t*	*Significance*
(Constant)	14,208.5	3721		3.818	.000
Village Unemployment Days	9,.209	3.130	.159	2.013	.003
Village Income – yearly Expenditure	-.092	.057	-.083	-1.635	.103
Dummy Construction	52,11.7	1416	.151	3.679	.000
Assets	-.028	.014	-.085	-2.002	.046
Migration Unemployed Days	-387.5	72.09	-.217	-5.375	.000
Per Capita Food Expenditure	-2.013	.525	-.190	-3.838	.000
Per Capita Non Food Expenditure	1.393	.616	.108	2.262	.024
Dummy location Dry	38,44 0	1791.4	.112	2.146	.032
Dummy Location Tribal	6,829.2	2109.7	.184	3.237	.001
Number of Observations R Bar Square F	502 0.25 19.6				.000

The choice of employment in higher paying work (dummy for construction) with increased unemployment, per capita non-food expenditure increases and movement from industrial dry to either dryland villages (dummy location dry) or tribal villages (dummy location tribal) takes place, remittances increase. On the other hand, when (i) village income is more than yearly expenditure, (ii) level of assets increase, (iii) percentage of unemployment in migration increases and (iv)per capita food expenditure, in source village, increases, the remittances decrease significantly. Using correlation analyses, it was found that those households who had higher unemployment at source have higher migration intensity. Households whose annual income from village activities is higher than their annual consumption expenditure have lower migration intensity. Households, whose food security from their own agriculture is for more days, have significantly lower migration intensity. Those households whose employment-days in village activities is higher, have significantly lower migration intensity. It is also been found that migration intensity is significantly higher in dryland villages and tribal villages compared to industrial dry villages. Using these as independent variable in regression analysis, we have tried to explain the variations in migration intensity (**Table 7**).

About 22 per cent variations in migration intensity are explained by the independent variables considered (**Table 7**). Among the variables, type of employment, expenditure gap and unemployment destination are the three most important factors (based on size of beta coefficient). In consequence of theoretical constraint, unemployment in village increases migration intensity, while higher (a) village income than yearly expenditure, (b) assets, and (c) annual expenditure, reduces migration intensity. We have also found that interactions of independent variables, rather than single independent variable are explaining the variations in migration intensity. The findings reveal that households with negative expenditure-gap, if also have low food security then their migration intensity is significantly higher than other combinations. Graph 1 depicts behaviour of migrants. If the income from activities in village is lower than annual consumption expenditure by Rs 2,750 or more and if side-by-side the households' food expenditure is low, than migration intensity shoots to 150 person-days. In all other combinations of expenditure gap and food consumption the migration intensity is significantly lower. This analysis vindicates our conceptual construct, at least partially.

Table 7: Determinants of Migration-Intensity using Linear Regression

	Coefficient	*Std. Error*	*Beta*	*t*	*Significance*
(Constant)	52.7	15.1		3.489	.001
Village Unemployment Days	.072	.016	.169	4.618	.000
Village annual Income – yearly Expenditure	-.001	.000	-.175	-4.526	.000
Dummy Construction	56.37	8.96	.221	6.293	.000
Assets	.00	.00	-.109	-2.758	.006
Annual Exp[Rs]	-.001	.00	-.127	-3.202	.001
Dummy location Dry	44.612	10.4	.175	4.281	.000
Dummy Location Tribal	40.86	11.99	.147	3.408	.001
Number of Observations R Bar Square F	688 0.22 29.3				.000

Impact of Migration

As labouring opportunities at the source dry up and wages remain unattractive, and meeting expenditure from village income becomes difficult, a section of labouring and cultivating households feel that seasonal migration is inevitable for survival. In the process, migrants in search of livelihood move to locations and employments that are relatively better but devoid of regulations that protect their rights. Migration does help them to survive but fails in creating environment of prosperity. The worst effected in the process are females that are left behind. This section presents impact of migration on employment and wages, living slandered of migrants as well as the contribution of females in migration and of the females who were left behind.

Employment at the Source

While casual labour and MNREGA provides about 72 per cent of total village employment to migrants, own agriculture, animal husbandry and traditional occupation account for only 25 per cent village employment. For tribal households, cultivation (53 person-days), Casual labour (70 person-days) and MNREGA (32 person-days) are main sources of village employment. But despite this, over 77 per cent of available labour of tribals remains unutilised (**Appendix I**). Among migrant households about 65 per cent of the available labour remains unutilised in village. In the case of non-migrants, own agriculture, animal husbandry and traditional occupation is important and accounts for over 51 per cent employment, while casual labouring and NREGA accounts for another 44 per cent of employment. Together, the village activities are able to provide employment to about 44 per cent of available labour with the non-migrant households. This shows that only about 56 per cent of available labour of non-migrant households remains unutilised in village activities. Thus, the relatively higher level of unemployment in village along with high unmet expenditure from village income (**Table 1**) is responsible for pushing-out the tribals in search of livelihood in cities.

Employment at the Destination

Labour relations at the destinations, though market-driven, are not free from exploitation. For tribal migrant households, who are predominantly employed in construction industry, the system of advance payment, their long working hours, payment mode and lack of formal work agreement result in exploitation of tribals. The state machinery, responsible for social security and work related disputes, remains unmindful to these facts. That is why about a fourth of migrants change their occupation. The search for new work starts by visiting the morning road-side labour-markets first, and then factories and construction sites. A third of migrants feel that received-wages were lower than the agreed wages, and about half of migrants faced delayed wage payment. About 85 per cent migrants work without any written agreement. However, over 60 per cent migrants working in security-agency and factories have written work contracts. Migrants also face problems of long working hours, misbehaviour at work place and disputes relating to payments. Despite these hardships, seasonal migration is inevitable, because about 45 per cent annual income of migrant households is accruing from migration. For tribal households, the migration contributes to about 51 per cent of the total income. Moreover, when casual wages, in source village, range from Rs 88 to Rs 92 per day, a migrant on an average earns Rs 162 per day in migration. Migrants however ascertain that migration remittance helps them in surviving the resourcelessness but is unable to pull them out of poverty.

Poverty and Migration

The evidence from this research reveals that over half of the migrants believe that (a) their consumption pattern has changed, (b) they could repay old debts, (c) education for their children and healthcare access has improved, (d) their agricultural input use has increased and (e) they have started some savings too. But a negligible proportion of migrants have reported that their agriculture production has increased and they are able to resist the depletion of their assets during abnormal years. Only 22 per cent of migrants believe that there is reduction in their poverty. The main reason for insignificant impact on poverty is lack of saving; remittance is used in sustaining their basic consumption. They believe that seasonal migration is able to maintain their expenditure level at respectable level and nine out of ten migrants retorted that they are just able to live because of migration, but are unable to improve their economic condition. This is mainly, because the seasonal migration has trapped them in a cycle of low skill and returning back to their roots for cultivation or labouring, without upgrading their skills. It is likely that generation after generation, these unskilled migrants will continue the work they are performing at present without any occupational mobility.

MNREGA and Migration

The impact of MNREGA on casual wage rate and employment generation in tribal Madhya Pradesh is mixed, but indicates its inability to support tribal livelihood (Sah and Tomar, 2014). It can be argued that locations which are near by cities where wages in construction industry are one and half to two times higher than MNREGA, the employment guarantee scheme do face a shortage of labourers. Even if work is taken up by Panchayats, in some of these villages, the MNREGA employment to labourers is by default; the most vulnerable of them — Tribal marginal farmers and agricultural labourers — seasonally migrate in search of livelihood. Those who remain in village, get MNREGA work, though they actually do not need employment. By default, MNREGA has excluded the marginalised and provided employment to above poverty households. The delayed payments, low wages, non-continuous employment, and insufficient employment create disinterest towards MNREGA. These marginalised groups prefer to seasonally migrate rather work in MNREGA. Evidence clearly recognises that wage rates in the Madhya Pradesh villages are governed by forces outside the MNREGA (*Ibid*). For one, the booming construction industry is one of the important pull factors that create shortage of labourers in village. But equally important is internal functioning of MNREGA that results disinterest of labourers in MNREGA work.

The shortage of labour in source villages has to be accepted for the sake of survival of landless labours and marginal farmers. The importance of relatively higher wages in migration notwithstanding, seasonal migration is constraining skill formation because employment to migrants is available mainly as unskilled labourers. Seasonal migrants, generation after generation, are slotted in this category of employment because attraction of unviable agricultural land, forces the migrants to return back to the source villages rather than get absorbed in non-farm activities and develop as skilled labours.

Gender Dimensions and Migration

Tomar (2010) has argued that contribution of females in tribal migration is equal to that of males. But bulk of the decisions about destination of migration, work and dwelling are taken by. As males, traditionally, are supposed to protect the family, so the type of work that has risks to female member of the family is avoided. Migration is also considered as an alternative of doing degrading labourers' job in source village, by middle and small landholders, in crisis. Interlocking their labour and credit market, by taking loan from village moneylender-cum-large farmer, and thus working on the farm of lender as attached labour is considered degrading by small and middle farmers. In order to avoid this, farmers under crisis, believing seasonal migration is safe, choose to migrate. This is corroborated by the fact that, by adjusting their working hours, creating safe dwellings in destination and living together with relatives and villagers, the migrant males are able to create similar environment as is available in their source village. But females, often disagree with such arguments. They find labouring in construction industry and mines extremely tiring. Females do not distinguish between loan from village moneylender and the middleman. They are not comfortable in living, cooking and doing their domestic chores in destination. They are also not comfortable by the idea of leaving children without proper supervision at the site. Therefore, the dignity that forces male to migrate, instead of working in village as labourer, is not that convincing to females that migrate with their husbands. Estimating the contribution of female in drylands, it is found that female contribution is much lower: among migrant households, males are 3.6 times more likely to migrate than females and the contribution of females in migration income is 4.5 times less than males (Sah and Tomar, 2014).

On the other hand, in absence of males, the left behind females have to work on fields apart from the managing family. In social realm, absence of the male breadwinner means families' access to social communication is broken. As a result, the households remain unaware of schemes and benefits available to them. These families also face serious security problems. Apart from these, in economic sphere, left-behind females are cut-off from information relating to agriculture technology, extension, inputs and markets. In about 60 per cent of migrant households, females did not accompany their husbands owing to household's responsibility at source. The three main reasons for not migrating were children's education, taking care of elders and availability of labouring opportunity in the village. Apart from these, adequate availability of foodgrains and livestock care was also reason for not migrating. Analysis of various familial and other activities before and after male-migration reveal that dealing with banks, using ATM, marketing activities, loan related meetings and labouring has significantly increased after male-migration. What did not change, however, are their household chores and their involvement in self-cultivation. These everyday jobs they were doing earlier too. Livelihood struggles and responsibility of looking after the children & elders, in absence of their husbands, did not leave much time with them for missing their husbands. The physiological and economical insecurity of these females, the work pressure on them and wait for their husbands is some thing that seasonal migration is bringing to females.

Conclusions

The governments should not see voluntary internal population movements as a threat. Indeed, internal migration offers societies an opportunity for economic growth and the convergence of welfare (HDR: 2009). For tribals, the assertion of HDR is like a fresh air, because it supports the internal labour migration. The internal migration from the poverty ridden regions to the developed regions has positively and significantly influenced the economic development across the globe (*Ibid*). These arguments are, however, contrary to the negative connotation given to it by the policy makers in India. The rural-urban migration, in Indian policy circles, is considered not only anti-development but also which brings poverty to urban areas, and is a major cause of unemployment, social disruption and overburdened urban civic amenities[1]. But, our findings show that migration has become inevitable in tribal drylands.

The seasonal migration from Tribal and Dryland Madhya Pradesh is inevitable, because over half of total income of tribal, poor and landless households, accrues from migration. The income from village activities fails to meet their annual expenditure. The larger this unmet expenditure, the more is the pressure on households to migrate. The remittances are able to sustain the tribals, though inability of remittances to pull-out the migrants from poverty is also evident. Higher unemployment, larger unmet expenditure-gap, choice of employment (in destination) and being in Dry-tribal areas significantly increase migration intensity. But in the social and economic relationships with the mainstream society, the

---

1. It can be argued that seasonal migration has resulted in labour shortage and thus is instrumental in hiking the casual wages in villages. This, we believe, is a price the economy has to pay if it is unable to protect the life, livelihood and rights of its migrant labouring mass.

migrants find themselves in a disadvantageous position. This disadvantage results in exploitation of migrants in wage payment, delays in payment, access to the social amenities and social security. The remittance, in this situation, works as insurance against poverty. Therefore, like employment and livelihood in agriculture and labouring, migration too is a livelihood option, though a bit dynamic. Unfortunately, state has failed to recognise this. Over 129 million persons in the India depend on migration for livelihood (Deshingkar and Akter, 2009). Our estimates show that this creates financial links, between urban and rural areas, of a tune of about 1.5 per cent of GDP of the country. But the migrants, who have established these financial links, remain invisible to policy makers and ignored by industry; both the industry and state have remained insensitive to the needs and rights of these labourers.

Two important policy implications are emerging from this analysis. First, crating environment that obstructs migration is desirable. The policy options that improve agricultural productivity and village employment, that ensure food security and improve access to PDS, fall in this category. Second, inevitability of tribal seasonal migration forces us to argue that if the current policy frame is unable to contain migration, it is time to support it. A way of reducing the incidence of migration is to intensify investment that conserves the soil-moisture and makes agriculture sustainable. Evidence reveal that civil society initiatives in central tribal belt of India have reduced seasonal migration significantly (Sah *at el*, 2008). Replicating such efforts may be helpful for the hapless migrants. Although a shock can push even a well to do household into a debt-trap and has to resort to migration as a coping mechanism, for a large section of households that are resourceless owing to population pressures, migration is the only coping mechanism. Therefore, the processes that facilitate migrants in the course of migration are as important as reducing migration. Making the lives of migrants at the place of destination less stressful, provide them with amenities there, and make their position stronger in the labour market, is as important as improving agriculture and increasing borrowing capacity of migrants, at the place of origin.

Appendix - I: Access to Various Capitals, Employment and Income and Food Insecurity

	Industrial	*Drylands*	*Tribal*	*F*
Access to Capitals				
Forest Income [Rs]	53	101	181	4.0 [.02][a]
Land Acre	1.27	2	3.07	8.9 [.00]
Assets Rs	63,714	52,818	58,404	NS
Percentage Trust Outsiders	43	40	14	48 [.00]
Per cent 5+ Educated	58	64	54	NS
Health Expenditure [Rs]	5,385	2,761	860	12 [.00]
Loan Taken [Rs]	6,702	4,862	2,017	5 [.02]
Village Income[Rs]	33,988 (202)[b]	26,404 (288)	18,137 (198)	28 [.00]
Employed Days				
Agriculture Days	70	66	53	NS
Forest Days	0.7	1.3	2.3	NS
Labour Days	200	152	70	51 [.00]
MNREGA Days	17	26	32	NS
Animal Husbandry Days	29	21	14	4 [.03]
Service Days	18	10	4	4 [.03]
Traditional Days	21	5	5	7 [.00]
Migration Days	36	87	111	37 [.00]
Total Labour Days in Village	355	281	181	44 [.00]
Annual Income				
Agriculture	4,241	7,714	7,962	3 [.03]
Forest	53	101	181	4 [.02]
Labour	20,472	13,969	6,288	62 [.00]
NREGA	1,841	2,698	2,559	NS
Animal Husbandry	2,462	810	513	17 [.00]
Service	1,168	413	1,096	NS
Traditional Occupation	3,751	699	578	8 [.00]
Migration	6,342	13,426	18,544	29 [.00]
Total	40,330	39,829	36,.681	NS
Unemployment in Village				
Total Worker	3.09	2.81	3.11	6 [.00]
Available Days	772	703	777	6 [.00]
Labour Days in Village	355	281	181	44 [.00]
Per cent Unemployment in village	54	60	77	27 [.00]
Migration Days	35	87	111	37 [.00]
Food Insecurity				
Agricultural Production [Rs]	4,241	7,714	7,962	3 [.03]
Foodgrains Production Qt	2	4	4	5 [.01]
Self Consumed Qt	1	2	1	10 [.00]
Self Consumption Months	2	4	2	11 [.00]
PDS Supply Rs	35	72	69	34 [.00]
Per cemt PDS in food Expenditure	4	7	10	34 [.00]
Food Expenditure [Rs]	1,331	1,345	1,017	22 [.00]

[a] Level of Significance NS Not significant
[b] Total number of households

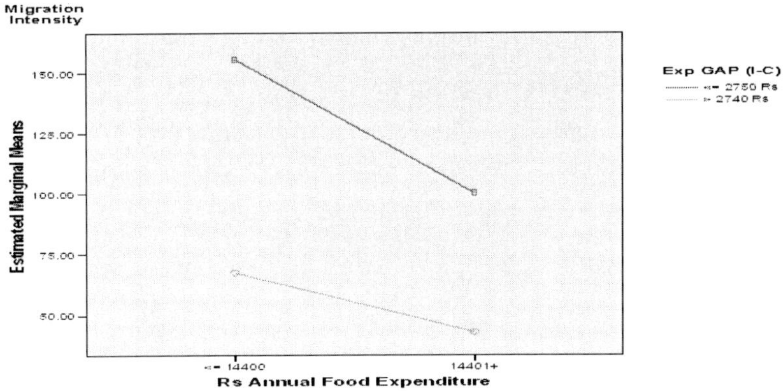

Graph 1: Interaction between Factors in Explaining Migration Intensity

Notes and References

Breman J, (1985): *Of Peasants, Migrants and Paupers*, Oxford University Press, Delhi.

Breman J, (1996): *Footloose Labour: Working in India Informal Economy*, Cambridge University Press, Cambridge.

Deshingkar P, Akter S, (2009): '*Migration and Human Development in India*', Human Development Research Paper 2009/13, UNDP.

Ellis F, (1998): 'Household Strategies and Rural Livelihood Diversification', Journal of Development Studies, Vol. 35 (1).

Ellis F, (2000): 'The Determinants of Rural Livelihood Diversification in Developing Countries, Journal of Agricultural Economic, Vol. 51 (2).

HDR, (2009): Human Development Report 2009: Shaping Human Geography, World Bank.

Lee ES, (1966): 'A Theory of Migration', Demography, Vol. 3 (1).

Lucas, Robert E. Jr., (2004): 'Life Earnings and Rural-Urban Migration,' *Journal of Political Economy* 112 (S1).

Mosse D, Gupta S, Mehta M, Shah V, Rees J and KRIBP Team, (2002): 'Brokered Livelihoods: Debt, Labour Migration and Development in Tribal Western India', *Journal of Development Studies*, 38 (5).

Oberai AS. and Singh, MHK, (1983): Causes and Consequences of Internal Migration: A Study in the Indian Punjab, Oxford University Press, Delhi.

Olsen W.K and Murthy R.R.V, (2000): 'Contract Labour and Bondage in Andhra Pradesh', *Journal of Social and Political Thoughts,* Vol. 1 (2).

Ray Chaudhari J, (1993): *Migration and Remittance*, Sage Publications, New Delhi.

Sah DC, (2007): 'Failing Agriculture and Marginalization: Evidence from Rural, Madhya Pradesh', *Man and Development,* Vol. 29 (1).

Sah DC and Bhatt A, (2008): *Trapped in Poverty,* Rawat Publications, Jaipur.

Sah DC and Shah A, (2005): 'Migration in Remote Tribal Areas: Evidence from Southwestern Madhya Pradesh', *Indian Journal of Agriculture Economics,* Vol 60 (2).

Sah DC and Shah A, (2008): 'Population Pressure, Migration, and Development', *Madhya Pradesh Journal of Social Sciences,* 13 (1).

Sah DC, Bhatt A and Dalapati Tapas, (2008): *Chronic Poverty in Remote Rural Areas: Evidence from Central Tribal Belt of India,* Research Conducted with support of Planning Commission, GOI, MPISSR, Ujjain.

Sah DC and Tomar S, (2014): *Livelihood Struggles and Migration in Drylands of Madhya Pradesh,* MPISSR (mimeo).

Saxena DP, (1977): *Rural Urban Migration in India: Causes and Consequences*, Bombay: Popular Prakashan.

Sjaastad LA, (1962): 'Cost and Returns of Human Migration', *Journal of Political Economy*, Vol. 70 (5).

Todaro MP, (1969): 'A Model of Labour Migration in Less Developed', *American Economic Review,* Vol. 59 (1).

Todaro MP, (1980): 'Internal Migration in Developing countries', in (eds.), Easterline R.A, *Population and Economic Change in Developing Countries*, Chicago University Press, USA.

Tomar Shubhra, (2010): 'Livelihood Struggles and Seasonal Migration in Tribal Madhya Pradesh', PhD Thesis Submitted to Vikram University, Ujjain (mimeo).

Widmalam Sten (2004): 'The Utility of Bonding Social Capital', mimeo, Department of Government, Uppsala University.

Chapter - 8

Tribal Livelihood in Contemporary Manipur

— M C Arunkumar

The State of Manipur is the homeland for tribal and non-tribal communities. There are 36 scheduled tribes in the State; predominately inhabiting the hill areas. The economy is, by and large considered as that of the shifting cultivation. There are tribes, who practice terrace and shifting cultivation. Urbanization and developmental works, other historical reasons have mobilized contemporary Manipur tribal communities to embrace different economic lives. These can be grouped into three: hill tribal, plain tribal and urban tribal communities. In spite of differences in ethnic affinities, three communities were distinct in their mode of livelihood and economic practices. The author studies only one tribe (the Kabui or Rongmei) as the case study. The Kabui (or Rongmei) inhabit in the hills, plain and urban settings.

The Kabui is one of the indigenous tribes, recognized as the Schedule Tribes. They settle in every nook of eastern and western regions of Imphal valley; it has the localities in the capital city, Imphal. The tribe has different and distinctive socio–cultural life. They speak a Tibeto-Burman language. Racially, they belong to southern Mongoloid. The tribe has its distinctive identity. The tribe is otherwise known as the Rongmei, despite interaction with the non-Tribal and dominant group the Meitei. In the present day literature, the word *Kabui* has been widely used within and outside Manipur and the name Rongmei is less known to other communities. The original home of Kabuis lies in the Tamenglong area, which has a vast tract of hilly regions, situated along the western borders. It is being reported that early settlers into the valley came from Tamenglong area. The earliest settlement in Imphal was more than a century (Marangmei 2010). A debate among the Kabuis has made the community prefer them as their ethnonym, while the hill dwellers as the Rongmei. Interestingly, the two ethnonyms of the same tribe find included in the Scheduled Tribe list of the State.

Livelihood of Hill Kabui

Tamenglong district falls in the western region. The district has a large number of Kabui. It has also other tribal communities, namely, the Zeme, Liangmai, Puimei, Thadou, Hmar, and Chiru. Kabui villages were also found in Senapati, Churachandpur districts. The districts are hilly. Kabui mostly practise shifting cultivation, while some are salariat and business. Census 1981 puts 40.34 per cent of the tribes as workers. Of them, 77.63 per cent were cultivators, 4.21 per cent were agriculture labourers, 2.82 per cent were engaged in household industries and the remaining 15.34 per cent finds engaged in other occupations (Sharma 2004).

Agriculture is the main economic pursuit. Every household has a share of cultivating field, which is distributed by the chief in the council. Rice is the main crop. They cultivate rice through slash and burn method. The crops are paddy, maize, millet, chilli, ginger, potatoes and other vegetables. Rice is grown in large quantity, as it forms the staple food. They also engage in tea plantation, out of which raw leaves were collected. Lemon plantation is also one of the important activities. The method of cultivation is different from other tribes. The Kabuis mostly practice *jhuming*, but the *jhum* plots are fixed and permanent; that is to say, these plots were well-demarcated, and the *jhumia* returns to old plot at the beginning of each *jhum*-cycle(Das 1989).

Live stock farming plays a prominent role in their economy, though agriculture is the main source of livelihood. Each and every house domesticates the animals. Piggery and poultry are of equal importance. They rear animals for necessary requirements to be used during *genna*, public functions, festivals and feast of the married. Today, their way of farming witness the remarkable changes and now, they have begun to adopt wet or terrace cultivation. Apart from the agriculture and farming, cottage industries like weaving and dying is being done by women folks. Expertise in weaving is still the merit of a bride and therefore, it is indispensable work among the Rongmei women folks. The Rongmei have techniques of dying thread into various colours. In order to dye the thread, the tribal people used various kinds of creepers, leaves, barks and other species (Beeju 2014). Forest is controlled by the chief in the council. It provides the raw materials for their house construction and daily needs of the villagers. Cane, bamboos and beams are important products of the forest (Kahmei 1995).

The works of cane and bamboos, wood crafting are some of the non-agricultural activities. The basket making is very common among them. They also produce the ornaments, made of canes, such as head gears, bangles, and leg-guards.

The land, generally speaking, belongs to the chief in the village council. Though the chief is only a nominal head, he has a class of intermediaries called *Rampaos* who own the lands of a village — each claiming the ownership of well-demarcated block. The cultivators can clear jungles with their permission only and became their tenants (*Laopaos*). These tenants pay regular rent to the *Rampaos*, and are liable to ejection on default (Das 1989). The individual household does not have permanent right in land. This restricts to a great extent to the livelihood of individual persons in the community.

The Peasant Community

There are many Kabui villages in the valley districts. It is not known about the migration and settlement of Kabuis in the Imphal valley. The distribution pattern of settlement shows the migration was not just a flow of population, in search of service or something otherwise. The villages in the valley were amidst the Meitei villages. Their economic lives are more or less similar except of the pig rearing job. They rear pigs for ritual life, consumption and business. Hindu Meiteis start rearing them, though it was not in their itinerary earlier.

The rural Kabui villages, unlike the hilly villages, have well-demarcated boundaries, mapped in the revenue maps. Every plot of land is being recorded in the revenue department; they have to pay revenue tax to the Government. Mainly, the villagers are agrarian by occupation. They cultivate rice and some cash crops. Many of them are in small scale business. Earlier, they were engaged in brewing and selling of liquor. Kabui women also weave; weaving is most important secondary occupation among them.

Urban Communities

Three waves of Kabui migration took place. It was being classified on chronological basis: Pre-Colonial Migration, Migration during Colonial period and Migration in Post-colonial period. The migration during the colonial period was mainly due to British officials' demand for services ranging from unskilled to household services. In the post-colonial period, the migrations were due to general push and pull factors of economy. In the pre-colonial period, the migration and settlement were internalized in the body social with a design of statecraft of the King. The King allowed them to settle in one or another place with assigned duties. Their services in religious ceremony, rituals and economy were part of the ritualistic state of Manipur. This explains why there were many Kabui villages around the sacred complexes of the State.

There were about 15 Kabui localities. In and around Imphal city, some of the notable are being Chingmeirong, Majorkhul, Keishamthong, Moirangkhom, Mahabali, Ragairong, Namthanlong and Kakhulong. Kakhulong was established with early settlers, who were employees in the bungalows of British officers (Thaimei 1995). The main occupation in alocality, till recent past, was small scale business, brewing and selling of liquor and piggery. Unlike some of the Kabui localities in and around Imphal cities, this locality does not have any economic relation with the villages in the hill areas. Many of urban tribal localities established in the post-colonial period have link with original villages. The individuals living in such localities have their affiliation to original villages, as they would get their share of plots of land and other associated benefits in the original villages. They have customary contacts with the village authorities of the original villages. The households in the Kakhulong localities do not have any such contact with their original villages. They have to earn their livelihood in the Imphal urban setting. This tribal locality is located in the busiest part of Imphal.

The tribal locality represents the urban tribal economy in a neo-liberal state. The neoliberal state should favor strong individual private property rights, the rule of law, and the institutions of freely functioning markets and free trade. These are the institutional arrangements, considered essential to guarantee the individual freedoms. Each individual is held responsible and accountable for his [her] own actions and well-being, while personal and individual freedom in the marketplace is being guaranteed. This principle extends into the realms of welfare, education, health care, and even pensions. Individual success or failure are interpreted in terms of entrepreneurial virtues or any personal failings rather than being attributed to any systemic property(Harvey 2005).

Urban Kabui with limited space and little capital cannot earn enough to support their lives. The piggery in the heart of the city creates problems. Brewing and selling liquor were no more good business, as the state became dry-state. Newly emerged source of income among the urban Kabuis is the renting rooms out to migrant population. However, these tribals do not have enough money or land to expand; so this source of income is very limited.

Class formation

There was no clear-cut class division in pre-colonial tribal society, which may at most be characterized as a two-fold stratification consisting of the commoners (cultivators) and the tribal chieftains. The two classes again represented two broad categories of livelihood: the commoners were the producers of food and the ruling chiefs appropriated a part, what the commoners had produced. As a matter of fact, the ruling chieftains practically depended on the labor of the common people(Dena 2011). Tribal communities undergone social change rapidly, with many governmental offers. Introduction of modern education and other developmental programmes changed the tribal rank society to a stratified society. Initially, a group of school-educated individuals, established by the Christian missionaries, played a role of intermediary between the masses and the colonial officials; in the post-colonial period, a class is emerged. This class includes politicians, bureaucrats, teachers, doctors, church leaders, wealthy businessmen and contractors.

The emergence of middle class among the communities has a great impact on their livelihood and subsistence economy. The wealthy businessmen and contractors became money landers to poor families. The poor families, in hill and urban settings, were still dependent of *jhum* cultivation with lesser production. The traditional pattern of livelihood and that of land distribution under the traditional leaders are under pressure, as the communities underwent the process of social stratification.

The emerging scenario of formation of tribal middle class and the existing land laws under customary authority is being further aggravated with the infrastructural development in the hill areas of Manipur. The road construction is inevitable; however, the opening up of the tribal economy and loss of land and forest exerts pressure on the lower class tribal families. The compensation of the loss of land, theoretically speaking, cannot reach the tribal households that occupy the land, because the ownership lies in the chief-in-council. In such situation, middle class men became the key intermediaries between the government and the chieftains.

References

Beeju, Kamei (2014) : "A Way of Life of the Zelianrong Nagas in Manipur with Special Reference to Rongmei (Kabui) Tribe". **International Journal of Social Science and Humanity**, Vol. 4, No. 2, March 2014 2(2): pp 151-154.

Das, J N (1989): **A Study of Land System of Manipur**. Guwahati: Law Research Institution, Eastern Region, Guahati High Court.

Dena, Lal (2011): **Emergence of Tribal Middle Class in Manipur**. *in* http://www.virthli.in/2011/09/emergence-of-tribal-middle-class-in.html Retrieved on 19 October 2016.

Harvey, David (2005): **A Brief History of Neoliberalism**, Oxford: Oxford University Press.

Kahmei, N (1995): "The Zeliangrong Nagas", **Manipur: Past and Present**, Volume 3. N. Sanajaoba, ed. New Delhi: Mittal Publications.

Marangmei, Gaikhamdim (2010): **Kabui Tribe: History, Society, Culture, Dress, Food, Economy**. Imphal: E-Pao.

Sharma, S K (2004): "The Kabui Naga", **.Encyclopaedic Ethnography of the Himalayan Tribes**: A-D. Narendra S Bisht, T S Bankoti, (ed). New Delhi: Global Vision.

Thaimei, Mangthoi (1995): "The Rongmei", **Manipur: Past and Present**, Volume 3. N. Sanajaoba, (ed.) New Delhi: Mittal Publications.

Chapter - 9

Livelihood Security of Tribes in Central India

— *Neelu Rawat*

The Livelihood Security

Livelihood is a means for living of people. It acquires the regular source of income to procure sufficient food, access to basic amenities – health, education and assets, necessary for survival etc. It revolves around the fulfilment of needs for food, cloth and shelter, in the laymans' parlour. In 1992, Chambers and Conway gave the holistic definition of livelihood with sustainability-

> A livelihood comprises the capabilities, assets (stores, resources, claims and access) and activities required for a means of living: a livelihood is sustainable which can cope with and recover from stress and shocks, maintain or enhance its capabilities and assets, and provide sustainable livelihood opportunities for the next generation; and which contributes net benefits to other livelihoods at the local and global levels and in the short and long term. (Chambers and Conway, 1992)

Broadly, the livelihood covers the availability and the freedom to own and use the tangible and intangible assets. Tangible assets refer to stores and resources, which include the availability of resources and its store like grain, cash, gold, tree, farm equipments, tools, domestic utensils and land etc. which becomes the base to earn livelihood and perform like shock absorbents at the time of crisis like gold, land, house and vehicle etc. can be mortgaged at the time of cash requirement. Intangible assets include the claims and access of which claims were demands and the appeal made for material, moral or any practical support. It can be made upon the person, organization, relatives, friends, government and NGOs etc. Access refers to the opportunity to use store, resource, service and income etc.

Attaining the livelihood security is the prime importance for developing countries like India, where about one-third populations is rural, who strive for day-to-day bread, lives in squalor, where the children were malnourished and having poor literacy etc. In recent years, the Government of India has been making a huge investment in promoting the livelihood security, through various programmes like Mahatma Gandhi National Rural Employment Guarantee Act (MNREGA), National Rural Livelihood Mission (NRLM) and National Skill Development Corporation. Currently, many of the definitions of livelihood security finds derived from the work of Chambers and Conway (1992) which includes capabilities, assets and activities required for a means of living as the livelihood. For Frankenberger (1996), the household livelihood security is adequate and sustainable access to income and resources to meet the basic needs (including the adequate access to food, potable water, health facilities, educational opportunities, housing and time for community participation and social integration). Several possible sources of entitlement constitute the livelihood of household, which are based on the endowments that a household has, and its position in the legal, political and social fabric of society (Drinkwater and McEwan, 1992). Livelihood is secure, when the households have secure ownership of/or access to, resources and income earning activities to off-set risks, ease shocks and meet contingencies (Chambers, 1988). These ideas of livelihood security involve both right-based and need-based approach and embody fundamental attributes- possession of capabilities, access to tangible and intangible assets and the existence of economic activities.

Tribal Livelihood

India is a home for over 700 tribal communities, residing in its provinces and union territories. The term 'tribe' is borrowed from the British, and is ambiguous but undefined, which has been carried for several decades in the independent India. In British India, the communities were defined on the basis of their characteristic that is being continued in the independent India. Lokur's Committee was the first setup constituted to outline the characteristics of tribal communities (Srivastava, 2008). The committee outlined the characteristics as - an ensemble of primitive traits, distinctive culture, geographical isolation, shyness of contact with the outside world and backwardness. The criterion outlined by the committee is hardly relevant today (Srivastava, 2008; Burman, 2006) but more or less these were being adopted by scholars and administrators galore. Further, several prefixes have been added to categorize a tribal community to provide special assistance for development, because they were being believed to be underdeveloped, as per the indices of development established by so called mainstream society, or the modern society- scheduled tribe, de-notified tribe, nomadic and semi-nomadic tribe and particularly vulnerable tribal groups. Article 366(25) of the Constitution of India refers to the Scheduled Tribes as those communities, who are scheduled in accordance with Article 342 of the Constitution. This Article says that only those communities who have been declared as such by the *president of India* through an initial public notification or through a subsequent amending Act of Parliament will be considered to be *Scheduled Tribes* (Annual Report, 2015-16).

Historically, the tribal economy was non-monetized and based on forest resource. They have earned livelihood from forest and their basic requirements revolved around forest. Their access to forest and its utilization became limited. This resulted into overcrowding over available forest, which turned into overexploitation, with extension and control of the government over forest. The forest resources proved to be meagre for the population, which squarely depended upon, threatening their livelihood security, inclining towards other sources of livelihood, like wage and agriculture labour to retain the livelihood sustainable. However, forest is still the source of livelihood earning, but any inclination towards occupations, other than traditional ones made their economy monetized. Earlier, the occupation of communities varied with climatic variation and geographical location, but inevitable changes brought uniformity, in terms of occupation and larger population of tribal communities have been turned into agriculture labour, whose share has been increasing in every decade.

The classical classification of tribe given - by Anthropologists - hunter and food gatherer communities, artists, shifting cultivator, pastoral and cattle herder etc. is proved to be irrelevant and a four-fold categorization has been given in census of India i.e., cultivator, agriculture labour, household industry and other work. Long ago, the expertise of particular community on particular occupation has been diminishing like blacksmithy by Agariya tribes of Madhya Pradesh and the knowledge of herbal medicine of Baiga tribes, etc. Interventions were being made for mainstreaming of tribal communities since they were believed to be underdeveloped and marginal in the context of socio-economic, health and educational status. However, the problems of less developed or underdeveloped remained the same, inspite of lot of developmental initiations with huge investment from pre- to post-colonial period[s]. Why does the communities are still at the cross roads of development? What are the impeding factors of their livelihood security? What were the perspectives of their livelihood security? This author made an attempt to ascertain the position through field work, trial-and-error tactics, to give their intrinsic conditions amidst host of environmental damages both manmade and natural.

Central India Tribes

The middle region is constituted by the states of Bihar, Jharkhand, West Bengal, Odisha, Madhya Pradesh and Chhattisgarh. More than 55 per cent of population resides in these states. [Xaxa, 2014]. Among the states, the largest number of scheduled tribe community reside in Odisha i.e., 62 followed by Madhya Pradesh (43), Chhattisgarh (42), West Bengal (40), Bihar (33) and Jharkhand (32) (Annual Report 2015-16). In the context of their population, Madhya Pradesh ranks first with

Table 1: Occupational Profile of Scheduled Tribes in Central India

	Madhya Pradesh	*Odisha*	*Jharkhand*	*Chhattisgarh*	*West Bengal*	*Bihar*	*Total*
Population	1,53,16,784	95,90,756	86,45,042	78,22,902	52,96,953	13,36,573	**48,009,010**
Sex ratio	984	1,023	1,003	1,019	998	958	**855**
Literacy rate	50.5	66.3	63.3	59.0	57.9	51.0	**57.2**
Total number of Workers	**76,40,148**	**47,69,659**	**40,58,020**	**41,31,903**	**25,09,166**	**5,48,000**	**2,36,56,896**
Cultivators	24,51,197 (32.1)	12,28,133 (25.7)	16,64,751 (41.0)	17,87,951 (43.2)	3,02,890 (12.0)	80,380 (14.7)	**75,15,302 (31.8)**
Agricultural Labourers	42,44,208 (55.5)	24,77,463 (52)	15,63,184 (38.5)	18,36,642 (44.4)	14,50,184 (57.8)	3,84,267 (70.1)	**1,19,55,948 (50.5)**
Household Industry	72,637 (0.9)	1,62,632 (3.4)	98,274 (2.4)	39,749 (0.9)	65,549 (2.6)	15,458 (2.8)	**4,54,329 (1.9)**
Other Works	8,72 106 (11.4)	9,01,401 (18.9)	7,31,811 (18.0)	4,67,561 (11.3)	6,90,543 (27.5)	67,895 (12.4)	**37,31,317 (15.8)**

Source: Census 2011, Office of the Registrar General, Census of India, Govt. of India.

1,53,16,784 tribals. Odisha ranks the second with 95, 90,756, followed by Jharkhand with 86,45,042 tribal people, Chhattisgarh (78,22,902), West Bengal (52,96,953) and Bihar (13,36,573).

It is evident from the Table 1 that 50.5 per cent of tribal working population is involved in agricultural labour, which reflects the failure of agriculture and other traditional occupations in procuring the livelihood security. The share of household industry workers in total working population is only 1.9 per cent. It is worth to mention that household and cottage industry among the tribal is close to its end, if such downfall still continue. The report of Anthropological Survey of India also highlighted the diversified occupation of tribes and emphasised on some of the occupations that are near to be vanished (cited by Xaxa, 2014). About 15.8 per cent tribal working population is engaged in works other than cultivation, agriculture labour and household industry. Change agents have done a lot on their part for the tribal development and to make their livelihood sustainable, but tribal inclination more towards agriculture labour, or the wage works than other works reflect the insufficiency of institutional inputs. About 31.8 per cent tribal population of Central Indian states are cultivators which also rely on the availability of cultivable land, irrigation facility and technological knowledge etc., which are historically very poor among the scheduled groups (Beteille 1972, Murdia 1975, Sharma 1994, Mohanty 2001).

Land Holding

Land becomes the pivotal property in terms of both income and employment in a country like India, where agriculture is the prime source of livelihood for majority of people, living in rural and tribal areas. By and large, the most disadvantaged and the deprived group is the scheduled tribe, who is at the bottom of economic pyramid and living in dire poverty with limited resources. Historically, land is the main earning source after forests for tribal people, so review of its availability among them is necessary.

Table 2: Landholding among Scheduled Tribes of Central India

Land Holding	*Year*	*Bihar*	*CG*	*Jharkhand*	*MP*	*Odisha*	*WB*	*All India*
Marginal	2005-06	87.75	42.92	NA	38.47	54.79	81.99	49.48
	2010-11	87.19	45.25	60.86	42.03	66.61	83.95	53.9
		-0.56	+2.33	NA	+3.56	+11.82	+1.96	+4.42
Small	2005-06	8.3	24.23	NA	28.19	29.6	13.97	25.62
	2010-11	8.41	25.16	17.75	28.72	23.55	12.88	23.99
		+0.11	+0.93	NA	+0.53	-6.05	-1.09	-1.63
Semi-Medium	2005-06	3.17	20.81	NA	21.17	12.46	3.8	16.44
	2010-11	3.8	19.4	13.15	19.64	8.3	3.04	14.82
		+0.63	-1.41	NA	-1.53	-4.16	-0.76	-1.62
Medium	2005-06	0.73	10.33	NA	10.84	2.94	0.24	7.38
	2010-11	0.57	8.82	6.97	8.66	1.46	0.13	6.32
		-0.16	-1.51	NA	-2.18	-1.48	-0.11	-1.06
Large	2005-06	0.05	1.71	NA	1.34	0.21	0	1.08
	2010-11	0.02	1.38	1.27	0.95	0.08	0	0.96
		-0.03	-0.33	NA	-0.39	-0.13	0	-0.12

Source: Agriculture Census 2005-06 and 2010-11, Agriculture Census Division, Department of Agriculture and Co-operation, Ministry of Agriculture, Government of India, New Delhi.

Note: NA- Not Available.

As per the agriculture census, the number of marginal land holding has been increased between 2005-06 and 2010-11 among the Scheduled Tribe. Increase of 4.42 per cent in marginal land holding has been witnessed at the national level. Odisha, with increase of 11.82 per cent is at the top in the Central India. Chhattisgarh, Madhya Pradesh and West Bengal also have rise in the marginal holding. Small land holding is decreased at the national level, Odisha and West Bengal, but has increased in Bihar, Chhattisgarh and Madhya Pradesh. If large and medium land holding is taken into account, then it can be seen that it has decreased in both state and national level. With moving from large to marginal land holdings, the number of land holders has been increasing, which is a threat to vast landlessness in future. As per NSSO (National Sample Survey Organisation), Government of India Report No. 516 (2006)- 4.9 per cent scheduled tribe population of Bihar, 3.5 per cent of Chhattisgarh, 0.4 per cent of Jharkhand, 3.0 per cent of Madhya Pradesh, 4.2 per cent of Odisha, 1.8 per cent of West Bengal and 3.6 per cent of the country are landless. On an average 3 per cent scheduled tribe population of central India is landless and 64 per cent possess marginal land. It becomes difficult for them to procure livelihood security in such poor condition of land holding on one and depleting forest resources on other hand.

Forest

The forest cover is also diminishing, on which they depended once upon a time and their access to forest is also limited with the extension of government control over forest. **Table 3** depicts the picture of forest cover situation among the states of Central India.

The overall forest cover of these states has been increased with 1.18 per cent in a decade [2005~ 2015]. Only Chhattisgarh state has declined by 0.2 per cent, which is nominal. Increase in forest cover is due to the initiatives of the state and central government, to increase the forest cover. The increase rate is not as the pace of forest resources has decreased. Some of the forest has been generated for industrial purposes and some for sanctuaries etc. The access of tribal in forest is still the same, and they are compelled to search other option.

Table 3: Forest Cover in Central India States

State	*Geographical Area*	*Forest Cover*				*Growth*
		In 2005	*Percentage*	*In 2015*	*Percentage*	
Bihar	94,163	5,579	5.92	7,288	7.74	+1.82
Chhattisgarh	1,35,191	55,863	41.32	55,586	41.12	-0.2
Jharkhand	79,714	22,591	28.34	23,478	29.45	+1.11
Madhya Pradesh	3,08,245	76,013	24.66	77,462	25.13	+0.47
Odisha	1,55,707	48,374	31.07	50,354	32.34	+1.27
West Bengal	88,752	12,413	13.99	16,828	18.96	+4.97
Total	**8,61,772**	**2,20,833**	**25.62**	**2,30,996**	**26.8**	**+1.18**

Source: State of Forest Report 2005 and 2015, Dehradun, Forest Survey of India.

Livelihood Security

The UK Department for International Development (DFID) had a Development of Sustainable Livelihoods Framework (SLF) to analyse about the livelihood security,. It understands those factors affecting the people's livelihood and how such factors interact with each other. The SLF provide the way to understand-

(i) Assets draw upon by people for livelihood.
(ii) Strategies of people to make a living.
(iii) Context within which livelihood is developed, and
(iv) Factors that make a livelihood more or less vulnerable to shocks and stresses.

The SLF broadly includes the livelihood assets, livelihood context, livelihood strategy, livelihood vulnerability and livelihood interdependency which have been discussed in further section in context of tribal.

Livelihood Assets

Asset here refers to any useful thing or person; it can be an item of property possessed by a person or organization; and it can also be skill, knowledge, language and culture. More specifically, assets can be both tangible and intangible, of which the former refers to resources, goods, equipments and machinery etc. the latter are non-material part of assets, like feelings, relation, claims and demands etc. The tangible and intangible assets are necessary to earn livelihood. The Sustainable Livelihood Framework (SLF) of the UK Department for International Development (DFID) categorizes livelihood assets as-

(A) Human Capital

The human capital is a combination of knowledge, habits, social behaviour and personality that contribute to economic benefits for an individual or community (Ellis, 1996) which also includes the health of an individual, household and community. In general, it can be said that human capital refers to skill, knowledge, health and ability to work. The education not only

of the skilled person with reading and writing texts, but it also exposes a person to other dimension of life. A person can acquire various skills through education, because it capacitates the individual to get information from books, posters and other literatures. Therefore, an educated family, individual or the community has higher chances of getting skills than a family, individual or community without education. Skill is also transferred from generation to generation, which in other terms also called as the talent, but loss of cultural heritage and language makes it difficult for skills to survive for more generations. For being educated and to acquire skill, the person needs to be in good state of health, because any person who is bread earner of the family falls ill, then that family may suffer livelihood insecurity. So, the health is also an important human capital as livelihood assets.

Historically, the tribal economy was autonomous and closer to the nature. Tribal communities were distinctively skilled with particular work based on geographical features and resource availability, such as - some communities were skilled in hunting animals and birds, and to utilize their body parts like feathers and nails for medicinal purposes, some were skilled in collection of medicinal herbs and its uses. For example, Baiga of Madhya Pradesh and Birhor of Jharkhand and Bihar were blessed with medicinal knowledge. Agariya of Chhattisgarh, Bhil of Rajasthan, Gujarat and Madhya Pradesh were known for making appliances of iron. Likewise, Khairwar tribe earned their livelihood from collection of *Khair (Senegalia Catechu)* tree products. Some communities were skilled in collection and processing of honey, while others collected forest produce like mahua *(Madhuca Longifolia)* and chironji *(Buchanania Lanzan)* etc. Youth of the communities collectively participated in economic activities and they had such a food pattern, which kept their mental and physical health sound. The health management was indigenous, within their control and without any side-effects, which reflects a favourable relation between the health and livelihood. On one hand, the resource availability was more than enough for a small population, their culture and customs were equipped with rituals for conservation and the protection of nature on the other. In this way, they depended upon the natural resources for livelihood and their culture protect and conserve the natural resources, which retain their ability to work. If we look at the tribal livelihood assets in the context of skill, health and the ability to work, then found it at crossroads, where on the one hand, tribal youth are unskilled for natural resource-based occupation, they are losing their indigenous knowledge from generation to generation, traditional healing practices are losing its importance, various complex diseases has been introduced in the region, as a negative results of industrialization and globalization, but the skill and the ability to handle modern economy has not been developed among them, on the other. There is the shortage of work availability, which is promoting the seasonal outmigration among the tribal lot.

(B) Social Capital

The social capital has an important role in the productivity of individual, organization and community (Ellis, 2000). It includes social resources including the informal network and the membership of formal groups. Social capital extends support in earning the livelihood and makes it sustainable at the time of stress or crisis. The community or collective ownership system is a better example under which the members of community earn, as per their capacity and consume as per their necessity; stress and shocks are being faced collectively. Maganga and Butterworth (2002) emphasized about the community ownership as a means of achieving the sustainability through community investment and commitment to the schemes. Borrowing believed the lending of money or goods is based on the informal relation without mortgaging of any valuable thing like gold, land or house, without interest. The repayment of debt seems to be the social obligation and be paid conveniently. Both formal and informal social networking is livelihood assets, which provide the sustainability to livelihood and enhance the overall productivity.

The sovereignty of tribal economy and mutual co-operation within the group or the community sustain their economy and fulfil the members need within the group. The informal institutions like family, kin group or community performed economic activity collectively; practice of exchange of goods and labour was there, which worked as the shock absorbent at the time of crisis. Over the time, the periphery of their social network has increased and reached the non-tribal community and their economic co-operation has shifted from within the community to outside community, but the system of exchange remained the same and they began exchanging of their forest produce and labour with money or goods of their requirements with the non-tribal community. However, they have developed a monetized economy, but still the nature of exchange is in formal and lacking in professionalism, except some newly emerged tribal elites. Hence, their social informal co-operation at the family level, the village level or the community level has lost its originality and function on the one hand and formal social networking with the outer world has not been developed, yet on the other.

(C) Natural Capital

Natural capital includes land, water, air, living organism and all ecosystems on the earth which are the basis of human economic activity and are necessary for human survival and well-being. In general, it refers to natural resources (Ellis 1996, 2000). In context of tribe, there was a symbiotic relation between tribal and their habitat natural resources, especially forest, so natural resources here refers to forest, soil, land, water, flora and fauna. Tribal communities lived in relatively remote isolated areas with their natural capital without much interference of outer world. Both tribe and their natural capital survive in this manner that their natural capital procures their livelihood and their culture protect and conserve their natural capital. In this manner, balance between both natural capital and their necessity were maintained which protected them from livelihood crisis and keept their economy sustainable. During British India, tribal right on their natural capital was encroached through various laws and policies like Forest Policy 1872, Categorization of forest and forest produce and Mineral Resources Act etc. After independence, the legacy of British India was continued with various changes. Selected integration approach was adopted and their access to natural capital was made limited. Although, their livelihood security was taken into consideration while formulating and implementing acts and laws but without ample acquaintance with alien occupation they were compelled to adopt it which resulted into livelihood crisis among tribal and after several decade they are still struggling for their livelihood.

(D) Physical Capital

The basic infrastructure like road, water sources, school building, health centres, sanitation facilities and machinery etc. refer to physical capital. Assets that help to turn raw material into finished products or services are physical capital (Ellis, 2000). Tribe had their indigenous infrastructures like zigzag path across the forest and wooden bridge over water stream for connectivity of house to house or village to village, natural water stream as source of water and they had their system of drainage and sanitation. Dormitories were there for education of youth where they were socialized with their culture and capacitated to earn their livelihood. These arrangements were present in every tribal community with meagre variations. Their traditional education system was replaced with modern education system, they were brought in contact with outer world and their economy was linked with modern economic system which increased their dependency on modern infrastructure which is lacking in tribal areas.

(E) Financial Capital

Historically, financial capital of tribes were in the form of storage of natural resources but monetization of their economy turned them towards cash and now they convert their labour and collected forest produce into cash to fulfil their requirement but saving cash is still absent among tribal at some sort because they are hand to mouth people. Whenever they require money, they sell forest produce, grain, labour and their cattle to earn cash. Their earning does not exceed their expenditure so they are unable to save money in cash even sometime it get shortage. Earlier, the mechanism of coping economic crisis was traditional where they helped each other with mutual borrowing and lending. Friends and relatives were the prime source of borrowing where they did not have to pay interest. Over the time, their informal institution of borrowing was replaced with formal institutions like *seth-sahukar* where they have to pay interest and problem of indebtedness increased among tribal that also resulted into bonded labour and land mortgaging among tribal.

Livelihood Context

The livelihood context or livelihood framework is a way of looking complexity of people's livelihood whether rural or urban and it is not only necessary to ensure appropriate development strategies but also for better monitoring, evaluation and a means of assessing potential for replication. Participatory Rural Appraisal (PRA), Rapid Rural Appraisal (RRA) and Participatory Learning and Action (PLA) are the approaches to understand context of rural development. The livelihood context can be understood through social, economic and political context.

The Social Context

It refers to the social settings in which people live or in which something happens or develops and institutions or people with whom they interact. In general, it is socio-cultural environment mainly the social relation, social structure and social organization. Weber in his work 'Protestant ethics and spirit of Capitalism' presented the ethics of ascetic Protestantism that in turn becomes the factor of establishment of capitalism (Weber, 1930). Weber also said it is the spirit of *varna* in India that militated against the establishment of capitalism there (Bendix, 1960: 208). In Indian context, he found social structure as resistance for emergence of capitalism. Similarly, when we look at the Indological and other interpretation of occupational structure in Indian society then found caste system at core to decide the occupation of any individual or community (Nesfield, 1885; Ghurye, 1961; Hutton, 1980; Klass, 1993). In Central India, tribal have interpretation of their origin and they have rich history which is inseparable part of their culture and religion. Social context differs from community to community but there is inter-linkages and few similarities among their cultural heritage. Their ethnic identity works as guideline to earn livelihood like shifting cultivation, gathering food, forest produce collection and craft work etc. Division of labour is also found among them and women participation in family economy is significant. Mutual co-operation among kins was found in economic activities whether in the form of labour exchange or good exchange. Social organization like traditional panchayat worked as decision making authority at community level for production, possession and consumption of produce for procuring livelihood security for each and every member of community.

The Economic Context

The resource access institutions and service delivery decide the economic context for livelihood security. Former refers to social norms, customs and behaviour that decide the attitude and nature of person to perform the economic activities and the later refers to effectiveness and responsiveness of delivery of services like education, health, water and sanitation by state and private sector agencies. Various factors among tribal community define the rule of the game means people's access to resources like *totem* and *taboo* which identifies the resources to be utilized and not to be utilized. State has intervened in tribal areas with formula of mixed economy which neither promotes capitalism not socialism for their development. With such an intervention, tribal are moving far away from their indigenous pattern of livelihood. State intervention has not been proved as effective and responsive and tribal alienation to their indigenous pattern of livelihood led them hanging between indigenous and modern economic system.

The Political Context

This includes form and quality of government system including structure, power, efficiency, right, representation, policy and policy processes. The country is governed by constitution through three branches executive, legislative and judiciary which works on principle of check and balance. Democracy made it possible to participate tribal in electing their representative at national and state level government. Reservation promotes their participation in administrative and other government services. The decentralization of power promoted three tier panchayati raj institutions for local administration which increased tribal representation in power structure. The constitution of the country gives fundamental rights and its directive principles of state for the development of weaker section for which various programmes and schemes have been formulated and implemented. The Ministry of Tribal Affairs looks into the matter of tribal development related to their health, education and living standard etc. Inspite of favourable political context they are still lagging behind their counterpart.

Livelihood Strategy

The livelihood strategies of rural and urban people are different within availability of livelihood assets, especially the livelihood strategies of rural people complex and diverse because not a single source of earning is ample as per their requirement. Tribal livelihood ends upon the forest but occurred changes have diversified their strategies too. Their strategies have been diversified to other strategies like subsistence production or production for market, planning for the sale of NTFPs, participation in labour market or labouring in agriculture or home and small household industries etc. Frequent institutional intervention for procuring their livelihood increased their hope towards external support. Their community based livelihood management system has lost its importance, their interdependency is losing its value.

Livelihood Vulnerability

The availability of livelihood assets may be affected by trends as well as shocks and seasonality. Livelihood vulnerability is external environment in which people exit and over which they have limited or no control. Trends in vulnerability context can be population trend, natural resource trend, national or international economic trend, political trend or technological trend. Shocks may be in distinct form like human, crop or livestock health shock, natural shock and economic shock which can make livelihood vulnerable. Seasonality of production; of price; of health; and of employment opportunities also affects livelihood security and downfall in such seasonality makes livelihood vulnerable.

Livelihood Interdependence

Very few livelihoods exist in isolation so the final characteristic of livelihoods is its interdependence. One livelihood may depend on other whether in form of assets or for exchange like manufacturer depend on producers of raw material, processers to prepare them and consumer to buy them. So, in preparing livelihood assistance programme it becomes necessary to consider the livelihood interdependence.

Conclusion

In order to look at the issues confronting the livelihood security of tribal people in general and tribal of central India in particular, it seems that at the transitional stage of occupational mobility which is diversifying their source of livelihood but insufficiency of livelihood assets makes their livelihood insecure and vulnerable. Human capital among tribe is weakening with loss of their cultural heritage and skill. Skill and knowledge among them is incapable to make them familiar with modern tools and techniques. This is not true that they are unwilling to accept changes but the pace of learning alien thing is quiet tough for them and they get it difficult to face the challenge of livelihood earning in an alien scenario. Their traditional education system has been vanished which was a platform of complete socialization. Dormitory was not a place of formal education but there were so many latent functions of dormitories like cultural teaching, economic socialization and moral development etc. It developed social capital among them but new education system is not sufficient for them in earning their livelihood because more or less the mode of earning livelihood among them is still in primary stage which is not covered in the courses. Their community based panchayats and community ownership are also getting out of the scene which is weakening their social capital. In this way both human and social capital are weakening against the requirement in alien atmosphere. Other natural and physical capital among tribal are also not much strong. Natural resources are depleting day by day and they are bound to exploit the resources at a limit. Infrastructural availability for basic requirements is lacking due to remoteness and dilapidated terrain of tribal areas. Their economy was non-monetized but with its monetization they are compelled to use currency also but their subsistence type of economy does not allow them to save money in hand which is hindering their strength of financial capital. Overall scenario of livelihood assets among tribal are being proved to be failure for livelihood security among them.

Social, economical and political context are not in favour for their economic empowerment. Technically, efforts have been made to enhance social, economical and political context among them but adherence to few old customs, financial crisis and ignorance towards statutory provisions for their development keeping them behind the bar of progress. It is necessary to fulfil the minimum requirement to avail the benefits of affirmative extensions but tribal are lagging in fulfilling it. Their old age practices to earn livelihood, their art and craft, their language and utilization of forest with conservational aptitude are seemed to be blurred in their mind and new practices are neither attractive for them nor easily amenable to them. With the poor livelihood assets and context, they are helpless to frame a livelihood strategy to make it secure. On one hand they do not have solid livelihood strategy their livelihood is prone to shocks and stress with natural resources depletion, unavailability of work, failure of crop due to climatic condition and less technical knowledge on the other.

In short, tribal economy of central India is at cross roads and their livelihood is not secure due to improper livelihood management. Various issues like literacy, basic infrastructure, health, revitalization of conventional skill and training etc. are required to be tackled properly.

Reference

Bendix, Reinhard (1960): "Max Weber: An Intellectual Portrait", New York: Doubleday and Company Inc.

Beteille, Andre, (1972): *Inequality and Social Change,* Delhi: Oxford University Press.

Burman, B.K. Roy, (2006): Draft National Tribal Policy of 2006: Creating Consternation, *Economic and Political Weekly,* August 26, Vol. 41, Issue No. 34.

Census (2011): Office of the Registrar General & Census Commissioner, Delhi: Government of India.

Chambers, R and G. Conway, (1992): *Sustainable Rural Livelihoods: Practical Concepts for 21st Century,* IDS Discussion Paper No. 296, Brighton, UK: Institute of Development Studies.

Chambers, R, (1989): Editorial Introduction: Vulnerability, Coping and Policy, IDS Bulleting, 2(2), pp.1-7.

Drinkwater, M & M. McEwan, (1992): *Household Food Security and Environment Sustainability in Farming Systems Research: Developing Sustainable Livelihoods,* Paper presented to the Adaptive Planning Research Team Bi-annual Review Meeting, Mangu, Zambia, April13-16.

Ellis Frank (1996): Rural livelihood diversity in developing countries: evidence and policy implications, (40). <https://pdfs.semanticscholar.org/6c8c/1e279da71ed5982580a2585389c9932b2549.pdf>

Ellis Frank (2000): The Determinants of Rural Livelihood Diversification in Developing Countries, *Journal of Agricultural Economics*, Volume 51, Number 2, pp. 289-302.

Frankenberger, T. (1996): 'Measuring Household Livelihood Security: An Approach for Reducing Absolute Poverty', *Food Forum*, No. 34, Washington DC, USA.

Ghurye, G.S. (1961): *Caste, Class and Occupation*, Bombay: Popular Book Depot.

Government of India, (2005), *'State of Forest Report 2005)',* Dehradun: Forest Survey of India, Ministry of Environment and Forests.

Government of India, (2006): 'Employment and Unemployment Situation among Social Groups in India', Report No. 516, NSS 61st Round, New Delhi: NSSO, Ministry of Statistics & Programme Implementation.

Government of India, (2012): *Agriculture Census Report 2005-06*, Agriculture Census Division, Department of Agriculture and Co-operation, New Delhi: Ministry of Agriculture.

Government of India, (2014): *Agriculture Census Report 2010-11*, Agriculture Census Division, Department of Agriculture and Co-operation, New Delhi: Ministry of Agriculture.

Government of India, (2015): 'State of Forest Report 2015)', Dehradun: Forest Survey of India, Ministry of Environment and Forests.

Government of India, (2015-16): Annual Report, New Delhi: Ministry of Tribal Affairs.

Hutton, J.H. (1980): (first published 1946), *Caste in India: Its Nature, Function and Origin,* Bombay: Oxford University Press.

Klass, M (1993): *Caste: The emergence of the South Asian Social System*, Delhi, Manohar Publishers and Distributor.

Maganga, F.P. and J.A. Butterworth (2002): Domestic Water Supply, Competition for Water Resources and IWRM in Tanzania: A Review and Discussion Paper, Tanzania, *Physics and Chemistry of the Earth,* Vol. 27, No.11, pp.919-26.

Mohanty, B.B. (2001): 'Land Distribution among Scheduled Castes and Tribes', *Economic and Political Weekly,* Vol. 36, No. 40, pp. 3857-68.

Murdia, Ratna (1975): 'Land Allotment and Land Alienation Policies and Programmes for Scheduled Castes and Tribes, *Economic and Political Weekly,* Vol X, No 32, pp.1201-14.

Nesfield, J.C. (1885): "Brief View of the Caste System of the North Western Provinces and Oudh Together with an Examination of the Names and Figures Shown in the Census Report 1882", Allahabad: North-Western Provinces and Oudh Government Press.

Sharma, B.D (1994): *Dalit Betrayed,* New Delhi: Har Anand Publications.

Srivastava, Vinay Kumar, (2008), Concept of 'Tribe' in the Draft National Tribal Policy, *Economic and Political Weekly,* December 13, pp. 29-35.

Weber, Max (2001): (First Published 1930), *The Protestant Ethic and the Spirit of Capitalism,* translated by Talcott Parsons, New York: Routledge.

Xaxa, Virginius, (2014): *Report of the High Level Committee on Socio-Economic, Health and Educational Status of Tribal Communities of India,* New Delhi: Ministry of Tribal Affairs, Government of India.

Chapter - 10

Credit Transactions and Tribal Land Alienation: [Kondh Tribe in Odisha Highlands]

— *Tapas . K. Dalpati*

Introduction

Tribal households face crucial challenge to maintain their livelihood in the present scenario. They could not resort to the traditional bases of livelihood due to widespread deforestation, narrowing down of habitat and fragmentation of land holding over the generation. As most of the tribes couldn't cope with financial turmoil in life, their land resources dragged into the process. However, the transfer of tribal land to the non-tribal is restricted under law; several informal tactics are being involved in the process of land transfer from the tribal to non-tribal. After independence, several measures have been undertaken to prevent alienation of land from tribal but the ruptured livelihood structure, informal credit transactions to maintain socio-economic liabilities gradually degraded their land resources.

Tribal land alienation has been widely discussed since long in India. In his seminal work 'Caste and Economic Frontier' Bailey analyzed the opening of tribal land to market in Bisipara village of Odisha. In this context, Bailey reiterated that sale of land of a peasant is directly related to his possession of other assets for meeting the contingencies in life (Bailey, 1957). Analyzing the informal credit practices among Kutia Kondhs, Mishra found that the informal credit practices are being the pivotal cause of land transfers from Kutia Kondhs through oral transactions. According to her for understanding the ongoing land transaction and intricacies of credit transaction, comprehension of Kondh's cycle of production season is very much necessary (Mishra, 2010). Viegas also analyzed the alienation of tribal lands and its dynamics in Odisha. He identifies the processes involved in land alienation and the ways and means devised by moneylenders, intermediaries and landlords in his study (Viegas, 1991). The present study is an empirical investigation of vicious cycle of lease-mortgage-sale of tribal land in Kondh dominated Thuamul Rampur region of Kalahandi district of Odisha.

The Field

The study covers two kondh villages from Thuamul Rampur block of the Kalahandi district. The two villages Mutachuan and Badchhatarang are located in the plateau of Thuamul Rampur Block of Kalahandi district. Mutachuan is a small remote village in the Kosabara Gram Panchayat of Thuamul Rampur Block. Kondh tribals dominate in Mutachuan village. Besides kondhs, dom, gaud and few paik families inhabited this forested village. There is less quantity of arable land under *bahal* and *berna* category available in the village. Most of the lands are of *mal* and *att* category. The village is being surrounded by Sringari Reserved Forest in the north and west, Semelpadar and Gondharamaska village is in the south and Kosabara village in the east. The villagers depend upon subsistence cultivation in the available arable land and most of the agricultural yields come from the shifting cultivation undertaken on the hills of Sringari Mountain. The village is full of fruit bearing mahul, mango, jackfruit tree, and deciduous forest including sal and piasal trees. In some of the hills, forest is protected by individual tribals for their sustainable use. The remote forested village is connected with the block headquarters with fair weather road. However, the village comes in between a track that connects the tribal area with villages of *hatti* river valley, which is now irrigated from the Indravati Irrigation Project.

In the lean agricultural season, the poor kondh tribal used to walk down up to 8 km for working in the irrigated fields of command area of Indravati project. The second village, Badchhatarang is one of the big kondh villages in the tribal land of Thuamul Rampur. The topography of Badchhatarang is relatively plain in relation to Mutachuan, but it also comprises the number of hillocks having scanty vegetation on it. Majority of villagers are Kondh residing with the *dom, gaud, paik* and distillrers *sundhi* caste people. The village is well connected with district headquarter Bhawanipatna through a crisscrossing road aside mountains. The kondh villagers generally walk down twelve kilometer to Thuamul Rampur to purchase weekly requirement from the local *hatt*. The village is surrounded by village Belangi in the west, Tasiguda and Dabiriguda in the south, Kamarghat in the east and Jamuguda in the north. The village history says that Badchhatarang is an important village in the *Langlabisi* a tribal clan area comprising group of adjacent villages Badchhatarang, Dabriguda, Champachuan, Kalduda, Sukli, Tasiguda, Balangi, Gandharamaska, Kumbharkani, Bagdiani, Jamguda and Kamraghat. The *Tara bisi, Banglabisi, Jhubia bisi* are the other kondh clan residing in the nearby forested tracts with whom kondh of Badchhatarang have matrimonial relationship. Badchhatarang is the biggest kondh village in the Mahulpatna area of Thuamul Rampur. The Odia meaning of Badchhatarang is 'big village mid way' perhaps the village is used for camping of travelers to erstwhile administrative head quarter Mahulpatna from Thuamul Rampur.

Livelihood Strategies - Challenges

Ancestors of kondhs established Mutachuan and Badchatarang by clearing the forest area in the Thuamul Rampur region. The kondh tradition says that 'seven hundred years ago, they (we) came to karonde or kalahandi and cleared the forest (rengal) and settled the villages...' (Deo, 2009: 155) In the pre-colonial and colonial period, kondhs are in charge of revenue collection and maintaining the law and order of the village, the kondh head is known as gountia at village level (Currie, 2000: 68). At present, both the villages the Kondh Gountias hold little land in his name and most of the land has transferred to other caste people through various means. Mutachuan is small village isolated from the mainstream society due to remoteness. Good quality land is scarce in Mutachuan and most of the villagers depend upon the *podu* (shifting) cultivation and collections from available forest products in the nearby Sringari forest range. Tribals from this village walk down to the irrigated village in the hatti valley for getting agricultural labour in the lean agricultural season, due to scarcity of agricultural land in the village. In Mutachuan, most of the farmers practiced settled cultivation in the available arable land and *podu* cultivation in the nearby Sringari forest range. In the available land Kondh farmers, produce paddy, mustard, mandia, maize. In the *Podu* fields of Sringari range, they produce alsi, kating, jhudung, jada, khedchana, kosla and kango. The village Badchhatarang has an undualting landscape with barren hillocks, once *podu* cultivation carried out in this hill slopes. Due to the undulating topography, farmers use bullock plough for cultivation of hill paddy, millets, ragi, grams etc. Besides cereal crops, various legumes, and grams are being sown with hoe in the hill slopes in the *podu* fields. In Badchhatarang villagers grow alsi, kating, jhudung, khedchana, kosla and kango in the hill slopes and paddy, surso, mandia and maize in the plain *bahal* and *berna* land available in the village.

Before initiation the process of *podu* cultivation in Mutachuan village, tribal council assesses the density of the forest for ideal patches. The hills with adequate vegetation without big trees are usually preferred for *podu* cultivation. After assessing ecological condition, the cultural conditions are taken into consideration for plot selection. According to kondh tradition, there should be a *dharni* altar established by earlier settlers in the patch to be selected as *podu* field. The hill god must permit the people to cultivate there. Therefore, before initiating clearing the forest rituals are performed to seek the permission of hill deity. In Mutachuan, slashing and clearing of the forest is usually done in the month of February- March. This act is known as *nel katkanaka* in kondh language. In the slash

Table 1: Main Occupation of the Households and Ethnic Groups in the Study villages

Occupation/Village	*Kondh*	*Dom*	*Gaud*	*Luhura*	*Paik*	*Sundhi*	*Total*
Badchhatarang							
Agriculture	60(80.0)	10(32.3)	25(56.8)	0	1(33.3)	4(57.1)	100(61.0)
Labour	14(18.7)	16(51.6)	18(40.9)	4(100)	2(67.7)	3(42.9)	57(34.7)
Service and others	1(1.3)	5(16.1)	1(2.3)	0	0	0	7(4.3
Total	75(100)	31(100)	44(100)	4(100)	3(100)	7(100)	164(100)
Mutachuan							
Agriculture	15(50.0)	2(40.0)	1(50.0)	NA	3(50.0)	NA	21(48.8)
Labour	15(50.0)	3(60.0)	1(50.0)	NA	3(50.0)	NA	22(51.2)
Service and others	0	0	0	NA	0	NA	0
Total	30(100	5(100)	2(100)	NA	6(100)	NA	43(100)

* Main occupation refers to the occupation that gives employment for more than 180 days in a year.

* Figures in the parentheses show percentage to the total

Table.2 Availability of Food in the Study Villages

	Kondh	*Dom*	*Gaud*	*Luhura*	*Paik*	*Sundhi*	*Total*
Badchhatarang							
Sufficient	6(8.0)	9(29.0)	5(11.4)	0	0	4(57.2)	22(13.4)
Average	11(19.7)	5(16.1)	9(20.5)	0	1(33.3)	2(28.6)	25(15.2)
Deficient	58(77.3)	17(54.8)	30(68.2)	4(100)	2(66.3)	1(14.3)	117(73.3)
Total	75(100)	31(100)	44(100)	4(100)	3(100)	7(100)	164(100)
Mutachuan							
Sufficient	4(13.3)	1(20.0)	0	NA	2(33.3)	NA	7(16.2)
Average	5(16.7)	2(40.0)	0	NA	2(33.3)	NA	9(20.9)
Deficient	21(70.0)	2(40.0)	2(100)	NA	2(33.3)	NA	27(62.7)
Total	30(100)	5(100)	2(100)	NA	6(100)	NA	43(100)

*Sufficient- Yield from agriculture provides foods for round the year and seeds for next agricultural season.

*Average-Yield from agriculture provides only foods round the year.

and clearing process, whole family contributes labour. The able men cut the big trees with axes and women cut and clear small bushes. If the patch for the *podu* is a big one and demands more labour, the owner seeks co-operative labour from the community or seek help of relatives from nearby villages. Kondhs of Mutachuan cultivate a patch of land for two to three years continuously. Then they abandon the field for vegetation to grow. This phenomenon is known as *pija manabu* (left to grow). In Mutachuan, tribals in the first year sow mandia, jhudunga, kangu, katinga in the *podu* fields. In the second and third year kosla, alsi are harvested from the same fields. As a rule, a patch of land may be cultivated for three to four years continuously. Then a fallow period of five to six years is being maintained to regrowth of vegetation. However, at present, it is being observed that even in the abandoned plot, vegetation growth is inadequate for *podu* cultivation, since last ten years.

The main occupation pattern in the study villages shows that majority of households in Badchhatarang (61 per cent) depend upon agriculture, whereas in Mutachuan, majority of households (51.2 per cent) depend upon labouring in agriculture and allied activities. The study of kondhs occupation in two villages show that majority of Kondhs (80 per cent) depends upon agriculture as main source of livelihood. In Mutachuan, equal numbers of Kondhs households depend upon agriculture and labour for their livelihood. One kondh household from Badchhaatarang serves the government of Odisha, in services and business sector.

Table 02 shows the pattern of availability of food from agriculture. The analyses of its availabilty pattern shows that, in Badchhatarang only 22 (13.4 per cent) households is able to get sufficient food, 25 (15.2 per cent) households get average food and majority of them consisting 117 (73.3 per cent) households are suffering from deficient consumption pattern. In the remote and forested village of Mutachuan, only seven (16.2 per cent) households are able to get sufficient food, nine (20.9 per cent) households have average food consumption and 27(62.7 per cent) households have deficient food consumption pattern in the village. Analysis across the ethnic composition of the villages shows that about 58 (77.3 per cent) kondh households

Table 3 Landless Households and Average Landholding

Village	*Total hh*	*Landless hh*	*Average land*	*Total land*
Badchhatarang	164	33 (20.1)	3.4	458
Mutachuan	43	9 (20.9)	5.2	180

* Figures in the parentheses show percentage to the total in the category

Table 4 Lands and Average Landholding of Ethnic Communities

Village	*Kondh*	*Dom*	*Gaud*	*Luhra*	*Paik*	*Sundhi*	*Total*
Badchhatarang	219 (3.5)	96 (4.1)	95 (2.8)	4 (1.3)	NA	44 (4.4)	458
Mutachuan	141 (5.8)	11 (2.7)	8 (2.6)	NA	20(4.0)	NA	180

* * Figures in the parentheses show average landholding (acre) among the landholders within the ethnic community in the village.

of Badchhatarang and 21 (70 percent) of Mutachuan kondh households have deficiently supported by agriculture for their food consumption. In the study villages only majority of sundhi caste households in Badchhatarang, are able to get sufficient foods from the agriculture.

Land and Credit Transactions

Before delving into analysis of the nature and process of land transfer, it is necessary to look into the land holding pattern of the two study villages of Kalahandi district. As mentioned earlier in the previous section, Mutachuan and Badchhatarang is located in the *dongerla* area of Thuamul Rampur Block. Mutachuan is a small *dongerla* village with 43 households and 193 acre of ryots land which is only 54.3 per cent of the total available land in the village. Likewise, Badchhatarang is a relatively plain village with 164 households and 335 acre of ryots land which is account for only 29.1 percent of the total land area of village.

Average land holding pattern in the study villages infer that in Badchhatarang 33 households (20.1 percent) are landless and in Mutachuan there are 9 landless households and they account for 20.9 percent of the total households in the village. Barring the landless households, the average land holding structure of the villages are 3.4, and 5.2 acres for Badchhatarang and Mutachuan respectively.

The average land holding pattern among different ethnic communities shows that ethnically kondhs holds an average of 3.5 and 5.8 acres in Badchhatarang and Mutachuan respectively. It is also evident from the table that non-tribal sundhi caste households are holding highest average land of 4.4 acres in Badchhatarang. However, in the remote village of Mutachuan kondh are still dominant demographically as well as in landholding position and they holds an average of 5.8 acres, which is highest in the village.

It is necessary to note here that Kondhs are the original settlers in the two villages. Other communities are new comers to the tribal kondh land of Kalahandi. Gradually the kondh community is exploited by various means by the incomers' caste either due to changing land revenue policies of colonial rulers or through dubious means of credit transactions. The sundhi caste people are also immigrated to Badchhatarang area from Umerkote region of Koraput district. They have acquired good quality tribal land illegally through selling liquor and lending money to poor kondh tribals in the region.

Analysis of landholding classes in Badchhatarang village shows that of the total 75 kondh households, 13 are landless which account for 39.3 percent of total landless households in the village. In the same group 8 dom, 11 gaud and one sundhi households are also there. In almost all the ethnic communities most of the households hold less than five acre land. Only one household from kondh tribe and two households of dom caste hold more than 10 acres land in the village. In this village though, Kondh are dominant in landholding position, dom and sundhi caste households have been acquiring good quality *bahal* land from tribals through lending money in the time of their necessity. It is important to stress here that all the four small shops located in the Badchhatrang are holds by Scheduled Caste doms from outside the village who usually lends money to kondhs in the time of their need.

Land holding structure of Mutachuan shows that out of 30 households of kondh six were landless, which account for 66.4 per cent of the total landless households of the village. Majority of households from all ethnic communities hold less than five acre land. Only one household from kondh tribe and another paik household own more than five acre land in the village, whereas only three kondh households hold above ten acres of land. In the remote village of Mutachuan kondhs were dominant ethnic community, but due to gradual interaction with non-tribal communities from the neighbouring villages, these Kondh households started lease and mortgage outland to the dom and gaud caste people, who resided outside their village.

The main reason for landlessness is the losing of lands through vicious circle of lease-mortgage-sale by the kondh tribal. Before discussing the credit transaction and its relationship with lease, mortgage and land transfer, it is necessary to understand different connotation for landholders and creditors in this region.

According to local kondhs; sundhi, doms and gauds are ryots in their village. Mishra's work decipher the verbatim from a kondh 'the sundhi never had land; they have been buying it from us and cultivating' (Mishra, 2010). Kondhs consider the landholding creditors as *mahajan* who lend them money at the time of their need.

Different types of credit transactions are prevalent in the kondh dominated Thuamul Rampur region. *udhar* (unwritten credit) is a form of simple borrowing of rice or maize for consumption, this does not have any interest as the period of repayment is of small duration, spanning for one or two months. When *udhar* is not paid, it charged with an interest *(kantar)* and it becomes *rina*. This is also applied to borrowing money for marriage, festivals and for even seeds for agriculture, which carries about 50 to 100 percent interest rate. This also involves the condition of mortgaging of different valuable assets like land, when *mahajan* feels that creditor is not capable enough to simply pay back the loan.

The above mentioned credit transaction operate in the interests of the *mahajans*. The *mahajans* give money to kondhs, because not only they want to get more money of the transaction but also they keep an eye over good quality *bahal* and *berna* land possessed by kondhs in the region. As agriculture is rain-fed and yields from agriculture last barely for three to four months. Kondhs need money at the time of distress situation like drought and emergency medical need. Another social vice that compel tribals to lending of money is the *Jula or harja* (bride price) practice prevalent among the kondh and numbers of festivals which need money for animal sacrifices and alcohol for merry making.

In the Thuamul Rampur region, the *mahajan* does not trust the *kondh* tribals in lending of money. They only lend money to those tribals, who have some asset in disposal. As the tribals have no other material assets, land is dragged into the credit transaction at the time of need of Kondh tribals. The kondhs never sale their land, as they consider it as their mother. Land is the most important natural asset and imperishable endowment, from which the kondhs derives his life and sustenance (Nayak, Boal and Soreng (1990: 97) To understand the complex process of money lending and its relation with land transfer is a very crucial issue because nobody wants to discuss it openly from the fear of revenue officials. In Mutachuan and Badchhatarang Kondhs are depending upon shifting cultivation, cultivation on encroached land and labouring outside the village. In the time of scarcity, they usually take *udhar* from the local mahajan assuring that they will repay the rice, maize, or money after the harvest. Where as in maximum cases tribal is unable to pay the *udhar* due to crop failure, drought and compel to lease out the land for one year or two year to repay the *udhar.* In case in between the period if the tribal needs more money, the mahajan (Money lender) convert the earlier lease to mortgage of the land of the concerned kondh tribal. In case of repayment of the loan, the tribal has to pay the interest on the loan amount. The Mahajan gives loan to those households, who have the repayment capacity, otherwise the defaulter kondh tribals have to mortgage some land as collateral item until the repayment of the amount calculated at the time of mortgage. However, most of the mahajans cheat the Kondh tribals while calculating repayment value of loan or fraudulently enhance the paid of money in case of mortgage, as most of the kondhs were illiterate. Unable to pay back the loan and having mortgaged the valuable land, Kondhs keep on asking for financial help to mahajan and gradually the debt become beyond the paying capacity of the poor tribal to get back their land. In Some cases, kondhs assume that they have sold land to mahajan, as they were unable to return debt. In some cases, tribals want to get back the land, but their financial incapacity constrained them to get back the same.

Therefore, in Thumul Rampur region credit transaction starts from udhar and gradually turns into rina and involve land initially as lease and subsequently, it is converted to mortgage and finally to sale. It is an astonishing fact that the tribal always not accept their land being sold to mahajans. On the other hand, mahajans say that they have purchased the land even if the land is under a lease agreement. From this, it can be assessed that how far the mahajans are optimistic about getting the land as sale from the kondhs tribal even at the initial phase of credit transaction.

In the highland of Thuamul Rampur lease of land is known as *katti bandha* and it is very often practiced by tribals to get small consumption loan that is udhar. In katti bandha the moneylender (mahajan) cultivates the land and supposed to return the land after specific years. During these years, the crop produced was retained as repayment of the loan. However, in most cases, the tribals need more money during the lease for various needs as the most valuable productive land was leased out. In this case, mahajan is in a very advantageous position and agreed to give more money against mortgage of the same land. In Thuamul Rampur region, mortgage of land is known as *kado bandha*. Under *kado bandha*, the creditor has to repay the loan totally to get back his land. In a rain fed economy, marginal and small tribal farmer unable to repay the borrowed huge amount finds the land under the control of mahajan, until the repayment of principal amount. In the meantime, if the creditor needs more money, the tribal have to sale the land to mahajan. As transfer of land to non-tribal is illegal in this scheduled area, the mahajan keeps on cultivating the land without going for the mutation process required for legal transfer. If in any case, the moneylender wants mutation, he does it under another tribal's name illiterate, obedient to the mahajan and agreed not to disclose anywhere. Therefore, most of the tribal land sale is not reflected in the record of rights of the villages.

Lease-Mortgage-Sale in Study Villages

In this study, it is being envisaged to understand the lease-mortgage and sale of tribal land to non tribal in the two kondh villages. For understanding of the credit transaction among various communities is very much important to understand its origin and spreading out of the same. For this comprehending self sufficiency regarding arranging food for kondh household is very-much needed. For the kondh tribals the best month of the year are '*bhudo lenju*' (September) and '*diar*' and *pusa' lenju* (November - January). The availability of food and credit is totally determined by the cycle of season and cultivation pattern of kondh tribals. '*Bhudo lenju*' comes after the usually hunger months (April to August) and hill paddy is being harvested from *podu* plots. For Kondh tribals, October and February to March months are easy to survive, because one can avail *udhar*, simple borrowing of rice and millets for consumption. Getting *udhar* is difficult in March, when it is regarded as *rina,* which accompany an interest rate of hundred per cent. The most difficult period for kondhs is lean period of April to August when output from one's own agricultural production is exhausted and *udhar* from *mahajan* is not available. It is in this period, most of the *udhar* converted to *rina* and lease agreements turned into mortgage of land, or the sale due to most distress conditions (Dalapati, 2008)

In Bachhatarang village, the analysis of buyer and seller of land transaction shows that two kondh households purchased 3.5 acre kondh land and 17 kondh households sold 28.5 acre land to various communities. It is important here to specify that most of land were lost to dom and sundhi caste households of Badchhatarang and neighbouring village of Latiaguda, Birikote and Gandhramaska. The dom, scheduled caste households were the highest buyer of land in last twenty years. Six dom households have purchased 11.5 acre of land in last twenty years and three dom households sold five acre of land in and outside village. Three sundhi caste households also acquired 6.5 acre of land in the village. Most of the lands acquired by non-tribals were kondh land through various fictitious means, but mostly practiced formula is purchasing of tribal land in the name of another tribal, who is illiterate and obliged to the purchaser. The land mortgage pattern of Badchhatarang shows that only two prosperous kondh households mortgage in 2.5 acre land in the village, whereas 11 kondhs households mortgaged out 16 acre land for various reasons. Six scheduled caste dom households mortgaged in 12 acre of land mostly from kondhs trifbals. Only two dom households mortgaged out four acre land due to various economic reasons. Three sundhi households also mortgage 8 acre land from kondhs. A sundhi household has mortgaged out 1.5 acre land to another sundhi household in the Badchhatarang village during data collection. Analysis of land lease pattern in Badchhatrang shows that three kondh household leased-in four acre land in the village. On the other hand, 12 kondh households leased-out 19 acre of land due to various economic reasons. Six households from dom caste leased-in 8.5 acre land and three dom households leased out four acre land for various socio-economic reasons. In the same pattern three Gaud households have leased- in 6.5 acre and three households of same caste leased out 2.5 acres of land. Three households from prosperous sundhi caste leased-in 5 acre land mostly from kondhs and one sundhi household leased out 1 acre of land to a sundhi household in Badchhatrang.

Land transfer pattern of remote village Mutachuan shows that only one kondh household has purchased 1.5 acre of kondh land, whereas six Kondh households lost 8.5 acre land to other communities of Mutachuan and neighbouring villages. In this village, two dom households purchased 5.5 acre of kondh land through various fictitious means. As most of the land in the village is Kondh land, it is transferred through mortgages to the non-tribals during last twenty years. Land mortgage pattern of Mutachuan depicts that only two prosperous kondh mortgage-in 2.5 acre of kondh land, whereas six kondh households mortgaged-out 14 acre land to other communities mostly to outside villagers of Gandhramaska and Birikote. In this village three dom household mortgage-in 5.0 acre kondh land, whereas one dom household mortgage-out 0.5 acre land to a same caste household. Lease of land in Mutachuan shows that two kondh households are being leased-in 2.5 acres of kondh land, where as many as nine kondh households leased-out 19.5 acres of land to other communities, mostly to dom caste households of the neighbouring villages. In this village, two dom households leased in 3.5 acre kondh land and one paik households 2.5 acre kondh land, whereas one household from dom and Paik caste leased out 1 and 0.5 acre land respectively to dom households in the village.

A close observation of lease, mortgage and sale of tribal land in the above two villages depict that all the land transaction are related to credit transaction with non-tribal communities. In Badchhatanang and Mutachuan most of the land has been passing to non-tribals through vicious circle of lease-mortgage and sale.

Kondh households were interviewed to understand trajectories of sale and mortgage of their land in the two villages, to evaluate over the above process. From the analysis, it was found that in Badchhatarang, 17 Kondh households have sold land amounting to 28.5 acre. Out of the total land sold 19.5 (68.4 per cent) acre sold by 11 households (64.7 per cent) preceded by mortgaging of the same land to others. In Mutachuan, six Kondh households lost 8.5 acre land through sale. Out of the total land sold 5.5 (64.7 per cent) acre sold land were being preceded by mortgage of the land to the some *mahajan* by three Kondh (50.0 per cent) households.

To ascertain whether the mortgaged lands were preceded by leasing-out of the same land in the two tribal villages leasing and mortgage practices were analysed. It was found that in Badchhatarang 16 acre kondh land have been mortgaged-out by 11 households. Out of the total land mortgaged nine (56.2 per cent) acre was earlier leased out to the some *mahajan*. In Mutachaun 6 Kondh households mortgaged-out 14 acre land out of which eight (57.1 per cent) acre involved in lease process earlier to the same *mahajan*.

In the analysis of land transfer from kondhs to non-tribal communities, it was found that in maximum cases sale of lands are preceded by mortgage of the same land in all the villages. Kondh households require money for various reasons, and they at first take *udhar* to compensate their day- to-day need. If the requirement is a big amount, the *mahajan* gives it as *rina* with an interest. If the creditor is borrowing money beyond his repaying capacity, his land is being mortgaged as collateral items. When the mortgage becomes unmanageable, kondh tribals compel to dispose off the land to *mahajan* orally and *mahajan* becomes the *de facto* owner of the land. All these process undertakes orally and transactions were not reflected in the village Record of Right, until the purchaser go for mutation process in the office of the Tahsildar. As the sale of tribal land to non-tribal is illegal and punishable under OSATIP Act, most of the land sale kept secret from the purview of revenue official or mutations are undertaken by bribing the revenue officials.

An analysis of causes of selling out of the kondh land in the two villages, it was found that in Badchhatarang maximum number of Kondh, households sold land for debt repayment

(3 households - 4.5 acre) and the expenses for solemnising festivals (three households 4.5 acre). However, maximum quantity of the land is lost for drinking habit of the kondh tribals in the village (two households - 5.5 acre). In Mutachuan maximum households sold land for debt repayment (two households - 1.5 acres), expenses for festivals (2 households – one acre) and alcoholism (two households - One acre), whereas the maximum quantity of land finds lost for debt repayment and paying of medical expenses in both the kondh dominated villages.

Analysis of the causes behind mortgage out of kondh land in two kondh tribal dominated villages shows that in Badchhatarang maximum Kondh households mortgaged land for festivals (three households - 3 acre), household expenditures (two households - 2.5 acre) and debt repayment (2 household - 3.5 acre). In Badchhatarang maximum land mortgaged out for debt repayment (3.5 acres). In Mutachuan, maximum Kondh households mortgaged out their land for debt repayment and payment of *Jula* (bride price) price in the time of son's marriage. Maximum quantity of land is mortgaged out for debt repayment to the *mahajan* (5.5 acre) in Mutachuan village.

The analysis of causes responsible for leasing out of Kondh land in the two villages shows that household expenditure requirement is the main cause of leasing out of Kondh lands for most of the households. In Badchhatarang, maximum land was leased out for debt repayment and Mutachaun maximum quantity of land was leased out for household expenditure.

To understand the circumstances under which kondh tribals were compelled to lease-mortgage and sale out their land; case studies are recorded from concerned households in the two study villages.

Case Study - 1

Leli Majhi lives with his wife Suni and their two children in Mutachuan village. Suni has developed some chronic gynecological disorder and suffering from bad health, since last twelve years. Rameshwar Naik, a quack from nearby Birikote village treated Suni since last ten years. Unqualified Rameshwar failed to cure the disease. Suni is under treatment of Rameswar's medicine, but cannot relieve from the ailment. Since last ten years Leli Majhi has incurred heavy debt from other fellow villagers. He could not pay the medicine and treatment charges of Rameshwar and sold his 1.5 acres of *bahal* land to him. Leli does not know about, how much amount he borrowed from Rameshwar in the form of medicines or treatment fees. However, the sold land has not been transferred legally to Rameshwar, but he has been cultivating the land since last four years.

Case Study - 2

Gardu Majhi is the present gountia of Badchhatarag village. After partition of the landed property from his father, he was left with 18 acres land in the village. Gardu living his life lavishly sold three acres land to Baya Majhi of Belangi village. He was an alcoholic, and lost 2.5 acres to Kalia dom of the Badchhatrang, who was a liquor dealer. Recently, he mortgaged four acres *att* land and subsequently sold the land for household consumption to Samdhu Naik of Birikote village. He himself told that his father has around 72 acres of land in the village, but his brothers lived like pauper, because they could not manage their land and livelihood properly.

Case Study - 3

Sitaya Majhi is the brother of Gardu Majhi of Badchhatarang village. He had 7.5 acres land in the village. Sitaya Majhi leased out 2.5 acres *mal* land to Santosh Naik of Badchhatarang for Rs 4,000 for four years in order to repay his earlier debt taken for household consumption and medical expenses. In the mean time, he had to marry his only son, for which he borrowed another Rs 2,000 from Santosh Naik. Now, the earlier leased land is mortgaged under *'kado bandha'* and Sitaya Majhi has to repay Rs 6,000 to get back his land from the mahajan. In the mean time, eight years have passed and Sitaya Majhi now realised it as difficult for him to get back his land.

Case Study - 4

Kalidesi Majhi of Badchhatarang had four acres of land in the village. He was an alcoholic person and consumes liquor of twenty rupee every day. This costly habit incurred him a heavy debt of Rs 2,500 to the sundhi *Mahajan* of nearby Latiaguda village. After repeated demand for the repayment of money, Kalidesi worked as labourer in the liquor factory of the mahajan for some days. However, he could not repay his debt by working for mahajan. At last, he compelled to sell his one-acre good quality *bahal* land to the sundhi mahajan to repay his debt.

Case Study - 5

Ramei Majhi of Mutachuan village had 5.5 acres land in the village. Ramei has a very big family of six children and his wife. All the children were below 14 years of age dependent upon Ramei and his wife. In 2003, Ramei's crops were damaged by scanty rainfall and he ought to incur an *udhar* of Rs. 1,000 for his family's food. He was unable to repay money to Sataru Naik of nearby Kosabara village and compelled to mortgage his 1.25 acres *mal* land to the mahajan. Since then, he was not able to pay back his debt under the *'kado bandha'* agreement.

Case Study - 6

Halmei Majhi of Badchhatarang village has three sons and two daughters. He owned 8.5 acres land in the village. During 1998, he mortgaged his 2.5 acre *berna* land to Sakli Naik of Berikote for paying '*Jula*' or '*Harja*' price at the time of marriage of his second son for Rs. 5,000. In 2004, he again married his third son and second daughter for which he again borrowed Rs. 3,000 from Gopal Sahu, a sundhi *mahajan* of the Latiaguda. Already indebted, Helmei Majhi, now does not know how to repay the debt for mortgaged land, and he know that he have to mortgage some land to Gopal Sahu, if he is not able to repay the *rina* within a year.

Case Study – 7

Rengo Majhi of Mutachuan village and his children starved during the hunger months of June 2001. He went to the village mahajan Dhansingh Majhi for an *udhar* of *Puti* rice (80 kg.). In the mean time, his wife expired and he was compelled to take a *rina* of Rs. 1,500 from the same *mahajan*. He could not repay the *rina* within one year and subsequently mortgaged 1.5 acre *att l*and to the kondh *mahajan*. Some four years went on and the poor Rengo Majhi couldn't repay his debt to get back his land.

Conclusion

The complex process of lease, mortgage, and sale in two villages of Kalahandi shows that most of the land transfers from Kondh tribals were enmeshed with the structure of credit transactions prevalent in the tribal region. As capacity of agricultural yield to supply the consumption need of the Kondh households was very weak, they usually take *udhar, rina* from mahajan. When they are unable to pay *udhar*, they lease out some land to clear the debt. If amount of money involved in the loan is substantial, the *mahajan* lend it as *rina,* with a high rate of interest. In case of lease, Kondh only loss access to the agricultural produce for one to three years, but when the land was involved in a mortgage transaction land was retained by the non-tribal *mahajan* till the payment of the principal amount. As kondh of Thuamul Rampur area living in undulating area, where the yield from agriculture was very meager, kondh were compelled to take loan for household consumption during the hunger months by leasing out land. In maximum cases, they were trapped by the moneylender, if the amount needed by them is big one. In these cases, they compel to mortgage their land in order to get the loan. In most of the cases, Kondh mortgage their lands, when they need a big amount for medical expenses, *Jula* price, or repayment of accumulated debt. It is found that in very few cases, kondh go for direct sale of the land, unless the requirement was extremely important and no other option was left to them. The kondhs were now facing dual challenge to manage livelihood after being displaced from the *dongerla* areas due to upcoming mining projects in the Kashipur and Lanjigarh area. In Mutachuan.forest village, majority of households have to walk down the irrigated areas of Indravati in search of agricultural employment. The condition of kondhs of Badchhatarang remains very deplorable, as they have no other option but to depend upon the agriculture in their degraded lands. Therefore, maximum cases of lease, mortgage and land transfer cases were found among the kondhs of Badchhatarang, which involved a substantial amount of land in the village. During the study, priority was given to understand the land transaction process. The tribal land involved in the lease-mortgage and sale processes identified during the study were only tip of the iceberg. A significant number of cases were difficult to capture during the study due to its dubious nature and involvement of revenue functionaries. Therefore, the new Forest Right Act may seems to be a silver lining for landless tribal in the Scheduled V areas of Kalahandi, but to ameliorate the real conditions of tribals, introduction of a more effective and sustainable policy to manage land resources held by tribal is highly necessary.

References

Bailey, F.G. (1957): *Caste and the Economic Frontier: A Village in Highland Orissa.* Manchester: Manchester University Press.

Currie, Bob (2000): *The Politics of Hunger in India,* Chennai: Macmillan India Ltd.

Dalapati, Tapas Kumar (2008): *A Sociological Study of Land Alienation of Tribals*, Unpublished Ph. D. Thesis submitted to Vikram University and M. P. Institute of Social Science Research. Ujjain.

Deo, Fanindam (2009): *Roots of Poverty: A Social History*, Bhubaneswar: Amadeus Press.

Mishra Arima (2010): *Hunger and Famine in India: An Anthropological Study*, New Delhi: Dorling Kindersley (India) Pvt. Ltd/ Pearson Education in South Asia.

Nayak Radhakanta, Barbara M. Boal and Nabor Soreng (1990): *The Kondhs: A Hand Book for Development,* New Delhi: Indian Social Institute.

Viegas, Philip (1991): *Encroached and Enslaved: Alienation of Tribal Lands and Its Dynamics*, New Delhi: Indian Social Institute.

Chapter - 11

Tsunami on the livelihood of Katchal Nicobarese

— Shailendra Prasad Sinha

Introduction

Wherever man has lived, the land underwent a set pattern of standardized interaction with the place of residing for survival. It is important to know the way man deals with the place of living in and interact for different needs. The latter depends on time and space. Thus bare facts of livelihood is the urgent academic need of the day, especially when the community of Katchal Nicobarese of Tihunyu island encountered *tsunami* devastation [December 2004]. It becomes more and more important to document their indigenous skills with indigenous knowledge of the self-development coupled with standardized behavior in their style of survival, before and after *tsunami*. The way of culture being constructed focused on their style of food for survival and related activities – gathering, producing, growing, storing, processing, consumption, distribution, exchange, trade and marketing etc, following the nature's fury. But in doing so gods, goddesses and ancestors for the Katchal were considered by them as very important in various way for e.g., food taboos etc.

Methodology

The author has taken account of the overall feedback, while supervising and guiding the PhD research work of Mr. K.M.

Sinha Rai of Anthropoligical Survey of India. His fieldwork was being done through *emic* and *etic* approach, as if the study forms a case study of Katchal Nicobarese in the light of pre and post Tsunami implications on the livelihood of Nicobarese. Census 1991 puts the Katchal population as 2,491 in Tihunyu Island out of 12 islands inhabited in Nicobar group of islands southeast of Bay of Bengal between 06° – 10° N latitude and between 92° – 94° E longitude. Nearly 10 kms of stretch got submerged following the fury. As sampled, it based on the data collected from villages – west bay and Kapand village of Katchal, besides Jula, Junshin, Upper katchal and Pounda villages as well. Tsunami occurred in the Indian Ocean [December 26, 2004 at 06:30 AM], the superficial fury in the history of mankind, the most powerful earthquake of its kind in 21^{C}. Katchals are Mongoloids, traditionally dependent on the forest and sea. They believed in the harmony of distinct ecological setting. They lost strength in both terrestrial and aquatic resources – an irreparable damage, following the fury. But Katchals are tried their level best for themselves with the existing situation even in their small surviving number in dismal figures with the help of welfare measures at their doorsteps from outside agency - governmental and non-governmental.

Andaman and Nicobar Groups of Island

A - N Groups of Island emerged in the deep sea during tertiary period. It comprised calcareous sand stone hills with long stretch of landmass having acreage of 62 square miles covered with dense forest, full of coconut, rubber plants in good number of fructifying and nonfructifying trees. Its soil solum was very good, worthy for plantation, surrounded by the sea stretch.

The group of islands was a heaven for hardcore criminals of the mainland peninsula in separate flock during the British era. The area developed mixed population. Largely, the Nicobar group of islands remained far-south with its inhabitants, except four villages with mixed multi-ethnic population. Jarwas, Shampens and Sentanales in isolation inhabited in the far south. Nicobarese inhabited nearly seventeen islands. It is larger in comparison with Andamanese and very less Jarwas, Shampens and Sentanales were there farther south.

The Katchal Nicobarese

Nicobarese inhabit the Katchal islands with 24 villages. Some 20 of which were near the sea and four were multi-ethnic villages farther from seashore. The Katchal Nicobarese had been homogeneous, shifting horticulturist and settled villagers. They maintained a distinct and unique cultural identity than others, as regards the inheritance of property, marriage rule and other traditional customs, best adapted to their habitats. Their tradition was imbedded in strictest monogamy exclusively conditioned by their ecosystem, in consonance with the livelihood. In general, the Nicobarese were nontotemic and indivisible group in clan and sub-tribes except the place of residence, to which they are being addressed like one Katchal Nicobarese and so many others. Either Katchal boy used to embrace "Gulam" tradition to serve his in-laws and shelter in wife's "Tuhet", which means family or Katchal girl used to settle in her in-laws "Tuhet" by becoming Gulam of her husband's family only due to the existing livelihood only to manage with the coconut orchards and shifting horticulture besides forest and sea as well. Katchal's family dwelt in a hut and remained small in size, different from eleven other islands. In majority, these were Christians and lesser animists. But, the uniqueness was reflected in their settlement pattern of patrilocal, matrilocal and bilocal tradition of living – a distinct feature of Katchal Nicobarese, totally an arrangement based on needs. They had been well translated in their spirit world known as "Iwi" of two types. Benevolent spirit was called "Iwi-ka" and malevolent spirit "Iwi-pat". The fear of Iwi was a guide to all people in all walks of life. Miniluana had been their spiritual head for all religious factions, accepted universally amongst Christians and animist as well.

Katchal Settlement [Pre and Post- Tsunami]

The tribals had good forest cover on one side, whereas on the other, they have settled. The "Tuhets" surround their "Golghar" i.e., Nyihopol. As such, everywhere they had "Iwi" in the forest and on the island, so in the Golghar, they had several anthromorphic form of wooden effigies to safeguard life all the time. The rhythm of their life was well-translated through the spiritual world developed in the effigies guided by Miniluana. "Reves" was their God, omnipresent to protect them all the time and brought rain for the Nicobarese. Yam, banana, coconut, pendanus, various other fruit and vegetables grew well, due to the mercy of Reves, on their belief.

Tuhet System

They were living in villages. The families ranged from nuclear to joint one. The few joint families made a "Tuhet" within the lineage group headed by "Nyitokarui-henlocha". Thus in Katchal, there were several Tuhets. Each Nicobarese was supposed to have a Tuhet and a Golghar.

Villages

There were 35 Tuhet, in the west Bay Katchal. The entire Bay along with 35 Tuhet and Golghar got completely submerged following the fury. Likewise, in Pounda village, there were 40 Tuhet and Golghar. They submerged together in the sea. In "Jula" village out of 27 Tuhet one Tuhet alone existed, but forest and coconut trees were completely destroyed. In Kapang village, out pf 36 Tuhet only two existed but the village was entirely destroyed. East Bay Katchal had seven Tuhets, where only three Tuhet existed.. Four out of 24 villages survived in Katchal islands, but with heavy damage. Seventeen Nicobarese and three multiethnic villages were found to have vanihshed without any trace of existence. There was no Golghar and no Tuhet was without loss of large number of family members following devastation.

Division of labor

They had a pragmatic division of labor system. Male performed hard labor, whereas the female used to do oil making, domestic work besides assisting male in shifting the horticulture, canoe making, gardening, pig herding and food gathering. The tsunami damaged their very division of labor system at heavy toll collapsing the cultural heritage. Loss of Tuhet member in large number brought a very difficult situation before the Katchal Nicobarese, as if, wits-end, as how to manage or regenerate things for survival and escape sudden developed precarious situation.

K-Nicobarese Livelihood

Forest and seas were so deeply penetrated in their way of life without which they even could not dream of surviving any more. Accordingly, they had developed their ethos and the world views along with the fear psychosis, embedded in their developed spirit world. The seas could be seen as an ultimate source of food and survival. Their livelihood was typolized in horticulture, coconut plantation, food gathering, fishing, hunting, herding and off late wage earning.

Food Gathering

They used to meet the basic needs besides collecting fuel wood, wood for making household, making Golghar and canoe (hori); they used to collect plenty of Pandanas, different types of fruits, roots and tuber, pigs, birds and medicinal plants, through exploitation of natural resources. The forest traditional foods– Yam, banana, pandanas, tapioca, coconut and plenty of wild fruits, root and tuber from the forest were usurped. Largely they had non-vegetarian dishes, preferably of fish, pork, mutton, beef, chicken etc. collected from forests and the seas, as well. Those included from the very sources - terrestrial as well as aquatic sources. From terrestrial resources, they used to get wild boar, python, pigeon, other birds, deer, wild goats, crocodile and bee-honey, as well for flesh as food besides varicty of fruits, roots, tubers, birds, leaves, nuts, jungle potato, nuts, areca nuts, which they used to collect from the forests. By way of aquatic sources, they had four ways – from deep sea, shallow water, creek and fresh flowing water. All the family remained busy daily in fishing and collecting edibles from the aquatic and forest sources.

Fishing

Fishing was very important for life to get food in terms of flesh in three ways: marine, creek and fresh water. Daily they used to do fishing through their small "Hori" canoe near the seashore to get material for daily consumption. At times in a group of five to six persons occasionally a voyage was arranged along with food for some 2-3 days. They used to sail in the deep sea farther the Tuhet and do large scale fishing. Huge quantity of fish caught for consumption was brought to the seashore and equally distributed among them. From the fresh water by applying mostly throwing nests they could get fishes, molasses etc. for immediate consumption on better taste. They used line fishing with nylon thread and hook, during rough weather in heavy rains. In all, they could apply indigenous wisdom of judging what to [not to] do by looking at the colour of water, wind weather conditions with the help of "Hinrio-kahe" traditional calendar.

Hunting and Bird trapping

Plenty of birds, deer, pigs, wild goat were found in the forest of Katchal. They used to keep bow and arrow, nets for trapping and fastening and other equipment made up of their own. Daily as well as occasionally hunting and trapping was the order of the day to get plenty of food in terms of flesh which used to constitute more than 50% of their food intake, rest beverages and then cereal product depending on availability.

Pig herding

Pig was essential for them and their ancestors. Pig was an important source of livelihood and to appease their ancestor's spirit. It was a gift by ancestors as per belief. Hence, the pig herding by the Katchal was indispensable for them, more or less, when phenomenally, each and every family used to herd the stock, as if, the very culture moved round. One who possessed more pig was considered a worthy man of pride. Feasting and gifting attracted the livestock. Besides, it was an asset for exchange all the time within the island, or even outside through voyage. On all occasions, the pork was used aplenty. It was thus a need-based flesh for consumption and appeasing of spirits, as if, pig was meant and the ancestors.

Horticulture

It played a dominant role in their livelihood. In Katchal Island, the Nicobarese used to do shifting cultivation. At first a patch of land was selected wherefrom wood and underwoods were cleared with the help of relatives (Tuhet members), neighbors, friends on the specific day fixed by the witch doctor i.e., Miniluana. Generally, it was done in between March and April. Logs and fuel wood were taken out for domestic use leaving twigs and leaves to dry in the scorching Sun. Generally, in the late April dried materials were burnt to ash. Thus with the onset of pre-monsoon on a fixed date by the witch-doctor, small holes were dug to accumulate stock of ashes in the dug hole, to work as a fertile bed for plantation. They used to prepare garden by fencing it in a typical jig-jag way from the wooden pieces. Miniluana was used to worship in presence of relatives and friends during May. That very day plantation of Yam, Tapioca, Banana and other crops were done after sacrificing pig and chicken to appease the concerned spirit. Oozing blood was sprinkled in the center for good harvest. The harvest was done known as "kin-ni-on", in the month of December. They used to face scarcity of food between April and December generally, the plot was used for two years and the next plot was selected for future for shifting cultivation. They went off-late for cultivating vegetables and fruits successfully for self-consumption.

Coconut Plantation

Katchal economy, a stable source of livelihood remains the backbone of their economy. Major areas of island forests were occupied by coconut, abundantly growing wild. They used to manage by their age-old identification mark to demarcate the area or plot for whose individual or Tuhet that belonged to. Coconut tree used to grow, bearing fruit after eight years of age and used to produce 50 ripen nuts every year (Mathur :1967) and having an average life span of about 40 years. Nut picking was done throughout the year. Ripened nuts keep falling down. Small nuts were eaten by pigs, rest nuts were collected by members of the owner. They used to pluck fresh nuts to get fresh water, toddy, kopra, coconut oil, broom, wood for pillar foundation, household, for Golghar and leaves for thatching huts and shells for drinking cups. They used to eat kernel, fed the pig, chicken and make oil from the coconut. On any function or occasions, they used to do spirit worship. Usually, they feed tender coconuts to infants as a staple food, in addition to breast feeding. As per statistics, it was believed, out of three coconuts, pig eats one, one was meant for kopra [dry kernel], leaving one for self-consumption. Coconut plantation was done in cyclic manner. Before hand, worthy coconut trees were selected and reserved. Good quality of nuts was plucked for sapling and seedlings. All were kept in a dampen area near indigenous water source. Nearly more than 100 coconut saplings were being planted, separated by 10 feet in between. Any of those beds used to grow well. At first for the foundry operation, they dug earth to plant the half covered sprouting nut, with the start of a registered co-operative. It was in. early 50's named "Manulamati Ltd.", Katchals started selling their products – kopra, coconut, arica nut etc. to the co-operative body. They learnt monetization and started to procure rice, wheat flour, dal, onion, potato, sugar etc. for daily consumption besides clothes, cosmetics and seasonal clothes. That has brought a fundamental change in the life pattern of Katchals.

The Barter Exchange

Katchal Nicobarese is the champions in their ageold barter economy. Taken together, materials from aquatic and terrestrial sources, they used to sail big boat on a voyage in a array of 3-5 boats across several islands of Nicobar area from North to South in clockwise direction. They used to barter coconut [copra], pig, fishes, vegetables and other materials of use as per the need in the neighboring island. It was done in their dumb barter system. That way they could get materials of their use in exchange. As if their barter exchange was another source of livelihood – A purely tribal way of life persisting in Nicobar area of islands. They had three sets of pursuits of livelihood – One from the forest, other from the sea and third one through the voyage of barter exchange across Nicobar group of islands. But, tsunami devastation destroyed all the voyage system putting a big fear psychosis among the Katchal Nicobarese.

Impact: Post – Tsunami

The deadliest action of Tsunami brought a big loss of human souls, wild life in the forest dismantled and washed away

Nicobarese Tuhet, their Golghar and all other material culture, which they had within five minutes in the early hours. In majority of the forests, the Tuhet along with villages were devoured by the sea and now the remaining ones started struggling as what to do [what not to do]. Various rescue operations by the government and NGOs from various corners came to serve the island dwellers. Since the edible and non-edible materials were washed away, they had to face starvation death, various types of ailments, complete loss of potable water, shelter, their ageold food system. That way the Nicobarese katchals had to rebuilt their infra structure for their survival. Obviously the food items supplied from the outside like bread, rice, potato, some fruits and other materials which they did not use earlier was a new thing for them with a new taste giving rise to a new way of dependency.

Conclusion

No doubt man makes his fortune for himself. Nicobarese Katchals have come on the path of livelihood regeneration depending on the three ultimate sources – forest, seas and barter exchange thereby. They have started to turn life in a meaningful way, step by step, which they have had in their memory mustering courage. In the absence of surviving knowledgeable persons, they face an impossible task to make it possible anyhow at the axis of self or with the help of others. Definitely, it will come up some day well translated with the ecological surroundings in future. Change in all walks of life and the emerging livelihood is witnessed but old ways of persistence re-emerge, as if a new pattern of culture is up by way of culture reconstruct mixed with largely persisting old camouflaged. An old perspective as such remerges with challenges galore!

References

Census of India; (1991): **The Andaman and Nicobar Islands**; Part-I and II, Vol.II Calcutta: Central Publication.

Mann R.S.; (1976): **The Bay Islanders** Calcutta: Institution of Social Research and Applied Anthropology.

Chapter - 12

Tribes of Jharkhand and their means

— Chaturbhuj Sahu

Jharkhand literacy means "land of forest and hills". It is a picturesque area with forest and hills galore. It has an area of 1,8746 sq km. The present state (created on the November 15, 2000) had only 7,9741 sq km. It ranges 380 km [north~south] and 463 km [east`west]. Of the total geographic area of 7,9741 square km, one-third of it falls under the category of agricultural land. There are vast forest resources. The total forest cover is 29.61 per cent of the total area. It includes teak, gamhar, mahua, sal, kusum, mango, ber, bel, tendu etc. Agriculture productivity measured by foodgrain yield includes the cereals and the pulses, which is lower than the bordering states. The overall backwardness of the state is evident from the infrastructural index besides various historical, political, social and cultural reasons. The state has remained economically backward and the limited availability of infrastructure has made the process of economic development slow (Sahu, 2009).

Jharkhand is one of the tribal populated states. The people have been categorized into 32 communities, which show heterogeneity in socio-cultural life. They are generally found to live in hilly regions, inaccessible to others, in the zones of lesser interaction. They constitute 26.3 per cent of the total population. Their socio-culture and religious life is quite different to the so called advance cultural groups of the society. They practice self-contained, self-sufficient and autonomous subsistence economy.

They have had some special salient features, which make them unique. The cultural identification or the way of living is still strong. So, they are culturally at widely different stages of social as well as economic development (Sahu, 2001, 2008).

Some of the tribes still cling to their abodes in forests. They emulate crude technology and simple ways of life at the same time there are others with higher levels of economy following gradual adoption to the nature and ecology. The latter practice pastoral economy, slash and burn cultivation or agriculture with ploughshare while some others depend on simple industries having some sort of socio-economic symbiosis with neighboring communities (Bhaowmick, 1990.) The basic economic activities of tribes force them to face economic crisis in poverty, isolation and segregation. In this way, we find the poorest of the poor, most backward amongst the backward people and they suffer from chronic poverty, economic insecurity and in many cases social injustice.

Means of livelihood

The Tribal livelihood is based on land and its related activities. They are primarily subsistence oriented and earn livelihood from forest, agriculture, livestock etc. Now, modern means especially for them on daily wages, where the laborers have been playing a big role in the livelihood.

The tribals fully depended upon forest for livelihood, due to simpler technology. The forest has two significance. Firstly, it acts as preservative agent through humus conservation of humus, retention of the top soil and governing the water flow. Secondly, it provides the basic needs to creatures including human i.e., edible forest products, timber, fuel etc. The tribals prefer to make their abode in forests due to availability of basic needs throughout the year on the basis of tangible assets, they decide upon their livelihood. Good levels of resources affect the quality of life and standard of living. Besides, forest satisfies deep rooted sentiments. However, the industrialization and big projects have destroyed their livelihood in particular and socio-economic life in general. Forest occupies a central position in the tribal economy. It is not only the hubs of their life, but has been a source of substance. The ecosystem for centuries had been inextricably bound up with the tribal communities. In way they, as forest dwellers, were the real custodians of the forest. The communities had their own customary laws for it and its resource management. They used to regard forest as their own property and hence, never exploited its devastating state.

The forest and tribals have had a symbiotic relationship through ages. They know better and still follow their own customary practices, as to which type of plant was to be cut at appropriate time of the year. They are familiar with and have a thorough knowledge about its growth, maturity and decay available in their own ecosystems. Their mode of management with other forest resources is based on age old experience. Tree felling is being undertaken with the advice of village council and performances of other necessary rituals. This phenomenon is indicative of the fact that the tribals have the perception of relative values of different plant types (Behura, 1982).

The tribals remain intimately associated with it from birth to death. A tribal life cannot be thought of without the forest. It is a supernatural entity for the tribal. He offers a twig to the presiding deity of the forest as a sort of obligation, on his day-break entry.

Tribal Economic grading

The economic condition of tribes varies from the region to region. There are few tribes who can be termed as 'pure hunters'. Many of them supplement their crude farming with hunting, fishing, and the few basically lead pastoral life. Thus on the basis of economy classification, the tribes had been made by the eminent anthropologist in whom L.P. Vidyarthi's (1975) classification has been widely accepted. His classification was based on the cultural affinities and technological achievements. He believes the tribes have been categorized into eight types viz., forest hunting, shifting or slash-burn cultivation, plain agriculture, simple artisan, pastrol, folk artisan, agricultural and non-agricultural laborers type and those engaged in service and trades. The *Jharkhandis* fall in the above mentioned type except pastoral and folk artisan type.

Forest hunting

Birhor and Korwa tribe are the examples. Hunting is very important source of livelihood of Birhor. Hare trapping is most important. They reach forest for its trapping, arrest for four or five days in a week around except during the rainy season. It is very difficult for any Birhor to live without forest because forest not only provides food but also remains the playground, right from the very birth to the death.

Their economy may be divided into the following categories–

- Traditional
- Modern
- Occasional

The traditional economy can be subdivided into two-main and subsidiary types.

Main economy –

- Hunting and trapping
- Rope and Rope made articles
- Food collection
- Herbal medicine
- Honey collection

  Mat making comes under subsidiary economy. Daily waged labourers have become the modern economy of tribes.

The earning from traditional type of occupation seldom provides enough resources to maintain their family, so they have been forced to accept the different labour jobs at different labour centres.

Shifting cultivation

Sauria paharia and Mal paharia tribes of Santhal Pargana division still earn livelihood by doing shifting cultivation on the hilly and denuded lands. However, the government attempts to ban such practice. Now, they are being compelled to adopt settled cultivation. They are in the transitional stage of settled cultivation, but it has become difficult task upon typical topography. The traditional shifting cultivation of subsistence crops finds supplemented by collection of various kinds of roots, fruits, leaves, honey etc.

Simple artisan

Asur, Birjia, Lohara, Karmali, Mahali, Chick bariak etc; are skilled in manufacturing several items in their respective home industries. Asur and Birjia are traditionally iron smelter while Lohara and Karmali are the manufacturer of agricultural and household articles from iron. Mahali is expert in making different kinds of baskets, winnowing fans, brooms etc; from bamboo for using agricultural as well as religious purposes. Chick baraik is very expert for making cloths. These items produced by the tribe of this category are very much demanded in the neighboring villages and weekly markets.

It has been observed that these tribes are not good bargainers in selling the goods, that is why the rate of their products varies from individual to individual.

Now smelting of iron is completely vanished but making of the items from iron is in practice among Lohara and Karmali tribes.

Pastoralism

Pastoralism has become one of the important sources of livelihood of almost all tribe. Rearing of goat to a great extent depends on the availability of different kinds of leaves from the forest. Forest is the huge resource for grazing the goat so they are seriously thinking over adopting this job. The goat is regarded as ATM machine. Rearing of pig is common while rearing of cattle is meant for well settled tribes viz Santhal, Munda, Oraon, Ho, Kharia, Chero, Kherwar, Bhumij etc. In this way we find that keeping of livestock plays a significant role in their livelihood.

Plain Agriculture

Land is an important asset for Santhal Orgon, Munda, Ho, Khari, Kherwar etc. The yields of remain is the main source of livelihood for them, but for others it will be the secondary source.

During 19th century, each tribe with more than ten acre of land has admitted it as the primary source, but now the situation has changed. Previously, all land was not cultivated every year. Some leftover followed in order to regain their fertility. But, now they try to cultivate *Aghani* as well as *Bhadai*. *Aghani* is the most important crop, which is followed by *Bhadai*.

The tribal communites maintain and manage economic activities well. For the economy is the base of those activities in life. It provides food, which is the foremost important need of any living organism on earth. Human beings are more systematic for their economic production and gains than animals, because they chose various ways and means to generate various articles of need and comforts in their daily chores (Soni, 1998).

Summer is the lean season. They remain free from agricultural work. They get involved in such activities on the onset of monsoon. Just after setting first shower in the month of June, the fields find ploughed and the seeds were podcast. They still follow the traditional Indian plough, which is being done with the help of bullocks. The agricultural implements are being indigenous to them.

Tribal Agricultural Areas

The term "Agricultural Regions" refer to an area characterized by homogeneity in agricultural conditions, especially of crops or crops grown and of scientific dissimilarities from the conditions in adjacent area in an entity in which agricultural scene finds essentially the same (Jha, 1991). On the basis of different crop associations, four types of agricultural regions in the tribal areas of Jharkhand were recognized.

Table 1: Agricultural regions and tribes of jharkhand

S.N.	*Agricultural region*	*District*	*Tribal community*
1.	Rice, Maze, Gram	Latehar,	Oraon, Chero, Birjia, Kherwar, Korwa, Parhaiya,
		Garhwa,	Birjia, Chero, Korwa
		Palamu,	Kherwar, Chero, Kisan, Parhaiya, Korwa, Munda, Kanwar

(Contd...)

		Lohardaga,	Kherwar, Mahali, Kisan, Asur, Parhaiya, Gond
		Gumla,	Oraon, Asur, Baiga, Munda, Kharia, Gond, Kanwar
		Hazaribag	Santhal, Munda, Bedia, Karmali, Parhaiya, Mahali
		Ramgarh	Santhal, Munda, Bedia, Karmali, Oraon, Birhor
2.	Rice, Maze, Ragi	Chatra	Munda, Kherwar
		Hazaribag	Santhal, Munda, Bedia, Karmali, Oraon, Birhor
		Giridih	Santhal, Munda, Mahali, Kol, Birhor
		Bokaro	Kora, Santhal, Munda, Birhor
3.	Rice, Ragdi, fruit and vegetable	Ranchi	Munda, Gond, Kisan, Savar, Lohara, Mahali, Chickbaraik
		Khunti	Munda, Gorait, Baiga, Khond, Chickbaraik, Lohara
		East singhbhum	Bhumij, Gond, Santhal, Munda, Bathudi, Savar, Hill Kharia
		West singhbhum	Ho, Bhumij, Gond, Hill Kharia, Savar
		Saraikela	Bhumij, Munda, Kharia
		Hazaribag	Santhal, Munda, Badia, Karmali, Oraon, Birhor,
4.	Rice, Maze, fruit and vegetable	Dhanbad	Kora, Santhal, Munda, Birhor

The **Table 1** shows that Hazaribag district is the only district, which comes under first three agricultural regions, while other districts are being specialized for having only one agricultural region. It seems that the suitability of the area and the food habits of tribal people is favourable for the district. Rice, maize, grams etc; are being the favorable cropping in Latehar, Garhwaa, Palamu, Lohardaga, Gumla and Ramgarh districts. Rice, maize, ragi region is found in Chatra, Hazaribag, Giridih and Bokaro districts. Rice, maize, fruits and vegetables were grown by the people including tribals in Ranchi, Khunti, Kolhan area and Hazaribag district, while fourth agricultural region occurs in Dhanbad district where rice, maize, jawar, ragi and other inferior crops were grown commonly.

Jharkhandis are very cautious for performing cultivation well, but their industrious labour mainly depends upon the nature. If the season remains favorable, they get good crop, else they had to languish like a beggar. Very few tribal people cultivate rabi and pre-kharif crop due to lack of proper source of irrigation. They grow different kinds of crop, but this is only meant for consumption of family members (Sahu, 1998,2001,2005).

Rice is the first ranking crop in all tribal districts. Besides, they also cultivate various types of paddy grown in Tanr, millets like Gondali (panium – millate), maize (zea- mays) and madua (elsie-coracana), pulses like sutru (phaseolus-calartus), urad (phasweolus-radaaus), kurthi (doicos-biflorus), massor (ervum-lens) arhar (cajnas-indicus), vegetables like potato, sweet potato, tomato and another seasonal vegetables. They are experts in growing different crops through crop rotation and different cropping method. More than 80 kinds of paddy are being grown from different types of paddy fields on the basis of qualities of field. Though some hybrid breeded grains were being used by them, but most of them are unhappy to use this rice. They are of the very bad opinion about the hybrid rice. They feel hungry immediately after lunch, whereas the food made of from traditional rice is being more durable. So they avoid the use of hybrid paddy seeds.

The improved technological methods were used by the non-tribals for getting much product, but the tribals are not in a position to adopt any improved technology due to the lower level of economic condition.

Cropping System

At the end of lean period, they eagerly wait for onset of monsoon, so that makes them fit for rendering services in the field. During the agricultural season, all the members of family remain busy in different works as per convenience, but women comparatively get no time to rest. The field is ploughed by men folks. For growing maize, the man ploughs the field and women follows the ploughing path for sowing, one by one, at a certain distance.

Madua is planted in the month of Ashar. They complete sowing of Gondali within the middle of Bhado. This is the season of harvesting maize and madua. In Ashwin, harvesting of Godadhan starts. Sravan is the best and favorable season for plantation of paddy on the appropriate soiled land. On the very first day of ploughing the field, the elder male member gets up early and after reaching the field with burning fire in a piece of tile, and offer the mix of dhup, ghee, jaggery in the field to the concerned deity to save the crop from evil eyes. He keeps regular watch thereafter till plant harvesting.

The tribals take care of Khalihan before harvesting. Women take special care for washing the floor twice or thrice with cowdung. Harvesting is being done by men and women. Thrashing is being done by bullocks and buffaloes. Winnowing is being done with the help of winnowing fan. Generally, two persons take part in this job. Boiling, drying, husking, cleaning, paddy pondering etc are being considered women's work.

Pattern Planning

Agriculture is the most important sector of the Indian economy. It contributes about one-fifth of the national income besides employment to about three-fifth of the working population of the country. The traditional method is the basic way of doing agriculture throughout the country. In some of the states, the farmers have adopted new technology for better yield. The adoption of new technology and use of varieties of seeds, assured irrigation, fertilizers, insecticides, pesticides etc. have been helping in transforming the subsistence of agriculture into the commercial one. Though the yielding is no doubt better, but it takes too much money within short interval. Adoption of new technology is unfavorable for them for they are not in a position to spend huge amounts of cash on purchasing market supplied farm inputs to carry their production operations.

Several tribal groups tried their level best to cultivate fields with the support of the money lender, which caused indebtedness among them. The existence of indebtedness among them has become serious matter. Hybrid seeds have made them handicapped, on adoption of new technology. It requires proper training. So, the government should provide maximum need-based facilities, comparatively for a longer period. It will ultimately make the glorious position in the field of taking multiple crops in the available land, and the youth will take care in the agricultural side. Besides, they are also in need of proper training for planning of maximum yield from the available land by adopting new technology and other required items, so that they may remain attach with their cropping pattern.

Skilled workers

Significant number of tribes come under this category. They earn livelihood from the employers of respective organization. They are happy with the job and attempt to maintain the quality of life.

Conclusion

The tribal people are concentrated in the hilly and forested areas from time immemorial. They have adjusted themselves in different ecological and eco-climatic conditions. There was no serious threat to their livelihood till the immigrants to their belt. The symbiotic relationship between tribals and forest was unaffected, but encroachment of their land by the outsiders has destroyed their livelihood and culture. Globalization, popularization of transportation and commercialization of cropping pattern have been making them unsafe and unsecure. It has negative effect on their means of livelihood and quality of life. Hence, it needs to be examined seriously from closer angle.

In the changing eco-system and increasing population, the agriculture situation has reached its critical position. The problems of agriculture have become deep-rooted, especially for the settled agriculturist tribals. For securing maximum crop production, the best use of available land ought to be made highly fertile. Modern methods of crop husbandry ought to be taken into consideration.

The National Bank of Agriculture and Rural Development (NABARD) has been supporting welfare projects for scheduled tribes in the country under its Tribal Development Fund. The Wadi Project is one such integrated tribal development initiative of NABARD. Its main features is the economic uplift of the tribal farmers through sustainable agriculture, social employment, and improvement in quality of life. The Wadi model started in Gujrat during the 1980s should be extended up to the tribal dominated areas of Jharkhand.

The present scenario of the forest and the question of livelihood of tribals, not only of Jharkhandis but the entire country have been raising issues galore related to the conservation of the forest. The forest department should be taken into consideration about the role of tribals as the real custodian and conservation of flora-fauna. Hence, it is imperative to reestablish symbiotic relationship between tribals and forests for conservation as well as for providing sustainable livelihood to tribals.

It is suggested over a need for collective intervention by the government and civil society organization to address various issues for sustainable livelihood of the tribal people with their active participation. It will make the glorious position for their means of livelihood and quality of life.

Reference

Behura, N.K. (1982): "Forest and tribal world-view", Journal of Social Research, XXV, I : pp 1-8.

Bhowmick, P.K. (1990): Applied-Action Development Anthropology, Calcutta.

Jha, G.P. (1991): "Agriculture", A Systematic Geography of Bihar (Ed.) L.N. Ram, Patna: Patna University, Geographical Society.

Sahu, Chaturbhuj (Ed.) (1998): *Tribal Culture and Indetity*, New Delhi: Sarup and Sons.

Sahu, Chaturbhuj (Ed.) (2001): *Indian Tribal Life*, New Delhi, Sarup and Sons.

Sahu, Chaturbhuj (Ed.) (2005): *Aspects of Tribal Studies*, New Delhi: Sarup and Sons.

Sahu, Chaturbhuj (2008): "Cultural Identity of Tribes of Jharkhand", *Jharkhand Journal of Social Development*, 1: pp 139-45.

Sahu, Chaturbhuj (2009): "Tribes of Jharkhand and their Cropping Pattern", V.B. Jr. of Economics, 1, 1: pp 45-52.

Soni, L.N. (1998): Cited from Chaturbhuj Sahu's Book *Tribal Culture and Identity,* op.cit.

Vidyarthi, L.P. (1975): *Rise of Anthropology in India*, Vol. 2, New Delhi: Concept Publication.

Chapter - 13

Livelihood Strategies of Kolam: A Case Study

— *Nisheeth Rai*

Introduction

There has been a focus on human well being and reduction of human inequalities, with the introduction of economic reforms in India. The foci are generally on the rural society and especially on the vulnerable social group like scheduled tribe (S.T.) and scheduled caste (S.C.). Besides guaranteeing them, the civil rights and protection against atrocities and crimes, well being also encompasses the individual attainment in the areas of education, employment, health, sanitation, housing, water and electricity. This is perhaps the inclusive growth, which is the essence of development strategy across the economies. For achieving inclusive growth, generation of productive and gainful employment with decent working conditions on a sufficient scale is critical. The development of the ST and SC are also critical, as they are the most marginalized section of the society.

There are some tribal groups, who are characteristically benighted in the different dimensions of their way of life. Some of them to have adapted to mainstream at one of the spectrums. Economically, they still indicate their specific trend of continuation of the archaic pattern of existence. Living very close to nature and their utter dependence on the bountiful natural resources, their way of life and basic philosophy have been molded accordingly. Any sort of severance from deep-rooted matrix results in an unbalancing situation. [Annual Report 2011]. They have been specially identified as the Primitive Tribal Groups (P.T.G.) or Particularly Vulnerable Tribal Groups (P.V.T.G.) by the Government of India. The basis of P.V.T.G. [See Figure 1].

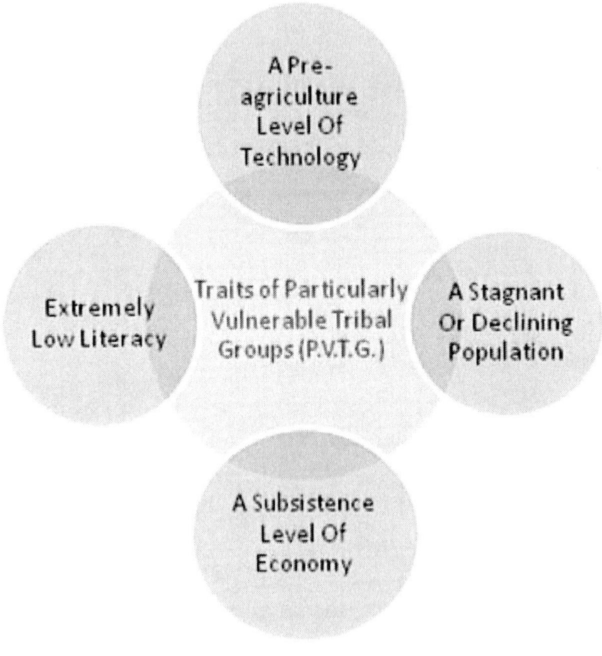

Figure 1: Traits of Particularly Vulnerable Tribal Groups (P.V.T.G.)

Kolam tribe is classified as Particularly Vulnerable Tribal Group (P.V.T.G.). It was mainly found in Yavatmal, Chandrapur, Nanded and Kinwat districts of Maharashtra state bordering Madhya Pradesh and Andhra Pradesh. In the latter states, they are classified as Scheduled Tribe, but in Maharashtra state they are being recognized as Primitive Tribal Group by the Government of India. Out of the four criteria mentioned above, the author finds only one which is subsistence level of economy applied to Kolam population of the study area. However, if we include **indebtedness as a criteria of P.V.T.G,**. then each and every family of Kolam will be a P.V.T.G.

The Kolams are of Dravidian ethnic group (Russell and Hiralal 1916). Census 2011 accounts their population in Maharashtra as 1, 73,646, when it stood at 1,77, 989 [Census 2001]. Research report (TRI, Pune) suggest it as being a settled cultivators' developmental programmes related to agriculture, irrigation, social forestry, health and education will be of immense help in for development of this primitive tribe.

The issue of development of Particularly Vulnerable Tribal Groups (P.V.T.G.) has been engaging the attention of the anthropologists, planners and administrators, since the planning process started in India. Despite almost six decades of planning, the Scheduled Tribes in general and Particularly Vulnerable Tribal Groups in particular continue to lag far behind in terms of infrastructure facilities, health, education and other social and economic development. On the other hand, due to urbanization, multipurpose projects etc., a large population of P.T.Gs. has been migrated from natural habitats and are facing biological, social, cultural and livelihood problems (Chaudhuri 2005). Most of the natural resources including minerals are being located in tribal areas.

The statistical profile of scheduled tribes in India (2013) shows that the main livelihood activity of the vast majority of PVTG in central India as labour and agriculture. The second major livelihood activity is being linked with the forest economy and pastoralism. The collection of minor forest produce particularly after harvest and selling them to various market provide them food security. Hunting is now no more a viable source of livelihood.

Review of Literature

Kurlanska (2011) defines the livelihood as the activities of individuals in relation to their resources and opportunities and how households manage these resources in an attempt to improve their living conditions. Whiteford (1985) and Cliggett

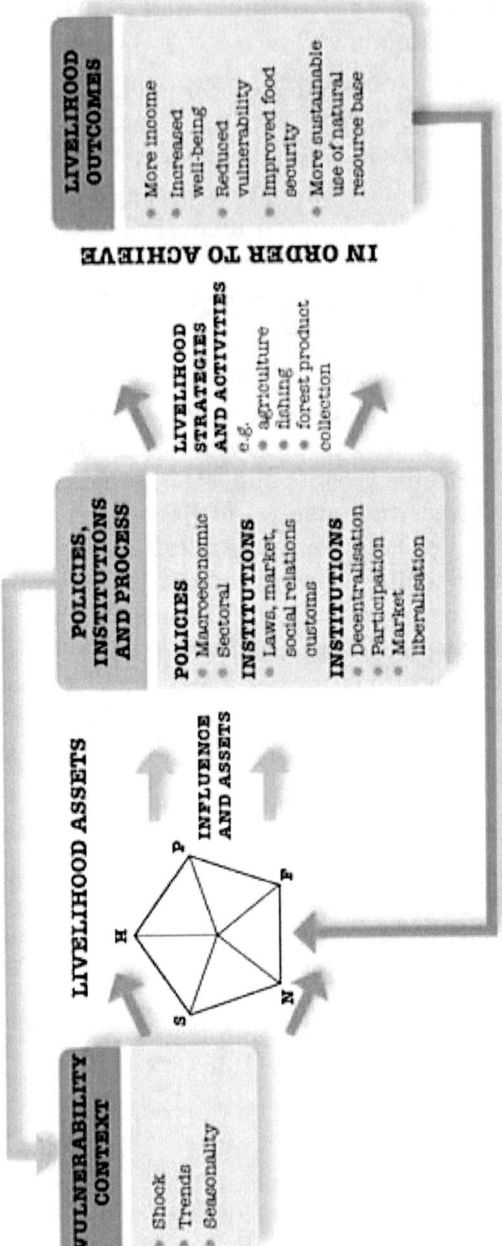

Figure 2: The Sustainable Livelihoods Framework (SLF from DFID).
Legend: H: Human; P: Physical; F: Financial; N: Natural; S: Social

(2007) observe that understanding the livelihood will help in understanding the social dynamics of households. At the center of the livelihood, the approach in development will be an understanding of the assets available to individuals and households, including social, human, financial, natural, and physical capital (Department for International Development ["DFID"] 1999) shown in **Figure 2**. In addition to assets, the two main facets that must be considered when examining livelihood decisions are structure and vulnerability (Rakodi 2002). Structural factors include organizations, institutions, policies, and legislation that influence livelihood decisions. Vulnerability is the uncertainty that individuals deal with due to changes in the political, economic, social, or ecological environment. Both dimensions are central to examining livelihood decisions associated with agriculture, labour and collection of forest product. Agriculture and collection of forest product involves high levels of vulnerability due to climatic uncertainty, while labour is dictated by structural factors and can have high levels of risk. Lont and Hospes (2004) call for the examination of how the livelihood strategies involving agriculture, labour and collection of forest product shape social process and constrain opportunities.

Methodology

An approach by development organization makes it easier to incorporate the academic research into applied realm. Their individual motivations and strategies are often very different, despite same household members working towards the common goal. Ethnographic research provides an excellent opportunity to uncover the differences. The author attempts to examine the livelihood strategies used to make ends meet by households in *Kolam* communities. Here each of the key factors specified in the above model forms an ethnographic perspective. The primary data arrives from the fieldwork of minor project related to bio-cultural analysis of *Kolam* under the supervision of the author [November 2012 to February 2013]. It is to be noted that the findings given below is related only to the Kolam[s] of the place at the above mentioned time following the telephonic talk on November 20, 2016 with the informant. [This portion of the data need not be included with the supplied data]. For, the data of *Kolam* community utilized in this study is located in village *Tejani*. The village *Tejani* is being located on Ralegaon Tehsil of Yavatmal district in Maharashtra, India. It is situated 16km away from the sub-district headquarter Ralegaon and 58 km away from the district headquarter Yavatmal. The total geographical area of village is 843.01 hectares. *Tejani* has a total population of 745. There are about 171 houses in the village, out of which 31 households belong to *Kolam*. Yavatmal is the nearest town to Tejani, approximately 58 km away. It has electricity, concrete road, wells, and hand pumps, with irregular bus service[s]. The residents are primarily farmers and labourers.

Objective

The author attempts to examine the strategies to make ends meet by households in *Kolam* communities. A DFID model with an ethnographic touch facilitated with the outcome.

Findings

The findings relates only to the Kolams of the place at the above mentioned time, but not to those of Kolams with the rest of India. The first thing to examine with a DFID livelihood's approach is **assets**. Narayan and Pritchett (1999) define the assets as resources that augment one's income, but are not entirely spent in the process. **The different types of assets include human, social, financial, natural, and physical capital.**

Human capital

This refers to the household members' 'capabilities' in terms of the number of members and their age, education and health. The Human capital (related to Age, Gender, Literacy and Health) of Kolam in Tejani Village is shown in the table 1 and 2 below.

Table1: The age, gender and education components

Name of the Village	*No. Of Households of Kolam*	*Population of Kolam*		*Pop. 0-6 yrs. of Kolam*				*Literate population of Kolam*		
		M	*F*	*T*	*M*	*F*	*T*	*M*	*F*	*T*
TEJANI	31	69	52	121	10	5	15	25	15	40

Source: Primary data collected by the author.

Table 2: The health components of human capital

Kolam of Tejani Village	*B.M.I.= Weight (kg.) Height^2(mt.) (Quetelet's Equation)*				*Nutrition = Weight (kg.) Height (cm.)^2 Rao(1961) and Singh (1971)*			
	Underweight		*Normal*		*Malnourished*		*Normal*	
Percentage of People	M	F	M	F	M	F	M	F
	44.5	51.8	55.5	48.2	40.7	47.1	59.3	52.9

Source: Primary data collected by the author.

The Kolam people are mainly dependent upon agriculture. It is their source of income due to the Yavatmal region, which subsists so. The contribution of hunting is low, generally they catch *tetar*, parrot etc., to sell for bird lovers. Most of the Kolam do Agriculture labour. Cotton is the main crop. It serves as their livelihood. Besides, cotton, soyabeen, *bazra*, *kanola* and other cereals are also produced and labour in which makes their livelihood. They are daily waged laborers. Men and women do labour equally. Neither take cash or crop. The main animals domesticated are hen, goat, cow and pig. The animal husbandry is for their use only. Different enclosures are being constructed. to ensure them properly accommodated. The egg and milk are for personal use.

The Human Capital is shifted from hunting gathering to labour. Sonba, for example, was trained in making nets for catching wild boaret, he cannot find work. As a result, his wife and children join him in the agricultural labour. The family still relies on human capital, but has shifted from skilled to unskilled

Social capital

It includes the kinship networks, associations, membership organizations and peer-group networks that people can use in difficulties or turn to in order to gain advantage.

Those of Tejani find divided into four totem groups *Kula Gats*, (phratries) namely, *Char Dev* (worshippers of four Gods). Though, the Kolams retain some very primitive customs, those of Tejani were hardly distinguishable from the Kunbis or Hindu cultivators. They were held to be lower than the Gonds, because a Kolam will take food from a Gond, but the latter will not return the compliment. In another respect, they are on a level with the lowest aborigines, as some of them do not use water to clean their bodies after performing natural functions, but only leaves. A Kolam is being forbidden to beg by the rules of the tribe, and he looks down on the Mahars and Matangs, who are often professional beggars.

The Kolam have a high sense of status and prestige as against other tribes. They consider themselves ethnically related to the Pandvas (Pandav- Vanshi) of the Mahabharat. Their love for their tribe and future finds reflected in the fact that they are being very conscious and proud of socio-cultural traditions and follow the rituals meticulously. They are true to their Kolami religion and hence no conversion to Christianity or buddhism were reported.

As stated by one of Kolam members, that Kolam society migrated long ago in the nearby areas of Andhra Pradesh mainly Adilabad and Warangal. Since Andhra Pradesh was under Nizam rule therefore Kolam came into contact with them. Nizam rule was abolished following Independence. Kolam were identified as non-hindu group. They were forced to live far away from the Hindu majority area. During the struggle of independence, the people revolted (1942) against the Britishers. In order to regain their identity for this purpose, they got protection from Nizam. For a longer period, their society was under pressure to maintain their indigenous identity, on one hand and being accepted by Hindu on the other hand. They accepted Islamic culture after Hindu opposition but support of Muslim. The government policies mobilized them migrate from

Andhra Pradesh to Maharashtra, where they met Rajgond in Chandrapur and Pradhan in Yavatmal. The author found the kinship terminology, such as ammi, abbu and celebrating Id, mourning during Muharram on their emulating Islamic lifestyle. In almost all villages, there was a tradition of middle name like in Marathi culture. The informant replied someone as Sonba Hussain using such middle name Hussain from many generations. It was however, certified by another informant Surghe Hussain Sorpam.

Kolam also mourn during Muharram. Muslims are pretty proud of their love to Muhammad Paigambar, at the same time express anguish when he was murdered. They prepare 'Tazia' inside the 'pond'. Tajia is made up of a special bamboo slice without nodes. It is taken across the village in which 'Pardhan' tribe also participate. Later it finds hung underneath tree so that it can't be destroyed by any animal. They believe Hussain alone can destroy the evil spirit coming from down and above. Ratan Hussain Meshram (Naik) says that on the id-day the spirit of Hussain enters in the body of Naik and helps in removing pain and sorrow of other people. It is to be noted that this area has no major Islamic institution, yet why the people participate in Muharram is the main question to be answered. Whether it is because of the reason that Kolam people migrated here from the Islamic region, or it was due to the cultural synthesis from Pradhan tribe. As they also use 'Hussain' as their middle name?

The Kolam culture depicts a beautiful synthesis of Islamic and Hindu culture. They celebrate the Hindu festivals like Holi, Deepawali, Dusehara, Navratra etc,; visit temple and worship gods and godesses, while on the other hand, they also celebrate *Id-ul-fitr* and *Muharram*. Their death ritual is a unique combination of two cultures. The dead body is washed with cow-urine and water for purification, and later buried (east-west). The mourner sacrifices some fowl and hosts fellow tribals over banquet and gets his pate and countenance shaved off hair. The spirit of ancestors find worshiped on any Monday in the month of 'Poush'.

For the tribe, the traditioned panchayat is more useful than modern panchayat [Panchayati Raj's]. They avoid going to courts of law. They believe their panchayat are better and cheaper. Sometimes, the tribe comes in contact with the policemen and courts, but their experience was horrible, as they believe there laws and acts were impractical. Today, the tribes are coming under the influence of modern political parties. They are now recognizing different political parties. Though, they were unable to self determine the party for whom to vote for, so they get easily lured by the political party for the exchange of vote for material gain.

Financial capital

It includes households' savings, credit and debt. .At the collective level, it may be accessibility of credit. 9.2 p c of Kolam are landless. The rest are only marginal farmers (having less than 0.1 hectare land. 63 p c of income is being spent on food items, 16 p c on medicine, and the rest on clothing and transportation) The type of employment is shown in **Table 4**. The amount of income depends upon the season. During crop sowing and reaping season, most of the families earn more than Rs. 3,000 per month. 5 p c families earn more than Rs. 5,000 per month, as they work in aanganwadi and private shops as the salesperson. As the research highlights, the availability of financial capital has changed dramatically over the past few years, and there is great variation of this asset among the households and their assets are increasing along with income.

Natural capital

They own natural productive assets, which provide them range of services. Households may privatize areas, through clearance for cultivation, and communities may evolve the customary institutions around common accessm and use of 'natural capital', such as forests, in order to ensure sustainable off-take levels. Farms include agricultural or forest land owned or accessed and so on. Tejani village lies in the plain region on the banks of the rivers Painganga, Wardha and their tributaries. The agriculture crops were mainly cotton, groundnut, rice and wheat. The crops like jowar, bajra, millets etc are not grown at present, as they were the low-priced food. The public distribution system has made availability of low priced or free food in the form of wheat and rice. Thus, PDS has decreased the crop diversity of the area. They pick-up minor produces like gum, honey, mahua, flowers, chironji etc., from the forests and hunting of wild boar is done. The community has had a reduction in natural capital. There are high levels of erosion, poor soil quality, and recent forest policy. Community members recognize such problems, but have difficulty in working together to address them

Physical capital

This refers at the household level about the physical equipment and tools that are used in production. At the most basic level, it can include buying of houses, bicycles, livestocks, and so on. It also includes the access to infrastructure such as, the road networks, clinics, schools and so on. 28 of the 31 houses were found owned by Kolam, out of which 20 (64.5 p c) are under Indira Awaas Yojana. The wall of the 25 p c houses was of burnt bricks and 10 p c were made up of mud. The roof and floor were mainly of asbestos (90.3 p c) and cement (64.5 p c) respectively. The 90 p c of the houses have radio, 29 p c of them have television sets and motorcycle/moped, 70 p c have bicycles and 45.2 p c have mobile phones. Hand pumps are the main source of drinking water.

At the community level, main road/state highway is 05 km from the village. Tejani do not have primary health centre, primary government school, post office or a nationalized bank. Nearest Public and private Bus Service is 5 km and 10Km respectively. The closest railway halt and post office is Khadki (12 km). While all community members use the same road for transportation, some households now have motorcycles, while the rest depend on the bus. Sorpam, for example, have a motorcycle, mobile, and television. His income is also high as he is using his physical capital for his livelihood.

Structure and Process

Each household in the study has its own set of assets or resources. It could be the conditioner for anticipated livelihood strategy. Simply having assets, however, does not mean that everybody finds employed. In some cases, households may not have the opportunity to use resources, or conditions may prevent the use of some assets. Some youth in the community have been educated, but are unwilling to leave the region; they are unable to find employment. Their education is a huge, untapped asset. In other cases, there are circumstances mobilizing or assisting the use of assets.

Structures

Government organizations influence the people. Everything from the laws and policies being implemented to available products create structures that govern daily decisions and long-term plans.

Table 3: Eeconomic Development of Kolam

S. No	*Name of the Programmes*	*S. No*	*Name of the Programmes*
1.	Providing Tools Related to Agriculture Development:	14.	Antyodaya Anna Yojana (AAY)
2.	Development programme for P.T.G	15.	Village Grain Banks Scheme
3.	Scheme for Motor vehicle driver training:	16.	Targeted Public Distribution System (TPDS)
4.	Scheme for recruitment in Police and Military	17.	TRIBAL SUB-PLAN (TSP)
5.	Khadyan Karz Yojna	18.	Grants under the First Provision to Article 275(1) of the Constitution
6.	Anaj Kosh Yojna	19.	Scheme for Primitive Tribal Groups (PTGs)
7.	Scheme for applying in different services for ST Candidates	20.	Vocational Training in Tribal Areas
8.	Scheme for Tribal Handicraft Exhibition	21.	Grants-in-Aid for Minor Forest Produce (MFP)
9.	Scheme for providing loan for self employment	22.	National Scheduled Tribes Finance And Development Corporation (NSTFDC)
10.	Scheme for opening center for Occupational training	23.	Adivasi Mahila Sashaktikaran Yojana (AMSY)
11.	Scheme for providing Electric pump	24.	Tribal Cooperative Marketing Development Federation Of India Ltd. (Trifed)
12.	Mahatma Gandhi National Rural Employment Guarantee Act (MGNREGA)	25.	Recognition of Forest Rights of STs
13.	Indira Awaas Yojana (IAY)	26.	Loan Waiver

Source: Annual report ministry of Tribal Affairs (2011).

Every government policy and law have three phases (i) Planning:- in which the goals, budget, people or the programme area and its duration is covered. This stage is being prepared by the MLAs and MPs i.e., legislature. (ii) Implementation: In this stage, the strategies for successful implementation of the programme at district, tehsil, village and block is finalized. It is being worked out by district magistrate/collector, block development officers and sarpanch and (iii) Evaluation:- the programme gets analyzed. Some of the concerns remained whether it has reached goals, or if not, the inherent loopholes, ought to be analyzed. This stage utilizes the expertise of sociologists, anthropologists, economists etc.

Processes

Some processes influence their ability within these structures. Issues such as who is given access to loans or which groups are aware to receive government assistance are examples of those processes that mediate access to and the use of assets. The key to understanding them is to examine them within the messiness of everyday life. Ethnographies contextualize the livelihood decisions, while taking into consideration the multiple factors influencing daily choices.

In order to assess the processes, a Programme Awareness Scale (PAS) has been developed in order to test the Awareness level of various policies run by the Government of India and Maharashtra. The data analysis shows that on an average the Antyodaya Anna Yojana (AAY), Khadyan Karz Yojna, Development programme for P.T.G and Indira Awaas Yojana (IAY), which really benefited the Kolam people as more than 80 p c of households were benefited by them. However, few Economic programmes like Scheme for Tribal Handicraft Exhibition, Targeted Public Distribution System (TPDS), TRIBAL SUB-PLAN (TSP), Grants under the First Provision to Article 275(1) of the Constitution, Grants-in-Aid for Minor Forest Produce (MFP), National Scheduled Tribes Finance And Development Corporation (NSTFDC) and Recognition of Forest Rights of STs are the ones whose name was not even heard by the Kolam people.

The scheme for waiving school fees of tribal students, midday meal, official *Ashramshala* group programme and ideal *Ashram* school, which really benefited the people as 64.3 p c to 84 p c of households were benefited from them. However, few Educational programmes like Eklavya English medium residential school, Tribal hostel, Scheme for providing Employment/Maintenance Allowance for ST students studying in professional courses, Grant-In-Aid to Voluntary Organizations Working For Welfare Of Scheduled Tribes, Rajiv Gandhi National Fellowship Scheme (R.G.N.F), Jan Shikshan Sansthan, Mahila Samakhya (MS), National Programme for Education of Girls at Elementary Level (NPEGEL), Kasturba Gandhi Balika Vidyalayas, Kendriya Vidyalayas (KVs) and Navodaya Vidyalayas (NVs) are the ones whose name was not even heard by the Kolam people.

The Kolam people only acts like a puppet and Pardhan and Kunbi represent them in local panchayati elections. In 'Tejani' village one of panchayat members says that the people are so innocent that all the benefits of government programmes were utilized by pardhan. They do not believe in anything, they only bother about food and liquor and they want us to remain poor. The role of traditional 'Naik Pradhan' (Sarpanch) has become limited. It is now restricted to organizing Gaon bandhni and other traditional function of Kolam. Most of the cases were taken over by panchayat's sarpanch, members and police. The control over panchayat is based on the needs of political parties rather than the needs of village people. Every society wants its share in political power so that they can accomplish other goals. Kolam have their totem as political unit but the share of political power does not depend on gotra. As a result, the political system became cooperative. The traditional political system is now represented by Panchayati Raj, Vidhan Sabha and Lok Sabha. The traditional leadership is losing its roots and its place is taken over by democracy.

Vulnerability

Another factor influencing asset use is vulnerability. It has three main aspects: trends, shocks, and seasonality (DFID 1999; Rakodi 2002). The trends encompass change in populations, economics, and politics among others. These impact the community members, and the relative instability of these issues increases household vulnerability.

Trends

They were hunters like other tribals and killing wild pigs was the favourite pastime. Now this has almost stopped. Originally, they lived on mountain slopes. They knew farming, but were shifting cultivators. They did'nt plough the land, but adopted broadcast method for sowing seeds like the *Gonds*. This was called *Podu,* which means shifting cultivation. Later, they adopted traditional method of cultivation with ploughs, axes and crowbars etc. In many of the villages, they were cultivators, but their lands were infertile and insufficient for livelihood of the families. Hence, many of them started working as labourers on the farms of landlords, while others migrated in search of labour. Some of them got wages as forest labourers, while others worked hard on stone cutting by hands. The state government gave them lands in some areas which were not cultivable. Stone cutting work was also given under the EGS (Employment Guarantee Scheme) of the state government, but due to reported corruption they could not get wages commensurate to labour. Women work on farms as labourers along with men. Some youths were employed on the farms of landlords with wages in kind (food-grains) and/or in cash, which may be a fixed sum.

Shocks

It includes environmental disasters affecting crops or livestock. During the research, farming suffered from drought. This area was suffering from water scarcity, the landless and landlord farmers were tackling this problem. The people faced double problem, firstly their dependence on forest was finished and secondly they have to adapt to agriculture. They received nothing in return due to dry nature of soil and redtapeism.

Seasonal changes

The seasonal changes in production, health, and employment opportunities ought to be dealt with on a regular basis. The unpredictability of the harvest, the changing price of goods, and irregular employment opportunities make it difficult for community members to make long-term plans.

The Livelihood Strategies

Community members have six livelihood strategies. Minor forest produce collection, pastoralism, agriculture, labour, government job and work in private jobs.

Table 4: Livelihood strategies in Tejani village

Type Of Employment		*Percentage of Males*	*Percentage of Females*
Agriculture	Owner	08.0	00.0
	Rented	27.0	29.0
	Labour	46.7	51.6
Jobs	Government	02.0	0.0
	Non-government	1.5	2.6
Pastoralism		05.0	17.8

Source: Author's field work.

Making the fallow land cultivable by uprooting of big trees and shrubs is a difficult job. Many tribals do this hard labour for earning livelihood like bamboo work, making of mats and grain-storage. They keep herds of goats and cattle for landlords from the village. It is one of the favourite occupations liking cutting grass, collecting firewood and selling. Some of them work even as wood-work artisans. Very few of them were educated and employed on white-collared jobs, but the percentage is negligible. Traditionally, they have been working as labourers and have migrated from place to place for work. Of late, their major occupation has been stone cutting and working as labours on forest-roads or forest.

Not all households could emulate all strategies, and the availability of each varies seasonally. Of course, it is important to distinguish between expected and actual outcomes. While community members want to increase their income or improve food security, this may not be what occurs. Making the distinction between expected and actual outcomes is central to analyzing decisions about livelihood strategies. The major portion of income (63%) is spent on food item, this shows that they are at the level of hand to mouth economy. The PDS is playing a vital role in supplying the staple food as 71% of rice & 49% of pulses consumption are met by them from it. IAY also plays a crucial role as 72.16% of houses were constructed under this scheme. However, there is no scope of maintenance in this scheme due to which most of the houses were found in very poor condition.

The Cultural Impact

Kolam believes in nuclear family, yet their social and individual life is bifurcated. The house and family of this society lives separately, with each generation. Kolam society gives due importance to social responsibilities of the individual. This aspect can be easily understood by the concept of cultural focus and cultural universal of Herskovitz (1958). He says that it is the very nature of the culture that some of its traits are projected as big and they undergo development with time whereas other traits were kept in background.

Firstly, their 'pond' which earlier used to be semicircular, has now taken the form of normal habitation. The 'pond' finds well separated and parted away from the colonies of 'Pardhan', 'Kunbis' and Gond tribe. Habitation of such village reflects the structure of traditional village wherein lower caste lives far away from the centre of the village. Since the tribe got the recognition as the lower strata of social stratification, they live in villages like dalits in Caste Society. However, the 'Up-Sarpanch' told us the tribe wishes to live in their own primitive way for which, they do not intermix with other society and make their 'pond' away from the centre of the village.

Secondly, easy availability of dress material has changed the traditional and normal life style of Kolam drastically. The youth now wears trousers, shirts etc, and women wear salvar-kurta and sarees, the utensils were generally of plastics, steel and aluminum. The food habits are like the societies residing close to them. The main food diet has become vegetarian and its process of preparation resemble with the societies around. Tea and 'kharra' (a special type of tobacco popular in Vidarbha) were not a part of tribal life have now become an essential part of life. The normal lifestyle of people changed, which can be noticed in entertainment, language and dance. The 'devasthan' known as 'chaupal' used to be evening meeting place for the tribe, now remains empty. Their famous 'Dandari Dance' is losing its interest among the youth. They now dance on filmy tunes and sing filmy songs instead of their traditional folkdance and folksong.

The 'Kolami' language which has 'Dravid' words in its structure is different from Gondi and other languages of simple societies. Its usage is decreasing at a very fast rate. The main reason for it is being their residence in Yavatmal, the main language being 'Marathi' as the first language for communication. The use of 'Kolami' language is only restricted to festivals, tradition and marriage folk songs.

The primitive economic system has some unique specialties. They are self-sufficient. Daily consumable items take the form of money. Money does not give birth to class system. The division of labour is based on sex and age. The basic specialties of economic system mentioned above have changed due to government policies and market pressure. The communal production changed into individual production due to influence of western economy. It got strength from modernization; the surplus production became the source of individual production. It gave rise to individual property rather than communal property.

Conclusion

An effective means for analyzing the complex decisions made by members of a household to meet their daily needs is the livelihood studies approach. This framework takes into account multiple factors, including assets, vulnerability, and structural forces that influence livelihood decisions and outcomes. Because, this approach is also used by the practitioners, it provides a common ground on which researchers can work with others to promote beneficial outcome. A greater depth of understanding is obtained when combined with an ethnographic approach. The interaction of livelihood assets, structures, and vulnerability can be understood in relation to livelihood strategies and outcome.

Ethnography provides the context needed to have a greater understanding of livelihood strategies. It is the ethnographic interview which reveals that although Sonba, for example, has been trained in making nets for catching wild boar, Yet, he cannot find work. As a result, his wife and children join him in the agriculture labour. The family still relies on the human capital, but has shifted from the skilled to unskilled. Such data is not available on a survey about the livelihood strategies. Simply describing the lives of community members is not sufficient to understand their situation or their livelihood decisions. Instead, they must be contextualized and understood as part of the wider economic climate.

In the name of globalization, the tribal people like Kolam are forced to migrate and adjust into the mainstream of economic system, where they can be utilized in the form of cheap labour. In this way, market gets cheap labour and Kolam people thinks that they cannot survive, if they do not become the part of the economic system. It is one type of colonial pressure in which on the name of the purchasing power and production the parallel economic system is destroyed so that a homogenous economic system can be formed. Kolam people are also not untouched with this phenomenon. If we look at the traditional economic system of the Kolam, we will find that they are hunters and gatherers. Their economic system was regarded as unreligious and primitive, so that they can be pressurized to be the part of market system. Now, the people do labour work in the same forest, which earlier used to be their communal property. Their traditional method of hunting and farming were declared illegal, and were forced to be a part of the economic system. As a result of which, their livelihood was dependent on daily wages through labour and programmes like MNREGA. Many tribes can be seen standing on the sides of the National Highway in search of labour.

Over the past few years, it has become clear that households cannot depend solely on farming for survival, due to the high levels of risk and unpredictability with the harvest. At the same time, alternate resources such as labor and pastoralism are becoming more competitive and difficult to acquire. As a result, the households have had to expand their livelihood strategies by starting small businesses and looking for the government assistance. Why such choices? Why the entrepreneurship and government programs remain most feasible options for these households?

P S: Author desires to express his gratitude to the Union Min of Tribal Affairs for using the data titled, "Impact of Migration and Development on Kolam: A Bio-Cultural Analysis".

References

Annual Report of Ministry of Tribal Affairs, (2011): New Delhi: Govt. of India.

Anderson, G.H., (1979). BControl of Protein and Energy Intake, C Can; Jr. Physiol. Pharamacol, vol.57

Chaudhuri S. Kumar and Chaudhuri S. Sen, (2005): *Primitive tribe in Contemporary India* New Delhi: Mittal Publication.

Cliggett, L. (2007): *Economies and Cultures: Foundations of Economic Anthropology.* Westview Press.

Dept for International Development. (1999): Sustainable Livelihood Guidance Sheets. <http://www.ennonline.net/resources/66>Position – 20.11.16.

Herskovitz, M. J. (1948): *Man and his works: The science of cultural anthropology,* New York: Knopf.

Kurlanska, C. (2011): *Ethnographic livelihood studies: the minutiae of microloans in Ethnology,* Vol. 50, No. 2 (Spring 2011), pp. 95-115.Pittsburg: University of Pittsburgh of the Commonwealth System of Higher Education.

Lont, H., and O. Hospes. (2004a): *Introduction. Livelihood and Microfinance: Anthropological and Sociological Perspectives on Savings and Debt,* eds. H. Lont and O. Hospes, pp. 3-24. Eburon Delf.

Narayan, D., and L. Pritchett. (1999): Cents and Sociability: Household Income and Social Capital in Rural Tanzania: *Economic Development and Cultural Change* 47(4):871 97.

Rakodi, C. (2002): A Livelihood Approach—*Conceptual Issues and Definitions. Urban Livelihoods: A People-Centered Approach to Reducing Poverty,* (eds). C. Rakodi and T. Lloyd-Jones, pp. 3-22. Earthscan.

Rusell R.V. and Hiralal, (1916): *The Tribes and Castes of Central Provinces of India;* New Delhi: McMillan Publication and Co. ltd.

Statistical profile of Scheduled Tribes in India (2013). Ministry of Tribal affairs Statistics division Government of India <.ww.tribal.nic.in>. Position - 20.11.16

Whiteford, S. (1985): The Political Economy of Rural Transformation: A Mexican Case; *Micro and Macro Levels of Analysis in Anthropology: Issues in Theory and Research,* (eds). B. DeWalt and P. Pelto, pp. 147-64. Westview Press.

Chapter - 14

Tribal Critique: Livelihood in Jharkhand

— *Abhik Ghosh*

Introduction

Anthropologists seem to have forgotten history, perhaps mobilizing me repeat that. They were the strongest critiques of the very idea of development. They believed a throwback to the Victorian classical evolutionist idea, calling for non-Western societies develop for ascending the ladder of evolution. Over the years, born, bred and sponsored by the very society we critiqued, we have become more complacent. We account for the development which needs to be undertaken and have even created forms of development that include local voices to save our conscience. We accept the fact that local forms are being superseded by new forms of globalisation in conforming to an imagined International standard of doing and being. At best, under such systems, local events and methods are tolerated by patronising experts. We seem to have forgotten that development as an ideal. It is flawed with own set of ethnocentric and ideological biases. These proliferated with the whole set of ideas and practices like a *habitus*, a stock-knowledge-at-hand, of practices and concepts, accepted without any critical evaluation or thought. It is as if thinking outside these contexts were itself not correct, that something was wrong with you if you did not conform to these practices. Many leaders were being elected into office around the world, upon their local and national nexus, rather than an International or globalised outlook. In a Brexit world, Donald Trump can win over the electorate by promising to be parochial, focussed on the majority White Anglo-Saxon American. In other words, globalisation has taken a back-seat. We, as anthropologists ought to rethink about our blind adherence to codes reverting to our more activist agenda against development. We need to really think through our ideas of development and what the concept of 'tribal livelihood' really entails. What it really meant was that tribal livelihood may not be contained within those safe categories that we usually like to think about. In fact, some of the tribal livelihood may really be something that we have never really liked to think about.

An Unbelievable setting

The tribals have traditionally been classified by anthropologists into different economic categories. Hunters and gatherers have been seen as those who hunt and forage for a livelihood. Thus, they are often seen within or near forests. The pastoralists base their livelihood on domesticated animals. Some of them needed to forage on long treks to assure animals, good fodder; while others are found to be settled. Next in the agenda, are the shifting cultivators, who use slash-and-burn or *jhum* cultivation methods, to ensure a good harvest by cutting vegetation and forests over a large area in a cyclical manner! Finally, there were the settled agriculturists, involved with the everyday practices of agriculture in a specific area, where they live.

Over the years, the researchers have classified the tribes in different zones, according to their livelihood (see, for instance, Majumdar; 1944). Others have attempted to show these forms of livelihood on a continuum, upon the evolution of economic life (see, for instance, Sahlins). These and other authors have seen livelihood as a part of a complex set of social and economic circumstances (see, for instance, Daryll Forde).

Whatever be the circumstances, livelihood are inevitably and unvaryingly one of the biggest methods of classifying tribal life.

However, tribals do not stick to one kind of livelihood. This is part of their definitional attributes and biggest strengths. This is the one feature that helps them to survive adversity, hunger, poverty and the lack of resources. In other words, we must remember them by definition accessible to multiple methods of dealing with economic, food and survival issues. This is why, in periods of extreme hunger and drought, tribes in India have had 'traditional' occupation to survive, while others in the same region perish.

One such region is Palamau in Jharkhand. Here many tribes live in close association with forests juxtaposed with Maoists. One such tribe in this region are the Parhaiyas. Our fieldwork in the region has shown a deep, abiding knowledge of a variety of forest produce by them and the results are being shared with other communities with whom they barter their produce, like the Cheros.

Tribals living the Life

According to a UNDP publication on Guidance Note on Recovery: Livelihood, the definition given of livelihood is as follows:

"A **livelihood** comprises the capabilities, assets (including both material and social resources) and activities required for a means of living. A livelihood is sustainable when it can cope with and recover from stress and shocks and maintain or enhance its capabilities and assets both now and in the future, while not undermining the natural resource base." (Chambers and Conway; 1991)

DFID (the UK Dept for Internal Development) who developed 'The Sustainable Livelihood Framework (SLF) has the following components (see Figure 1):

1. **Livelihood Assets:** It has five further components.

[a] *human capital:* skill, knowledge, health and ability to work; [b] *social capital:* social resources including informal networks, membership of formalised groups and relationship of trust that facilitate co-operation and economic opportunities; [c] *natural capital:* this involves

natural resources like land, soil, water, forests and fisheries; [d] *physical capital:* This includes basic infrastructure like roads, water, sanitation, schools, ICT, producer goods like tools, livestock and equipment.; [e] *financial capital:* it has resources like savings, credit, income from employment, trade and remittances.

2. Livelihood Context: This includes the social, economic and political background. Some of these situations may create obstacles while others create opportunities for livelihood. They may be classified under these six heads: [a] *Social relations:* This involves the way on their gender, ethnicity, culture, history, religion and kinship affecting livelihood of different groups in that community. [b] *Social and political organisation:* Decision-making processes, civic bodies, social rules and norms, democracy, leadership, power and authority, rent-seeking behavior.

Governance: the form and quality of government systems including structure, power, efficiency and effectiveness, rights and representation.

Service delivery: The effectiveness and responsiveness of state and private sector agencies engaged in the delivery of services like education, health, water and sanitation.

Resource access institutions: The social norms, customs and behaviours that define the access of people to resources.

Policy and policy processes: The processes through which policy and legislation are determined and implemented as well as their effects on people's livelihoods.

3. Livelihood Strategies: This includes the way people use social, economic, political and environmental contexts for livelihoods assets and strategy. These strategies are very large in number. Any individual may take up several ways to meet his/her requirements. Individuals may also cooperate to create a collective strategy. This kind of strategy is often used cooperatively within households to help the family to sustain and grow. Within some cultures this level of cooperation may go to the extent of a small community, where individuals work for the betterment of the community.

1. Livelihood Vulnerabilities:

The outcome of production is not the only measurement of livelihood. It is also seen in the way it copes with shocks, seasonal changes and trends. These shocks may include natural disasters, wars and economic disasters. Resources, incomes and demands for products and services may fluctuate seasonally. Trends in politics, governance, use of technology, economics, availability of natural resources can pose gradual and unpredictable effects on livelihoods. They may affect the availability of assets as well as opportunities for transforming them into a mode of 'livelihood'. In such circumstances, individuals have to either modify existing strategies or develop new ones to live.

2. Livelihood Interdependence:

Most livelihood strategies are not brought out in isolation but are in conjunction with the interdependence of whole communities. Any livelihood may rely on other livelihoods to access and exchange assets. Livelihoods may also compete with each other for assets and markets. So livelihoods have positive and negative impact on others. This is very important when thinking of a planned intervention (see Figure 1).

Tribal Practices of Livelihood

We seem to have accepted the fact of multinational corporations and globalisation as if the world of anthropologists had never objected to this form of development in its history. The fact remains that the present forms of development supported by world leaders as well as its economists as a foregone conclusion, is not accepted as a viable solution by many anthropologists. From time to time different conceptualisations of development have been put forth by a number of anthropologists which have been largely ignored by economists, politicians, development experts and the like.

In other words, development practices have been taken as granted and the fact that tribal livelihood have to 'toe the line' when it comes to development. It is quite simple to state this as a development expert in an air-conditioned office than it is to implement. This was seen in the 1960s when the development experts went to South America to attempt to change the economy there according to the way the American economy was operating. It was a resounding failure, leading the anthropologists to propound that alternative economic pathway should be recommended, especially for developing countries.

Today, most such alternative forms have been tailored to become offshoots of the major economic development fronts of the government rather than independent economic pathways. This has led many to ignore the complex pathways by which tribals in different moments strategize their multiple sources of livelihoods.In other words, they have had to lie to development agencies.

Hunter gatherers deal with certain kinds of livelihood over others. Very few groups have actually left the job but resorted to 'mainstream' activites. We perhaps often tend to think that our hunter-gatherers are of no consequence and do not merit a separate development programme for them. However, an unpublished report by D. Venkatesan cited by Hitchcock and Bisele claims them constituting 1.3 million. In addition, about 600 more on the Andaman and Nicobar Islands, constitute some 25 p c of the world's hunter-gatherers. This is a significant number by any standard. It is claimed that perhaps this high number was achieved due to the tolerant nature of India's religious communities and political structures (Gardner; 2013).

Hence, the hunter-gatherers need to be a major part of our efforts to understand and record before we eradicate them through our development processes. This is especially so, because we may need their local knowledge and expertise to survive climate change in our own ecospheres (see Ghosh; 2016 discussed in this very forum).

In India, pastoralists have recently been acknowledged, as being a group that required special attention. Indian pastoralists have been in a bad spot. The Gujjars of North India have been claiming a tribal status. They claim selves to be of eight p c of the overall population. That is a huge number! If this is a major economic mode of livelihood, then we have to really rethink our economic policies. In fact, there is no mass evidence from Gujarat that the early origins of plant cultivation in India were linked to herders, who were planting millets and pulses (Garcia-Granero, *et al.*; 2016). Today, our government promotes this lot as the basis for our next level of Green Revolution.

Over and above, environmentally most abused group had been the slash-and-burn agriculturists. However, a lot of research in the North East of India, where this kind of agriculture mostly recurs has no deleterious effect on the environment. In fact, the effects may also be beneficial and sustainable over long periods of time due to local practices. Perhaps, some of these practices need to be taken up by our farmers to make our farming practices better.

We have pondered over the settled agriculturists. Many of the tribals have shifted from becoming peasants to farmers; others have opted out of agriculture to other vocations on their falling interest in land and land affinity. Over and above, such classical divisions of a preliminary kind of livelihood classification, they become traders as well as gone out for different kind of labour, seasonal to permanent. Some have gone to other countries for plantation labour, others have stayed in India to work in plantations or in tea gardens. Others went for construction or brik kilns. Occasional labour as a tribal mode of livelihood has often been noted, but has not become a major calculation among economists.

An occupation among tribes that has often been ignored is the fact that the lot has often been involved in crime – robbery, extortion, guns for hire, guards or as gunmen for organised syndicates and insurgent groups. These have regularly provided them with some livelihood. The author accessed some aspects of their livelihood by taking up Jharkhand cases.

Tribal World views

Jharkhand species have become problematic in theory. However, even after these issues have been covered, it seems apparent that proximity to forests and markets play an important role in the marketing and sale of forest produce in significant amounts (Belcher, Achdiawan and Dewi; 2015). The fieldwork in Thakurgaon, close to the forests with a weekly market within the village with good connectivity to local areas and transportation has justified the position.

Modern irrigation and other agricultural support groups cluster, like birds of a feather, to regions where other facilities are also available. They require the support from markets, pesticides and fertiliser agents, as well as good quality seeds for best effects. They refuse to acknowledge those who are outside these support areas. This creates major anomalies in the way rural wealth finds created and distributed among the groups. This is especially seen in reports published by such support groups (see, for instance, Satapathy; 2002, Barla; 2013).

"For selection of clusters availability of water sources, tribal communities, marketplaces and banks should be considered. Villagers having access to market area better choice for investment irrigation. The interior villages should be covered on a later date. Ideally the service area of a single bank located in a place that is or can be connected to distant markets should be selected as a cluster." (Satpathy; 2002: 31)

Other reports from the entire central Indian region projected better irrigation facilities and water control are key factors ensuring better development indicators for the people in the region.

An arena, consistently been ignored is that of the indigenous health practitioner. Such people carry wealth of plant and animal knowledge, as well as a huge practice of using for better results in curing of a large number of ailments (Gupta, Sahu and Sharma; 2009). In the case of the rural population away from health centres, this is a very big boon. They are also a big help in reducing the out-of-pocket expenditures of the public on healthcare. This fact has been borne out by our own studies on the tribals of Jharkhand, like the Oraons of Ranchi, Gumla and Lohardaga districts, Mundas of Khunti and Tamar regions, the Cheros and Parhaiyas of Palamau and Latehar, the Hos of Singhbhum, among others.

Non-Timber Forest Produce or NTFP has been the saviour and major resource of many tribal families. Thus being cut off from these resources has not helped many of these families

(Islam, *et al.*; 2015). The return to these families of the Rights to Forests has been a bit more complicated. The list of those who were entitled has grown over the years while the forest resources have not. The Forest officials have also lost out on power and authority. They have protested strongly responsible for and a lot of issues, regarding this transfer (Sarangi; 2013). In fact, the issue served the rest of humanity has never once been stated in all the arguments for and against FRA in the state.

Rare among these literature, was the study of Sanjay Kumar in 2002. He analyzed the common pool resources in connection with the poverty alleviation as a result of 40 years of JFM activities. It was concluded by him that separate programmes were needed to develop the poor within the villages.

Traditional knowledge of rare and little-known forest produce used as food or medicine is also very deeply embedded in the tribal psyche in Jharkhand. Many studies have shown different aspects of these tribes to indicate new varieties of such kinds (for instance, see Singh and Kumar; 2014).

An important factor in the region from the past has been migration for short or long-term for work. This has been a major amount of income in many households. This condition has remained like this for over 200 years or even more. To some extent, this kind of migration is irrespective of caste, or even household income, though higher castes and those having a higher household income migrate less for work in Jharkhand. For all the groups, household income increases due to remittances sent in by those who migrate. This has also saved the men and especially the women in their dealings with local money-lenders. In brick kilns, other studies show, workers are segmented, with different kinds of labour preferring to do different kinds of labour. There were different categories of work for tribal women and tribal men as well as for the Bengalis, who only cut the soil and help to mould the bricks (Deshingkar and Farrington; 2006).

In recent times, the failure of MGNREGA for adequate work and money as per rules, has made them migrate in search of pastures anew. This made many of the families dysfunctional or partly functional at best (Kumar; 2012).

In fact, Jharkhand has recently passed an Act under which this kind of illegal money-lending, especially to the poor and the tribals has been banned.

Another aspect of tribal livelihood in Jharkhand was dairy farming, though on a very small scale. The major constraint was the lack of credit availability. The authors could not understand why much of the economy moved through barter or by minimal inputs of cash for the majority (Eqbal, Singh and Khan; 2013).

Sometimes, agriculture has not been enough to sustain the family. Other solutions were arrived at like pig-farming (Kumar, *et al.*; 2015). However, the tribal villages aligned to Muslims may hesitate to take up the issue so readily. The livelihood under different ecological and social settings however, varied. (See **Table 1, Figure 2**).

Other options include making leaf-cups out of Sal leaves as a part of livelihood (Islam, *et al.*; 2015).

Table 1: Livelihood under Different Systems (after Petare, *et al.*; 2016)

Rainfed agriculture-based livelihood system	*Rainfed and forest-based livelihood system*
Agriculture is the main source for more than 60 p c house holders.	Similar with the rainfed livelihood system.
Less than 10 p c of net sown area is under irrigation.	The community is partially dependent on forest to augment and buffer livelihood.
Paddy is the major crop in the *kharif* season (monsoon), oilseeds and pulses are cultivated on residual soil moisture.	Paddy is staple crop, *kharif* vegetables initiated.
Increasing trends toward cultivation of vegetables.	Income augmented during lean period from sale of fuel wood, from nearby forest and sale of non-timber forest produce, such as Mahua (*Madhuca longifolia*) flower and lac.
Decreasing trend for finger millet with increasing area under vegetables.	More than 33 p c of geographical area is covered by forests in these locations.
Uncertainty of rainfall and unavailability of water, community is more dependent on casual unskilled labour. Villages well connected with major towns find involved in this mode.	Current holding of goats is 2–3, which are used as a buffer in the crisis period or used during festival for meat.
Migration is more prominent in youth. It was earlier only during non-crop periods. Now all migrants return only during peak period of agriculture; migration to the towns for casual labour create increased pressure on women in crop production and harvesting.	

How is Tribal Livelihood different?

Some studies have started dealing with the issue of what is so different about tribal livelihood. The received idea is that tribal knowledge of forest produce is so good that they are able to make better use of these resources when they are available, than do other caste groups. Recent studies have shown that when resources are sufficient, then tribes as well as other communities benefit from forest-produce at almost the same rate (see Figure 2). Most can only suggest ideas in the same line of development that has been carried out so far, only with more intensity (Belcher, Achdiawan and Dewi; 2015). This is also seen in the case of plate-making technologies in Bundu area (Islam, Rai and Quli; 2014, Islam, *et al.*; 2015, Islam, Rai and Quli; 2015).

Shifting skill sets is also a major problem for the farmers. They are used to rainfed farming. Once irrigation facilities become available, they do not immediately shift to it. Once they observe others around them, they start using irrigation and new high-yielding crops and chemical fertilisers. However, the new skill sets required are more complex. Even here, it requires skill to understand which seeds to use, which fertilisers and pesticides to use and when and how to use the irrigation water available. Recent studies from Dumka show how tribals are often abandoning traditional knowledge and old methods for such new and unsure methods without having the requisite skill sets. Those who have lowland or *don* are not shifting while medium or uplands are being converted through irrigation.Knowledge of agriculture in the family is definitely a sorely required skill. Thus different kinds of farmers have different kinds of practices and thus livelihood requirements and differences in skill. An important issue is that a mix of schemes are required (Satpathy; 2002).

This same set of results are obtained for different kinds of livestock and pig farming among the tribes of Jharkhand, wherever new schemes have been introduced (Kumar, *et al.*; 2015). It is called CGP, (cattle, goat and pig) as well as chicken (Kumar, *et al.*; 2015).It was also seen that microfinance was a good way of funding costs for the initial stage of cattle farming, since poor farmers rarely had cash at hand for such activities

(Sinha, Dhaka and Meena; 2012). Further, the development of local breeds of cattle and other livestock is an absolute necessity (Sirohi and Chauhan; 2010, Deka and Wright; 2011).

An important part of local and rural livelihoods is the usage of local biota for preparing and using medicines. This becomes a cheap and handy pharmacopoeia that may readily be used by a majority. Development programmes about livelihoods ignore these issues unless it is about marketing these plants. Without these, loss of life, manpower days and general wellbeing would be an issue that would affect livelihood (see, for instance, Gupta, Sahu and Sharma; 2009, Singh and Kumar; 2014, Islam, *et al.*; 2015).

The issue of decentralisation of water and in ensuring greater control over it is also considered to be key to increasing tribal livelihoods (Phansalkar and Verma; 2004).

Tribals had been pushed in Eastern and Central India to occupy hilly and forested terrain that turned out to have rich mineral deposits. Now their earlier land tenures and uses of land are being violated by a government keen to take over this land for its resources (Hebbar; 2006, Meher; 2009). Having the justifiable share in this land is thought by many to be their right. Working out the right negotiable dynamics of this process is the most difficult step in this line.

Overall, then, the issue is about the use of common-pool resources by the majority of people in forested areas. If they are not using these resources then survival becomes difficult. However, one wonders if the use of such resources is at all sustainable. With adequate diversity and density, using resources is still a problem for the poorest, who needs it the most. This is because a majority of these poor tribals, as was seen by a study among the Mundas in the Bundu area, do not get access due to local political or structural issues (Kumar; 2002).

Migration among the tribals for livelihood may also be seen as a strategy used over more than a century by the communities of the region (Kumar; 2012). This has its own effects and specific resources and methodologies should be used to deal with the effects of migration among the tribal communities. In fact, this kind of migration has specifically led to trafficking among women. Also, such migrations are used by many to enact a different story from the mainstream one. Many stories of exploitation and hardship seem to be fake, perpetuated to maintain a structure of relations within the society so that people do not migrate out. They seem to give the idea that the tribals need protection from such kinds of practices (Shah; 2006 MS).

The above conclusions are in line with my own findings in the region among the Mundas. It is also apparent that the use of these forests by a larger number of people may not be supported by the carrying capacity of the forest. Climate change has also caused to decrease in production drastically causing huge losses to local sellers, users as well as the tribals.It is also apparent that many of the local crops may be grown year after year, while use of High Yielding Varieties of rice lead to intensification of cropping and thus resulting in successively increasing damage to the land. The land then does not recover completely and fertiliser is required to support further yields from the same land (Barla; 2013).

Conclusions

The author attempts to create some kind of background to ascertain about the issue from various studies. What we see is a chaotic hodge-podge of issues running higgledy-piggledy into each other without any holistic ideas or thought. All of them seem to have missed the human element out, but the fact that beings have culture and economic system, as an integral part of the cultural whole. The entire exercise can become a farce, which was seen, without linking up livelihoods to the local culture.

It is a fact that government departments dealing with tribal development seldom have the idea about original plans. They work by rote, ensuring certain numbers to be maintained, but not really caring about the kind of development sought (Prakash; 1999).

A second issue would be the idea that plants, animals and human beings are in interaction over millennia to wrest out the forms of livelihood. In the process, they have co-evolved together.

Introduction of new agricultural or animal species willy-nilly in the name of livelihood, without adequate thought or study seems to create the very thing we dread – the dissociation of human beings from the source of their livelihood, whether it is the farm, the dairy, or what have you. This is what eventually happens. One of the results of livelihood loss or shock, there is an increase in conflict in the region.

A third issue would be the fact that farmers do like making and spending money. Today, our economists and politicians seem to hate the idea that money should be saved. They believe money be spent or invested, whether it leads to security or not. Imagine the fate of some penniless farmer who ends up in suicide over asign of our degraded sensibilities and the poverty of a good development approach.

A fourth issue, tribal farmers often earning in crore through farming and other non-farming practices. However, like the general public, their number is a fraction of the total. We need to really look into the disparities and attempt to deal with them. So far, our development theories lack in this aspect, as well as address such issues of inclusion [exclusion] within select livelihood coteries or secret groups. The issue of vulnerability is only addressed as an afterthought.

A fifth issue, leave alone welfare capitalism, this kind of development seems to be just like a system of doles, rather than any theoretical approach, perspective, thought or concept of development. It is as if we have completely forgotten many aspects of development as downright wrong; have failed or are against humanity. It is also apparent that ideas on a new way of development seem to have been abandoned with new forms being an added agenda to the 'mainstream' of development. The idea of a tribal development would be paternalistic, autarchic, hegemonic and an academic folly, without any good critique of development.

References

Barla, Marcus. (2013): 'The Impact of New Agricultural Technology on Tribal Farming: A Study of Ranchi District of Jharkhand State', *Journal of Economic and Social Development*, Vol. 9, No. 1, pp. 121-31.

Belcher, Brian, Ramadhani Achdiawan and Sonya Dewi. (2015): 'Forest-Based Livelihoods Strategies Conditioned by Market Remoteness and Forest Proximity in Jharkhand', India *World Development*, Vol. 66, pp. 269-79.

Deka, Rameswar and Iain A. Wright. (2011): *Potential for Livelihood Improvement through Livestock Development in Jharkhand*. New Delhi: ILRI.

Deshingkar, Priya and John Farrington. (2006): 'Rural Labour Markets and Migration in South Asia: Evidence from India and Bangladesh', Background paper for the *World Development Report 2008*.

Eqbal, Md Shahid, Manish Kumar Singh and Nazam Khan. 2013: 'Constraints Faced by Tribal Dairy Farmers Regarding Dairy Farming Practices in Lohardaga District of Jharkhand', *International Journal of Scientific Research*, Vol. 2, No. 6, June, pp. 546-8.

Garcia-Granero, Juan Jose, Carla Lancelotti, Marco Madella and P. Ajithprasad. (2016): Millets and Herders: The Origins of Plant Cultivation in Semiarid North Gujarat (India) in *Current Anthropology*, Vol. 57, No. 2, April, pp. 149-73.

Gardner, Peter M. (2013): 'Understanding Anomalous Distribution of Hunter-Gatherers', *Current Anthropology*, Vol. 54, No. 4, pp. 510-3.

Gupta, Ishwari Parsad, H.B. Sahu and H.P. Sharma. (2009): 'Studies on Ethnomedicinal Uses of Plant Resources in Ormanjhi Block of Jharkhand', *International Journal of plant Sciences*, Vol. 4, No. 2, pp. 607-9.

Hebbar, Ritambara. (2006): 'Forest Bill 2005 and Tribal Areas: Case of Jharkhand', *Economic and Political Weekly*, Vol. 41, No. 48, 2-8 December, pp. 4952-5.

Islam, M.A., R. Rai and S.M.S. Quli. (2014): 'Manpower Potential, Employment Status and Forest Based Livelihood Opportunities among Tribal Communities of Jharkhand, India', *Journal of Human Ecology*, Vol. 47, No. 3, pp. 305-15.

Islam, M.A., R. Rai, S.M.S. Quli and M.S. Tramboo. (2015): 'Socio-economic and Demographic Descriptions of Tribal People Subsisting in Forest Resources of Jharkhand, India', *Asian Journal of Bio Science*, Vol. 10, No. 1, April, pp. 75-82.

Islam, M.A., S.M.S. Quli, R. Rai and P.K. Singh. (2015): 'Livelihood Promotion through Value Addition to Household Traditional *Sal* (*Shorea robusta* Gaertn.) Leaf Plate Making in Jharkhand, India', *Indian Journal of Natural Products and Resources*, Vol. 6, No. 4, December, pp. 320-5.

Islam, M.A., R. Rai and S.M.S. Quli. (2015): 'Forest Resources Use for Building Livelihood Resilience in Ethnic Communities of Jharkhand', *Trends in Biosciences*, Vol. 8, No. 5, pp. 1256-64.

Kumar, Ashwani. (2012): 'Economics of Migrating Villagers of South Chotanagpur Region of Jharkhand: An Empirical Study', *Journal of Economic and Social Development*, Vol. 8, No. 1, pp. 125-33.

Kumar, Mukesh, Jancy Gupta, Aparna Radhakrishnan and Minu Singh. (2015): 'Pig-based Production System Contributing Towards the Sustainable Livelihood of Tribes of Jharkhand', *International Journal of Farm Sciences*, Vol. 5, No. 1, pp. 290-8.

Kumar, Mukesh, Jancy Gupta, Aparna Radhakrishnan and Vikram Singh. (2015): 'Contribution of Livestock Production Systems Towards the Sustainable Livelihood of Tribes of Jharkhand', *Indian Journal of Animal Sciences*, Vol. 85, No. 5, May, pp. 519-21.

Kumar, Sanjay. (2002): 'Does "Participation" in Common Pool Resource Management Help the Poor? A Social Cost-Benefit Analysis of Joint Forest Management in Jharkhand, India', *World Development*, Vol. 30, No. 5, pp. 763-82.

Majumdar, D.N. (1944): *Races and Cultures of India*. Lucknow: Universal Publishers Ltd.

Meher, Rajkishor. (2009): Globalization, Displacement and the Livelihood Issues of Tribal and Agriculture Dependent Poor People: The Case of Mineral-based Industries in India', *Journal of Developing Societies*, Vol. 25, No. 4, pp. 457-80.

Phansalkar, Sanjiv J. and Shilp Verma. (2004): 'Improved Water Control as Strategy for Enhancing Tribal Livelihoods', *Economic and Political Weekly*, 31 July, pp. 3469-76.

Prakash, Amit. (1999): 'Decolonisation and Tribal Policy in Jharkhand: Continuities with Colonial Discourse', *Social Scientist*, Vol. 27, Nos. 7-8, July-August, pp. 113-39.

Sarangi, Tapas K. (2013): *Legalising Rights Through Implementation of Forest Rights Act 2006: A Critical Review on Odisha and Jharkhand*. Working Paper No. 126, RULNR Working Paper No. 20. Hyderabad: Research Unit for Livelihoods and Natural Resources (supported by Jamsetji Tata Trust) and Centre for Economic and Social Studies.

Satpathy, Manas K. (2002): *Irrigation for Livelihoods Improvement: Small Holder Tribal Irrigation in Jharkhand*. IWMI-Tata Water Policy Research Program, International Water Management Institute, Annual Partners' Meet 2002.

Shah, Alpa. (2006): *The Labour of Love: Seasonal Migration from Jharkhand to the Brick Kilns of Other States in India* (MS).

Singh, Geetanjali and Jyoti Kumar. (2014): 'Studies on Indigenous Traditional Knowledge of Some Aquatic and Marshy Wild Edible Plants Used by the Munda Tribe of District Khunti, Jharkhand, India', *International Journal of Bioassays*, Vol. 3, No. 2, pp. 1738-43.

Sinha, Mukesh Kumar, J.P. Dhaka and M.S. Meena. (2012): 'Milk Production Economics and Micro Financing Impacts in Chotanagpur Plateau of Jharkhand', *Indian Journal of Animal Sciences*, Vol. 82, No. 7, July, pp. 757-61.

Sirohi, S. and A.K. Chauhan. (2010): *Current Scenario of Livestock Development and Potential Interventions for Livelihood Improvement: Case of Jharkhand, India*. ELKS Publication Series 2. Kenya, Nairobi: ILRI.

Figure 1. Sustainable livelihoods framework

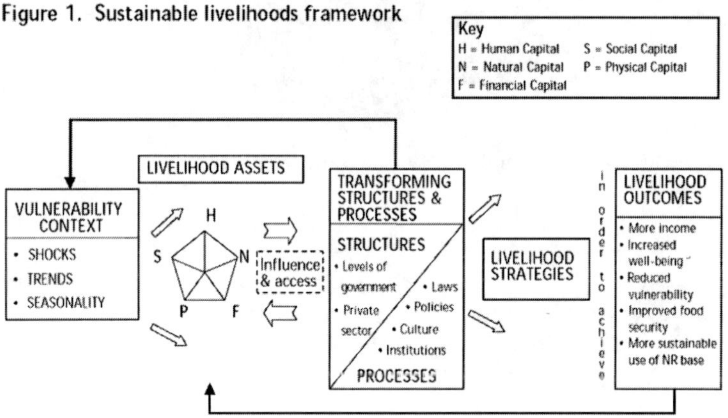

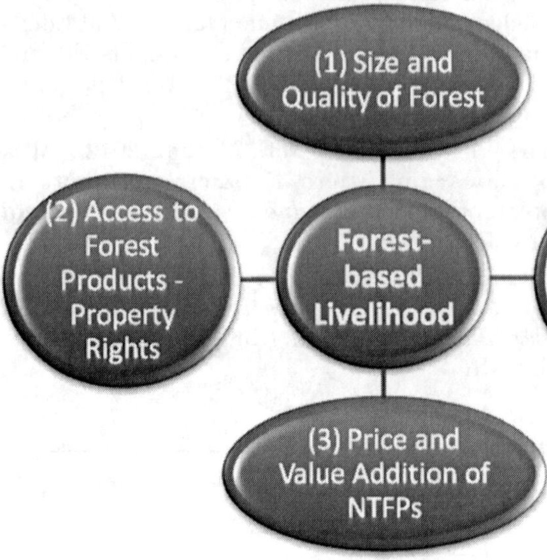

Figure 2: Forest-Based Livelihood Schemes (after Sarangi; 2013).

Chapter - 15

A Tribal Village of Odisha

— ***Satya Ranjan Mahakul***

Introduction

In the process of livelihood production, various communities across the world have evolved their own social institutions and cultural mechanisms for utilizing natural resources. Very often this process forms an integral part of culture. Anthropologists are in a privileged position to study the social and cultural mechanisms by which the communities have managed their commons[1]. Common properties are the resources accessible to the whole community of a village and to which no individual has exclusive property rights. They consist of village pastures, community forests, wastelands, common threshing grounds, waste dumping places, watershed, drainage, village ponds, tanks, rivers/rivulets, and river beds, etc., (Jodha,1986). Its survival depends upon the character of the communities and the institutions that have evolved around CPRs. These local natural resources are of more social, cultural and economic value to the dependent population, and are vital assets in the form of livelihood support for the community. These properties are not openly accessible and outside communities are not allowed to use these resources.

These community properties are under crisis due to outsiders' involvement in the form of privatization, encroachment and development. It is leading to depletion of resources and decline of its management. The significant outcome of different studies proposes that for the management of CPRs, participation of the local people is required. Management in this context implies human intervention in a common property resource system with a view to restore it, conserve it, or to sustaining its productivity, and regulating its use. The intervention could be in the form of application of labour and material inputs, creation of institutions or modification of existing institutions, enhancement of laws and so on (Kartar Singh, 1996).

The communities use their cultural knowledge sustainably, to manage with such natural resources. People adjust to natural changes by using their cultural knowledge. In a natural setting, they negotiate regularly with nature using such knowledge for livelihood. However, when people are being introduced to new intervention made by the State, the relationship between them and their resource alters. It leads to a break in the nature-culture relationship. People are the forces into a new setting, which is unfamiliar to them. This has serious implication for people and the environment (Siva Prasad 2001). This leads to depletion of community's natural resources.

I

The depletion of natural resources and its impact on the local communities were highlighted in the works of Jodha (1986), Fernandes and Menon (1987), Chambers (1989), Guha (1989), Nadkarni (1989), Gadgil (1993), Agarwal (1999), and Siva Prasad (2002). They clearly point out that development of a uniform process of reduction in diversity leads to resource depletion and decline in traditional management systems of resources. It is ultimately leading to destruction of traditional institutional arrangements, which facilitated the sustainable use of resources earlier (Karanth, 1992).

One of the reasons for deterioration of CPRs is outsiders' intervention with local resources. Increased uncertainty in the property rights is another reason. Suppose a community thinks that they together own the forest which their forefathers passed on to them, but the community does not possess any legal document regarding such forest, its rights to resources find insecure. When people are uncertain of their rights to a piece of property, they hesitate to make the investment to protect and improve them. If the security of CPRs is uncertain, then the collective responsibility of the people and its management system may collapse.

Another reason for the degradation of CPRs is that management practices at the local level are sometimes reversed by governing authority. It is found that a number of States in the Sahel, Western Africa, for example, imposed rules, that in effect destroyed communal management practices in the forests. Villagers stopped operating their authority to punish those who violated locally instituted rules (Thompson et. al 1986; Somanathan 1991; Baland and Platteau 1996).

Social norms of behaviour, established on reciprocity, can be breakable. The institutions based on reciprocity are especially fragile in the face of growing opportunities for private investment in substitute resources (Dasgupta 1993 and 2003; Campbell et. al. 2001). This is a case where institutions deteriorate when traditional systems of management collapse and are not being replaced by institutions that can act as substitutes, the users of CPRs become neglected. Balasubramanian and Selvaraj (2003) have found the oldest sources of irrigation in a sample village in southern India, 'village tank', deteriorated over the years due to gradual decline in collective investment in their maintenance.

History tells us that CPRs can be expected to decline in importance in tandem with economic development (North and Thomas 1973). Ensminger's (1990) study of the privatization of common grazing lands among the Orma in north-eastern Kenya established the transformation to have taken place with the consent of tribal elders. She attributed this to cheaper transportation and widening markets, which made private ownership of land more profitable. The elders were from the economically stronger families. She found that privatization brought out inequality within the tribe. In view of this, designing and adopting new institutions to solve CPR problems were a difficult task, no matter how homogeneous the group was, how well informed those members were about the conditions of CPR, and how deep-rooted were the generalized norms of reciprocity.

Hence, looking to the above reasons, the question arises how to prevent such degradation of resources, when the carrying capacity was mounting? The rapid population growth can trigger resource depletion, if institutional practices were unable to adapt to the increased pressure on resources. The growth in rural population was accompanied by the increased deforestation and reduced fallows.

Keeping the above questions in mind, a theoretical model was evolved to understand Juang perception towards common property, private property and government property in relation to their natural environment. The theoretical framework adopted in the study assumes that people who utilize common property resources [CPR] have their own logic in considering a resource as common property, in contrast to the understanding of the government, and in the utilization and management of such CPRs. This operates on the internal logic of the community that uses CPRs. This logic is hinged to their perception, management and resource utilisation. Common property for the community is shared and belongs to the community collectively. Natural resources are respected in the form of supernatural beings. If resources are to be appropriated and used sustainably, these beings have to be appeased in culturally prescribed ways. The logic of the Juang or any traditional community for that matter in the utilization of such resources is misunderstood by the State. The State constantly attempts to regulate people's use of resources. Further, the State introduces development programmes without considering people's logic of sustainable use of resources. In order to grasp how people perceive, utilize and manage natural resources, an understanding of the user's logic becomes essential to prevent further depletion of resources.

The study further assumes that outside interventions in common property resource affects the people's ownership and their utilization. Hence, people negotiate with the changing circumstances to utilize the common property. In the process, they redefine their relation with natural resources by perceiving the States property as common property. Government proposes the community which has lost ownership over natural resources belong to the State, but people feel the moral responsibility to take care of those available within their reach, as they earn their livelihood from them. Hence, they have an interest in their upkeep and conservation.

In the changing situation, the resource use pattern by the Juang though has not changed much; the form of use has changed. Some of the resources have acquired monetary value in the market. They use the new resources and accommodate them in their cultural knowledge using their cultural logic, thereby making it normatively accepted. They extend their belief, faith, rituals and gratitude to the new resources, by this process they make it fit into their system. In order to avoid the cultural imbalance within the community and environment, any aspect taken out of its context needs to be replaced by another cultural mechanism. The development measures have to progress along people's logic of resource use, if new intervention ought to become operational and participatory. Anything new to the community should be demonstrated to them in a way they can culturally adjust with it.

II

In this regard, this study analyse the utilization of CPRs, in general, and its sustainable consumption in the context of extensive tribal development of the Juang in Odisha. In order to test the validity of the theoretical perspective, fieldwork – using the traditional anthropological methods, i.e., participant observation, key informant and unstructured interviews, and case studies – was carried out among the Juang of Kadalibadi village, one village out of seven villages of *Satakhandia Pirah*, which comes under Gonasika Gram Panchayt in Banspal Block of Keonjhar districts, Odisha. *Pirah* is the federation of traditional, territorial socio-political unit of the Juang.

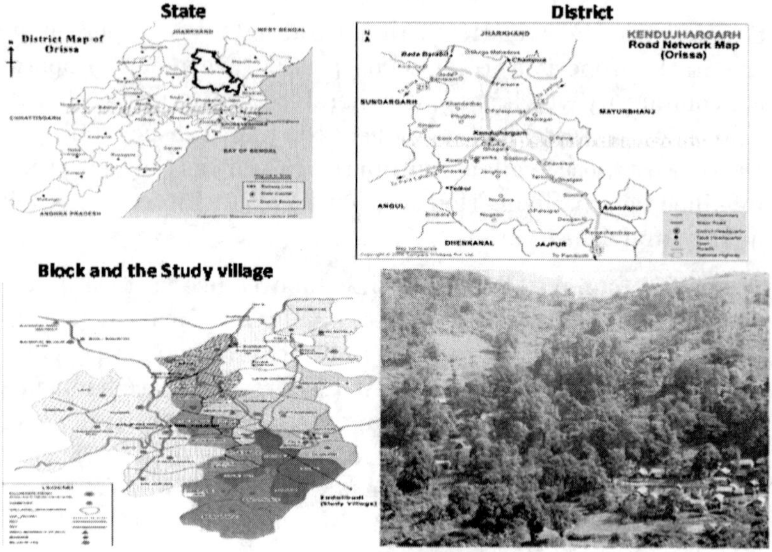

Objectives

1. To examine the changing pattern of utilization and management of CPRs in the study village.
2. To explore the socio-economic impact of CPRs management in terms of livelihood support and the problems faced by the village communities.
3. To understand the change in development context and its impact on livelihood and institution.

Methodology

Satakhandia Pirah villages come under the Scheduled V Area. Keonjhar district has extensive forest cover and consists of 46 Scheduled Tribes and Juang are more concentrated in Banspal than Telkoi, Ghatagaon and Harichandanpur Blocks. Major criteria for selection of the village are the presence of forest, CPR land and traditional institutions, like *kutumba* (kinship organisation), *majang* (community house), *barabhaika* (village council), etc., relating to CPR management. Common properties like village forest, stream, well, tube well, open land, fruit bearing trees, cultivable waste lands and degraded forest, un-demarcated forest, hilly areas, irrigated and un-irrigated land, grazing land and wastelands are found in the study village. The village has 23.3 hectares of forest, including 2.05 hectares of village forest. State has undertaken different developmental interventions, like Vana Surakya Samiti (VSS), Juang Development Agency (JDA), and other Constitutional measures to strengthen community institutions, like *gram sabha*. Juang have community forest protection committee named *Kadalibadi Jangal Surakya Samiti*, which comes under Community Forest Management system (CFM).

Village Resource Map

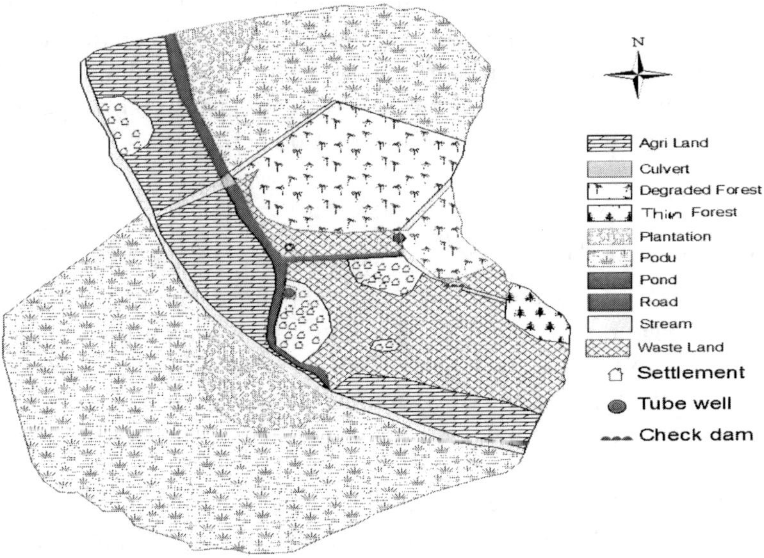

The village has fifty households forty belong to Juang and the rest with Gauda. This has provided a framework for identifying the quantum of CPR availability to the village community and also helped in rapport building. Techniques, like participant observation, resource mapping, social mapping, structured and unstructured interviews, key informant interviews, informal interviews, were used in collecting primary data. The study employed detailed checklist (interview guide), census schedule, recording of oral histories and case studies in data collection.

Study Significance

The significance lies in understanding the Juang cultural perceptions and social institutions for managing access to and use of CPRs. The study aims at understanding the reason in utilizing and managing natural resources by the Juang. This understanding can contribute to better strategies for sustainable development. It focuses on the impact of external interventions, including developmental activities, on the traditional modes of life and livelihood systems besides the existing resources in the village. In order to incorporate cultural and environmental considerations in developmental planning, there is a need for formulating a comprehensive strategy for CPR based development planning and management. This study strives to provide a broad normative framework for resource planning and development based on the proactive community participation accounting for their cultural perceptions and values.

III

Important Findings

This study explains how Juang perceived common property resource and their management and utilization patterns based on their cultural knowledge to earn their livelihood. However, a gap exists between the Governments understanding and Juang perception and their logic of resource use. New practices are required to utilize the resources simultaneously, when they were introduced into the community. At this juncture, a gap exists between new and the traditional method of utilizing those resources. Here, the Juang do not have the knowledge of the new resources and its practices. What the Juang have in the new context is their traditional knowledge and practices. Hence, to make sense of the new resources which is entirely new and unknown world, the Juang attempt to work out using their traditional cultural knowledge and practices. It is somewhat similar to approaching or understanding the unknown through the known.

In the new context, the resource use pattern by the Juang though has not changed much, the form of its use has changed. Some of the resources have acquired monetary value in the market. They use the resources anew and accommodate them in the cultural knowledge using cultural logic, thereby making it acceptedc normatively. They extend their belief, faith, rituals and gratitude to the new resources, by this process they make it fit into their system. In order to avoid the cultural imbalance within the community and environment, any aspect taken out of its context needs to be replaced by another cultural mechanism.

Traditionally, the Juang had perception towards property as one that is communal which was socially, culturally and ecologically sustainable. During the King's rule and the colonial period they have been introduced to the concept of private property ownership. The ownership pattern was imposed upon them by the State. Gradually, property owned by the community has shifted to the State (*sarkari*, according to Juang), wherein the individual derived ownership rights through the State.

Juangs perception towards property began to alter through the interventions of colonial and post-colonial rule. It changed from a communal ownership to private ownership. Hence, the Juang distinguished between private, community and government property. Land survey and settlement[2] operation and strict forest laws have enhanced the process of privatization of common property resources. The privatization of CPRs in the name of development, settled cultivation, diversion of grazing land for the purpose of community development, plantation in the *podu* land and its distribution for horticulture are constraints for the Juang to practice their livelihood. These changes are being introduced by the State with the idea of strengthening the livelihood options of the Juang. The consequence of these interventions resulted in the depletion and degradation of CPRs on which the Juang depend for their survival.

The Gauda's as outsiders were allowed by the Juang to access their ancestral land in a humanitarian gesture. However, Gauda have encroached eight per cent waste land by bribing revenue officials during survey and settlement operation. During this process seven per cent of *guda* land is given to 21 Juang families for private horticultural development. This conversion of CPR land to private land is a major change found in the study village.

Further, Forest Department has taken over 28 per cent of *podu* lands (nine patches) for social forestry plantation on the ancestral cultivable *podu* land of Juang.

The ancestral settlement site is also occupied by the Gauda. This is the root cause of conflict between the Juang and the Gauda. Gauda households were closer to the wet land and horticulture land, which helps them exploit CPRs. The grazing land finds degraded in the name of conversion and reservation for development purposes. We have found that 63.4 per cent of such land found reserved for future development purposes out of the total grazing land. Six Juang families have 4.6 per cent of land for homestead. Thirty seven per cent of grazing land found merged with the village forest. This has led to the reduction of grazing land; hence, the cattle were deprived of fodder. Currently, through settled cultivation, they get paddy straw for the purposes of thatching and fodder. Hence, they were not totally dependent on grasslands for such purposes, but still preserve and protect, whatever patches of grasslands exist within the territory. Among the other CPRs, since cremation ground is being declared as protected land, villagers search for alternative option of such activity in the forest or *podu* land closer to settlement.

Among other form of degradation, privatization of CPRs is often found in the study area. The privatization of *podu* land by revenue and Forest Departments in the name of development has reduced the access to land by the Juang. The Juang have a sentiment attached to the land as their ancestors depended on it. At present, 40 Juang households are only accessing 15 per cent of *podu* land for their livelihood.

Podu lands managed by the community are a major significance in the context of livelihood production. Juang community plays a major role in the selection of sites, its distribution, selection of crops, fixing the time of sowing and harvesting with the help of *nagam* and *pradhan*. The plots are being distributed according to the family need, size and cultivating capacity. Here, temporary ownership of land is being given to the cultivating family and later it reverts to the community after three year cyclic period of cultivation over.

Separately, communal plots (*ganaria ekan*) were allotted to young men (*kangerki*) and women (*selanki*) of the *majang*, which they cultivate on a cooperative basis. The produce from such plots are being utilized as funds to entertain and buy gifts for boys and girls coming from the *bandhu* villages. As *podu* cultivation is labour consuming, the community has developed its ways and means to solve the problem of labour exchange during such cultivation. In their community, factors like mutual help, exchange of labour, reciprocity have facilitated them carry shifting cultivation cycle. For example, the helpless widows and physically challenged lot in the village were given *podu* plots, so that they were not a burden on other people in the village.

The communal plots (*ganria ekan*) are being cultivated by villagers collectively on a cooperative basis. The produce of plots are kept in common village fund (*gan bua*) to be spent for entertaining guests, meeting expenses for common village disputes, litigations, arranging communal rituals, feasts and festivals, paying annual land revenues, and any kind of customary tributes, granting aids and advancing loans to villagers at the time of need and meeting various contingent expenses when sought. At present, the community land finds degrading due to privatization by government and encroachment by outsiders. Hence, there is a shortage of communal land to cultivate.

Land for *Podu* is cultivated for three consecutive years, namely *surilok, bualok* and *nala*. During these years, they mostly do mixed cropping like *rasi, sulur, suturi, gadari, batatas, bua, kudu, akayang, kudu, gingari, kesada, kalar*, etc. An important reason for mixed cropping is that the crops grown in the patch have different periods of maturation and are being harvested one after another. The scientific view is that the crops derive benefits from the associations of one another [as experimentally, there are more than one crop, which needs such phrase]. The pulses are being the source of nitrogen fixation. Millets and cereals are soil binders. The climbing pulses like *suturi* and *kalar* get support on *gingari*. The photochemical smell of one plant keeps insects and pests affecting the other plants away. After continued three years of *podu* cultivation, they leave the land uncultivated for three to four years to regain its fertility. This depicts the Juang's understanding and efficient communal management of land.

In comparison to the labour invested, the productive output from *podu* cultivation is very minimal, which hardly sustains three to four months in a year. But the process of *podu* cultivation keeps them occupied for about three-quarters of a year. The output from such cultivation is always uncertain and unpredictable, as it depends upon the climatic conditions, wild animals and birds, pests and diseases. Population pressure on land, prohibition and restriction by Government further limited the area and scope of *podu* which compelled them to cultivate the small area available to them continuously by shortening the recuperative period from eight years to three to four years at present. This has aggravated the situation further by causing serious damage to the soil and natural environment. Gradually the production has declined.

The Juang have adopted settled cultivation due to the influence of Gauda. Settled cultivation gives a higher yield of crops on which the Juang sustain for seven months. They have started cultivating at the valley bottom, besides the stream, for summer (*kharif*) and winter (*rabi*) crops. Though the *bilaw* (plain irrigated) land gives more yields, the Juang do not have enough land and knowledge to cultivate it. Therefore, forest and forest products offers them additional source of livelihood in comparison to wage labour, agricultural labour, migrant labour, timber collection, small business and government service.

Along with shifting and settled cultivation, forest produces as CPRs are major support to the community during lean period. In the village 90 per cent of households depend on NTFP collection which provides them a safety net. The average household income of Juang is Rs.537, which varies annually. During summer and winter they invest maximum time and manpower in the collection of NTFPs. The contribution of sale proceeds of *sal* leaf, *sal* seed, mango, mango kernel, *mushakani* root and *patalagaruda* root to the household income is quite important. For household consumption they use mushroom, jackfruit, *pitalu* and mango kernel. During NTFPs collection

92.4 per cent are collected individually, whereas earlier the whole community used to collect the NTFPs collectively and shared it amongst the households. The change is because of the introduction of market economy to develop the households and not the community. This also shows the lack of togetherness of the *kutumba* as well as the community.

The important role of CPRs is in reducing income disparities when other sources of livelihood fail. For example, all the households in the study village have poor income, less access to markets and are closer in location to the forests. Household data represents NTFP collection as a subsistence activity. CPRs are providing the basis of income generation for households with multiple options. For the economic development of Juang, socio-cultural and religious setting in relation to existing CPRs needs to be understood and recognized, that would be sustainable.

The method of collection, harvest and management of forest resources are based on rational and controlled process of management. The utilization processes of forest resources convey their management and conservation skills. They categorize forest based on their tree composition, forest position on hills, its size and religious beliefs. They do not cut the fruit bearing trees even if it is in the *podu* field as well as in the locality, because they treat them as their children. While collecting various plants or their parts, they apply certain practices like they burry the upper portion of the tubers in the pit and cover it with soil so that it will regenerate. They do not cut the trees which they are fond of, like the *mahua* and *kusuma* plant, even though they may need it urgently. They collect fruits, leafy vegetables, roots required for one day. So the products are not exhausted in a short time. Certain areas in the ecosystem like *salo* (sacred grove) were never harvested for any purpose, so that the trees get maximum protection to grow and decayed plants were left to decompose.

The traditional practices and its cultural relevance in the context of CPR land and forest cover are important factors for management. They are being emotionally attached to natural resources which make them quite possessive to treat as their own communal property. In Juang community, the process of social-cultural arrangements and supernatural sanctions in utilization pattern of resources restricts the growth of individualism.

They perform number of rituals related to the selection and distribution of *podu* land. Major one is *Pus-Punai* or *Magha Poda* festival when they perform rites to honour the ancestors (*pitruki*), village goddess (*Gramasiri),* other gods and goddesses, ghosts and sprits dwelling in hills, forests and streams by offering cooked food. *Tritia* festival is the symbol of beginning the sowing of crops, which is kept in *majang*, by the religious head, followed by others. *Amba nua* and *nua khai* are the festivals observed during the harvest by worshiping village deity. They observe these communal rituals and offer the seasonal fruits to those deities and ancestral sprits, before consumption. This acts as the survival measure. For example, in the *amba nua* (new mango eating) festival, they offer green mature mangoes to deities and ancestral sprits, before first eating. Similarly, in *asadi paraba*, they offer *bangrur* (*kusuma*) fruits to deities before eating. If such a ritual would not exist, these fruits would probably have been already consumed by the beginning of lean period. The ritual, thus, is a survival measure and ensures food security. There are other such rituals to control the use of food resources. New paddy is being consumed after observing *nua khai*, new pulses, vegetables, millets and tubers are consumed only after observing *kalarb*. Similarly, *siali* fruit, cakes made out of cereals and millets are consumed only after the observance of *pus punei*.

Sacred grove (*salo*) is conserved for the sacredness attached with it, It is regarded and worshiped in remembrance of ancestors. Trees are being protected with religious sanctions, so that no one can use any species of the area. Thus, the species in *salo* gets maximum protection. Safeguarding of totemic plants, animals, sacred groves and fruit bearing trees are viable approach of indigenous method for forest protection, conservation and management.

In the context of traditional management of CPRs in India, according to Chopra, (1990) three factors like; community organizations, community set norms and various forms of community management function at different levels have declined due to population pressure, state intervention and operation of market forces, found similar in the study village as well. The community organizations are like *kutumba* (members of the whole community), *gan bua* (village common funds), *majang* (mandaghara), *barabhaika* (village council), and the community forest management institution like (*Kadalibadi Jangala Surakhya Samiti*) play a major role in CPR management. The community norms like *paichala* (customary payment), *thengapali* (watch and guard system), and *padia* (a system of grazing) are decided by the community which is followed by all without any violation.

The traditional village council (*barabhaika*), at present is not being recognised by the Forest Department, Panchayat and *palli* sabha. So, they do not have formal village head. The active members of the VSS are the influential people supported by Forest Department. There is always a conflict between different new institutional member, like the VSS and Panchayat members, who represent the village in *palli* sabha, Panchayat sabha, and *pidha* sabha, etc. Functions and decisions taken in zilla parishad and *palli* sabha are not known to the villagers due to the above reasons. This shows that the management practices at the local level are most of the time reversed by the governing authority.

It leads to some conflict between the community and the governance system, which has usurped the community ownership over local natural resources. This enforces the community to think positively about the management of its resources. It is clearly reinforced along with measures like PESA and Forest Rights Acts by Government. These measures were not defined and explained clearly in Odisha context. For example, Odisha government had conformed, though not fully, to the provisions of the Central PESA Act while modifying its Panchayat Raj Institution Acts. Mandatory provision in the Central Act, ensures tribal communities control over natural resources, grant licenses for minor minerals and exploit and/or acquire such land by government for development projects, which is proposed to be enforced through Gram Sabhas have not been conformed yet.

Traditional institutions, through rational and controlled mechanisms utilize common properties. They are being *Desha* organization, *Pirah* organization, and village council (*barabhaika*). *Desha and Pirah* are the traditional, regional, and territorial socio-political units of the Juang which are managed and headed by their respective leaders. These leaders play key role in resolving territorial resource conflicts in intra and inter village managements. Nowadays, they do not have any functional power but continue to enjoy the respect of people.

Further inquiry can be taken up to ascertain about the sustenance of CPRs and traditional knowledge within a community [a particular environmental and cultural setting], when outside impacts were unavoidable. Many scholars were doubtful about the future survival of traditional lifestyle and some claim that could hamper the communities' development in other directions and integrate into civil society (Patnaik, 2003). Verrier Elwin with a vast research experience and a deep personal knowledge of/affection for the Indian tribes, called it a "sort of abstract power dwelling in the tribe so long as it does not turn from traditional customs and beliefs (Elwin, 1954). The point Elwin stated as back as in the late 1950s is still valid in its core. He demands for the understanding and respect for tribal communities without which no policy and laws can impact on their social situation. He says this process leads them to a situation like, "progress into nothingness" (Elwin, 1954). For decades, tribals have been alienated from their cultural setting and tradition by outside interventions which adversely impact the resource utilization and management practices. On the other way, it leads to the loss of their cultural identity.

The alternative solutions suggested by Demtez and Johnson about the CPR degradation find confirmed to be wrong through our study. Also, suggestions in favour of giving full authority to an external agency, usually the State, to regulate the commons is also wrong as per our study. Even though PESA Act is accepted by the State, but actual power was not given to the traditional institutions, because of the dilution in the State Act as mentioned in the fifth chapter. The State retained the power through this process. *Gram Sabha* (*palli Sabha*) lost its authority to ownership, control and management of natural resources in

Schedule V areas. Empowering the people over natural resources leads to its better access and management. In situation, where the State became inefficient, there was a case for strengthening community organizations by creating institutions that can manage common property.

The study reinforces theoretical position held in the thesis that for better management and conservation of natural resources, including forests, the government and other agencies involved in the business of development needed to understand the logic of resource users, as they are the ones who have interest in the upkeep and conservation. Unless, this perspective was not internalized into the programmes and interventions of the government and other agencies, the health of the natural resources and their conservation only remains a mirage. In fact, this approach can ensure a healthy partnership and trust between the traditional forest dwellers and the government and other agencies. This can ensure a better and healthy environment for the natural resource dependent communities.

References

Agrawal, A. (1995): 'Dismantling the Divide between Indigenous and Scientific Knowledge'. *Development and Change*, 26: 413-39.

Agrawal, A. (1999): *Greener Pastures: Politics, Markets, and Community among a Migrant Pastoral People.* Durham, NC: Duke University Press.

Agrawal, Arun, (2001): 'Common Property Institutions and Sustainable Governance of Resources'. *World Development*, 29(10): 1649 - 72.

Baland, Jean-Marie and Jean-Philippe Platteau. (1999): 'The Ambiguous Impact of Inequality on Local Resource Management'. *World Development*, 27(5): pp 773 – 88.

Balasubramanian, R and K N Selveraj. (2003): 'Poverty, Private Property and Common Pool Management: The Case of Irrigation Tanks in South India'. *South Asian Network for Development and Environmental Economics*, Kathmandu.

Campbell, Bruce, Alois Mandondo, Nontokozo Nemarundwe, Bevlyne Sithole, Wil de Jong, Marty Luckert and Frank Matose, (2001): 'Challenges to Proponents of Common Property Resource Systems: Despairing Voices from the Social Forests of Zimbabwe'. *World Development*; 29(4); pp. 589 - 600.

Chambers, A. (1991): 'The Paradox of the Commons', presented at the second annual conference of the International Association for the Study of Common Property (IASCP), Winnipeg, Manitoba, September 26-29.

Chambers, Erve., (1989): 'Thalia's revenge: Ethnography and theory of Comedy', *American Anthropologist* 91(3): pp 589-98.

Chopra, Kanchan, Gopal K Kadekodi and M N Murthy. (1990): *Participatory Development, People and Common Property Resources*. New Delhi, Newbury, London: Sage.

Dasgupta, P. (1993): *An Inquiry into Well-Being and Destitution,* Oxford: Clarendon Press.

Dasgupta, P. (2003): "Population, Poverty, and the Natural Environment", in K.-G. Mäler and J.Vincent, eds, Handbook of Environmental Economics, Vol. 1 (Amsterdam: North Holland).

Ensminger, J. (1990): 'Co-opting the Elders: The Political Economy of state Incorporation in Africa'. *American Anthropologist*, 92.

Fernandes Menon and Veigas, (1987): *"Tribal Women and Forest Economy, Deforestation, Exploitation and Status Change* New Delhi: Indian Social Institute.

Guha, Ramachandra. (1989): *The unquiet woods: Ecological change and peasant resistance in the Himalaya.* New Delhi: Oxford University Press.

Jodha N. S. (1986): 'Common property Resources and Rural Poor in Dry Region of India'. *Economics and Political Weekly*, 21(27): pp 1169-81.

Nadkarni, M.V. (1989): *The political economy of forest use and management.* New Delhi: Sage Publications.

Singh, Katar. (1994): *Managing Common Pool Resources.* New Delhi: Oxford University Press.

Siva Prasad, R. (2001): 'Changing Frontiers and resources Depletion in South Asia'. In Sudhir Jacob Geroge, ed., *Intra and Inter-State Conflicts in South Asia.* New Delhi: South Asian publishers, pp. 203-12.

Somanathan, E., (1991): 'Deforestation, property rights and incentives in central Himalaya', Economic and Political Weekly 26(4): pp 37-46.

Thompson, M., M. Warburton, and T. Hatley. (1986). Uncertainty on a Himalayan Scale. London: Ethnographica.

Chapter - 16

Building for Tribal Livelihood: The Wadi Experience [Odisha]

— *S. N. Tripathy*

Backdrop

Forest dwellers, mainly the tribes are among the poorest lot in India, for whom the forests are the source of livelihood, identity, customs and traditions. The forest dwelling scheduled tribes and other traditional forest dwellers inhabiting forests for generations were in occupation of the forest land for centuries. However, their rights on their ancestral lands and their habitats had not been adequately recognized despite being integral to the very survival and sustainability of the forest eco-system.

Thus, it is inferred that an enormous section of the tribal people has been traditionally depending on the forests for their livelihood and hence, their life and work is intimately connected with the forest. The forest laws have ruptured the organic link between the forest and the life of the tribes. One of the tragic aspects of tribal life has been their alienation from traditional habitat.

The draft National Tribal Policy (NTP) aptly remarked, "Land is the most important source of livelihood for STs. However, and in spite of state enactments to prevent alienation of tribal land, its wrongful alienation is the single most important cause of pauperization of tribes...." Further, they are being prevented from exercising traditional rights over the forests, even as the forests have been opened up to all sorts of plunder and destruction by the process of so-called development.

Suggesting that the "deep sense of exclusion and alienation" among the tribes was responsible for unrest in certain tribal areas, the NTP states candidly: "A situation is thus developing, where the STs view the state as their exploiter and enemy, and the preachers of violent actions as their protector and friend. Tribal people tend to support these violent movements as they feel that it would help them get their rights, protect them from exploitation and redress their grievances."

The studies have shown that there is a high percentage of population below the poverty line in forested areas, varying from 69.02 p c in south Orissa to 44 p c in Chhattisgarh, as against 37.2 p c being the national average (Saxena, 1999). This clearly indicates that the local population is not being benefited by the revenue generated by forest as a natural resource. Therefore, the existing situation needs corrections through policy interventions, under which the forests are used for livelihood requirements and the dependents for their poverty alleviation.

Moreover, the simplicity of tribes and their general ignorance of modern regulatory frameworks excluded them from asserting their genuine claims to resources in areas, where they belonged and depended upon. Insecurity of tenure and the fear of eviction from lands where they had lived and thrived for generations were perhaps the biggest reasons why tribal communities felt emotionally as well as physically alienated from forests and forest lands. This historical injustice needed correction and, therefore, the Government enacted the Scheduled Tribes and Other Traditional Forest Dwellers (Recognition of Forest Rights) Act, 2006, which is commonly known as Forest Rights Act (FRA). The Act came into operation with the notification of Rules on January1st 2008, for carrying out the provisions of the Act. The Act goes beyond the "recognition' of forests rights and also empowers the forest rights holders, *gram sabhas* and local level institutions with the right to protect, regenerate, conserve and manage any community forest resource. This marks a decisive step forward in resource governance itself for the tribes.

Sustainable livelihood

In view of their abject poverty and century old tradition of depending on forests and moreover, due to lack of alternative viable option for livelihoods, the indigenous tribal people have to retain their traditional right over forest resources. The tribes as forest dwellers conceived themselves as the trustees of forest resources, preserving the forest for the benefit of future generations. The tribes adhere to the sustainability principle by the economic and rational use of the minor forest produces, based on their traditional knowledge of protecting and conserving forests for generations. In view of the fact that the life of the tribal people is being linked with forests and land as an integral part of symbiotic relationship between the forests and the local dwellers, the tribes desire that they should be accorded full control over resources.

The confrontation between the tribal people and the government, across the country has been on the issue of land, water and forest resources, be it in South Bastar of Madhya Pradesh, Adilabad in Andhra Pradesh, Gadchiroli in Maharashtra and Malkangiri in Odisha.

Notwithstanding the ground reality presented in the aforesaid paragraphs, the tribal development policy embarked upon more than six decades was to integrate and change the development paradigm, by taking away the land and forest – the two aspects around which the community life of tribes is centred for the national interest.

In most of the tribal concentrated districts, ecological degradation, erratic rainfall and a high risk of drought in the area have resulted in the food insecurity, increasing outmigration and periodic deaths from starvation. The ecological imbalances in recent decades have seriously undermining the livelihood patterns and increasing the vulnerability of the tribes.

A small land base, low agricultural productivity and low incomes have led to the mounting indebtedness, trapping tribes into a vicious circle of exploitation. The life of the tribes is increasingly vulnerable due to a persistent lack of assured entitlements to their resource base. Land alienation has deprived them of their land; forest legislation has turned them into encroachers on land, which they have always used; and they have also been impacted adversely by the displacement due to mining operations, irrigation projects, wildlife sanctuaries, etc. For instance, the project affected a total of 427,000 villagers (89,000 living within the PAs) in and around the Periyar Tiger Reserve (Kerala), Buxar Tiger Reserve (West Bengal), and Palamau (Bihar), Gir National Park (Gujarat) Pench Tiger Reserve (Madhya Pradesh/Maharashtra), Ranathambore National Park (Rajasthan) and Nagarhole National Park (Karnataka) in which a sizeable section of the tribes have been victimised.

It is thus, inferred that tribal land alienation is the most important cause of the pauperization of tribal people, rendering their economic situation, which is extremely vulnerable even at the best of times, or more precarious. The access of tribes to forests for livelihoods has shrunk, both because the forests have shrunk by themselves, and because the regulatory regime continues to restrict tribes from collecting and processing non-timber forest produce for their livelihoods.

There are frequent occurrence of malnutrition related deaths in the tribal communities in different states including Rajasthan, Bihar, Jharkhand and Madhya Pradesh. The higher number of these deaths and the continuity proves that the tribal communities are more exposed to livelihood insecurity leading to food insecurity and child malnutrition in these states.

The ground-level observations indicate that the roots of the problem is the marginalization of tribes and their access failure to natural resources, especially land, forest and water. Low productivity, dispersed habitation, shifting cultivation, weak cooperative and marketing infrastructure, continued tribal land alienation leading to their dispossession and exploitation, physical complications etc. are some of the manifested features, which characterize the tribal areas.

The prominence of tribal peoples' concerns stems from the realization that they have not benefited from development projects, while the mainstreamed societies have prospered at their expense, pushing them deeper into the poverty trap. Deforestation, exploitation and recurring droughts and other natural calamities drove them into relentless grip of diseases, sufferings and starvation. About the decision which ends up destroying their land, livelihood and survival, leading to perpetual misery, the tribes were never consulted. These are voiceless people and unfortunately nowhere on the political agenda appear the restoration of their traditional rights to harvest and sell non-timber forest produce at fair and remunerative prices.

Moreover, the large scale direct and indirect displacement of the tribal poor, in the name of development has contributed to creating a huge army of disaggregate casual workers, pushed into the migrant sector, while the state completely abdicates on the responsibility to regulate or govern this most vulnerable section of the society.

Tribal development policy, despite the facts, embarked upon more than six decades was to modernize and 'mainstream' and make capable of participating in nation building. Despite the new provisions under the scheduled tribes and other traditional other forest dwellers (Reorganization of Forest Rights) Act 2006, arbitrary takeover of forest resources, establishment of state monopoly over forest resources and the conservation of traditional occupants of forests into encroachers, to be victimized , market and anti-tribal policy over the period. The tribe's rights upon basic resources such as land, forest and water, in fact in the entire environment have been seriously eroded, as non-tribal peasants, traders, businessmen and other categories of aliens have moved into tribal land, with the opening up of tribal areas, and with industrialization (Singh K.S. 1993, p.7).

Objectives

The paper focuses on the following:

(i) to evaluates the genesis of Forest Rights Acts, its dimensions in the context of forest management and possible constraints and challenges in its effective implementation as has been practiced in the tribal belts of India.

(ii) To identify the bottlenecks, and explore the ways for proper implementation of the Act and to know its impact on the livelihood, and

(iii) to evaluate the impact of Wadi-project on income, employment and livelihood of beneficiary households.

Methodology

The methodology adopted in the study is both historical and non-participant observation; based on primary and secondary sources of data. The quantitative changes have been analysed on the basis of sample obtained by employing quick appraisal techniques like rapid rural appraisals (RRA) and focus on group discussions with the beneficiaries in three simple randomly selected villages of Dasmantpur block in Koraput district. Three villages namely Bonasil, Marchiguda, Girliguma were selected and ten beneficiaries from each village aggregating 30 households from the villages were selected on the basis of same random sampling method in order to collect the primary data. Different socio-economic and environmental parameters were considered to assess the impact of Wadi- program on the development of livelihoods of tribes in the study regions.

The socio- economic impact of watershed has been examined by comparing the present status of different indicators during 2015-16 (Post project periods) with the corresponding figures in the year 2006-07 (Pre-project period). The marginal changes have been calculated through percentage changes and analysed accordingly.

The Rationale

There is a justification to take up this study to understand the nature of problems; emerged in the recent decades in the tribal pockets and the viable alternative livelihood programs necessitated to mitigate such important issues. Many of the issues interconnecting with the problems of tribes, their socio-economic problems emerged due to restrictions imposed on the use of forest and common property resources, are detrimental to their sustenance and livelihood; which have been portrayed in this paper.

Further, it is conceived that the study will be of immense benefits to the policy makers, administrators, farm scientists and extension agencies in taking appropriate decision to accelerate the diffusion of Wadi program as an appropriate intervention relating to agriculture and allied enterprises for the enhancement of productivity in terms of employment and income supporting the livelihood of the tribes in India.

Area Profile

Orissa is the poorest state with 46 p c of people below the poverty line in 1999-00, as against 26 p c for the country. As per expert group constituted by the Planning Commission, Government of India, under the chairmanship of Dr. C Rangarajan, 45.9 per cent of Orissa's population and 47.8 per cent of rural population continue to live below poverty line (Planning Commission, 2014).

Tribes constitute about 23 per cent of total population, who are the backward, marginalized and poverty stricken. Koraput is the most backward district, which forms one of the KBK districts of Odisha. The district accounts for 19.72 p c populations over 30.59 p c geographical area of the state and the tribes constitutes 38.72 p c (District Statistical Handbook, Bureau of Statistics and Economics, Bhubaneswar, Orissa, 2009). Several socio-economic indicators highlight the backwardness of KBK region, which is one of the poorest regions in the country.

The low level of income in the region, large scale unemployment, under employment and poverty, ultimately distressed migration of tribes has been due to the lower growth rate in agricultural sector. Such migrant tribes fall prey to exploitative contractors and suffer bondage, social isolation and identity crisis (Tripathy, 1989). There are evidences, which enlighten that because of deforestation, restrictions imposed by the Government for the use of forests, pressure on land, recurring drought, unemployment and poverty- the tribes of KBK migrate to outside the state in search of employment and livelihoods in construction projects and brick-kiln and other manual works (Tripathy, 2006, p.17).

Ecologically, rainfall is generally erratic and irrigation facilities are unevenly distributed. All the present eight KBK districts are ecologically fragile and problems of soil erosion and land degradation are common. Other socio-economic indicators such as population composition, net area irrigated, availability of hospital beds and connectivity to growth centres are far from satisfactory.

The state of Odisha though is endowed with abundant natural resources, yet it continues to be one of the poorer states even after six and half decades of planned development. An important feature of the state population is the presence of about 40 (S.Ts 22.85 p c and S.Cs 17.13 p c) per cent (2011 census) of weaker section comprising scheduled tribes (ST) and scheduled castes (SC). As per 2011 census, Orissa is ranked third (numerically) in terms of ST population, whereas its position is eleventh (numerically) in terms of SC population in the country. The census 2011 shows that density of Koraput district for 2011 is 157 people per sq. km. Average literacy rate of Koraput in 2011 was 49.21 and its gender wise, male and female literacy were 60.32 and 38.55, respectively.

Koraput stood at 1,032 per 1000 male, in respect of sex ratio. The average operational land holding in the district is 1.81 hectare in comparison to the state average of 1.34 hectare; in fact, it is the third highest in the state. The 27.6 per cent marginal farmers hold 9.71 per cent of the total agricultural land, the 57.8 per cent small farmers hold 78.46 per cent and the 14.6 per cent big farmers hold the other 11.82 per cent of the total agricultural land. Of the total land holding, 14 per cent of the agricultural land belongs to the SCs, while 71.7 per cent of the total land remains with the STs; other caste groups hold the remaining 14 per cent of the agricultural land (District Statistical Hand Book-2009, Koraput). The district Koraput is situated in the south-eastern region of the state. Rayagada, Nawarangapur and Malkangiri are the neighbouring districts of Koraput. As per 2011 census, sixty five per cent of the total population of Koraput comprises of SCs and STs with high incidence of poverty. The district very often comes in the news for naxalism, starvation death, death due to eating of roots, kernels, and malnutrition etc.

The district Koraput even with availability of abundant natural resources is virtually cut off from the mainstream of development. Shorter cycles in shifting cultivation, weaker linkages between forest and agriculture production systems, increasing fragmentation of land holdings etc. pose a threat to the subsistence agriculture practiced by the rural communities. Besides, the presence of Left Wing Extremists (LWEs) in some parts of the district has worsened the development scenario in the district in the last couple of years.

Genesis of 'Wadi' [Agro-horticulture Dev. Program]

Originated from a Gujarati word, "Wadi" implies a 'small orchard' usually covering one or two acres of land, has been initially introduced in the tribal district of 'Dangs' - as an effective tool for tribal development. This program later on has been experimented and replicated in other part of India dominantly inhabited by tribal population with great degree of success. The "Wadi" may be of any fruit crop suitable to the area or a combination of these tree crops, with forestry species on the periphery of the land holdings. Two or more tree crops are selected in the"Wadi" model to minimize biological and marketing risks. As the program progresses with "Wadi" establishment and income generating activities, loan assistance is also given to the participants to support income generating activities, micro enterprises, water resources development and other emergent needs under Alternative Credit Delivery System. Thus, a unique feature of the funding mechanism is blending of grant with credit not only to ensure participants' stake and involvement in the program, but also for self -reliance of the participants.

The "Wadi" model of tribal development is holistic in approach addressing production, processing and marketing of the produce and also other needs. Though, the focus of the program is "Wadi", other development interventions were also built around, addressing the concerns in the areas of environment, gender and health viz., soil conservation in the wadis, water resource development, agriculture development, women development and health.

One acre model of "Wadi'" accommodates around 60 fruit plants (depending on spacing) and 600-800 forestry plants, which can provide adequate income and livelihood security under climatic vagaries. In five years, a village gets converted into an orchard of proportionately equal numbers of families and acreage of land producing hundreds of tons of fruits. While the fruit plants generate income after 4-5 years, the forestry species provide a fence and also act as a shelter belt. The species mix planted meets the families' needs for fuel, fodder and small timbers and helps in reducing the pressure on existing forests.

An important aspect of Wadi concept is that any beneficiary under the scheme cannot sell the land covered under the project till the expiry of economic life of the orchard or for a minimum of twenty five years, which thus not only retain the land resource at disposal, but also secure the most valuable asset for the future generation.

The "Wadi" project, named after a system for land-based production in local parlance, has especially promoted agro-horticulture and agro-forestry, thereby enhancing the socio-economic status of the resource-poor families, and in improving livelihoods of tribes.

NABARD sponsored an ambitious project in 15 villages of the tribal-dominated Anandpuri block in Banswara district of Rajasthan. It has strengthened the rural livelihood scenario by successfully connecting missing links of resource management in agriculture, forestry, animal husbandry, pasture, medicinal products and fruits.

Banswara-based non-government organization 'Vaagdhara' has implemented the project sanctioned by NABARD under its Tribal Development Fund with the objective of bringing about a transformation in the rural landscape within the next couple of years. The initial results have depicted an increased access to nutritive food, better resource maintenance and reduction in migration to cities.

The main features of a Wadi model are economic uplift of the farmers through sustainable agriculture, social empowerment, improvement in the quality of life including health and women empowerment in tribal dominated areas of the country. The broad interventions are in the areas of land use planning, soil and water harvesting measures and improved farming based agro-forestry practices. Therefore, Wadi not only strengthens the agrarian livelihoods of tribal households, but also increases food and nutritional security. Wadi programme is introduced as the strategy to improve horticulture development. Tribal families having less than five acre patta land is being given one acre Wadi each for raising 60-75 fruit plants suitable to local area and 200-300 forestry plants on the boundary. Other development interventions in the Wadi areas are soil conservation, water resource development, agriculture development; women development, health, income generation for landless etc. are woven around the Wadi.

The socio-economic impact of Wadi program has been depicted in the **Table- 1**. It has been revealed that due to intervention of Wadi Program, there has been crop shifting from traditional cereals and vegetables to high value off season vegetables. The advantages accrued from the Wadi project to the tribal households can be summarised as [i] sustainable income from orchard every year, [ii] till plants starts fruiting, inter cropping provides earlier return to family, [iii] due to assured irrigation, farmer can take 2-3 crops in a year, [iv] ensuring food security to the family, [v] minimising the cost of production and [vi] collective marketing and processing of all produce because of bulk availability for sale.

It was found from the **Table-1** that with the introduction of Wadi program, the farmers have grown new vegetables. It has been demonstrated that the yield rate of paddy has increased by 71.42; cropping intensity has made a record growth of 101.51 per cent. The spectacular increase in the gross revenue per hectare has also been manifested. Consequent upon the hike in agricultural production and availability of fodder, livestock population has increased, which in turn enhanced the production of milk. It is heartening to mention that fish yield exhibited an increase by 50 per cent in the project area.

Further, it was revealed from the focus group discussion that the key factors explaining the highest incidence of poverty in the study region are: (1) tribes' low bargaining capacity; (2) their low degree of political representation and poor quality of local governance; and (3) constrained access to forest, land, and water. The issue of control, power and access to natural resources is contentious, both at the economic and the political level for tribal groups, apart from the deep-rooted corruption and massive pilferage of development funds by the Government officials (Tripathy, 2014).

Water harvesting through structures like vegetative check dams, brush wood dams, earthen gully plug, sand bag structures, farm/dugout ponds etc. were undertaken with a view to enhance the vegetation through raising nurseries, block plantation, afforestation of barren hills, bund plantation, live fencing, dry land horticulture, fodder development etc.

One of the most important strategies of the programme was to converge with various departments and programmes, to bring in a holistic impact. An effective convergence arrangement is being established with other programmes (MGNREGS - Mahatma Gandhi National Rural Employment Guarantee Scheme, a rural employment programme of the government) and departments (Department of Agriculture, Animal Husbandry, Forestry, Horticulture etc. for undertaking interventions.

Dasmantpur block Tribals' Livelihood

A survey conducted at the project's initiation included the indicators of agricultural production and economic value, existing trees and their productivity, cattle population, farm practices and fodder production. On the basis on these inputs, the results of livelihood interventions were estimated.

Large-scale deforestation forced them shifting on to the farming activities on a sloping land, causing degradation, while communities in the region have had forest resource-based livelihood. Continued and damaging run-off resulted in the loss of agricultural land along the stream course and led to an adverse effect on the ground water conditions in the district.

There are nine blocks in Koraput - Koraput, Similiguda, Pottangi, Laxmipur, Nandapur, Bandhugaon, Narayanpatna, Lamtaput, Dasmantpur. The villages selected were from the Dasmantpur; which is a tribal block in Koraput district of Odisha. Here, on the hilly and denuded land, the tribal communities have been traditionally practicing shifting cultivation of subsistence crops like millets and pulses supplemented by collection of forest fruits, roots, honey etc. However, destruction of forests due to commercial over-exploitation over the last 3 to 4 decades has decreased the productivity of the soil. This has severely threatened the well-being of the tribal community which depends on agriculture and forest, forcing them to be bonded and migrant labour; increasing their indebtedness; and exploitation of forest produce for income.

The fragile eco-system of the upland tribal regions has also been affected by deforestation and rampant shifting cultivation practice, causing extensive soil erosion, reducing the capacity of land to rejuvenate and affecting natural vegetation and water resources.The National Bank for Agriculture and Rural Development (NABARD) has been supporting various welfare projects for Scheduled Tribes in the country under its Tribal Development Fund. The Wadi project is one such integrated tribal development initiative of NABARD.

Objectives

(a) to facilitate creation of 1,000 acre of self-managed mini orchards for 1,119 tribal families;

(b) to empower and capacity building for farmers and women groups in 37 villages through different trainings for income generation.

(c) to provide nutritional food and safe drinking water for the families of the 37 villages;

(d) to achieve convergence with government schemes such as NREGS, National Horticulture Mission, National Rural Health Mission etc.

(e) to enhance their quality of life through basic services like health, sanitation, safe drinking water etc. in those project area villages

NABARD sanctioned a Wadi project in 37 villages covering 1,116 tribal families of Dasmantpur block and Agragamee [NGO] became the Principal Implementing Agency of the project in the targeted region, considering the extreme poverty, land and climatic conditions.

Water and Soil conservation

Although, Dasmantpur receives moderate to high rainfall, due to its steep slopes and rocky terrain, water retention is poor resulting in severe soil erosion and nutrient loss. To protect the fertile top surface runoff during the monsoon, and to increase moisture retention in the Wadi plots, earth and stone bonding, platforms, trenches and ring basis were introduced. Protective irrigation systems such as ring wells, check dams and diesel pump sets were used. The gully treatment and bunds slowed down the flow of water and stemmed erosion; the groundwater levels improved. This significantly increased the cropping intensity.

Intercropping [Organic farming]

Intercropping is used to cultivate a range of crops like grams, millets and vegetables [to optimise land use and cater to short-term needs]. Tomato, brinjal, beans, chilly, pumpkin and various pulses like arhar, chickpea, pigeon pea, black gram are being grown by farmers, which provide rich nutritional food to their family, while the sale of surplus crops supplements their income. The Wadis were supplied with organic manure for growth and soil revival. Sixty-five vermicompost pits were constructed under the project, where cowdung and goat droppings were used for composting. The rich compost improves the soil fertility and reduces the dependence on chemical fertilizers, thus facilitating the production of organically grown produce in the region. Measures were taken to prevent termite, bacterial and fungicide attacks by using neem cake and cow urine. All these efforts have increased the natural fertility of the soil and boosted production.

Local community building

It is highly important for the local communities to ensure sustainability of the project, participate and own the very process. A group of 10 farmers, who have compact land up to a minimum of five acre form Udyan Vikash Samiti (UVS), was formed. The concept behind forming these organisations is to assure better aftercare activities, and marketing. Till date, some eighty three UVS have been formed, and each has been provided capacity building and skill upgradation training on the orchard development, income generation and resource mobilisation. Fifty women Self Help Groups (SHG) consisting of 741 members were also formed and many of them have been involved in successful micro-enterprises. These factors have collectively helped in their saving habits, reducing dependence on moneylenders with growing self-confidence.

Table 1: Socio-Economic impacts [Wadi program] on Koraput tribes

Sl. No.	*Indicators*	*Pre-project*	*Post-project*	*percentage of deviation*
1.	Cropping pattern (Number of crops)	Only four crop (Paddy, brinjal, lady finger, cabbage)	(Paddy, brinjal, lady finger, cabbage, patato, adish, tomato, sunflower, peanut, maize, and beans) 11 crops	275
2.	Yield rate of paddy In quintals/acre	14	28	100.0
3.	Gross revenue per acre	Rs. 6,000	Rs.14,000	133.33
4.	Cropping intensity (Gross cropped area as percentage to land holding)	56.66	124.33	219.43
5.	Incidence of out-migration (No of persons reporting in a year)	10	Nil	-100
6.	Incidence of hunger (no of households remaining hungry for some days in a year)	15	Nil	-100
7.	Continued income from orchard every year	04 (cashew)	30 (cashew, lemon, orange, mango)	65.0
8.	Extent of multiple cropping in a year	nil	30	100
9.	collective marketing and processing of produce	04	30	65.0

Source: Field study.

A special attention has been given to 157 landless households by extending support for animal husbandry, a multi-purpose utility shop, tailoring unit, vegetable vending unit, and bicycle repair shop. Under the Wadi project distress migration in the region reduced by 30 per cent. On average, each farmer is able to earn Rs 8,000 to Rs 10, 000 per year from his Wadi, which has given him funds to invest in repairing their houses and purchasing other household needs. In each acre fruit, trees like cashews, mangoes, litchis etc. are planted with the agricultural crops.

The Wadi program has empowered the tribes as demonstrated from the evidence-based insights in directing the resources for maximum impact, while bringing the better prospects of employment and optimum use of land and forest resources. The Wadi-experience has shaped the socio-economic conditions of the stake holders in the study villages, opening new avenues of economic support and building new skills to the tribal households. On the whole, the sample tribal households of the villages namely Bonasil, Marchiguda, Girliguma have expressed that Wadi has ameliorated rather transformed their living condition through dependable and rewarding livelihood.

It was seen from the **Table-1** that because of the crop demonstration program, the farmers have adopted new vegetables. It has been demonstrated that the yield rate of paddy has increased by 100; the cropping intensity has made a record growth of 219.4 per cent. The spectacular increase in the gross revenue per hectare has manifested.

The socio-economic conditions of the tribes in the study villages were deplorable prior to the Wadi's drive. After the advent of Wadi, in these villages with the active cooperation of ***Agragamee***, the initial task was to develop land through earth and stone bonding; priority was accorded to fencing for protection from cattle. After the land was developed and fenced, provision of water facilities was created for extensive use of fruit saplings and intercropping which consequently transformed the rocky and uncultivable land into green Wadi plots. On its conclusion, the project is expected to make the target tribal households "drought-proof" with better nutritional resources and increase per hectare unit yield of different crops. With the livelihood available locally, production efficiency is set to improve and linkages for sustainable development strengthened.

Table 2: Abstract of the NABARD funded WADI Project in Koraput

District	Koraput	Total beneficiaries	1,119
Block	Dasmantpur	Border plantation	1,000 acres
Total villages	37	Supply of diesel pump for the irrigation purpose	36
Name of Panchayats (four panchayats)	Dasmantpur Chikamba Girliguma Dumbaguda	Check dam	2
Project period	2009 to 2017	No of landless beneficiaries	101
Total area covered	1000 acres	Funding agency	NABARD

Source: *Agragamee*, Annual Report-2014-15, Kashipur, Koraput, Odisha.

Bonasil village - A success

Out of three sample villages selected, for our study, the village Bonasilhas made tremendous success in its performance and conferred benefits to the participating households. Bonasilis a tribal dominated village consisting of 90 households; the majority of them are tribes belonging to the Kondha Paraja community. Bonasil became a model village under the Wadi project implemented with the support of *Agragamee*- a local NGO, has attracted the attention from the neighboring villagers, government officials and development activists for its lush green Wadi plots with mixed cropping of vegetables, grams and orchards. The project was designed to address the vulnerability of targeted tribal families, including those in the BPL and near poverty line, against fluctuating climatic conditions.

Concluding remarks

A perusal of the analysis reinforces the ground reality that forest-dependents are highly impoverished community. They are constrained to migrate urban settlements in subhuman living conditions without basic requirements. Deforestation, exploitation and recurring droughts and other natural calamities drive them into relentless grip of disease, suffering and starvation. About the decision, ending up destroying land, livelihood and survival, leading to perpetual misery, the tribes are never consulted. These are voiceless people and unfortunately nowhere on the political agenda appear the restoration of their traditional rights to harvest and sell non-timber forest produce at fair and remunerative prices.

Forests have not only been disregarded in economic policy but also have been plundered for short-term gain. Sustainable development of forest resources and their effective/optimum utilization is crucial for alleviation of rural poverty. Hence, what are needed are a strong institutional framework- and an effective legal and regulatory environment ensuring the rights of specific groups among the tribes and forest dwellers being recognized and protected simultaneously providing opportunities to develop sustainable forest business to these communities (Lahiri, Souparana , 2010).

Deforestation, shifting cultivation, over-grazing and improper cropping of undulating land, plugging of natural drains and other kinds of poor land management have been instrumental for runoff , reduced ground water recharge and water scarcity.

Such activities further result in the deterioration of soil, loss of valuable nutrients, lower yield, flooding of lower lands , sedimentation of small tanks and wastages of precious water to the ocean. Changes in land use, in particular degradation of soil, loss of vegetation cover and over extraction of ground water are likely to affect water availability through their impact on hydrological parameters determining recharge (Chopra, 2003).

In the Indian context, its position in the terms of population and forest resources, it possesses around 16 per cent of the world's population and 15 per cent of world's livestock, with only 2.4 per cent of the world's land area and 1.7 per cent of the world's forest stock. Apparently, land and forest resources were not commensurate with the proportionate burden of population and livestock on India's soil. Thus, there has been shrinking forests and land resources on the one hand and escalating population on the other, gave rise to the series of environmental complications.

The tribes have been demanding three basic issues: i) right of confirmed use of resources by those dependenets, ii) right of unbreakable link between the means of production and the worker and iii) rejection of those unconstitutional and anti-rights laws.

In the light of above, we can forward some suggestions for better policy implications:

(i) Reforms needed to focus on achieving secure tenure and management rights for the forest tribal dwellers; strengthening of forest management, providing access to more efficient market systems; and developing more effective and flexible institutional models for creating prospects of tribal livelihood.

(ii) Tribal participation could be evoked only by creating and sustaining their interest in plantations and utilizing their indigenous knowledge, preserving resources as the forests provide a wide range of services, which include prevention of soil erosion, floods, landslides, maintenance of soil fertility, and fixing carbon from the atmosphere as biomass and soil-organic carbon.

(a) scientific management of forest resources is the imperative to reduce the exploitation of natural forests, which requires plantations of mixed species and the recycling of forest products for better avenues of tribal livelihood.

(b) multiple livelihood options ought to be created for their sustenance in the absence of livelihood strategy and pervasive poverty, else they may revolt and sabotage the national interests. Hence, the issue of livelihood needed to be on priority, to arrest of any unrest with consequent outcomes.

(c) the productivity need to be increased for growth in income, development of human resources; elimination of exploitation with infrastructural development (D.C. Sah, 2008, p.35).

(d) non-farm enterprises such as leaf plate making, weaving, mushroom cultivation, basket making, group trading, edible and non-edible oil units, tamarind processing and packing of pulses ought to be promoted among the poor households.

(e) investment in social forestry, reclamation of agricultural land, provision of free and compulsory education, health services and guaranteed employment or source of employment with multiple livelihood options, equitable sharing of resources with utmost priority for tribes, immediate implementation of Panchayats Extension to Schedule Areas (PESA, 1996)in the fifth schedule areas, will certainly ameliorate the socio-economic conditions of tribes in Koraput through ensuring sustainable livelihood.

It is imperative that the agricultural productivity be enhanced by governmental efforts in the tribal pockets of Odisha, to harness the natural resources.

Notes and References

* Scheduled Areas are the areas; which are included in the Fifth Schedule of the Indian Constitution (Article- 244) declares certain tribal areas as Schedule Areas in the States of Andhra Pradesh, Orissa, Madhya Pradesh, Bihar, Himachal Pradesh, Maharashtra, Gujarat and Rajasthan. Similarly, Article 244(2) provides various provisions under Sixth Schedule for the administration and control of Scheduled Tribes in the North–Eastern States. On the basis of expert advice, as contained in the Bhuria Committee Report, 1995, an Amendment to the Act was enacted in December 1996 enabling extension of the 73rd Amendment Act, 1992, in a modified form to the Schedule Areas. The Act extends Panchayat to the Scheduled Areas (PESA) of eight Sates namely, Orissa, Andhra Pradesh, Madhya Pradesh (including recently formed State of Chattisgarh), Himachal Pradesh, Gujarat, Bihar (including the recently formed State of Jharkhand), Maharashtra, and Rajasthan, which intends to empower the Gram Sabha and Gram Panchayat in tribal societies to preserve their customs, values and traditions and ensure their traditional rights over natural resources. The main objective of all these initiatives is to bring sustainable development in tribal areas and, especially, to sustain the livelihoods of tribal communities.

Agragamee, Annual Report (2014-15): Kashipur, Koraput, Odisha

Chopra, Kanchan, (2003): 'Sustainable use of water: The next two decades', *Economic and Political Weekly,* Vol. 32, August, 9, p. 3362.

D.C. Sah, Ashish Bhatt Tapas K. Dalapati (2008): Chronic poverty in remote rural areas: Evidence from Central Tribal Belt of India (A Project financially supported by Planning Commission, Government of India, New Delhi), Madhya Pradesh institute of social science research, Ujjain

District Statistical Hand Book (2009): Koraput, Government of Odisha

Lahiri, Souparana (2010): From Colonialisation to Commodification: The Saga of India's Forests and its people, Globalization Governance Grassroots series No. 16, National Centre for Advocacy Studies (NCAS), Pune

Report of the Expert Group to Review the Methodology for Measurement of Poverty, Planning Commission, Government of India, 2014

Saxena, N. C. (1999): World Bank and the forestry sector in India, in World Bank, Alleviating poverty through participatory forest management; an evaluation of India's forest development and World Bank assistance, Washington, D.C., Operations Evaluation Department

Singh, K.S (1993): 'Tribal Perspectives – 1969-1990', in miri M (Ed.) *Continuity and change in tribal society,* Shimla: Indian Institute of Advanced Study, pp.5-10

Tripathy, S.N (2006): *Dynamics of tribal Migration,* New Delhi: Sonali Publication.

Tripathy, S.N (2014): 'Naxalism and the Development of Tribal Youths', in *'Tribal Studies: A Journal of COATS',* Koraput, Orissa, vol.2, Issue-2, December

Tripathy, S.N. (1989): Bonded labour in India, New Delhi: Discovery publishing House.

Chapter - 17

Forest, Governance System and Livelihood Pattern of Tribes: An Analysis

— *Jayanta Behera*

Introduction

Historically, tribals living within and on the fringe of forest areas have derived their livelihood from forests. Forests, in fact, have influenced their collective imaginations, belief systems, and culture, thereby shaping their very identity. Even today, there is evidence of the coexistence of tribals and forests (Poffenberger and McGean 1996). Although romanticized to some extent, the dependence of Indian tribal people on the forest was characterized by customary rules of use and extraction, governed by religious beliefs and practices that ensured forests were not degraded. Beginning with the arrival of colonial forestry, however, there has been unabated deforestation.

The British administrators in the 19th century viewed vast tracts of Indian forests as impediments to the prosperity of the colonial exchequer, as these lands could otherwise be utilized as revenue-yielding property (Pathak 1994). Thus, forests were rapidly razed to the ground both for revenue earned from timber supplies and for maximizing land revenue by putting the cleared tracts into cultivation (Guha 1994). The growing ship-building industries in England in the 1800s and the expansion of the railway network in India in the 1850s further spurred the demand for timber, leading to rapid deforestation. The risks inherent in unregulated logging were noted by some imperial officials, and they created the Forest Department to protect and govern the use of forests. They pointed out that continued exploitation of forests would severely impair the potential of forest stock to yield timber, and they advocated insulating forests from the pressure of local use. Toward this end, legislation to curtail the previously free access enjoyed by village communities was proposed. A debate ensued within the colonial bureaucracy, finally resulting in the passing of the Indian Forest Act of 1865.

A privilege, not a right!

The Imperial Forest Department was established in India in 1864. The state monopoly over forests was first asserted through the Indian Forest Act of 1865. This law established the government's claims over forests. Thirteen years later, however, it was reissued with far-reaching amendments as the Forest Act of 1878. This version curtailed centuries-old, customary-use rights of local communities over forests and consolidated the government's control over all forests. The Forest Act of 1878 established that forest use by villagers was not a right, but a privilege of concession was given by the government.

The Indian Forest Act of 1927 consolidated the existing laws relating to forests, the transit of forest produce, and the duty leviable on timber. It introduced three categories of forest distinguished by the degree of privileges enjoyed by communities over forests. The forests free from all claims were categorized as "reserve forests". These were exclusively designated for the use of the Forest Department, and forest-fringe communities had no rights other than the ones explicitly permitted by the state. The category of "protected forests" provided communities with certain rights solely for household consumption and not for commercial purposes. Their exclusion from forest management was, therefore, physical and social—physical, because they were denied or restricted access to forests and pasture, and social, because as "right holders" they were allowed only a marginal and flexible claim on the produce of the forests. The act formed a third category called "village forests", which provided village communities with more concessions in using forests for their livelihood. According to the act, the state government may assign to any village community the rights of government to or over any land that has been constituted as a reserve forest. But, the state government can cancel such an assignment. The government makes rules for regulating the management of village forests: how the villagers may use timber and village produce and pasture, and their duties for the protection and improvement of such forests.

The stereotypical attitudes of colonial administrators toward tribal uses of forests were most acutely captured in colonial policy on shifting cultivation, or *jhum* agriculture. Shifting cultivation, also known as *swidden*, is not an exclusively tribal practice, but it characterizes tribes, as it is different from the dominant culture of the plow that has been a key characteristic of the mainstream Hindu society. The prohibition of *jhum* in the Forest Act of 1927 led to an acute sense of deprivation among tribal communities, violating, as Guha puts it, "the aboriginals' notion of property, wherein the forests and forest produce belonged to the community, every member of which had a prescriptive right to harvest what they needed" (Guha, 1994).

When a forest settlement officer of the Forest Department decided to take over a forest as reserve or protected forest, the officer gave three months' notice to the communities to contest this decision. If communities failed to respond and file a claim within this period, the forest was vested in the state, and communities lose any user-rights that they have had. The official procedures for the settlement of claims and the demarcation of the forest boundaries were written in a way that was ostensibly favorable towards the local communities. But in practice, the communities could not benefit from such processes, because of their illiteracy and marginal social status. Their lack of capacity to negotiate effectively excluded them from benefiting from the complicated rules of notice, appeal, and settlement. As a result, most communities were physically displaced without appropriate compensation (Poffenberger and Singh 1996). Moreover, the local high caste elite and landowning households have exploited the limited access to forests that the communities had to their personal advantage.

The colonial state radically redefined the nature of private and communal property rights. While private property rights were limited to lands that had been cultivated regularly, resource-use practices such as grazing, forest product collection, and shifting cultivation were not considered as a basis for land ownership, even if land taxes had been paid for such lands. The priorities of the new system of forest management and control, imposed by the colonial state, conflicted sharply with local systems of forest use and control. In short, the forests of rural communities were being taken over by the state, and the rights of the village communities to such forests were progressively eroded.

After India gained independence in 1947, a landmark policy to take over the princely states controlled by the independent rulers impinged further on the customary rights of forest dwellers, although it did not entirely eliminate them. And the decision to nationalize the forests in those areas created a rush for exploitation, as people tried to beat the deadline of the new governmental authority. As a result of these changes in control, over 20 million hectares (ha) of forest were either logged or converted to agriculture throughout India (Poffenberger and Singh 1996).

The forest policies of colonial India continued into the postcolonial period, as exemplified by the National Forest Policy of 1952, which has further reinforced the right of the state to exclusive control over the forest protection, production, and management. Just as the fulfillment of imperial needs was the priority of colonial forest policy, the demands of commercial industry became the cornerstone of postcolonial forest policy. While communities were excluded from using those forests, many industries were granted raw materials at extremely low prices. Large tracts of forests were diverted for agriculture, hydroelectric projects, and other development projects in the years after independence. It is estimated that between 1950 and 1980, the rate of diversion of forests to sites of commercial industries was about 150,000 ha per year (Saigal et al. 2002).

At present, about 95 per cent of the total forest area belongs to the government, and the tribal population of India has been divested of much of its legal communal rights. This is a major practical concern, because the rural economy of India is largely biomass-based. People are directly dependent on forests and common lands for a variety of non-commercial-timber forest products for food and fuel, small timber for housing, and herbs and medicinal plants for meeting their subsistence livelihood needs. In the absence of alternative sources of livelihoods, or an ability to eke out sustenance from marginal landholdings, there is a continued high level of dependence on forests for survival.

The relationship between the ancestral land rights and the tribals has perhaps been most acutely brought into focus in the forestry sector in India and continues to be fraught with contention as communities experience new forms of encroachment on their customary rights by developmental interventions such as large dams, mining, and conservation. Saxena (2005) states that "nearly [8.5 million] tribals had been displaced until 1990 on account of some mega project or the other reservation of forests as National Parks, etc. Tribals constitute at least 55.16 per cent of the total displaced persons in the country." This is visibly acute in a mineral-rich state such as Orissa, the developmental history of which is spattered with conflicts between tribals and the state on mining-related issues. The violence witnessed during the tribal resistance to mining projects in the Kashipur area of the Rayagada district in Orissa is a grim example of this struggle. There has been a sustained and exacerbated threat to the rights of tribals to forest land that has been both a cause and a consequence of a larger process of political, economic, and cultural marginalization during the colonial and postcolonial eras.

Xaxa (1999b) argues that the root cause of the tribals' demand for "indigenous peoples" status is their complete loss of power over natural resources. The forest dwellers of India, who have been so severely disenfranchised have seized on the term as a rallying point to gain development assistance and demand back their lost rights.

The encroachment of the state on forests and customary tenure rights of the tribal forest-dwelling communities did not go unchallenged during the colonial and postcolonial periods. Environmental history in India has directed a significant amount of attention not only to the fate of forests in the country and its effects on forest-dwelling tribal/adivasi peoples and their subordination, but also to their resistance in increasing the commercial exploitation and the state control (Arnold 2001).

Undeterred by the provisions of the Indian Forest Act of 1927, many tribal groups have mounted a sustained challenge to the continued denial of their communal rights over forests. Gadgil and Guha provide us with one such example. "In 1957, a movement broke out among the Kharwar tribals of Madhya Pradesh, which called upon the people to stop payment of rent to revenue-collecting agents, utilize the timber and the forest produce without making any payment, defy magistrates and forest guards, and flout the forest laws which violated tribals customary rights. The movement slogan *Jangal, zamin azad hai* (forests and land are free) succinctly expressed tribal peoples' opposition to state control and commercial use of forests" (1995).

However, until the 1980s, the tribal resistance to the Forest Policy of 1952 had been sporadic, and as a result, the Government of India did not pay much attention to tribal peoples' rights or the need for recognizing their communal rights over the forests and other common property resources. In fact, it has been argued that tribal peoples' alienation and eventual physical eviction from forests in the post-independence era have become increasingly entrenched, as the postcolonial state has been even less responsive to the tribal claims than the colonial government was. The example of the *van panchayats* (forest councils) demonstrates this point. In response to agitations, the colonial government had gradually recognized the existence of some local community rights over forests and their resources, and these were incorporated in the Indian Forest Act of 1927. The act provides for constituting "village forests" to meet local needs, and this led to the creation of forest councils in Uttar Pradesh through a new state law passed in 1931. All the "de-reserved" marginal reserved forests were reclassified into Class 1 forests and placed under the jurisdiction of the *van panchayats,* in which local tribal communities play a key role in forest administration. More than 4,000 van panchayats were created, although the area under their control did not exceed 8 p c of the total forest area of India. Nonetheless, they represent an example of a forest tenure system in which the communal tenure is recognized by law (Sarin 2003). Moreover, as mentioned earlier, the India Forest Act of 1927 provides for declaring the intention of the state to reserve an area as forest. It also provides for the appointment of a forest settlement officer to arbitrate preexisting claims of occupants and users. These safety clauses, Sarin argues (2003), have often been dispensed with after independence, whenever the state appropriates tribals' communal land. The issue of what is deemed by the Forest Department to be encroachment on forest land has been highly contentious. The state has taken over many areas that tribal people considered as their ancestral property and has classified them as state forests and labeled tribals as encroachers on state land. These actions have undermined the application of Article 338(9) of the Constitution of India, which places the protection and welfare of tribal people as a "sacred trust" of the state.

Tribal areas in India are being governed by two separate schedules of the Constitution—Schedules V and VI—and by the Panchayats Extension to the Scheduled Areas (PESA) Act (1996). However, the constitutional guarantee that the tribal people could earn their living from forests was seriously eroded by the Forest Conservation Act 1980 and the Wildlife Protection Act of 1972 (Sarin 2003). For example, in Andhra Pradesh, almost all tribal areas under Schedule V of the Constitution have been designated as "forests". About 77,700 acres of land in Andhra Pradesh's reserve forests were cultivated by the tribals before the enactment of the Forest Conservation Act of 1980. A government memorandum in 1987 required the regularization of all cultivated lands by tribal communities. This memorandum remained unheeded for eight years, before it was superseded by another memorandum issued in 1995. The latter directed that all such lands should be brought under the World Bank-funded Joint Forest Management Project, a participatory forestry program. This effectively changed the legal status of such tribal lands into state-owned forest lands. Thus, environmental concerns regarding forests have clearly been accorded higher priority than tribal peoples' communal rights, despite their constitutionally guaranteed right to use forests for survival.

Forest Rights Act 2006 (FRA)

This law is an attempt to arrest "historical injustice" through the acknowledgment of tenurial rights of tribals and other forest-dwelling communities. Along with this legislation, the Draft National Tribal Policy of 2006 acknowledges that there has been "no single policy which looks at the issue of protection and development of Scheduled Tribes in an integrated and holistic manner." The government's acknowledgment of historic injustice and policy neglect is a definite leap forward toward recognition and legalization of the "third generation" rights-75 years prior to December 13, 2005. Essentially, the act aims to provide a framework to record the rights of forest dwellers, allowing them cultivate forest land that they occupy, up to a limit of four ha, guaranteeing them the right to collect, use, and dispose of minor forest produce, and ensuring rights inside forests that are traditional and customary, like grazing and maintaining homesteads. But, the most significant provision is under section 3(i), which pertains to the right to protect, regenerate, conserve, or manage any "community forest resource" that they have traditionally protected and conserved for sustainable use. The FRA also makes it mandatory for the rights holders to ensure sustainable use, conserve biodiversity, and maintain ecological balance, thereby strengthening the conservation regime of forests across the country.

Various tiger reserves have already been designated as the critical tiger habitats and as out of bounds for human beings in keeping with the requirements of the amended Wildlife Protection Act. Thus, the village communities lying in those areas will be relocated. Tribal rights activists, however, see this as an effort to arbitrarily sabotage the rights of indigenous peoples and remove them from forest areas (Anon 2007).

Even the rules of the act have attracted criticisms. For instance, it is argued that they were inadequate in the matter of eco-conservation by the *gram sabhas* (village assemblies). The act forbids diversion of forest land without the consent of the *gram sabhas,* but the fear is that they could be manipulated by commercial interests, particularly when those forces are too powerful and deeply entrenched. The law itself is not explicit enough on this matter (Roy-Burman 2008).

Man is a social animal and hence a man cannot live without his society and culture. While defining culture, Sir E. B. Tylor in his book '*Primitive Culture*' (1871:1) mentioned 'Culture as that complex whole, which includes the knowledge, beliefs, arts, morals, laws, customs and any other capability acquired by man as a member of society'. This culture can be divided into two types, *i.e.*, material culture and non-material culture. This material culture, also known as the tangible culture, is the physical evidences of a culture, which is visible, touchables and have a particular shape and size, made by man for a particular purpose. The material culture of a tribal and rural people is very much associated to their various activities related to livelihood and economy, like hunting, gathering, fishing, pastoralism, agriculture, household activities, means of land and water transportation, dress and ornaments, music and dance etc. on the other hand, non-material culture or intangible culture is the invisible culture, which does not have any physical shape and size and one cannot see or touch it. It includes, song, music, folklore, religion and rituals etc. the tribal and rural people are very rich both in tangible and non-tangible culture heritages. Preservation of heritage generally refers to tangible heritage, which has to be kept safe from innumerable hostile factors, which attack the materials of objects of art or daily utility and break them up (Harinarayana, 2007:11). Some of these cultural heritages are tribe or community specific where as some are area or region specific. Both tangible and intangible cultures are changing from time to time. Because of the interaction with the other neighbouring tribes and communities, invention of new technologies, availabilities of raw-materials etc the material cultural heritage of a particular tribe or community is changing rapidly in comparison to the non-material cultural heritage. To understand the level of change, the development of any people can be judged from the different materials used by that respective society.

Problems of the Study

Most tribal people in India lead a hard, materially poor life. That is a fact, but multiple natural sources along with strong community ties makes life possible, even under difficult circumstances. Displacement destroys these two important bases of individual's life - natural resources and the community. Adivasis largely depend on agriculture as their main source of livelihood. But, minor forest products, fishing, cattle supplements are their income and a means of livelihood in numerous ways. Tribes of the river bank, never go to work as wage labourer. The forest is our moneylender and banker. From its teak and bamboo, we built our houses. From its riches we are able to make our baskets and cots, ploughs and hoes. From its trees, leaves, herbs and roots, we get our medicines. Our cattle and goats, which are our wealth, graze here freely as they have always done, said by tribals (Sainath, 1996: 106-107) who lives in one of the villages in the study area. It has to be recognized that even a relatively liberal rehabilitation package cannot compensate for the loss of forest, river, ancestral land, which is intricately woven in the social, cultural and religious practices of a community. Only after we pull water ten to fifteen times from the well, is it enough for our cattle to drink. There is no water for them to bathe in. We are waiting for the rains when small puddles will form and our cattle will be able to drink and feel the wetness of this pond.

Objectives of Study

The objectives of study reflect a clear focus on the main goal and target despondences of the research work. The following are illustrative examples of objectives for survey:

- To find out economic profile of the respondents in the study area;
- To find out the role of government and Non-Government organization aimed to tribal development; and
- To suggest measures for the betterment of the livelihood patterns of the tribals.

The rationale behind the choice of the district is the following: (1) the tribals of Dindori district (M.P) mostly inhabit the hilly regions, mainly in close proximity to forests comprising near more than 64 per cent of population in the district. (2) The district in which almost all of the Primitive Tribal Groups (PTGs) live for centuries, being far away from the mainstream in their relatively isolated, inaccessible, less fertile and less agriculturally productive regions of forests, hills and mountains; (3) the role of governmental scheme is very important in these areas for enhancement of the standard of tribals.

The tribals living in such a remote area, where facilities are unavailable, for which they depend on agriculture, forest. In agricultural system, they have had to follow the traditional method due to lack of modern technique. Most of the tribals in these areas live below poverty line. A large percentage of adult tribals are not educated and not aware of their rights and thus unable to access to various opportunities meant for them. On an average 60 per cent of tribal farmers were forced to migrate in search of jobs, after the harvest season. They are prone to various forms of exploitation when they migrate. Migration also negatively affects the education, health and overall development of their children. The study in such areas is directed to underline the rate of success of governmental scheme to reduce the problems of tribals.

Methodology

The field survey have been undertaken in 30 remote tribal villages and the forest areas among Baiga, Gond, Koal, Pradhan, Dhulia, Bhoumia and Agaria tribes in Karanjia block of Dindori district. Dindori district has a special distinction of accommodating about one-sixth of the total tribal population of the State. Tribals constitute 64 per cent of the total population of the district and thus, it stands fourth among all fifty districts of the State with highest proportion of tribal concentration. Dindori district is situated at the eastern part of Madhaya Pradesh touching Chhattisgarh state. It touches Shahdol in east, Mandla in west, Umaria in north, and Bilaspur district of Chattisgarh State in south. It is 144 Km from Jabalpur on S.H 21, 104 km from Mandla and 88 km from the holy place

Amarkantak. It is located at 81.34° longitude and 21.16 ° latitude. The holy river Narmada passes through the district. It is situated at a height of 1,100 m above sea level amongst the herbal-rich, Maikal mountain ranges. Dindori has many historical as well as spiritual places. Some of the spiritual places are Laxman Madva, Kukarramath, Kalchuri Kali Mandir etc. The Kanha Tiger National Park is 180 km and Bandhavgarh National Park is 140 km away from the district headquarter. It was created on May 25th, 1998 with total 927 villages. The district is being covered in seven blocks namely Dindori, Shahpura, Mehandwani, Amarpur, Bajag, Karanjiya and Samnapur. The Baiga are PTG and very Particularly Vulnerable Tribal Groups, which can be found only in this district of Madhya Pradesh. The Baigas are known as the "National Human" (Official Website of Dindori District, 1998.)

The survey sample is the set of respondents, who are selected from a larger population for the purpose of participating in the survey. They are being studied to gain information about the population as a whole. Sampling plans address generalize ability, certainty and precision of results by defining who is included in the survey, how many people are needed and how respondents are selected? The study is mainly based on primary data collected from selected respondents in the affected district of Dindori through multi-stage random sampling procedure.

The researcher has conducted this study in Karanjia block of the district. Under the block numbers of GP (07 GPs such as: bhusanda, gopalpur, harratola, jhanki mal, jogi gwara, khannat mal, khari deeha) was selected. Field survey have been undertaken in 30 remote tribal villages and the forests areas among Baiga, Gond, Koal, Pradhan, Dhulia, Bhoomia and Agaria tribes in Karanjia block of Dindori district. Old and experienced men and women were interviewed for the first hand information on socio-economic condition. The numbers of villages were selected from the districts for studies. In the villages of district, 150 head of the households were selected on a random basis aggregating a total sample including male and female available during the interview. 92 men and 58 women were interviewed. The selected sample respondents were contacted in their respective residence and required primary information was collected with the help of a semi-structured interview schedule by trained local investigators. Some of the important variables covered in the study in respect of impoverishment risks include the customary rights and privileges, traditional knowledge system. Further, with the help of focused group discussion, additional data were procured regarding the awareness campaign among the tribals. The interviews were individually carried out during the first contacts with the local population, "native specialists" were identified, in other words, the people who consider themselves, and are considered by the community as having exceptional knowledge about their socio-economic problems. Several field trips were undertaken for collection of the data during different seasons. The information was gathered through oral interviews of the local tribal people, especially older persons. These data can be analysed quantitatively or qualitatively depending on the objectives and design of the study. Survey can be designed specifically to gather the information about the knowledge related topics.

Environment and Human Ecology

The forests have remained the usual abode of the tribal people in most parts of the world in general and the India in particular. Hilly tracts with the forest covers have become permanent shelter grounds for them due to obvious and non-apparent politico-economic reasons. Forest provides a suitable hunting ground and definitely a gatherers' paradise for most of the hunting and food gathering tribes of India. It is call of the time to have a sensible exploitation of the forest resources along with substantial aforestation in the same area for keeping the balance of means and consumption in the forest. About a couple of decades ago, the population was less and the forests were plenty in quantity and variety. Now, the situation is almost reverse. Forest reserves have gone down, while the population has increasingly gone up. The tribals are still the greatest friend of the forests and co-existence of both is essential

The tribals live in a forest environment on the hilly areas and developed some techniques to exploit their local environment for their livelihood. Their dependence on the forest ecological niche is unique for their adaptation as well as survival. They developed a nearly self-sufficient livelihood practices in the mountainous ranges and practiced slash-and-burn cultivation, and later on practiced settled cultivation on the valley areas between two mountains where water supply was available from natural perennial streams. The tribal settlements are situated on the valley areas surrounded with the forests. The settlements are devoid of any particular form which is a dispersed type of settlement. There are many fruit-bearing trees in the forest-environment and in their locality which help them to sustain in different seasons.

Most of the households have the homestead areas, where they grow vegetables, especially in the rainy season. They used to take it with boiled green leaves and vegetables and sometimes with the help of roasted fish; and salt, chili, onion are added with their staple food. In scarcity of availability of food items, they eat different types of boiled roots and tubers. They have had the knowledge of the specific roots and tubers in the forest, which are edible and collect it for their consumption. Rice and vegetable curry are taken mainly in the ceremonial occasions, and sometimes by the wealthy families of the tribals. Economically, the tribals were mainly food-gatherers and hunters in their forest environment. They still perform these two kinds of economic activities along with agricultural activities. The new-items of food-bearing trees have been introduced in their locality. The walls of the houses are being built with the help of bamboo strips applying mud on it. The roofs are being thatched with the help of a kind of locally grown grass, but tiles and tins are being used for making the roof at present.

Economic Life

Economy is the base of all activities in human life. It provides food which is the foremost important need of any living organism on earth. Human beings are more systematic for their economic production and gains than animals, because they choose various ways and means to generate various articles of need and comforts in their day-to-day life. For food and related activities, they acquire foods, which vary from region to region and community to community. Hence, the tribal form the hunters-gatherers, primitive agriculturists and so many other categories on the basis of their economy. Now, some groups have acquired knowledge and means to adopt neo-technique ecotypes, *i.e.* the year-round cultivation of arable land aided by the development of crop rotation and the use of fertilizers. It is, somehow, depended on irrigation facilities available to them and their interest to adopt the new techniques and implements needed for cultivation of land. The tribals of the study areas are deemed to be the good cultivators in the region due to their hard work, adoption of new agricultural techniques and use of fertilisers.

The researcher has conducted the study in such areas, where the villages were being surrounding by the forest of *Sal* trees, where the natural beauties fascinate every individual. The water of Narmada and Sono River brings fertility of land, where the farmers can generate lot of production on their land. They have adequate agricultural land, but could not produce the yield. Tribal farmers concentrate on their agricultural land and hope to produce lot of grains for discharge of the bailey. They have to do hard labour to fulfill their basic requirements. The area covers with biological diversity, which may promote eco tourism. The coming of tourists can develop the area. The tiger, forest and folk culture of tribals may attract the people.

The tribals directly depend on agriculture and forest to earn their livelihood. They collect small forest products such as *Harra* and Baheda (local name) in the month of March, April and May, *Amala* (local name) in the month of October, November and December, *Tendu Patta* (local name) in the month of March, April, May, June, November and December, *Dhup* (local name) in the month of January, February and December, Honny (local name *Saheda)* in the month of January, February, March and Appril, *Chironji* (local name) in the month of May and June, *Mahul Patta* (local neme) in the month of March, April, August, September and October. All the above forest products collected by them and sold in the week village market fetch least rate. They sell it to the small businessmen. These are the secondary source of income for them. Another secondary source of income of the tribals is that, they domesticate cow, buffalos, goat, pig and poultry etc.

Livelihood resources

(a) Hunting

The hunting-and-gathering was their main economic pursuit, and is still continuing, but in a decreased manner. They have opted new pattern of tools and techniques for hunting the wild animals. Nowadays, they are using the high power electricity in the forest for hunting. They are flatting/trapping the electric wear in the forest to catch the wild animals. On the other hand, their forest-environment provides many wild fruits, roots, tubers, vegetables and the like, for gathering activities for their livelihood. They used to subsist on hunting the wild games. Besides, they have practiced the slash-and-burn cultivation in the surrounding forest land, and at present, they are involved in settled cultivation with the help of their traditional tools and techniques. These activities provide them food and the forest-products provide them ingredients for making shelter.

(b) Agriculture

Agriculture is the backbone of tribal communities. The shifting cultivation is related to tribal myths and is the product of their culture. The shifting cultivation as a subsidiary means of livelihood is found among some of the tribal communities of Madhya Pradesh. A great majority of people of the study areas, with very few exceptions, practice shifting cultivation on the hill slopes, even on precipitous one and this is closely linked with their social customs and mythology. In present times, the shifting cultivation is being replaced by settled cultivation with the help of their traditional tools and techniques. In agriculture, the corps like different types of paddy, maize, *ragi;* varieties of vegetables, pulses, oil-seeds, etc., are cultivated by the tribal people. The varieties of pulses are like *kangu*, *kandual*, *jhudunga,* etc. The varieties of oil seeds are like *alsi*, castor, *til,* etc. In the study areas it was found that the tribal have opted a new pattern of technique to destroy the different types of tree from their agricultural field. Here, the researcher has observed how the tribals eliminate the trees from their agricultural field by opting a new technology. When the tribals of the remote areas have practiced shifting cultivations, at that time they have practiced a new technique to remove the trees from their agricultural field. At first, they have flatted the dry grasses and small fire wood around the root of the big tree, and then started to burn in the night. After few days that particular tree has to be dying, and then they have followed the same process to burning or cutting that dry tree. After few days it became agricultural land.

(c) Collection of Forest Products

People are directly dependent on forests and common lands for a variety of non-commercial-timber forest products for food and fuel, small timber for housing, and herbs and medicinal plants for meeting their subsistence livelihood needs. In the absence of alternative sources of livelihoods or an ability to eke out sustenance from the marginal landholdings, there is a continued high level of dependence on forests for survival.

The seasonal collection of varieties of minor forest-products supports their subsistence economy almost throughout the year. These activities are inherent in their life-activities; they start it from a very early age by both males and females. The edible roots and tuber roots, green leafy- vegetables, bamboo-shoots, mushrooms, tandu patta, mahua, chironji or char, honey, gums wood, etc., are collected to consume in different seasons. Sometimes, they sell it in the weekly market to local businessmen on very marginal price.

The most common tribal communities of the areas are the Baiga, Gond, Agariya, Pradhan and Kol. These communities live close to the forest and are largely dependent on the wild biological resources for livelihood. They utilize various plant parts, such as bark, leaves, roots, fruits, stems etc to enliven selves and remain comfortable. These ethnic people use to prepare simple formulations with single plants or combinations of two or more plant resources, which are easily available (Wagh and Jain 2010:715-20). The bulk of herbs traded still derive from wild harvesting. Only a very small number of species are cultivated.

(d) Domestication of Animals

Animal husbandry is the main source of livelihood among the tribal communities of the Madhya Pradesh. The tribals domesticate some animals, like cow, buffalo, goat, ship, pig, chicken etc., in their respective households. They are herding the domestic animals near by the forest. The buffalo, bullock are being used for agricultural purpose. The meat of goat, ship, pig and chicken are being consumed by themselves on different occasions. The meats of different types of birds are being consumed by them. All their activities are being centred around the buffalo-keeping and rituals associated with this.

(e) Dairy work

Even dairy work is being followed by certain rituals for the care of animals. The milch cattle are being considered sacred and are being attended by men especially. Besides the haunting, agriculture, and as a labourer, they have practised dairy work. Milk and dairy products are the main source of livelihood of few tribals. Dairy farming has been recorded as an amelioration of tribal poverty by way of providing assured, constant income on the day one itself, in the habitat providing nutritional security to the family members. It is an important instrument to fight against the poverty in tribal communities has come to limelight. The sources of income from dairy farming are through selling of milk and dung. It was observed that except agriculture and laborer work, the tribals are getting very small income from dairying and livestock directly by self sources in the study areas. In respect of seasonal labourers, since the amount of marketable milk was not constant, their income was on lower side. The field data clear that the dairy farming does not play a significant role in sustaining the tribal livelihoods, for which the phenomenon of migration, malnutrition/ill health are widely prevalent in tribal communities.

(f) Labour

Modern occupations are not widespread among tribals, some tribals are working in factories as labourers. In the same way, the Bhils and the Gonds are engaged in industrial labour in Madhya Pradesh. After completion of the seasonal cultivation, they are engaged in labour works in the construction of roads, clearing of forests, and also in agricultural works. In this way, they are engaged in wage earning to run their livelihood but their main source of livelihood is agriculture. Maximum contribution in household income comes from labour work including agricultural labour work and other labour works. In the absence of proper land and land holdings and declining traditional occupation, tribal people are diverting towards labour work and most of them are becoming labourers/seasonal labourers these days.

The actual magnitude of unemployment in the study areas has not yet been correctly estimated. But it is a well-known fact that there is large scale underemployment in the tribal areas, as the people mostly depend on agriculture, more or less seasonal in nature. Due to lack of employment opportunities, the seasonal migration of such workers from this district to another districts of M.P. as well as to the bordering districts of C.G. occurs during the time of transplantation of paddy plant in the rainy season and at the time of harvesting in winter season each and every year. While MNREGA implementation of the state has gained significant achievements, many job cardholders have alleged that although payment against their work is ensured, it takes prolonged period to get money after the work is completed.

(g) Art and Craft

The craft has remained a pursuit of interest and income since time immemorial, tribal people depending upon art and craft practice as a means of their livelihood during the lean period of their major economic activity, *i.e.*, agriculture. Art exemplifies a level, where the life and creativity are being inseparable. In its archetypal nascent state, the tribal arts have a unique sensitivity, as the tribal people possess an intense awareness very different from the settled and urbanized people. Their minds are supple and intense with myth, legends, epics and multitudinous gods born out of dream and fantasy. Their art is an expression of their life and holds their passion and mystery. Craft is a process of industrial production and form of artistic action. According to the dictionary meaning the word craft denotes "skill' art, trade etc. in India however, craft is always associated with art and that is why a craft example is usually considered to be a specimen of folk art or people's art.

Different types of utilitarian, decorative and ritual objects are still being produced by them, which serve the needs of the common people mostly in or around the centres of production, and satisfy the artistic taste of the sophisticated community.

The craft examples have their age-old traditions of production, their own designs, colour schemes and individual shapes. The objects may be made of textile items, baskets, vessels for keeping domestic articles, oil containers, water pots, musical instruments, measuring bowls, stools for sitting fishing traps, smoking pipes, tobacco cases, hunting arrows, combs etc. The decorative objects mainly include jewellery and ornaments such as the bangles, amulets, necklaces, finger-rings, forehead ornaments, ankle-bands, head gears and Bison horn headgears. Among other decorative items, special mention may be made of wall decorative items, which still play a significant role in the socio-cultural life of the people. The magico-religious objects mainly represent figures of deities which are worshipped by the indigenous people in their own way of ritual complex (Coomaraswamy: 1909).

(h) Common Land

Common lands are vital for the livelihoods of millions of people in India, which is still largely an agrarian economy. Only a single crop a year could be cultivated in most rain-fed farming areas. The dry, harsh, and risky environmental conditions of a large part of India have discouraged the privatizing of large tracts of land to be used as agricultural fields. As a result, many of the rural communities supplement their meager household incomes by depending on common property resources such as forests for their basic subsistence and livelihood. "Balancing of intensive (by cropping) and extensive (by pasture/forest) uses of land, as required by the resource characteristics, became a part of collective strategy for risk management and production enhancement" (Jodha 2001).

A vast majority of tribals thus depend on forests for meeting their basic needs of fuel wood, fodder, small timber for agricultural implements and house construction, and food and medicines. Resources from the "commons" provide the poorest of the poor with last-resort livelihoods as well as security of tenure in the form of a "place in the world" (Ellsworth, 2002).

A large number of tribal groups in the study areas live off the communal land. Even where some households own land, the area is usually very marginal (less than one ha of land holdings) and therefore largely unproductive (Brits et al. 2002). Where land reforms have taken place, such reforms have not been complemented with better literacy, development of skills, and provision of access to extension services. Moreover, the substitution of customary law with the codified law has progressively limited communal management of common lands. In many areas, rich farmers have taken possession of land parcels previously held by communities. The laws have sometimes regularized such encroachments. This was possible because the traditional institutions that used to control common property resources are no longer recognized by national and state laws (Gadgil and Guha 1995).

The role of Government

The traditional livelihood system of tribal people was based on shifting cultivation and collection of non timber forest produce. The customary rights of tribal people on livelihood resources and their territorial sovereignty increasingly came into the conflicts with the forces of development. Since independence, from time to time, several polices based on the positive discrimination and affirmative action for development for tribal people have been adopted by the State and National governments, but the situation of tribal people have not been much improved. The tribes of Sonebhadra district, Uttar Pradesh are facing the problem of displacement under the project of Rihand Dam, Kanhar Dam and consequently by forest department. The study establishes a link between the level of early deprivation and that of present development programmes. The development projects in the tribal areas displaced the people in a row. Adjustment has become troublesome in the new resettled areas. The present paper has narrated that how these tribes adjust with the resettlement after these displacements and they have faced lot of problem related to their livelihood.

Most of the development projects in tribal areas have resulted adverse effects in the form of displacement of people from traditional habitats and the way of life and denying them of their basic right to livelihood. Development induced displacement is one of the major social problems in tribal areas. The National Planning Commission estimates that some 50 million people have been displaced since 1950 on account of various development projects, of which more that 40 per cent are tribals. These projects include large irrigation dams, hydroelectric projects, open cast and underground coal mines, super thermal power plants and mineral-based industrial units. In the name of development, the tribals are being displaced from traditional habitats and livelihoods with little or no rehabilitation (Status Report, 2008: 33).

Displacement, in tribal areas forcefully evicted people from lands and natural resources created a serious problem. The displacement took place in the wake of implementation of development projects, industrial and mining project, power plants, like Hindalco, NTPC and construction of dam. Due to the larger displacement in tribal areas, the larger part of the local tribal people has been displaced from the original habitats. Their traditional and subsidiary occupation has been changed due to displacement of local tribal people. The traditional occupation of the local tribal people is sand quarrying from river. The secondary occupation of local tribal people is animal husbandry, farming etc.

In the study areas, the tribal people depended on the forest for livelihood. The life in the present time is full of struggle in the affected villages. The people deal a life of crisis in economy and get deprived from a list of civil amenities. The people of these villages grow mostly *arhar*, maize, paddy, wheat and occasionally vegetables on their small land holdings and depend on collection of *Mahua*, Tendu Patta, honey and dry twig, which offer them a supplementary income. Some people are doing work as a daily wage labour. The important thing is that women participate in these works equally with that of the men folk. Some of the women labourer are working as a daily wage labour in Industries and MNREGA. During the working period few of them, they get sexually exploited by the contractors. The children remain engaged in collecting *Mahua* and *Tendu Patta*, which made them absent from schools.

In the present study, it has been observed that the government of India and the state of Madhya Pradesh had started various training progrmmes to train the tribal people. Training programme (as in the participating training programme) also influences the income and employment generation activity. The training programme has made a positive impact on the generation of employment and income and it generated more employment for the member's households. In recent times, the government and the voluntary organisations have been endeavouring to tap the latent entrepreneurial talents of tribals. To that end, a number of training capsules on subjects like the agricultural practices, fisheries, poultry, dairy farming, weaving, disc making, rope making, handicraft by using of local raw material and basket-weaving etc., are being organized for tribal communities. The intention behind such initiatives is to empower tribal communities so that they can gain a greater degree of financial independence. It should be logical to expect that with enhanced self-confidence and own income, tribals would be more articulate in expressing their views in household matters.

Self-Help Groups

There are numbers of SHGs functioning in the tribal areas of Dindori district. The women are being attracted to the benefits such as savings, availability of loans for purchase of sheep, buffalo and other cattle. After the formation of one group, people have realized the importance of such groups and slowly but steadily new groups have emerged. The group members meet regularly and decide on the future course of action. In these meetings, the SEDS (Students for the Explorations and the Development of the Space) functionaries educate them about savings and healthcare. Due to regular meetings and *Gram sabhas* conducted by SEDS, their awareness level has increased enormously about their healthcare, children's education and most importantly their savings. As savings accumulates, women members could withdraw money during emergency. According to the statement of one of the respondents at the time of interview that before the formation of the groups, if anybody was ill in the family, they had to rush to moneylender for help, whereas now, there are SHGs to help. They borrow money from the group. The lending of money for one's own or children's is decided on the severity or necessity of the person which they feel urgent, such as health care, or children's school fees or any other urgent need." Women found to be active in such leadership in SHG. Women are sharing their views or dissatisfaction very freely and there is no undue interference. What types of facilities to be provided by the community so as to benefit the tribals have emanated from the group deliberation, it clear from the following data.

There are fewer number of NGOs/SHGs working in this area for the benefit of the tribals. The field work data clearly revealed that 26.66 p c respondents have taken loan from such institutional facilities for starting business. Another 40.84 p c respondents have taken loan for the agricultural production purpose. 22.5 p c respondents have availed the help of such loans to get rid of debts from moneylenders. Residual 10 p c respondents have obtained the deposit facility. From the above data, it was clear that the bank facility was unavailable in that area, it means it is far away from the tribal villages which made them face many problems, such as being debarred from different kinds of loan facility. Consequently, they are always exploited by money lenders' exorbitant rates of interest on the loan amount. The problems of poverty and drought that plague the region continually, but the work of other like-minded NGO's, both the local environment and population have seen improvements that change the situation for today's community for better future. Their saving levels according to them have improved enormously due to the efforts of the SEDS. Majority of the women are sending their children to schools, as they have realized the significance of education. They also have plans to contest and win the elections in the village and thus participate in the village administration and policymaking process.

In the study areas, it was found that SHGs fulfills the livelihood pattern of the tribal women. After a study the researcher got the knowledge that the midday meal is to be managed by the SHG group of the villages. The scheme was also seen as an opportunity for women's self help groups (SHGs) to take the responsibility for regular procurement, cooking and distribution process. In this context, an account of the self-help group managed midday meal programme was introduced in those schools. The self-help groups looks at the responsibility of midday meal more as a service for children rather than as a work for their group. They were of the view that since the responsibility of cooking has been taken by their SHG, they are continuing it. The money lasted for past few months have not come, so they were managing expenditure from their own funds.

In the study areas, it was found that the midday meal was assigned to an elderly woman from the village, had it been a primary school. Where the SHGs women were hired to cook, they reported long delays in receiving the funds. Some of them were unaware of the amount they receive, expenditure and planning for the purchases, as they were illiterate. The presidents of the SHGs were responsible for cooking the midday meal in the assigned school. During survey, they were called for discussion regarding the matter, but could not give much information. In spite of having above problems, they have opted it as an income generating source

In the study areas, it was found the individuals, who were landless or holding marginal lands and may not have direct benefit from the government schemes, they may, however, benefit indirectly through initiating income-generating activities such as dairying, rope making, basket weaving, tailoring, vegetable vending etc to sustain their livelihoods. Some of the cases have also encountered where, the SHGs were formed due to pressure of district authorities such as ZP-CEO, Collector, Commissioner, etc. It was observed during the field visit that basic principles of group formation in terms of caste, class, income level, gender equalities etc, were not followed in those villages.

The groups were formed by assuring the group members accessing financial assistance in terms of Revolving Fund and/ or as Bank Loan. The group activities were largely focused over women's groups rather than men's groups. A total 20-25 SHGs were formed and by and large, they have started as thrift and credit groups later on some of them provided some income generating activities through subsidy, but in the absence of adequate capacity building inputs in group dynamics and group process, these groups became defunct. Hence, the study has revealed that no substantial efforts were being made for awareness generation and community mobilisation at the entry point phase.

The Role of NGO

The NGOs facilitate the undertaking of subsistence activities, and income generation activities, either equal to or less than the existing wage income. These activities made a difference to the people insofar as they may be undertaken during the lean season and that the problem of seasonal unemployment be solved to some extent. It has been recognized that the task of the development of Scheduled Tribes cannot be achieved by government efforts only. The role of voluntary or non-governmental organizations, with their local roots and sense of service has become increasingly important. They supplement the efforts of the State in ensuring that the benefits reach to large number of populations. In certain cases, it is the voluntary organizations, who were found to have been in better position to implement the schemes of the government in a more efficient and objective manner than the government itself. This is primarily attributable to the highly committed and dedicated human resources that are available to some voluntary organizations.

Some 18.33 p c of the respondents have bad ideas regarding the NGOs, 41 p c respondents in the surveyed village have good ideas regarding the NGOs, 22.33 p c respondents express better views regarding the NGOs, and 18.34 p c respondents have very bad views regarding them. Thus, it is clear from the above data that those respondents who have derived benefits have positive attitude regarding the NGOs, and those who have negative opinion regarding them are either exploited by it or facing some other related problem. Thus, the level of knowledge towards the NGOs would be of critical value. Through this, the major numbers of tribal shall come forward to share the work of their own development. Tribals are aware of the importance of NGOs; large number of them are of the opinion that it plays a vital role to solve some different problems for those residing in the region and work for development of the region.

The role of Non-Governmental Organizations/Voluntary Organizations has been recognized since the beginning of the 1st Five Year Plan. Many voluntary organizations have done a commendable job in the uplift of tribals and are still continuing their efforts. However, in view of the mushrooming growth in their number approaching the ministry for financial assistance, efforts have been made to ensure that only genuine and committed organizations shall undertake developmental activities as the partners of government.

Conclusion

The tribal communities living in and around the forests are being disenfranchised of the customary rights to forests and forest produce. Today, they do not have *de jure* communal tenure rights, and there is much conflict between the communities and the state over the continued though limited exercise of de facto rights over forests. This historical loss of access to land has been central to the crystallization of an *adivasi* identity among such tribes in different parts of the country. This is also reflected in a number of social movements wherein "adivasi consciousness" is inextricably tied to the struggles over ancestral land, water sources, and forests.

In a poor and backward State, it is least expected that the development scenario of the village and the pace of socio-economic transformations could be better. Our socio-economic survey of different types of villages in different regions of tribal areas clearly reveals that the State has to make a longitudinal perspective plan for the transformation of the subsistence oriented backward agricultural economy in order to solve the problem of poverty and to improve the 'quality of life' of tribal people. Dependence of population on primary sector occupations is quite high, whereas agriculture with its present State of infrastructure and technology and, above all, operational holdings is itself not in a position to provide a substantial form of gainful livelihood to the majority of tribal. Development projects have failed to achieve desired goal across space and people. Often this serves the interest of only large, medium and semi-medium farmers. Like this, the welfare programmes and Minimum Needs Programme implemented by the State under social sector development to lessen poverty and improve the 'quality of life' of poor in tribal areas hardly reach the targeted population. With regard to law and Acts, there is no end to their formulation yet little beginning of their implementation.

In a poor and backward state showing highest incidence of rural poverty, the development of hardcore backward districts requires special attention. It is found that the socio-economic conditions of people have worsened over the years. The deforestation and erratic rainfall causing recurring droughts and famine like situation, the areas having more than 70 per cent of agricultural dependent population show bulk of the poor and destitute. This shows that the study areas have been affected by the 'backwash effects' of development, which may probably be due to their inherent disadvantageous factors like poor quality of human capital, backward and unsustainable agriculture coupled with reckless exploitation of forest resources. While economic indicators of development are poor, which produce acute poverty conditions, there are a number of social conditions of deprivation that tend to perpetuate poverty which, in turn, hold back social development. This is a kind of vicious circle, which calls for stepping up the investment in productive sectors to increase the pace of growth and improve the economic and social well being of the poor.

References

Anon. (2007): Government Notifies Forest Rights Act. Infochange Environment. infochangeindia.org/200801026795/Environment/News/Govt-notifies-Forest-Rights-Act.html (accessed on 24 Oct 2008).

Arnold, D. (2001): 'Disease Resistance and India's Ecological Frontier, 1770– 1847', In Scott, J. and N. Bhatt, (eds). *Agrarian Studies: Synthetic Work at the Cutting Edge.,* New Haven: Yale University Press.

Brits, A. M, C. Grant, and T. Burns. (2002): 'Comparative Study of Land Administration Systems', Paper presented at the Regional

Workshop on Land Policy Issues, Asia Program. <www.landequity.com.au> Coomaraswamy, A.K. 1909. *The Indian Craftsman*. London

Gadgil, M., and R. Guha. (1995): *This Fissured Land: An Ecological History of India,* Delhi: Oxford University Press.

Government of Madhya Pradesh. (1994): *Participatory Natural Resources Management.* Bhopal: Rajiv Gandhi Mission for Watershed Management, Department of Rural Development.

Guha, R. (1994): 'Fighting for the Forest: State Forestry and Social Change in Tribal India', In Mendelssohn, O., and U. Baxi, eds. *The Rights of Subordinated People.* Delhi: Oxford University Press.

Harinarayana, N. (2007): *Heritage: Essays on Museology and Conservation*. Chennai; New Era Publications.

Jodha, N.S. (1986): 'Common Pool Resources and Rural Poor in India'. *Economic and Political Weekly*. 21.

Pathak, A. (1994): *Contested Domains: The State, Peasants and Forests in Contemporary India*, Delhi, Thousand Oaks, and London: Sage Publications.

Poffenberger, M., and B. McGean, eds. (1996): *Village Voices, Forest Choices: Joint Forest Management in India,* Delhi: Oxford University Press.

Poffenberger, M., and C. Singh. (1996): 'Communities and the State: Reestablishing the Balance in Indian Forest Policy', In Poffenberger, M., and B McGean, (eds). Village Voices, Forest Choices. Delhi: Oxford University Press.

Roy-Burman, B.K. (2008): 'Ambiguities, Incongruities, Inadequacies in Scheduled Tribes and Other Technical Forest Dwellers (Recognition of Forest Rights) Act 2006: A Case for Constructive Engagement,' Mainstream. 46 (15).

Saigal S., H. Arora, and S.S. Rizvi. (2002): The New Foresters: The Role of Private Enterprise in the Indian Forestry Sector. Instruments for Sustainable Private Sector Forestry series. Ecotech Services and International Institute for Environment and Development.

Sainath, P., (1996): *Everybody loves a good drought*, New Delhi: Penguin Books, pp 106-107.

Sarin, M. 2003. 'Bad in Law', *Down to Earth*. 12 (4).

Saxena, N.C. (2005): Draft National Policy on Tribals: Suggestions for Improvement. National Advisory Council, Ministry of Tribal Affairs, Government of India.

Soni, Lok Nath. (1982): 'Economic Spheres of Indian Tribes: With Special Reference to Gonds', *Vanyajati* 30 (2):12-17.

Status Report, August, (2008): Land right Ownership in Orissa, pp. 33.

Tylor, Sir E. B. 1958 (Ori. 1871): *Primitive Culture.* New York; Harper Torchbooks.

Wagh, V. Vijay and Ashok K. Jain. (2010). Ethnomedicinal Observations among the Bheel and Bhilal Tribe of Jhabua District, Madhya Pradesh, India. *Ethnobotanical Leaflets* 14: pp 715-20.

Xaxa, V. (1999a): Tribes as Indigenous People of India. Economic and Political Weekly. 18 December.

Chapter - 18

Tribal Livelihood in Jharkhand: An Anthropological Explanation

— Gaya Pandey

Introduction

The state of Jharkhand has 32 scheduled tribes. Their traditional means of livelihood has been hunting-gathering, cattle rearing, livestock keeping, shifting cultivation, settled agriculture, artisan, labour and folk artist type work since time immemorial. But urbanization industrialization, modernization and introduction of development interventions to bring them in the mainstream of national development have allowed a change in the traditional livelihood and life style among them. These changes have brought positive as well as negative impact on traditional livelihood of tribals of Jharkhand.

Traditional livelihood

The tribes of Jharkhand accordingly, have been grouped as:

- Hunting-gathering livelihood – Hill Kharia, Hill Korba, Ulthalubirhor, Prachiya.
- Shifting cultivator: Sauria Pahariya
- Settled Agriculturists : Santhal, Oraon, Munda, Ho, and Bhumija

Animal husbandry and livestock

This means of livelihood is related to agricultural tribes. The agriculture tribals do animal husbandry and have livestock to supplement their income. No tribe is attached collusively to this particular means of livelihood. Livestocks are found even in the houses of shifting cultivation, artisans, artists and labouers.

- Sifting Artisn Crappnancialps

  Labour Harmali, meheli and chickbasaik are artisan tribes by tradition. Their traditional lifestyle revolves round craftsmanship. Lohara and karmali are black smith and prepare different kinds of iron tools. The mohali are kasnofmaters. The chickaraik are beavers. They weave traditional clothes for the local people.
- Labour

  This means of livelihood has found significant place after urbanization, industrialization and modernization. This means of livelihood is prevalent in almost all tribes of Jharkhand. After transplantation and harvesting of crops, each tribe supplement their livelihood by working as labourers and getting wages in cash.

Folk artist

This is also not tribe specific livelihood. Some numbers of each tribe earn livelihood by working as folk singers and folk dramatists.

Modern livelihood

The tribals came into contact with industrial society and modern society, after Independence. Due to contact communication and modern education, they have also brought a change in traditional livelihood. They are employing modern technology in the traditional means of livelihood, such as agriculture, animal husbandry, livestock, sheeping and craftsmanship. The modern means of livelihood in tribal Jharkhand are as follows:

Tribals of Jharkhand have been attracted towards modern technology related to agriculture. These include HYV seeds, chemical fertilizers, pesticides, weedicidos, ploughing by tractor, in place of spade plouging and oxen ploughing. Some have their own assured means of irrigation, such as tank, well and diesel machine. They are trying to get more and more yields from their downlands. In their kitchen yard some of them are producing vegetable for their own consumpsion, they are cultivating vegetables as cash crops. Some of them have become progressive farmers, in place of simple peasants. They are selling their agriculture produce in the market to get money.

Animal husbandry and livelihood

The tribals of Jharkhand have also been attracted towards the modern technology of animal husbandry ad livestock. They are domesticating cows and buffalos to get milk and earn money by selling them in market. They are also using veterinary services and cattle insurance scheme. They are rearing goat, pig, cocks, hens, and ducks through modern technology to supplement their livelihood, besides cows and buffaloes. They are selling them in market to get money.

Fishery

Some tribals are also engaged in fishery by modern technology with the help of governmental or non-governmental agencies. They are also having a good earning from the source.

Workshop

Some households of lohara and karmali are engaged in tracking, hunting, gathering and agricultural activities. They have established their own workshop. They are engaged in making modern windows and door frames and grills. They are getting regular order from the people.

- Basket supplier

  Some members of Hehala tribe have taken up the job of supplying different kinds of baskets in the local and urban market. They have a good earring from this work.
- Wearing modern clothes

  Some members of chickbaraik community have been engaged in handloom and Khadi industries. They are preparing modern handloom and khadi, *dhote, sari,* towels and *gamcha.*

- Sewing clothes

  Some women members of each tribal with the support of *Self-Help Group* have received training sewing clothes. Some of them have also own sewing machines. They do the job of sewing clothes of children, adult male and female.

- Small business

  Some members of tribal are now engaged in small business like shops, tea and breakfast shops, sweet shops, etc. They are having good income from this work.

- Rickshaw puller

  A number of tribal members are engaged in rickshaw pulling. They have their own rickshaw and earn by them. Nowadays, some of them have also battery-operated rickshaw.

- Auto-taxi driver

  A good number of tribal members are now engaged in driving autorickshaw and taxi. They have either own autorickshaw or taxi, or they have it on daily payment-basis from the owner.

- Meson

  Some members of tribal have received training in meson work. They remain engaged round the year in building construction and have a good income.

- Reja Collie

  The rapid growth of urban and industrial centers and different types of institutions and centres has provided opportunities to tribal adult males and females to get work as *coolie* and *Reja* in construction of building, roadbridge, roadways, hospitals and other types of governmental and non-governmental establishments. The male daily labourers are known as Reja. They get payment in cash at the end of each week. Different kind of construction works have brought opportunity for traders to got employment and payment in cash during off agricultural season.

- Contractor

  A number of members of tribal communities are involved in the construction work as contractor. For example, construction of buildings, roads, bridges, tanks, wells, and riverbanks and soon, they are being engaged as the contractor in governmental or private works.

- Land broker

  A good number of tribes are also engaged nowadays in the work of land brokers. They are involved in the buying and selling of tribal land as well as non- tribal lands.

- Migrant labour

  Nowadays, the tribals are also migrating towards the metropolises to earn more and more wages. They have become more and more aware that the wages of a labour in metropolises is nearly four times more than the rural and town areas. The willingness to earn more and more wages and leading a metropolitan life, the members of tribal community are migrating in different parts of the state.

- Service

  The spread of modern education has brought opportunities of doing service in different governmental, nongovernmental and private institutions on different posts. For example, they are employed by doctor, engineer, professor, manager, civil servant, police, cleark, nurse and so on. They are getting monthly salary and other benefits. The development of modern information technology has opened scope for them in multinational companies, private and government institutions.

- Establishment of company

  Some well-to-do tribes have established their own company and are doing their business. They are constructing multistoreyed flats, schools, hospitals and so on.

- Politicians

  A number of tribal members are working as MLA, M.P., Minister, Mukhia, Sarpanch, Ward member, Panchayat secretary, chairman, Zila parishad member and chairman, Mayor and deputy mayor etc.

- *Livelihood change*

  From the above accounts, it is quite clear that continuity and changes are true for the tribal livelihood in Jharkhand. Now, tribals are not dependent on one means of livelihood. They are involved in multiple means of livelihood. Traditional means of livelihood are also continuing with some modifications. New means of livelihood are being adopted by young members of the community. The impact of livelihood change can be discussed under two headings:

  - Negative impact
  - Positive impact

- *Negative impact of livelihood change*

  Livelihood changes has brought some negative impact on traditional means of livelihood, such as hunting, gathering, fishing, shifting cultivation, agriculture, artisan and folk artist occupation. A number of Forest polices/Act and decrease in forest areas have worked against the foraging livelihood. It is in the way, things of the past. Very few tribal families are engaged nowadays in these kinds of livelihood. Only those families are engaged in this livelihood, where members do not have any alternative. Some of them do the collection of minor forest produce under the forest contractor, as contract labour. The shifting cultivator faces a number of problems. Educated and service doors are not opting this kind of livelihood. They have either group-three livelihood or have left for other uneducated and unemployed family members.

  Lack of assured means of irrigation and continuous drought has forced tribal families to migrate to cities and metropolises to get work and wages. The migrant labourers are not coming back to houses for doing agriculture. They are leasing out lands for sharecropping to other members of the community. Service doors engage labourers and persons involved in other occupations won't prefer to do agriculture. Thus, agriculture livelihood is facing a great problem. Some antisocial elements are also exploiting tribal peasants. This has also gone against their traditional livelihood. Young and adult members are leaving villages to work in metropolises as laboures. Service doors prefer to live in towns and cities.

Industrialization has given a big jolt to artisan tribals. It is because machine made iron implements, clothes and baskets are available at cheap rate in the market. They also look beautiful than tools, clothes and baskets made by artisan tribes. Artisan tribes face problems related to raw material. They are not in a position to compete with machine made articles. As a result, craftsmanship of artisan tribes are in the way of becoming the thing of past. Majority of families, artisan tribals have given the livelihood of artisan or craftsmanship. Craftsmanship related tools can be seen in their houses as unused. They have become labourers from artisan. Nowadays, they do not have jajmani relation with families of other tribes and castes. Very few families are carrying on their traditional profession with the help of modern technology. They have migrated to towns and cities. They have their own shop. They are now not maintaining jajmani relationship. They have become order supplier by receiving cash. The educated tribal youths are also facing the problem of unemployment, because they do not like to carry out hereditary livelihood.

- *Positive impact of livelihood change*

Change in livelihood has brought a number of positive changes in tribal communities of Jharkhand. Due to livelihood change, the tribals have become cash earners and town dwellers. They have created *pucca* house with having all modern facilities. They have become aware of the education of child and health of family members. Their children are getting education in good English medium school, medical, engineering, management and post graduate institution. They have developed the concept of saving. They invest their savings to get more and more profit. They have also become aware of their rights and duties as citizen of nation.

Conclusion

After going through a good deal of discussion on various aspects of livelihood change in tribal Jharkhand, it becomes clear that the livelihood of tribal Jharkhand is witnessing continuity of traditional means and existence of modern means. This denotes that the livelihood of tribal Jharkhand is not static, rather it is dynamic. It has incorporated changes in traditional system of livelihood and accepted itself with new technologies in time. Nowadays, the change in livelihood can be seen in a number of families. The old member is carrying out traditional livelihood and young members are engaged in different kinds of modern livelihood. Women are now, not only confined to households chores, they are also contributing in family income through modern livelihood. The change in tribal livelihood has followed both positive and negative paths. This change has resulted in the rising standard of living of a good number of tribal families on the one hand, but it has given a big jolt to traditional livelihood of tribals. Due to changes, the concept of multi-livelihood has also come into existence.

Reference

Atal, Yogesh (1965): *Adivasi Bharat*, Delhi: Rajkamal Prakashan.

Bose, N.K. (1970): *Tribal life in India,* Bombay: Asian Publishing House.

Ghurye, G.S. (1959): *The Scheduled Tribes,* Bombay: Popular Prakashan

Guha, B.S. (ed) (1950): *The Tribal of India, Two Volumes*, New Delhi: Bhartiya Adimjati Sewa Sangh.

Pandey, Gaya (2007): *Bhartiya Janjati Sanskriti,* New Delhi: Concept Publishing Company.

Roy, S.C. (1912): *Munda and Their Country*, Kalkatta: City Bar Library.

Vidhyarthi, L.P. and B.K. Rai (1976): *Tribal Culture of India,* New Delhi: Concept Publishing Company.

Chapter - 19

Tribal Livelihood: A Study of Continuity and Change [Bharias of Patalkot]

— *Sunil K. Yadav*

Introduction

Livelihood refers to the fulfilment of basic needs of food, shelter and cloth. It can be extended to fulfil the requirements of medical, education and other needs. Robert Chambers and Gordon Conway (1991) in a classic paper proposed three components of livelihood viz., livelihood capabilities of a person, tangible assets and intangible assets. Tangible assets refers to stores and resources, which includes land, water, trees, and livestock; and farm equipment, tools, and domestic utensils and intangible assets refer to claims and access; claims are demands and appeals; which can be made for material, moral or other practical support or access. In other words, livelihood comprises capabilities, assets and activities required for a means of living.

In the context of tribe, their livelihood was based on natural resources of the surroundings especially on forest. They depend on natural resources, they had the capability to store the resources and had claim and access over the resources. Every tribal community had its distinct livelihood pattern on distinct ecological and geographical location. Several social

Anthropologists presented their views on their historical dependency on forest for livelihood earning and gave economic typology of tribes - Majumdar (1966: 153) suggested three typology, (a) hunting and collectional stage, (b) shifting or jhum cultivation, lumbering and manufacturing etc., (c) settled agriculturists, who also keep poultry, weaving, spinning and farming. Atal (1965) presented fourfold tribal economy classification. In 1968, Das presented fivefold division of tribal economy viz. Nomadic food collector and pastoral, shifting cultivator of hill slope, plough cultivator of plateau and tarai area, tribes who are partially assimilated in Hindu Social System and tribes who are totally assimilated who got a good social status among Hindu. Dube (1969: 247) categorized total six types under two main categories of economy as *important and semi-important*. Majumdar and Madan, again in 1970 gave six folds economic typology of tribes. Taking these classifications into consideration, Vidyarthi and Rai (1976: 116) suggested eight categories of tribes exclusively on their livelihood basis-

(i) The forest hunting type;
(ii) The hill cultivation type;
(iii) The plain agriculture type;
(iv) The simple artisan type;
(v) The pastoral and cattle herder type;
(vi) The folk-artist type;
(vii) The agriculture and non-agriculture labour type; and
(viii) The skilled, white collar job and traders type.

The above classifications are scholarly given by social anthropologists. For administrative purposes, nomenclature of tribes finds associated both in colonial and post-colonial period like criminal tribe in British India and de-notified tribe, particularly vulnerable tribal groups and scheduled tribe in independent India. The term 'tribe' is a colonial construct (Beteille, 1986) in itself and this colonial legacy is carried in independent India with certain modification. Those groups, enumerated in schedule of Indian Constitution are treated as Scheduled Tribes. Indeed the Constitution defines a scheduled tribe, as such tribe or tribal community or part of or groups within such tribes or tribal communities as are deemed under Article 342 to be scheduled tribe (Xaxa, 2008). According to Tribal Annual Report 2014-15, nearly 748 such communities are spread over States and UTs of India. In 1871, Criminal Tribal Act was enacted by the British Rule and imposed on communities supposed to be the habitual criminals and groups listed under such act were prohibited to move out of their area and they were termed as 'criminal tribe'. Till 1924, the act finally incorporated all such groups and implemented to the territory of British India. After independence, the list of such communities was carried by Indian government with mere modification of the term as 'nomadic' and 'de-notified tribes' with Habitual Offenders Act, 1952. As per National Commission for Denotified, Nomadic and Semi-Nomadic Tribes, there are about 313 nomadic tribes and 198 denotified tribes spread over the territory of country (MoSE, 2016). The misnomer of the tribal communities was again repeated in 1977 with the categorization of 'Primitive Tribe' (PTG) which was replaced with 'Particularly Vulnerable Tribal Group' (PVTG) in 2006, since the term 'primitive' is derogatory, but as per the Report of National High Level Committee on Socio-Economic, Health and Education Status of Tribal Communities of India (2014: 60) chaired by Virginius Xaxa the term 'primitive tribes' is still used by government, NGOs and media. There are 75 such communities residing in 18 states and one Union Territory over the country (Annual Report, 2014-15: 178).

Livelihood pattern is one of the important features taken into accoung while categorization of tribes whether Scheduled Tribe, denotified, nomadic or particularly vulnerable tribal groups which was termed to be under developed and was at the core of strategy of development. Taking into account their under development, various acts and laws have been formulated and enacted, several schemes and programmes are being implemented for their economic development. Subsequently, other process of change like industrialization, urbanization and globalization accelerated the process of acculturation and assimilation etc. and tribal economy and livelihood strategies have undergone subsequent change. *People of India* report by Anthropological Survey of India incorporated the diversified livelihood and economy of tribal. According to the report, the hunting and gathering activities has declined by 24.08 per cent, trapping of birds and animals has declined by 36.84 per cent, pastoral activities has declined by 12.5 per cent, shifting cultivation by 18.14 per cent and traditional craft has been declined by 25.85 per cent (Singh, 1997). Rise in number of agricultural labour and fall in cultivator and household industry (as categorized in census) raise questions like- At what sort, these changes are beneficial to them? Have their livelihood sustainability been affected? and, Whether they have uplifted in development ladder or their vulnerability is still the same? The study is based on these alarming questions in the context of *Bharia* (a Particularly Vulnerable Tribal Group of Madhya Pradesh) of Patalkot.

Objectives

To know the status of livelihood earning among Bharias;

1. To overview the continuity and change in their livelihood pattern; and
2. To analyze the impeding factors of livelihood earning and perspectives of its development to come up with suggestion for fruitful implementation of livelihood development programmes.

Study Area

Madhya Pradesh is geographically occupying a central position of the country with Bhopal as its capital. The state came into existence in 1956 and split to form a new state of Chhattisgarh in 2000. It holds the second position in the country in terms of area with a medley of ethnic groups and tribes, castes and communities. It ranks first in context of tribal population with 15,316,784 tribal populations (Census, 2011) which belongs to 43 tribal groups and sub-groups (Annual Report (2015-16). The scheduled tribe constitutes 21.1 per cent population of the state which is dominated by Gond, Bhil and Korku tribe. The state is predominantly rural because 72.4 per cent of population resides in villages (Census, 2011). As per census 2011, the state has 54, 903 villages, 23, 012 gram-panchayats, 313 developmental blocks, 342 sub-districts, 10 divisions and

50 districts of which Chhindwara is one where the present study was conducted.

The District

Chhindwara district is situated at 2,236 feet above the sea level on Satpura Plateau of Madhya Pradesh (Kalia, 1972). It is spread over 11,815 sq. km. of area (District Census Handbook, 2011) lying between 21° 28′ and 22° 49′ North and 78° 10′ and 79° 24′ East (Russell, 1907). It is surrounded, on the north by Hoshangabad and Narsingpur districts, on the east, by Seoni district, on the south by Nagpur and towards the west, by Betul district (Kalia, 1972). The district occupies 8th place in the state according to population with having 2,090,922 persons in 442,366 households (District Census Handbook, 2011). As per Census 2011, the scheduled tribe population is 769,778 constituting 36.82 per cent of district population residing in 1965 villages which falls under 11 development blocks of which Tamia is fifth scheduled area.

Tamia Development Block

Tamia is completely rural spread over 1,282.68 sq. Km. of area having 191 villages (District Census Handbook, 2011). There are 23,290 households in the block with 114,176 persons (Census, 2011). The scheduled tribe population of Tamia is 89,431 from 17,549 households. The main tribes living in the Block are Gond, Bharia, Pardhan and Korku. Gonds are numerically largest and Bharia, who are supposed to be most primitive and one among the three particularly vulnerable tribal groups are mainly concentrated in Patalkot region, where they earn their livelihood through collection of minor forest produce and agriculture partially.

Bharia and Patalkot

The Bharia of Patalkot call themselves "Bharia" distinguishing themselves from the Bharia outside the Patalkot who call themselves "Bhariya Bhumiya", Bhumiya means 'owner, lord or master' of the soil but the meaning of Bhariya is obscure (Kurup, 1986). Its simple meaning can be taken as 'bhar'

Table 1: Village-wise Population in Patalkot.

Sl. No.	*Gram Panchayat*	*Village*	*Total HH*	*Total Population*	*Bharia HH*	*Bharia Population*		
						Person	*Male*	*Female*
	1	*2*	*3*	*4*	*5*	*6*	*7*	*8*
1.	Kaream Rated	Chimtipur	49	250	19	85	43	42
		Ghogri Gujjadogri	15	80	0	0	0	0
		Kaream Rated	110	539	104	556	269	287
		Palani Gaildubba	65	361	35	158	80	78
		Total	**239**	**1,230**	**148**	**799**	**392**	**407**
2.	Ghatlinga	Ghana Saldhana Kodia	107	523	57	342	174	168
		Ghatlinga	133	486	62	247	117	130
		Gudhichhatri	69	300	47	300	139	161
		Total	**309**	**1,309**	**166**	**889**	**430**	**459**
3.	Harrakachhar	Dhurni Malni Domni	41	180	10	56	33	23
		Jadmadal Harrakachhar	68	342	41	188	104	36
		Jhiran	1	6	0	0	0	0
		Khamarpur Sehra Pachgol	104	597	95	472	251	221
		Sukhabhand Harmau	34	171	33	157	80	77
		Total	**248**	**1,296**	**179**	**873**	**468**	**357**
	Grand Total		**796**	**3,835**	**503**	**2,665**	**1,290**	**1,271**

Note: For column 1, 6, 7 and 8 Bharia Development Agency Survey Report 2009-10, For column 2 Tiwari (1985), for coloumn 3, 4 and 5 Primary Census Abstract, Census 2011.

or 'weight', the Bharia then so called load carriers or coolies. Bharias have forgotten about their affinity so knowledge about their origin is apparent, one of the stories of origin says that Arjun, when matters were going badly with the *Pandavas* in their battle against *Kauravas*, took up a handful of *bharru* grass and, pressing it produced men who fought in the battle and became the ancestors of the Bharias. Russel and Hiralal consider that Bharia is the contemptuous form of Bhar and belong to the great Bhar tribe who were once dominant in the eastern part of the United Provinces (Russell and Hiralal, 1916). One of the stories says that when the Maratha terrritories were taken over by the British, Raghuji III hide in the Patalkot and men who carried belongings of Raghuji III settled there and they are now called Bharias.

Patalkot, the residence of Bharia (PVTG of Madhya Pradesh) is a bowl-shaped valley, situated approximately between 22° 24′ and 22° 26′ North, and between 78° 40′ and 79° 10′ East is about 31 sq. Miles in area falls under the Tamia Development Block (Russell, 1907). It is a land locked area surrounded by hills rises to about 1500 ft. The inhabitants of these villages are Gonds and Bharias who were practicing shifting cultivation (Kalia, 1972) but now they have moved as settled cultivators with state interventions. There are 796 households in these twelve villages comprising 3835 persons in which 1923 are males and 1912 are females (Census, 2011).

The universe of the study is 503 Bharia households with 2665 Bharia population of twelve villages. Bharia Development Agency survey report 2009-10 says - two villages viz., Ghoghrigujja Dogri and Jhiran have no Bharia household and the remaining villages of Patalkot has been categorized on the basis of percentage of Bharia household with total households of Patalkot and these categories are as under-

(1) Villages with 100 per cent Bharia households:

- (i) Kaream Rated
- (ii) Khamarpur Sehrapachgol
- (iii) Sukhabhand Harmau

(2) Villages with either or above 50 per cent of Bharia households:
   (i) Gudichhatri
   (ii) Palani Gaildubba
   (iii) Ghana Saldhana Kodia
   (iv) Ghatlinga

(3) Villages with below 50 per cent Bharia households:
   (i) Jadmadal Harrakachhar
   (ii) Dhurni Malni Domni
   (iii) Chimtipur

Sampling

Four villages have been selected from the categorization mentioned above viz. Kareamrated, Palani Galdubba, Ghatlinga and Jadmadal Harrakachhar for the purpose of the study of which 200 households were selected as main respondents by adopting convenience sampling technique for which 100 households from category I, 75 from category II, and 25 families from category III village.

Table: 2 Socio-economic Profile of Studied villages

		Palani Geldubba	*Ghatlinga*	*Kareamrated*	*Jadmadal Harrakachhar*
Area of Village (in hect.)		5.21	3.58	4.29	2.31
No. of Household		65	133	110	68
Population	Total	361	486	539	342
	Male	176	243	275	177
	Female	185	243	264	165
0-6 Age Population	Total	59	78	100	67
	Male	32	42	55	34
	Female	27	36	45	33
Literacy	Total	55.6	85.2	54.8	36.7
	Male	59.7	73.6	61.3	49.6
	Female	51.8	79.7	48.4	22.7
Sex Ratio	General	1,051	1,000	960	932
	0-6Age	843	857	818	970
Total Worker	Total	181	293	267	195
	Male	88	148	132	95
	Female	93	145	135	100
Main Worker	Total	15	45	33	166
	Male	12	30	26	82
	Female	03	15	07	84

(Contd...)

Cultivator	Total	05	10	00	110
	Male	04	08	00	55
	Female	01	02	00	55
Agriculture labour	Total	01	06	10	49
	Male	01	04	08	23
	Female	00	02	02	26
Marginal Worker	Total	166	248	234	29
	Male	76	118	106	13
	Female	90	130	128	16
Cultivator	Total	57	64	62	20
	Male	48	58	59	11
	Female	09	06	03	09
Agriculture Labour	Total	104	175	169	08
	Male	23	54	44	02
	Female	81	121	125	06

Source: Census 2011, Office of the Registrar General, Govt. Of India.

Materials and Method

The study is exploratory in nature. Semi-structured interview schedule was used to collect data from main respondents. Interview guide was prepared for key respondents. Other tools and techniques were also adopted like observation, informal interaction with villagers, photographs and group discussion to comprehend the reality. For secondary data, various reports and surveys of governmental and non-governmental organizations were used alongwith review of earlier studies was made.

Findings and Discussion

Findings of the study have been discussed broadly in five sections. The first section deals with traditional livelihood activities performed by Bharias followed by second section, which is based on newly emerged wage work and emergence of migration in the region. Earning, expenditure, saving and indebtedness have been presented in third part. The fourth part deals with initiatives by change agents and its impact. Finally, conclusive remark and suggestion have been given in fifth part.

I

Collection /Marketing NTFPs (Non-timber Forest Produce)

Historically, tribal livelihood revolves around forest

characterized with non-monetized economy and it was the only means of their food, shelter and cloth from the beginning (Chaudhary, 2012: 192). They hunt in the forest, collect roots, bark, fruit and nuts, leaves and wood etc. from the forest to earn their livelihood. Prohibition on hunting and on forest with its categorization as protected forest and national park delimited their access to forest which compelled them to collect only non-timber forest produce from forest upon which once their entire basic requirements of livelihood were fulfilled. Patalkot valley, the habitat of Bharia is covered with forest having various herbs, shrubs and trees with their exclusive features of nutrition, medicinal and domestic utility. Bharias hunted animal in these forest and gathered forest produce for their meal and constructed their houses with wood, bamboo, leaves and grass found in nearby forest; as an agriculturist they practiced slash and burn cultivation which they called *dahia* in local term in these forest. Earlier, they collected produces for self-consumption and as per requirement, but within the impact of monetized economy and exposure to outside they started marketing of forest produce. Taking into account the use of forest produce by Bharias, these can be categorized as-

Table: 3 NTFPs Collected by Bharias of Patalkot

Sl. No.	*Categories*	*NTFPs*
1.	Domestic use	1. Firewood 2. Date leaves *(Phoenix Dactifylera)* (for broom making) 3. Dev-bahari grass (for broom making) 4. Bamboo *(Bambusoideae)*
2.	Marketing	5. Chironji *(Buchanania Lanzan)* 6. Amla *(Phyllanthus emblica)* 7. Harra *(Terminelia Chebula)* 8. Bahera *(Terminalia Bellirica)*
3.	Both Domestic and Marketing	9. Mahua Flowers *(Madhuca Longifolia)* 10. Gulli (Mahua Fruit) 11. Tamarind *(Tamarindus Indica)* 12. Bhilma *(SemecarpusAnarcadium)* 13. Honey 14. Medicinal Herbs

Source: Field data.

Collection and marketing of NTFPs in the region has witnessed multi-fold changes due to various factors like-availability of produce, market demand, and the price of NTFPs besides the required labour input etc.

Once upon a time, cottage industry of basket making from bamboo and broom making from *devbahari* grass was prevalent in the region, Bharias made basket and broom, which they sold in nearby weekly market, but this cottage industry has disappeared from the region due to limited access to forest and decreasing bamboo and *devbahari* grass in the forest and now their craftsmanship has been limited to their domestic use only and not for market.

Literature on Bharias of Patalkot says that Mango Kernel was being collected by them and they ate bread of kernel flour but while study not a single family was found collecting mango kernel because other grains flour like maize and wheat are easily available and also there is no demand of mango kernel in the market. Now, Bharias of Patalkot inclined themselves towards those NTFPs, which are easily sold in market and give instant cash like chironji, harra, bahera, amla and mahua etc. which is evident from the **Table 4** that above 80 per cent of studied families collected Mahua flower, Chironji and Amla; 46.5 and 47.5 per cent families collected Mahua fruit and Harra respectively; and only 10.5 per cent families collected Bahera because of its meagre availability. Other NTFPs like Bhilma, Tamarind and edible fruits etc. were collected by negligible number of families. Firewood collection is done by cent per cent households but its marketing was done by only two families of

Table 4: Households Collecting NTFPs

Sl. No.	*NTFPs*	*HH*	*Per cent*
1.	Mahua Flowers *(Madhuca Longifolia)*	182	91
2.	Chironji *(Buchanania Lanzan)*	168	84
3.	Amla *(Phyllanthus emblica)*	162	81
4.	Harra *(Terminelia Chebula)*	93	46.5
5.	Bahera *(Terminalia Bellirica)*	21	10.5
6.	Gulli (Mahua Fruit)	95	47.5
7.	Bhilma *(SemecarpusAnarcadium)*	2	1
8.	Tamarind *(Tamarindus Indica)*	1	0.5

Source: Field data.

Rated hamlet of Kareamrated village which they sold to hotels owner of Chhindi and medicinal herbs were also collected by two families of Kareamrated for marketing, the rest collect only for self requirement.

Agriculture

From their early stage, the tribal community did not perform agriculture, but in due course, they have started shifting cultivation which is called as transitional stage between the food gathering and hunting and settled agriculture. Therefore, the agriculture is new and an alien concept for them, so they are lagging behind in use of modern tools and technology of agriculture in comparison to community practising settled agriculture much earlier than them.

On one hand, they have lack of knowledge about modern agriculture the topography of their habitat is not much favourable for agriculture on the other. Similarly, Bharia practiced shifting cultivation which they called *dahiya* but 1965 had been a turning point in their life as settled cultivation began to be practised due to legislation (Kurup, 1986: 37). The land of Patalkot region is stony, hilly, sloppy and undulated making difficult to perform agriculture. As per Kalia (1972: 9), there was practically no land available for the allotment for permanent and settled cultivation in the area but over the time registration of land had been given to the resident of Patalkot under various provisions and the process of registration is still going on under Forest Right Act 2006 provision of giving permanent *patta* of 'forest land'[3] occupied by them.

In this way, problem of landlessness is not in the region, but land holding has been shrinking with its partition and majority of the studied families i.e. 124 out of 192 families having cultivable land had marginal land holding (as per Agriculture Census, GoI, below 1 hectare land holding is marginal). It means about 64.6 per cent families are surviving with small patch of land which on the other side had been equipped with less irrigation facility which can be observed from the fact that only 14.9 per cent of total cultivable land in twelve villages of Patalkot region is irrigated.

In the context of agricultural tools, it was found that Hal and Bakkhar[4] are found in above 75 per cent of households which is the main equipments in the region to plough the field with the help of bullocks. In many of the land there are bulk of big rocks which makes difficult to plough field with hal and bakkhar even slope of the field do not allow to plough with tractor. These are the factors that tractor is also not successful in the region for cultivation and only one tractor was found in Ghatlinga village which was mainly used for threshing wheat connecting with thresher and was partially used for ploughing in plain land. The other agricultural tools that were found in studied family are- thresher in 15 households, sprayer machine in 75 households and motor pump in 43 households.

Most of the equipments were distributed by government under agriculture development schemes and projects without considering its requirement and utility in the region. For example, motor pump were distributed in Kareamrated village where most of the time there is electricity cut and which has lack of well, boring and perennial stream etc. so people took the motor pump and gave it to their relatives living outside of Patalkot, since that motor pumps were useless for them in absence of sources of water. In context of techniques of agriculture it should be noted that their poor economic condition on one side and agriculture productivity of land on the other do not allow them to invest in seeds, fertilizers and pesticides so they follow their traditional way of preserving seeds, use cow dung as manure and negligible person use pesticides which was observed from the fact that of 192 households having land only 182 cultivate their land of which 51.1 per cent used self stored seed, more than 50 per cent used cow dung as fertilizer and none of them used any chemical pesticide nor any herbal pesticide.

Bharias used self stored seeds, cow dung as fertilizers and manual care of crop from the beginning of settled agriculture and grow crop like maize *(Zea mays)*, jawar *(Sorghum)*, bajra (Pearl Millet) *(Pennisetum Glaucum)*, balhar *(Phaseolus vulgaris)*, rahad and jagni *(Guizotia abyssinica)* etc. With institutional intervention new crops were introduced in the region like wheat

(Triticum), rice *(Oryza sativa)*, gram *(cicer arietinum)*, urad *(Vigna munga)*, moong *(Vigna radiate)* and pea *(Pisum sativum)* etc. and use of chemical fertilizers and pesticides was taught to them and provided free of cost by government. Kharif was the main crop raised by them and they grew kutki *(Panicum sumatrense)*, kodo *(Paspalum scrobiculatum),* maize and jowar in month of June-July and harvested in October-November; in winter, during December–January rabi crops like wheat and gram were sown which was harvested in month of April-May after Holi (Kurup, 1986: 39). At present, maize, balhar and kutki were found main kharif crop sown by above 60 per cent of total cultivators. The other kharif crops- tuar, kodo, paddy, jawar, ured and pea were sown by insignificant number of cultivators. Wheat and gram are the main rabi kharif crops sown by 81 and 56 cultivators respectively. Before 10-15 years, the main crops in the region were maize, balhar, kutki and kodo, of which kodo is in verge of extinction. Only 25 cultivators sown kodo Kutki which was sown by 122 families during the previous year of the study.

At present, 81 households is cultivating wheat, which is about six times, more than the number of households cultivating wheat earlier i.e., 13. Similarly, the cultivation of paddy has been increased from one household to 13, pea- from two to 10 households, gram- from nine to 56 households and tuar- from 18 to 40 households, which shows an abundant increase in cultivation of these crops. Although, they are moving towards the crops, which were not prevalent in the region, but maize and balhar are still important for them; because of the region's topography and available resource of agriculture. This indicates continuity and change among Bharias of Patalkot in the context of crop. However, vegetables are not grown in the region, yet except five to ten plants of chilli and tomato in *badi* (kitchen-garden) of every household for domestic purpose only, not for market.

Animal Husbandry and Poultry

Subsidiary to NTFPs collection and agriculture, animal husbandry and poultry was practiced by Bharias but it has witnessed a significant fall. Earlier, Bharias produced dairy products especially *ghee* which was bought by businessmen of Chhindi (Sharma, 1978: 74). The elderly persons of above 50 years of age also told about the production of ghee and its sell to Chhindi shopkeepers; a technical man of Public Welfare and Engineering Department of Madhya Pradesh who worked in the valley in 1980s also told that Bharias tamed cow in large number and discussed about sell of dairy products. The mostly found livestock in the region are bullock, cow, goat, cock and hen of indigenous breed. Total 279 bullocks were found in 147 households constituting 73.5 per cent of total studied families since fields in the region are ploughed by hal and bakhar with the help of bullocks. The number of cow was 174 in 114 family accounts 57 per cent of total family. Only 90 families were found rearing goat which counts 45 per cent but the number of goat was quite high from bullocks and cow as well i.e. 284. In context of poultry, 158 cocks and 310 hens were found in 115 and 114 households respectively.

Table: 5 Livestock in the Respondent Households

Sl. No.	*Livestock*	*Household*	*Per cent*	*Total Number*	*Cost (in Rs.)*
1.	Bullock	147	73.5	279	2043500
2.	Cow	114	57	174	447200
3.	Goat	90	45	284	610300
4.	Cock	115	57.5	158	71250
5.	Hen	114	57	310	66250
	Grand Total			**1,205**	**32,38,500**

Source: Field data.

The above table 5 shows that bullock rearing is dominant over other and the use of bullock in ploughing field is the main reason behind this because the field in region is hilly, stony and undulated so ploughing with tractor is quite difficult on one hand and lacking knowledge of modern agricultural technologies of Bharias is on the other. It is also noticeable that, of 182 households practising agriculture, only 147 has bullocks which shows that 19.2 per cent of total agriculturists do not have bullocks. If total number of family having bullock and total number of bullock is taken into account than it is found that the average number of bullock in a family is 1.9, which also indicates scarcity of bullock in the region. However, the tradition of mutual co-operation is still continued in the region, which makes their work easy to borrow bullock from one another to plough the field without any rent, but the question arise here that - what will be the scope of agricultural development in the region with high scarcity of resources?

There is also scarcity of fodder in the region as 36 persons reported that they have left a part of land uncultivated for cattle grazing. Animal food supplement is neither provided by the government nor it is within the capacity of Bharias to afford. They depend on forest and their agricultural residues for their animal fodder, which is not sufficient resulting into weakness of cattle and deteriorating their breed too. Bullocks are so weak that they are unable to perform ploughing for long hour and unable to plough most elevated fields, as reported by the people. The milk production capacity of cow has also been decreased and its utility has been shrunk to fulfil the need of dung as fertilizer and for the application in the floor of houses, since the houses in the region is *kuchcha* type and the people apply cowdung on its floor, once or twice in a week.

Rearing of goat is performed as the coping mechanism for economic crisis, because it can be sold immediately to the nearby market at the time of necessity. It has also been observed that only those families are taming goat, who has extra working hand to graze goat, since it requires a full day labour and care; but Bharia is inclining towards wage work, which get them engaged in work other than their traditional cores and generating disinterest towards cattle rearing.

Hen and cock are also kept by Bharias due to its importance in worshiping their god besides being consumption of egg and meat, since they are non-vegetarian, except the few who do not eat egg and meat with the influence of other community, who are pure vegetarian. They sacrifice hen or cock[5] in performing rituals for good agricultural production, their safety and pleasing god etc. The sacrificed hen is being eaten by the gathering and this is the occasion, when they can eat chicken; otherwise, their economic condition hardly allows them sacrifice hen only, for the purpose of meal.

Hunting and Fishing

The game of hunting and fishing, which were enjoyed by

tribal and associated with livelihood, for long ago has been disappeared. Hunting is completely left by Bharias, but occasionally, they go for fishing into Doodhi River, which is also situated beneath steep valley, so it also seems to them cumbersome.

II

Wage Work and Migration

Wage work has emerged as main source of earning after NTFPs collection and agriculture, which is promoting seasonal outmigration of Bharias. Both men and women are involved in wage work, both within village and outside of it, but their involvements are partial and depend on the availability of wage work. Of 599 persons above 15 years of age, 169 male and 156 female are involved in wage work, besides other economic activities. There are 13 male and 11 female, who mainly depend upon wage work to earn their livelihood and NTFPs and agriculture are secondary to them, since they do not have cultivable land or having small patch of land, and not having possession on tree for NTFPs. Within the village, they are involved in governmental work, such as construction of road, well and school buildings etc. and they work as agriculture labour outside of village. Insignificant numbers of person are involved in wage work in the nearest towns and villages and it is occasional, but a large population seasonally outmigrates to places such as Pipariya and Hoshangabad to work as agriculture labour.

Migration of Bharias for work is a new phenomenon in the region. The effective area of the area command of Bharias has sharply declined due to passage of command of maximum area in hands of forest department, which has resulted into overexploitation of available resources; over the time land holdings also shrank; decreased number of fruit bearing trees and their decreased yielding capacity; besides their grown needs due to greater contact with outside world etc. lead them to seek more options of earning and finally culminated into seasonal out migration in large number which can be seen in Table 6.

Table: 6 Migration among Bharia

HH	*No. of Migrated Persons*				
	Total	*Male*	*Percentage*	*Female*	*Percemtage*
126	179	128	71.5	51	28.5
Age Group					
15-29	76	54	71.1	22	28.9
30-59	100	71	71	29	29
60(+)	3	3	100	-	-
Occupation					
Wage work	173	123	71.1	50	2.9
Govt. Job	6	5	83.3	1	16.7

Source: Field data.

There are 179 persons belonging to the age of above 15 years reported to migrate for work. It means every third person among working population of Bharias migrate for work. Members of 75 per cent families migrates atleast once in a year in search of work. Number of male migrants with 128 of total migrants is higher than the female migrants i.e., 51. In the context of age of migrants, the age of 55.9 per cent migrants was ranging from 30-59 years, 42.6 per cent migrants belonged to 15-29 years of age and a negligible number of persons were senior citizens. Of the total migrated persons, only six persons were in permanent job of teacher, or peon in the government school outside village and the rest were migrants, who seasonally migrated to work as agriculture labourer.

Bharias migrate in group and reside in working place in a cottage, which is self constructed by them or sometimes provided by the farmer. They get money or grain as wage and return with their saving, which makes their economy sustenance at some sort. The duration of migration is 15 to 30 days as per the availability of work and once or twice in a year. Thus, they earn necessary cash for their cash requirement to purchase grain from PDS shop and consumer commodities from the market.

Self -Employment

It has been mentioned earlier that Bharia perform several economic activities together so few of them are also self-employed, beside agriculture, wage work and NTFPs collection and selling, but their number is insignificant. Only 26 households perform such type of activities, of which 12 persons were involved in broom making and its selling, three persons sell indigenous liquor of mahua, two persons do sewing work, three sell medicinal herbs and one person is involved in each of the work of basketry, flour mill, NTFPs purchasing and selling in market, kirana shop, carpentry and cattle grazing.

III

Income and Expenditure

Historically, forest is at core of tribal economy and was one and only source of the earning livelihood, but over the time their economy diversified in the influence of various developmental initiatives through change agents. Tribal economy has reached at the crossroads of development (Chaudhary, 2010), but forest is still the prominent means of livelihood earning among tribal. Similarly, the livelihood pattern of Bharias has been diversified, yet the forest contributes major in their earning followed by agriculture, wage work (including agriculture labour) and other. Bharias' involvement in multi-economic activities makes their livelihood sustainable, which is continuing the nature of their old age economy because it is said that tribal have self developed mechanism to sustain their economy.

In context of source of income for Bharias, not a single source is exclusive for their income except those who are in government job and getting fixed and regular salary. The income of persons involved in other activities fluctuates due to many factors like up and downs of NTFPs and its price, agriculture production, wage work availability and wage rate etc. In such a scenario, it is difficult to find their exact monthly income so earning[6] from all sources was calculated and variation in income of families has also been seen among them. Maximum, 102 families that constitutes 51 per cent of total studies families earned Rs. 20,000 to 50,000 annually, 47 families (23.5 per cent) earned 50,001 to 1,00,000 INR. in a year, 32 families (16 per cent) income ranging from 10,001 to 20,000 INR, 12 families earned 1,00,001 to 2,00,000 INR, the annual income of six families was upto 10,000 INR and only one family's annual income was above 2,00,000 INR.

It should be noted from the fact that major population i.e., 70 per cent lives with annual income below 50,000 INR. Such disparity in income is an indication of emergence of elites among themselves and beginning of class formation in the community, whose one of the main features was homogeneity. Various scholars have given their view on stratification and class formation among the tribes of India - according to Oommen (1977: 189) there is emergence of prosperous class among the tribes, which gives birth to intra-tribe division based on income and wealth. Kothari (1988) talked about the class polarization among the tribes and Sharma (2001: 170) accepted stratified peasantry among the tribes in India. Dhebar Commission Report (1961) stated about the layer among the tribes, which was reiterated by Shilu Aao Commission Report (1969). The commissions have recommended for special assistance to such communities, which were at the bottom and a new classification emerged called 'Primitive Tribe' (now called 'Particularly Vulnerable Tribal Group) and the task of their development began. If such type of class formation is going even in PVTGs then a question emerges - Is there any need to review and re-categorization of PVTGs within the community?

Similarly, with the limited and the primary source of income Bharias' expenditure is also very simple and confined to the basic requirements, especially on material not produced through agriculture. Their regular expenditure is in the weekly market and the PDS (Public Distribution Shop), 187 and 146 families have reported to spent money in weekly market and PDS respectively, a month immediate before study. With the exposure to outer world, they are becoming familiar with consumer culture and market forces has been established with the development of transportation facilities, so they are slightly inclining towards luxurious good. Luxurious here doesn't mean life of five star hotels and expensive vehicles rather it refers to alien commodities not much useful for them, which only refers to status symbol and generates 'relative deprivation' among them. Mobile is one of the commodities, which has attracted them much, where 108 of 200 families have had mobile phones, of whom 28 persons were asked whether they spent money on mobile recharge worth 4, 040 INR. Many other new expenses have been introduced with consumer culture, but they are nominal. Such changes indicate any possibility of expansion of their expenditure in future instead of the small and limited sources of earning, which is also a reason of indebtedness.

Saving and Indebtedness

Bharias are 'hand to mouth' people so culture of money saving is not popular among them, but it should not be fully neglected, if we look at the mechanism of their management. They store NTFPs in their house. When the cash in hand gets exhausted, they pick some NTFP and sell it to the nearby market to get cash for their requirement. Many times, the storage of their NTFPs support them at time of emergency like illness of any family members, even NTFPs is a great support for expenses of marriage. In this way, the storage of NTFPs is like bank for them, which do not require formalities for transaction. Although, every family have bank account, whose credit goes to the mandatory provisions of governmental schemes, where money is directly transferred to the beneficiary bank account, but they never deposit money in their account after withdrawal of money they get through schemes due to their poor economic condition. Fifty per cent of the studied families were not found having any saving from their income (three month immediate before study) in cash except storage of NTFPs and the rest had saved money in hand or in bank account ranging from 200 INR to 50,000 INR of which majority were persons doing government jobs or those, who had good NTFPs collection or recently got their wage.

The poor economic conditions and cashless hand may suffer financial deficits at the time of sudden cash requirement like marriage and treatment etc., which can pull them into indebtedness. Growing aspirations within the influence of outer world or so called modern non-tribal communities results into the increased unnecessary expenditure and indebtedness as also warned by Sharma (1978) in the context of Bharias of Patalkot. People in the region lead a simple life and mostly depended upon their indigenous mechanism in every sphere of life, but their movement from traditional health practices to modern treatment, monetization of their economy, establishment of the consumer culture and entrance of market forces etc. has increased the sphere of their expenditure, which has enabled presence of indebtedness among Bharias. Indebtedness was found among 68 Bharia families, which constitute 34 per cent of total studied families. They borrowed from various sources for various reasons. If number of borrowing is being considered, then total 80 borrowings were found in 68 families, of which maximum 45 people took loan from friends/relatives followed by 17 loans from doctors for treatment, other borrowings like from kirana shop, cloth store and sahukars[7] etc. were in insignificant number. With regard to purpose of borrowing money, treatment is at the top followed by marriage, which shows the vulnerability of their traditional healing practices, believed to be very rich. Cash was borrowed from friends, relatives and sahukars, while borrowings from doctor and shops were in the form of service and commodities respectively.

It is clear from the above description that Bharias borrow money for their basic requirement at time of financial crisis, not for business or for profit making. Their maximum borrowing is based on social bond, where the interest is not levied, where they co-operate with each other at the time of necessity. But the fact is that their income is lagging behind their necessity and the gap may be wider in future with growth in exposure to the outer world. Increased indebtedness in the region may result in the bonded labour and land alienation, with which they are untouched.

IV

Institutional Initiatives

The developmental programmes and schemes are being implemented by both the governmental and non-governmental organizations in the region for Bharias development and livelihood security is one among those. Inspite of various interventions, training and expenditure of bulk amount Bharias are still struggling for livelihood earning, so it is needful here to take an overlook on the schemes and programmes. Some of the initiatives have been discussed below-

Wadi – A Commendable Attempt by NABARD

Wadi or *garden* project is the initiative of NABARD (National Bank for Agriculture and Rural Development) since 2004 to promote horticulture in rural areas. Nabard provide financial assistance in the form of loan or grant or a mixture of these two to people having less than five acre of agricultural land and willing to develop a garden for horticulture. NABARD has made a fund, known as the Tribal Developmental Fund (TDF) for the implementation in tribal area and the project is being run through some organizations like social organization, NGOs, voluntary organizations and trusts. In Patalkot, the project has been implemented through Madhya Pradesh Vigyan Sabha[8] (MPVS) and Nageshwara Charitable Trust[9] (NCT). As per information provided by MPVS and NCT, the beneficiary is being provided 25 plants of Mango, 15 plants of Guava and 15 plants of Indian Gooseberry to plant in one acre of unused agricultural land. Further assistance is also provided like distribution of manure and spray machines, guidelines to manage garden and facilities of transportation etc. The organizations has extended assistance to dozens of Bharia beneficiaries, but not a single Bharia family was found with a well nurtured garden; they show their interest for the scheme, but the establishment of garden requires a disciplined effort and Bharias are neither habituated in such gardening, nor have much time to spend due to their involvement in wage work and agriculture. They are hand-to-mouth and expect for the instant benefit so they do not have patience to wait for a longer period and their economic conditions also does not allow them, because they have to secure their bread for today.

Skill Development Programmes

Training programme for skill development was provided like training for cooking, making of *dona*, masonry and sewing etc. which were also associated with free distribution of tools and equipments required for particular skill but outcome of these programmes had not been as expected. Not a single person was found utilizing the equipments for actual purpose given after training for self- employment. In the training of cook, a plastic table, eight plastic chair, mixer grinder and utensils etc. were given so that the beneficiary can run a *dhaba* or small restaurant, to earn livelihood, but after receiving the training and equipments he resumes his earlier work and leave the given material unused. Similarly, Bharias were given training for dona making and were provided a machine for this, so that they can make dona and sell it in the market for livelihood, but the machine was left in badi (kitchen garden) or at home unused, and no one was making dona at the time of study. In similar manner, other programmes also failed, but the interesting thing is that they collect whatever they get free of cost, and carry home whether willing [un] to use. Such type of scheme failure shows that they like and adhere to their old age occupation, except fixed and sure wage work but in business they believe with the certainty of risk, which they seldom wish to bear.

Public Distribution System (PDS)

The scheme of GoI to provide grain in cheaper cost is very helpful for Bharias, as they were able to include wheat and rice in their meal, since these are not grown in the region and cannot be afforded from market by them as well. Sugar and iodized salt was also given through PDS, the former has introduced tea intake and the latter fulfill the iodine requirement of their body and cure them from iodine deficiency. Although, maize is the main crop in the region and not a single family face its shortage over the year other than purchasing from PDS, because they get cheaper than the market rate and if its quantity exceed their requirement, then they sell it in the market for more money than invested in buying from PDS shop, so it earns money for them to buy other food items like oil and spice etc. They also get kerosene from PDS, which they use in chimney or diya to light their house when electricity was tripped.

The ration card was available with 177 families and the rest of the 23 families did not have due to delay in fulfilling the documental requirement for ration card. Of 177 ration card holders, 160 card holders have lifted the complete or partial quota from the PDS shop the month immediate before the study and the rest did not, because of reasons like shortage of money, unavailability of coupons, was out of the village for wage work and stock was not exhausted last month, especially in the case of kerosene and sugar. Lifting the quota of material from the PDS by a large number of family shows its importance for them and above 50 per cent of families were found satisfied with the quantity and quality of material provided through PDS. A negligible number of families complained about the behaviour, quantity of material and its quality. However, about 20 per cent of the families suggested to include other material like cooking oil, spices, dal and cloth etc. in PDS shop.

V

In short, it can be said that Bharias of Patalkot are moving towards modern agriculture with limited availability of resources adhering themselves with certain traditional equipments, which replicate both change and continuity in the context of agriculture. It is needful to mention that crops like kodo and kutki, which have been termed as stigma of primitiveness by non-tribal community or so called modern society are in the verge of extinction from the region and new crops have been introduced with new agricultural tools and techniques. The remarkable quality of kodo and kutki should not be ignored as quoted by Jain (1988: 107) that these can survive in drought-stricken areas having low rainfall and poor soil. Government has gone much to root out cultivation of millets like kodo-kutki. Neither state nor any agency undertook a scientific study of its merits. Shiv Kumar (et. al, 2010) conducted research to compare the soy-based millet biscuit and kodo-kutki millet based biscuit and found kodo-kutki millet based biscuits the best. Centre for Advanced Research and Development (CARD) also says that kodo-kutki millets are three to five times nutritionally superior to widely promoted rice and wheat in terms of proteins, minerals and vitamins.

Historically, the forest played vital role in the livelihood of Bharia and Gond as well in Patalkot region. The facts show that it has been proved insufficient to ensure their livelihood security, so they are moving in search of other option. The potential of forest has been decreasing day by day because all the fruit bearing trees are getting old which is affecting fruit protection. On one hand, tribal are exploiting forest at their maximum but do not plant new trees and care the tree on the other because they have a notion that these entities belong to government. The emotional attachment of tribe with the forest had been weakened and eco-friendly cultural practices, which were performed is getting weak. Once, who was the nurturer of forest has become its exploiter. The government has failed to establish a sound mechanism to get them benefitted with NTFPs. Their old art and craft has disappeared except broom-making and bamboo craft by few people for domestic use, but not for marketing, because the raw material for these art and craft have been exhausted and has become rare.

The inadequacy of NTFPs and agriculture has compelled them move towards wage work, which has resulted in the seasonal outmigration in the region. Migration is affecting their NTFPs collection, agriculture and their children's education. The scope of wage work availability within the village is poor, so they have to go outside in search of work. The government opened work within the village under MNREGA and the construction of governmental buildings like schools, anganwadi and PDS shop etc. but these could not provide them work for full year.

The government has initiated various schemes for their development, but the lacuna is resource availability and geographical and ecological context. Initiatives are being taken without considering the distinctiveness of one community to another, one geographical location to another and the climatic condition of one location to another. Both Bharia and Gond of Patalkot region share similar climatic conditions and resource availability etc., but they are treated distinctively, the former as PVTG and the latter as the scheduled tribe. Similarly, the two communities of distinct location are being treated similar to PVTGs, termed to be backward, whether they have similar problem. Policies and programmes are being formulated and implemented uniformly for all communities categorized as PVTGs. For example, motor pump had been distributed among Bharias of Kareamrated village, where there was lack of well without any perennial sources of water; the bicycle is being distributed to girl child to promote education without taking into account wether there is road connectivity or not. There were so many lacunaes traced in the implementation of development initiatives in the region during the study. Any scheduled tribe is declared as PVTGs, if it fulfils any of the criteria outlined by the state, but while implementing the developmental programmes, all were treated as the same instead of better input in that particular field, for which particular tribe has been declared as PVTGs. Specific programmes and schemes for the specific community should be formulated and implemented based on the resource availability and ecological aspects.

References

Analysis of Value Chain- Kodo and Kutki (Minor Millet), Bhopal: Centre for Advanced Research and Development (CARD). <http://www.cardindia.net/mksp-pdf/report-on-value-chain.pdf>

Annual Report (2014-15): Ministry of Tribal Affairs, New Delhi, Government of India.

Atal, Yogesh (1965): *Adivasi Bharat*, Delhi: Rajkamal Prakashan.

Béteille, A. (1986) 'The concept of tribe with special reference to India', *European Journal of Sociology*, 27(2), pp. 296–318

Census (2011): Office of the Registrar General & Census Commissioner, Government of India, Delhi.

Chambers, R and G.R. Conway (1991): 'Sustainable Rural Livelihoods: Practical Concepts for the 21st Century', IDS Discussion Paper 296.

Chaudhary, S.N. (2010): 'Changing Pattern of Tribal Economy and Its Implications: Case Study of a Betul Village', in (ed.) S.N. Chaudhary, *Tribal Economy at Crossroads*, Jaipur: Rawat Publications, pp. 84-118.

Chaudhary, S.N. (2012): *In Search of Sustainable Development: Scenario in a Tribal Village of Madhya Pradesh,* New Delhi: Serials Publications.

Chaudhary, S.N. and R.P. Singh (2006): *Tribes of Pachmarhi Biosphere Reserve and their Indigenous Knowledge,* Intangible Cultural Heritage of India-4 (ed.) Kishore K. Basa, Bhopal, Indira Gandhi Rashtriya Manav Sangrahalaya and Delhi, Pratibha Prakashan.

Das, T.C. (1968): A Scheme for Tribal Welfare in Applied Anthropology In India, (ed.) by L.P. Vidyarthi, Allahabad: Kitab Mahal.

Dhebar, U. N. (1961): *Dhebar Commission Report,* New Delhi: Government of India.

District Census Handbook (2011): Directorate of Census Operations, Bhopal: Madhya Pradesh.

Dube, S.C. (1969): *Manav and Sanskriti,* Delhi: Raj Kamal Prakashan (1960, 1st edition).

Government of India (2016): "Draft List of Denotified, Tribes Nomadic Tribes and Semi-Nomadic Tribes of India", National Commission for Denotified, Nomadic and Semi-Nomadic Tribes, New Delhi: Ministry of Social Justice and Empowerment. <http://social justice.nic.in/writereaddata/UploadFile/Draft%20List%20of%20Denotified%20Tribes%20for%20Mail.pdf on 24/01/2017>

Jain, C.K. (1988): *Patterns of Agricultural Development in Madhya Pradesh*, New Delhi: Northern Book Centre.

Kalia, S.L. (1972): 'Survey Report of District Chhindwara (Based on Area Development Approach)', *Bulletin of The Tribal Research and Development Institute* Bhopal, Vol. X, No. 1& 2., pp.1-10.

Kothari, Rajni, (1988): *The State against Democracy: In Search of Human Governance*, Delhi: Ajanta Publications.

Kumar, Shiv, Rekha and Lalan Kr Sinha, (2010): Evaluation of Soy Based Millet Biscuits, Advances in Applied Science Research, 1(3), USA: Pelagia Research Library, pp. 187-196. <http://www.imedpub.com/articles/evaluation-of-quality-characteristics-of-soy-based-millet-biscuits.pdf>

Kurup, A.M. (1986): *Continuity and Change in a little Community: A Study of the Bharias of Patalkot in Madhya Pradesh,* New Delhi: Concept Publishing Company.

Majumdar, D.N. (1966): *Races and Cultures of India,* Bombay: Asia Publishing House.

Oommen, T.K. (1977): Scheduled Castes and Scheduled Tribes, in S.C. Dube (ed.) *India Since Independence,* New Delhi: Vikas Publications, pp.153-93.

Russel, R.V.(1907): (ed), *Central Provinces District Gazetteers,* Chhindwara District, Bombay: The Time Press, pp. 2-33.

Russell, R.V. and Rai Bahadur Hiralal (1916): *The Tribes and Castes of the Central Provinces of India,* Vol II, London: MacMillan Publishing Co. Ltd.

Sharma, K.L. (2001): "Social Stratification among Tribes in India", in (ed) K.L. Sharma, *Reconceptualising Caste, Class and Tribe,* Jaipur: Rawat Publications, pp. 167-203.

Sharma, Sushila (1978): "Bharias of Patalkot", (eds.) Surajit Sinha and B.D. Sharma, *Primitive Tribes: The First Step,* New Delhi: Ministry of Home Affairs, GoI, pp.72-82.

Shilu Aao, P (1969): *Shilu Ao Commission Report,* New Delhi: Government of India.

Singh, K.S. (1997): *The Scheduled Tribes,* New Delhi: Anthropological Survey of India.

Survey Report, (2009-10): Bharia Development Agency, Tamia.

Tewari, D.N. (1985): *Primitive Tribes of Madhya Pradesh*, New Delhi: Govt. of India, Ministry of Home Affairs, Tribal Development Division.

The Gazette of India (2007): The Scheduled Tribes and Other Traditional Forest Dwellers (Recognition of Forest Rights) Act, 2006, New Delhi: Ministry of Law and Justice, Government of India.

Vidyarthi, L.P. and Binay Kumar Rai (1976): *The Tribal Culture of India,* New Delhi: Concept Publishing Company.

Xaxa, Virginius (2008): *State, Society and Tribes: Issues in Post-colonial India,* New Delhi: Pearson Education India.

Xaxa, Virginius (2014): *Report of the High Level Communities on Socio-Economic, Health and Educational Status of Tribal Communities of India,* New Delhi, Ministry of Tribal Affairs, Government of India.

Notes

1. These are protective provisions (Article 15, 16, 19, 23, 29, 46, 164, 330, 332, 335, 338, 339, 342 and 371), development related provisions (Article 15, 16, 19, 46, 275 and 399), administrative provisions in the 6th schedule (NE States) areas (Articles 344, 338 and 339) and reservation facility (Article 330, 332, 334, 335 and 340).
2. A "common" is any resource that belongs to the public domain and is used by all those who depend on it. Put differently, when anyone uses a shared resource one is using a common. Commons can be better managed when its management responsibilities can be shared by a geographically localized community or communities.
3. After the Orissa land survey and settlement Act 1958, several changes were introduced in the land classification. As shifting cultivation has been the major source of livelihoods for the tribals, the Government of Orissa is yet to recognize it as a legitimate land use and has declared all such cultivation areas, including forest land, as Government land. During the Survey and Settlements, the shifting cultivation lands on hill slopes were categorized as government land, with no recognition of tribal rights over it, either individual or collective (UNDP, cited Kumar, 2008).
4. Under Section 1(d) of 'The Scheduled Tribes and Other Traditional Forest Dwellers (Recognition of Forest Rights) Act, 2006 'Forest Land' refers to land of any description falling within any forest area and includes unclassified forests, undemarcated forests, existing or deemed forests, protected forests, reserved forests, Sanctuaries and National Parks. In the Act, there is also a provision